D0082677

Restoring the Faith

Restoring the Faith

The Assemblies of God, Pentecostalism, and American Culture

Edith L. Blumhofer

University of Illinois Press
Urbana and Chicago

Illini Books edition, 1993
© 1993 by the Board of Trustees of the University of Illinois
Manufactured in the United States of America
1 2 3 4 5 C P 5 4 3 2

This book is printed on acid-free paper.

Library of Congress Cataloging-in-Publication Data

Blumhofer, Edith Waldvogel.
  Restoring the faith : the Assemblies of God, pentecostalism, and
American culture / Edith L. Blumhofer
    p.   cm.
  Includes bibliographical references and index.
  ISBN 0-252-01648-3.—ISBN 0-252-06281-7 (pbk.)
    1. Assemblies of God—United States—History.   2. Pentecostalism—
United States—History.   3. Popular culture—Religious aspects—
Christianity.   4. United States—Church history—20th century.
5. United States—Popular culture—History—20th century.
I. Title.
BX8765.5.A4B59   1993
289.9′4—dc20   92-23888
                                                        CIP

2616 00 72

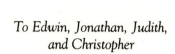

*To Edwin, Jonathan, Judith,
and Christopher*

Contents

Acknowledgments

In the years since I began studying American Pentecostalism as a graduate student at Harvard University, many others have focused their research on aspects of the same subject. I am indebted to a host of them, especially to members of the Society for Pentecostal Studies, for helping me think about the history and the meaning of American Pentecostalism. The network of scholars in American religious history linked by the Institute for the Study of American Evangelicals at Wheaton College has also contributed perspective and encouragement. The Institute's project, Pentecostal Currents in the American Church, funded by the Lilly Endowment, has brought together a stimulating group that shares my interests and has taught me much.

During the course of research and writing I have become indebted to many individuals. William R. Hutchison and George H. Williams provided invaluable advice as they guided the early parts of this work through the dissertation stage at Harvard University. Mark A. Noll of Wheaton College and Grant A. Wacker of the University of North Carolina at Chapel Hill read the entire manuscript and offered constructive criticism. Joel A. Carpenter of the Pew Charitable Trusts and Russell P. Spittler read and commented on substantial parts, as did Larry Eskridge of the Institute for the Study of American Evangelicals at Wheaton College. Paul B. Tinlin willingly read, listened, discussed, and helped me clarify my conclusions. He co-authored "Decade of Decline or Harvest?: Dilemmas of the Assemblies of God," *Christian Century*, July 10–17, 1991, that, slightly edited for this study, is the Epilogue.

Wayne E. Warner, Joyce Lee, and the staff of the Assemblies of God Archives in Springfield, Missouri, graciously assisted in countless ways.

Archivists and librarians at Oral Roberts University, Central Bible College, the Billy Graham Center Archives, Moody Bible Institute, Southwestern College of the Assemblies of God, the Apostolic Faith Bible College (in Baxter Springs, Kansas), and Wheaton College helped me locate research materials. The staff of the secretariat at the Assemblies of God international headquarters responded to many inquiries. The faculty development committees at Southwest Missouri State University and Wheaton College and a summer grant from the National Endowment for the Humanities provided financial assistance that enabled me to complete research.

I also owe much to the many Assemblies of God adherents I have come to know over the years. The support and interest of Thomas F. Zimmerman, longtime general superintendent of the Assemblies of God, facilitated access to denominational materials. Other students of the Assemblies of God, especially Grant Wacker, Margaret Poloma, and Robert Mapes Anderson, have greatly influenced my perceptions. I am grateful for their encouragement and have benefited from their written work.

Over several years, my research assistants at Wheaton College, Teri Kondo, Kristin Helmer, Candace Wegner, and Katherine Tinlin-Vaughn prepared the final manuscript. My thanks to Kurt Berends for his work on the index. Becky Standard made this a better manuscript than it would have been without her perceptive editorial eye. I thank her and Elizabeth Dulany for their assistance.

This book is dedicated to my family with thanks for the cooperation and encouragement that enabled the completion of this project.

Restoring the Faith

Pentecostalism through a
Restorationist Lens

L ATE ON THE first Friday night in January 1901, Agnes Ozman spoke in tongues during prayer at an out-of-the-way residence on the south side of Topeka. A burst of public curiosity quickly subsided, and she faded from the scene. Five years later on a foggy spring evening in Los Angeles, a *Los Angeles Times* reporter visited a nondescript mission on Azusa Street and wrote about the howling, fanatical rites and wild theories that characterized the devotees of a new sect. These events at the turn of the century marked the unlikely beginnings of public awareness of Pentecostalism, a religious movement that relentlessly extended its influence until by the 1990s its progress had become a central theme in the story of twentieth-century Christianity. Pentecostalism not only spawned new denominations, it also interacted with virtually every existing Christian form, often influencing both the worship and the message of the church around the world.

Pentecostalism comes in a bewildering variety of forms, each marked by tremendous internal diversity—Catholic and Protestant; classical and charismatic; black, white, Hispanic, Asian; trinitarian and oneness. The sheer size of the movement is staggering, and its immensity issues in confusion. It is impossible to give precise parameters for this experience-oriented tradition, but adherents generally share at least two suppositions. They agree that the gifts of the Holy Spirit described in the New Testament should operate in the church today. They also believe that Christians should experience a distinct "filling" or "baptism" with the Holy Spirit, but they disagree about how this will be evidenced. Some believe that tongues speech always attests Spirit baptism; others insist that any New Testament spiritual gift (1 Cor. 12, 14) can appropriately manifest the Spirit's filling; still others deemphasize spiritual gifts and regard Pentecostalism as a means to gain power over evil spiritual forces and life's difficulties.

The Pentecostal movement is usually dated from January 1901 when Charles Fox Parham, the leader of a small Bible school in Topeka, advanced the view that tongues speech would always mark an authentic baptism with the Holy Spirit and, in response, Agnes Ozman spoke in tongues. Because many of Parham's contemporaries across the United States shared his experience-oriented interest in the person and work of the Holy Spirit with a wide array of theological nuances, Pentecostalism disentangled itself only slowly from other popular religious movements that also worked toward realizing the dream that motivated Parham of restoring the power and message of the New Testament church in the twentieth century.

American Pentecostals who trace their heritage from 1901 are often called "classical Pentecostals." This book examines part of their story, focusing on the world's largest Pentecostal denomination, the Assemblies of God. There are obvious limitations in using one denomination to generalize about a religious movement. For one, in the United States the Assemblies of God is predominantly white with a sizable (15 percent) Hispanic membership. Its story virtually ignores the large and thriving segments of American Pentecostalism that are predominantly black. For another, the Assemblies of God is both trinitarian and non-Wesleyan while large portions of American Pentecostalism, white and black, are nontrinitarian or Wesleyan. Huge sectors of classical Pentecostalism are fiercely independent, and no denomination's story can fully reveal the power or extent of this vast Pentecostal subculture.

On the other hand, there are several compelling reasons for studying the Assemblies of God and using the denomination as a lens to illuminate larger issues in American Pentecostalism. First, the denomination's size, affluence, and influence merit attention. In the past decade the Assemblies of God was cited more than once as America's fastest-growing denomination, and its adherents regularly rank among the highest in the nation for per capita world ministries giving. Second, much of American Pentecostalism in all of its forms has interacted at some point with the Assemblies of God. The denomination's story, though admittedly atypical for sizable segments of American Pentecostalism, illustrates the issues and tensions that have shaped the larger movement's course. Some of America's biggest churches and best-known (and most notorious) media ministers have at one time or another been part of the Assemblies of God: Jim Bakker, Jimmy Swaggart, Kenneth Hagin, and Paul Crouch.[1] The Assemblies of God has provided leadership and resources for cooperative

Pentecostal endeavors around the world. It has also served as a bridge to other segments of conservative Protestantism through its leading role as a supporter of various evangelical voluntary associations. Third, because the Assemblies of God always had a national (as opposed to a strictly regional) constituency and because it drew together people from many denominational backgrounds, its history perhaps reveals more about the extent of the movement's early appeal than do the stories of other Pentecostal denominations that focus more on either a geographic region or a dominant personality.

For reasons like these, then, it seems to me that the story of the Assemblies of God offers instructive insights into a single denomination and a much larger religious movement. My interest in Pentecostalism is also part of a broader inquiry into the nature and fate of restorationist movements as they acculturate. Early Pentecostalism was most basically the expression of a yearning to recapture in the last moments of time the pristine purity of a long-gone era. Its agenda was the end-times restoration of the apostolic faith, but for some, it was deeper, involving the realization of personal Edenic perfection in this life. Pentecostalism's most devout followers wanted to live in the present amid the powers of the world to come. They believed that the way to accomplish this had been committed by Christ to New Testament believers through their endowment with the Holy Spirit at Pentecost.

Since 1901, successive bursts of restorationist fervor have animated the Pentecostal worldview. During the 1940s, Pentecostals who deplored institutionalization and acculturation heralded a new restoration they called the "latter rain." Since the 1960s, participants in Pentecostal movements have worked toward the restoration of New Testament forms of ministry to the church. A recent issue of *Charisma,* the publication that perhaps best traces current trends in popular Pentecostalism, called for the restoration of apostles and prophets in the church of the 1990s. Contemporary Pentecostalism has moved beyond the hope to restore New Testament spirituality to call for the restoration of New Testament authoritative offices and vigorous spiritual warfare. Both of these have potentially frightening implications. In the course of a century, prominent media voices in this movement have shifted from advocating the recovery of such New Testament virtues as humility, gentleness, and love to boasting about dominion and authority. In its extreme forms, contemporary popular Pentecostalism is brash and aggressive, unabashedly meshing its image of God and the American way of life. Such popular forms of Pentecostalism, promulgated especially in print and broadcast media, are found in Pentecostal denominations such as the Assemblies of God as well as in the vast independent sector.

The story of the Assemblies of God, then, suggests that restorationism is often a basic component of a Pentecostal movement, expressing itself differently as the movement improves its economic and social position. Assemblies of God history helps elucidate what happens when the restorationist dynamic clashes with cultural norms. The narrowing or redirecting of the restorationist dream helped the Assemblies of God come to terms with modernity but also assured the persistence of a large and growing independent Pentecostal sector that exists in considerable tension with the denomination.

At least four stages have marked the process through which the Assemblies of God has found its bearings in the broader religious and secular culture. (1) Restorationism marked the denomination's early ethos. (2) The perception of affinities with fundamentalists in the 1920s led Assemblies of God adherents to understand themselves as "fundamentalists with a difference." (3) The charismatic renewal after World War II introduced a new stage emphasizing the view that Pentecostals represented a "third force," a potential for renewal for the church at large. (4) Since the 1970s, a growing predilection for popular culture has marked yet another stage. The Assemblies of God did not necessarily pass through these stages chronologically; rather, in the course of its history successive stages have been added to earlier ones. Today one can find restorationist, fundamentalist, middle-class "third force" impulses, and pop expressions of Pentecostalism coexisting in the denomination at large, in local congregations, and among individual leaders. Yet the four, examined in chronological order, offer an organizing device for a selective look at a complex history.

Restorationism

As restorationists, early Pentecostals intentionally ignored historical tradition, opting rather for biblical terminology and precedent. Those who note the absence of theological reflection in the tradition should not be surprised to discover that Pentecostals have always squabbled frequently and fiercely over doctrines: they are not doctrinally unconcerned, but they are suspicious of theological finesse. As millenarian restorationists, the people who established the Assemblies of God in 1914 intended only to mobilize their resources for a brief and intense spurt of activity they thought would usher in Christ's return. They had no plans to create a denomination that would spawn its own traditions and significantly modify the restorationist drive.

Early Assemblies of God adherents assumed that as citizens of another kingdom—heralds of divine activity that would issue in history's climax—

they had little stake in this world's affairs. For most, this meant pacifism during the patriotic frenzy that accompanied World War I. It implied reservations about the scope of women's sphere in the church and affirmations of male prerogative in the home and the culture. It offered a fresh vision of racial equality. Politically and socially, however, early Pentecostals professed to desire no place in the public arena. But they did demonstrate a pragmatic proclivity to use anything and anyone to accomplish their ends.

The restoration was dynamic, fluid, and progressive, and as it became more amorphous, divisive tensions surfaced. Two years after the Assemblies of God was formed in 1914, the denomination began attempts to contain the restoration by defining appropriate doctrines and excluding efforts to restore culturally unacceptable New Testament usage (wine at communion) and unorthodox views of the Trinity (which zealous primitivists noted was not mentioned in the New Testament). When Christ's failure to appear in the clouds mandated attention to worldly affairs, Assemblies of God adherents found in contemporary Protestant realignments affinities that suggested an alternative way of understanding themselves. With fundamentalists they affirmed the basic points of Christian orthodoxy, a sense of cultural loss, and devotion to a Christian America. Gradually, assertions that they were heralds of the "full" gospel replaced earlier millenarian restorationist rhetoric.

The Full Gospel: Fundamentalism with a Difference

Amid the stormy public confrontations between modernists and fundamentalists in the 1920s, Assemblies of God adherents proclaimed their essential unity with fundamentalists. In fact, the two groups had common assumptions about America, similar economic and social standing, and similar educational experiences at vocational and Bible institutes. Both movements were popular—even populist. They both mirrored and shaped the deepest longings of common people.

For Assemblies of God adherents in the 1920s and 1930s, the "full" gospel was fundamentalism with a difference. They added to the standard fundamentalist profession of faith (which most basically included the verbal inspiration of scripture, the virgin birth, the substitutionary atonement, and the physical resurrection) two components that made their gospel "full"—the insistence that physical healing was "in the atonement" for all believers and the expectation that tongues speech and other spiritual gifts listed in 1 Cor. 12, 14 should be manifested in the contemporary church. This stress on affinities with fundamentalists distanced Assemblies of God adherents from many other Pentecostals and charted

a course that would result in easy formal cooperation with the new evangelical heirs of the fundamentalists in the 1940s. In opting to emphasize
right belief and to identify with fundamentalists and their new evangelical
heirs, Assemblies of God adherents conceded (perhaps unwittingly) that
Pentecostalism was far less fluid than they had once assumed. And Pentecostal experience was not an essential part of Christian faith: it was,
rather, an optional though desirable benefits package for those who
shared evangelical commitments, an "add on" for those who espoused the
fundamentals. Espousing the fundamentals was functionally prerequisite
to receiving Pentecostal experience. An increasing percentage of adherents never proceeded from affirming the fundamentals to experiencing the
Pentecostal distinctives.

Third Force

A third perception of their place on the landscape made sense to some
Assemblies of God adherents after World War II. Amid a general increase
of interest in religion and in response to dramatic growth of Pentecostal movements in developing countries and their emergence in historic
Christian churches, some proposed that adherents consider themselves
participants in a "third force," or a renewal movement parallel to Catholicism and Protestantism but distinct from each. In the Assemblies of
God the tensions this view aroused were best revealed in the denomination's prolonged and uneasy relationship with one of its ministers, David
Du Plessis.

Du Plessis was a pivotal figure in the charismatic renewal in mainstream Protestantism and Roman Catholicism, and his activities revealed
deep division at the popular level within the Assemblies of God. He proposed that Pentecostalism was, most basically, a religious experience.
Right doctrine was less important in the quest for an authentic Christian
witness than was shared experience. Pentecostal experience, then, might
well occur in spite of—rather than because of—adherence to the tenets
and practice of fundamentalist Protestantism. This stage in Assemblies of
God history was marked by carefully nuanced middle-class terms attuned
to an acculturating constituency that had once addressed moral perplexity
with rigid proscriptions but by midcentury found itself in considerably less
tension with society.

Popular Culture

In recent years, the popular nature of Pentecostalism has increasingly
influenced content, style, and agenda in the Assemblies of God. The

Assemblies of God (like Pentecostalism generally) has always been an audience-conscious popular expression of Christianity. At the local level, it has adapted readily to the styles of American popular culture, and that has been its strength and its weakness. Its appeal to the masses rather than to an elite and its cultivation of the talents of media stars and entrepreneurs have assured it a wide hearing. Its upbeat message promising joy, peace, and wholeness attracts a wide spectrum. Nathan Hatch has noted that the strength of evangelical movements has been their identification with the people and their passion about communicating their message.[2] Pentecostalism, he notes, is democratic in structure and spirit. Since Pentecostalism belongs to the people rather than to elites, its adherents tend to measure the importance of an issue by its popular reception, the worth of a book by the number of copies sold, or the adequacy of a method by the number of people it attracts. They are likely to value quantity over quality.

While Assemblies of God adherents (like other Pentecostals and evangelicals) often formally object to secular popular culture, they have participated enthusiastically in the creation of a parallel popular culture that offers Christian variations on everything from rock bands and night clubs to soap operas, talk shows, sex manuals, and exercise videos. Kenneth Myers, former editor of *Eternity*, a highly regarded evangelical monthly, noted about this Christian pop culture that takes its cues from the secular counterpart "but sanitizes and customizes it with 'Jesus language' ": "Popular culture has the power to set the pace, the agenda, and the priorities for much . . . social and spiritual existence without . . . explicit consent."[3]

In the Assemblies of God as in Pentecostalism more generally today, popular culture appears increasingly to do just that. Almost entirely unacknowledged, it influences perceptions of success, goals, professions of belief. Heroes are the media stars and entrepreneurs who lead megachurches, not those who reflect critically on the relationship between religion and culture. The denomination has grown at least in part because at the grass roots it is so thoroughly attuned to the tastes and jargon of the popular culture and has embraced and exploited modern technology. Membership cards reflect growing accommodation to the culture: since the late 1970s a new membership form without the behavior and dress proscriptions listed on earlier cards has been available. Even so, barely half of those who attend Assemblies of God churches officially join.

The ability to communicate with the masses accounts for much of Pentecostalism's success, then, but popular culture also poses a subtle challenge. Its greatest influence, Myers suggests, is its shaping *how* people think and feel rather than its determining *what* people think and feel.

While this constituency loudly opposes the content of television programming (enthusiastically endorsing boycotts of sponsors of the shows to
which it objects) and the lyrics of rock music, it does not acknowledge
the basic changes that pop culture has worked in local churches. Popular
culture's impact on *form* rather than on *content* may, Myers proposes, be
"as serious a challenge for modern Christians as persecution and plagues
were for the saints of earlier centuries."[4] The Assemblies of God offers a
setting in which to consider how popular culture has quietly come to
influence the agenda of a populist religious movement. In this fourth
stage, earlier hopes to make the church an alternative to the methods and
message of the popular culture fade as the parallel Christian popular culture is embraced.[5]

The story of the Assemblies of God is a blending of legacies from these
four stages. This book is at once a denominational history, an overview
of the ideas that describe this constituency's beliefs, and a look at how
Pentecostal people have related to American culture. The first chapters,
exploring the period in which organization was less important than grass-
roots activity, depend heavily on popular sources—periodicals, letters,
hymnals, diaries. The later chapters cite more formal sources at least
partly because the centralizing tendencies and economic constraints of
the denomination began to limit the number of periodicals produced.
The *Pentecostal Evangel*, formerly a more inclusive publication, became a
house organ. Minutes and committee reports give the story of leadership's
vision and document the denomination that became a significant player
in some evangelical circles but they neglect the grass roots, where the
strength of religious movements becomes most evident. Despite the
choices I made in selecting sources for the recent past, I am convinced
that the denomination's large headquarters enterprise, with its one thousand employees, is less relevant than leaders suppose to the denomination's grass-roots strength.

The real story of the Assemblies of God is the story of hundreds of
thousands of unnamed women and men who sustained it at the local level
and carried its message around the world. Their experiences illustrate the
tensions inherent in restorationist dreams of recovering an elusive pristine
past untainted by culture. Less selective looks at that past not surprisingly
indicate that it, too, was culture-bound and socially influenced. The Assemblies of God began with professions of allegiance to a higher kingdom,
enjoining adherents to live as "pilgrims and strangers" in the world. In
time, its adherents improved their economic and social standing and
carved out a niche for themselves on the American religious scene. The
restorationist urge erupted occasionally as a troubling reminder of their
earlier identity; it spawned popular movements that continued to have

wide appeal in a constituency that professed to yearn for spiritual authenticity but often yielded to the enticements of the times.

Pentecostalism's message, Martin Marty has noted, was once assumed to be true because the following was small and pure; by the 1980s, when the Assemblies of God was cited several times as America's fastest-growing denomination, the message seemed true because it had such wide appeal.[6] While contemporary adherents profess to long for the spiritual vigor they find in their past, they generally do not covet the social experience that early adherents believed sustained that power.

Events in recent years have helped unveil the diversity that thrives under the Assemblies of God umbrella. How the Assemblies of God has responded to internal diversity and cultural pluralism as well as to the legacies of the stages that have helped shape its ethos constitutes an important part of the story that follows. For if accommodation to the values of middle America and affinities for the forms of Christian pop culture are prominent features of the Assemblies of God today, they did not always so blatantly shape its identity. For the first generation at least, Pentecostalism had appeal because it offered common people a transforming perception of reality that invested life with meaning and promised transcendence of life's problems. Early adherents discovered a gospel that resisted the lure of secular society and issued more than a superficial challenge to the culture. The historian Grant Wacker has noted that in crucial ways Pentecostalism is less mature today than it was in its early years.[7] The convictions of women and men who insisted that being in step with God meant being out of step with the times gave the Assemblies of God the dynamic that carved out its place on the American religious map.

NOTES

1. Michael Horton, ed., *Agony of Deceit* (Chicago: Moody Press, 1990).

2. Nathan O. Hatch, *The Democratization of American Religion* (New Haven: Yale University Press, 1989), 214–19.

3. Kenneth A. Myers, *All God's Children and Blue Suede Shoes: Christians and Popular Culture* (Westchester, Ill.: Crossway Books, 1989), 18, xiv.

4. Ibid., xii.

5. Ibid., xvi.

6. Martin Marty, *A Nation of Behavers* (Chicago: University of Chicago Press, 1976); see also Grant Wacker, "America's Pentecostals: Who They Are," *Christianity Today*, 16 Oct. 1987, 18–21.

7. Wacker, "America's Pentecostals," 21.

CHAPTER

1

Pentecostalism's Roots in the Premillennial, Healing, and Holiness Movements, 1880–1901

I n 1897 two popular Midwestern Church of God preachers, Barney Warren and Andrew Byers, edited a songbook for use in "general gospel work." Entitled *Songs of the Evening Light,* the book opened with a preface about the prophetic significance of the times:

> We are in the evening of the last dispensation of time. In fulfillment of the prophecy—"At evening time it shall be light"—the pure gospel is shining now as it never has shone since the days of primitive Christianity. The ransomed of the Lord are returning from their apostatized condition and are coming to Zion with songs and everlasting joy upon their heads.[1]

Warren and Byers were not alone in expressing such convictions. Preachers and exhorters in congregations scattered across the country echoed the message: the closing years of the nineteenth century were the last days, the time of the "evening light." To the faithful, the phrase evoked a biblical image of restored perfection. Divine judgment was fast approaching, but so was a renewed experience of apostolic Christianity. Those who basked in the rays of the clear "evening light" or others who anticipated refreshing "showers" of the "latter rain" confidently announced with excitement and awe that God was doing a new thing: the church stood on the verge of both history's greatest revival and history's consummation. It was about to enjoy again the full blessings of the primitive faith. "Nothing can stay the onward march of God and His kingdom," the convinced confidently asserted.[2]

Pentecostalism gradually emerged as a discrete religious movement among people who were certain that they lived in the days of prophesied restoration, revival, and consummation. Molded by a view of history that anticipated that an intense, brief recurrence of pristine New Testament faith and practice would immediately precede Christ's physical return to earth, early Pentecostalism is best understood as an expression of resto-rationist yearning that was shaped in significant ways by the hopes and dreams of disparate groups of late nineteenth-century restorationists.[3] Various expectations energized this constituency. Millenarian fervor characterized their expectation of Christ's imminent physical return to earth, while the form of radical evangelicalism embodied in the holiness movement drove the pursuit of religious experience. The doctrines of the "fourfold Gospel" (salvation, healing, baptism with the Holy Spirit, and the second coming) were all vigorously proclaimed in sectors of American evangelicalism long before a Pentecostal movement could be identified.[4] In affirming each of them, Pentecostals later confirmed their participation in a religious heritage with a broad base in American culture.

A brief, selective overview of the major strands of thought and practice that molded American Pentecostalism reveals how multifaceted Pente-costal backgrounds are. And it suggests, too, the significance of cultural influence in the formation of this religious movement. Pentecostals, like other radical evangelicals, were often people who experienced a deep sense of cultural loss, even betrayal. They perceived encroaching moder-nity as a sinister enemy eroding social values, bankrupting theology, and displacing individuals. They responded by embracing a religious world-view that assigned alternate meanings and values, promised them divine wisdom, and gave them status as the despised few who were really God's victorious army in disguise. Full initiation into the group ultimately came through the manifestation of God's choice in the exercising of a spiritual gift. The power of this worldview is obvious in their rhetoric. It gave them definite goals, but in the quest to achieve those goals, they tended to exploit the means afforded by the modernity they rhetorically rejected. In significant ways, over time, American Pentecostalism has succumbed to aspects of modernity.

In making their initial appeal, however, Pentecostals drew on themes with deep roots in American evangelicalism, reviving hopes that had sur-faced repeatedly in the past. Restoration, health, and empowerment were common concerns in American society and religion. Early Pentecostal views on such themes mattered deeply to the constituency and were shaped in part by radical evangelicals in the last quarter of the nineteenth century.

Restorationism

Restorationism/Primitivism: "The impulse to restore the primitive or original order of things as revealed in Scripture, free from the accretions of church history and tradition."[5]

Attempts to recapture the presumed vitality, message, and form of the apostolic church have spawned countless movements in the course of Christian history. Owning to a nostalgic sense of the pristine purity of early Christian experience, restorationists often remember selectively and yearn for the return of "the good old days."[6] In the closing decades of the nineteenth century, some restorationists sought to restore the apostolic faith; others anticipated a divine restoration. Since the people whose restorationist hopes most directly shaped American Pentecostalism were premillennialists ardently committed to the belief that theirs were the last days, they generally expected God's imminent intervention in history; they also sought ways to cooperate with God's presumed intentions.

Among such people, the restorationist impulse served various practical functions, four of which had particular significance for Pentecostalism. Each of the four also coincided with widely assumed fundamental American characteristics. First, in a nation historically devoted to political and social reform and perfection, restorationism sounded a call to Christian perfection and religious reform. It ran counter to late nineteenth-century evolutionary optimism, however, because it assumed that the best had already been realized. It proposed instead an agenda that eliminated patterns associated with progress and development. Perfection meant a return to the norms of an earlier era. History—with its accumulation of tradition—was irrelevant. The church was called to be ahistorical, or at least to exist untainted by historical currents. Those who influenced early Pentecostals yearned to discover a spiritual Eden.

Restorationists, then, advocated purifying religious forms and testing practices and beliefs against the New Testament. Bennett F. Lawrence, the first historian of Pentecostalism, aptly conveyed this conviction when in 1916 he wrote of Pentecostalism: "This movement has no history. It leaps the intervening years, crying 'back to Pentecost.' "[7] Historylessness was a badge of honor. It also was a trait valued in large sectors of American culture.

Second, restorationists promoted assumptions of Christian unity and simplicity. They reminded believers of their fundamental oneness in Christ. In focusing on the unity of the early church, they ignored the turmoil and heterodoxy that had characterized Christian beginnings. An emphasis on shared origins promoted hopes of renewed family harmony and optimism about rediscovery of the "pure" gospel.

Third, American restorationists grappled with eschatological issues. Some understood themselves as promoting America's destined millennial role. Others considered restorationist emphases an integral part of end-times Christianity and noted their intrinsic apocalyptic assumptions. They tapped emotions that ran deep in the American experience where America itself was assigned eschatological significance. Joseph Smith

called his restorationist group The Church of Jesus Christ of Latter-day
Saints; Alexander Campbell—whose restorationist hopes spawned the
Disciples of Christ—titled his publication the *Millennial Harbinger*.

Fourth, restorationist expectations occasioned and nurtured antidenominationalism. The turn-of-the-century restorationists who influenced
Pentecostalism tended to find submission to church authority intolerable.
In what they regarded the best Protestant tradition, they insisted on the
priesthood of all believers and on the ability of all to read and interpret
Scripture for themselves. Impatient with both tradition and creeds, they
concluded that God had long since abandoned organized religion. The
popular holiness preacher John H. Brooks spoke for many when he urged
"come-outism" as a necessity rather than an option.[8] This persuasion
molded the subculture in which Pentecostal views flourished: early Pentecostals were often radical evangelicals whose preferences had marginalized them from the mainstream before they embraced Pentecostalism.
The conviction that cultural values necessarily opposed the true faith
shaped their understanding of the world and worldliness. They interpreted rejection and persecution as measures of spiritual strength. They
volubly opposed the personal behavioral norms of the modern culture and
the conviction that they offered a viable, satisfying alternative to worldliness attracted adherents. In effect, however, they often objected more
to specific features of the culture than to the core of the culture itself. As
restorationists, they believed they had discovered the biblical way to transcend the struggles of daily living. Restorationism offered not only certainty and divine immediacy but also a new way of perceiving reality.

Groups of restorationists sometimes succumbed to the temptation to
regard themselves as a spiritual elite by insisting that they had recaptured
more fully than others the dynamic, the message, or the form of the early
church. The quest to restore any or all of these gave identity to fledgling
popular religious movements. Establishing that their distinctive views and
practices had apostolic precedent shaped their goals and lent a certain
audacity to their pretensions. As restorationists, for example, in 1886 a
few women and men created a congregation in rural western North Carolina that they called the Christian Union. Undaunted by their lack of
social influence, local support, or contact with the world beyond the
mountains that isolated them, they avowed their intention "to restore
primitive Christianity and bring about the union of all denominations."[9]
Similarly, during the 1890s, the followers of Charles Fox Parham, an
obscure healing evangelist in eastern Kansas, claimed that their movement had—for the first time since the second century—fully restored the
apostolic faith.[10] A community in southern Maine known as Shiloh rallied around Frank Sandford, a one-time Free Will Baptist who had re-

nounced denominational "shackles" to lead God's earthly kingdom.[11] And thousands of Americans flocked to healing revivals conducted by the intractable, Scotland-born Australian John Alexander Dowie, who established a restorationist denomination, the Christian Catholic Church, in Chicago in 1896 and five years later opened the first of several projected Christian utopias called Zion.[12]

Efforts to restore New Testament Christianity—or at least the expectation that God would sovereignly restore the faith in the end times— were not confined to any specific denomination or to Christian orthodoxy. Gnawing uncertainties about the present helped incline some to expect the end of the world and nudged them toward restorationist sympathies. The conviction that their endeavors coincided fully with God's end-times calendar made them confident of their ultimate success.

The hope of full restoration of primitive Christianity through the proclamation of the gospel and the reform of religious institutions—together with the sense that such thoroughgoing reform was uniquely possible in America—had motivated thousands of Protestants throughout the American experience. Closely related to an understanding of America's place in history and its special mission, this hope continued to attract new advocates in the closing decades of the nineteenth century. Restorationism was compatible with various millenarian schemes. When it combined in particular ways with premillennialist expectations, it became a powerful incentive to some who fully expected to live to see the day when "the windows of the heavens shall be opened, / And the floods be poured upon the world's dry ground."[13]

Premillennialism

During the closing decades of the nineteenth century increasing numbers of people with essentially conservative religious inclinations seemed disposed to embrace radical millenarian views. Russellites (or Jehovah's Witnesses) published prophetic tidings of the rapid approach of the end. Adventist groups rooted in the Millerite excitement of the 1840s became more visible. More significantly for the story of Pentecostalism, a growing number of evangelicals in both traditional denominations and independent institutions, prompted by restorationist inclinations, popular evangelical literature about the "signs of the times," and a haunting sense that the waning century might well conclude in Christ's return, concurred with one of their leaders, Arthur T. Pierson, who noted that by twelve independent methods of prophetic calculation, "some great crisis lies between the years 1880 and 1920, or thereabouts."[14] In a small town in Kansas, a group of friends huddled expectantly on a lawn at midnight on

31 December 1900. "Everyone felt that something strange, some extraordinary phenomenon would take place as 1900 rolled into 1901 and the twentieth century began. . . . This was an evening of evenings for the entire Christian world," one recalled. When nothing dramatic happened, they disbanded undaunted, still confident that something of eschatological significance would soon be manifested.[15]

Animating this conviction of a rapidly approaching consummation was a view of history articulated by John Nelson Darby, an Irish Anglican priest who helped shape the Plymouth Brethren movement in mid-nineteenth-century Britain. Darby divided history into seven time periods called "dispensations" and insisted that events detailed in biblical prophecy were about to begin, inaugurating the seventh (and final) dispensation. This would begin with the "secret rapture," or miraculous sudden removal, of the church from the world. The rapture would be followed by a seven-year tribulation that would precede Christ's return to earth to reign for one thousand years. Claiming that Christ's return for the church was "always imminent" and "any moment," Darby and his popularizers stressed the believer's obligation to be ready and to be making the world ready. As an incentive to personal holiness and militant evangelism, Darby's teaching played a significant role in shaping the context in which Pentecostalism emerged.[16] The first Pentecostals assumed that their movement alone assured escape from the tribulation by participation in the rapture.[17]

Darby and other Plymouth Brethren "came out" from established religious institutions and abandoned traditional liturgical forms. Stressing the importance of a thorough knowledge of the English Bible, they developed popular Bible study handbooks that greatly extended their influence. Replacing the typical sermon with a "Bible reading," they devised a teaching form that dismayed some of the era's pulpiteers but had enormous influence on popular evangelicalism.[18] In the United States Darby's view of history and his emphasis on Bible study influenced people who considered themselves conservatives in contemporary disputes about inerrancy and science.

Although American evangelicals argued about Darby's views on dispensations and the rapture (some rejected them entirely; others insisted that end-times prophecies were already being fulfilled; some questioned Darby's radical separation of Israel and the church), many concurred with his underlying premise that Christ's coming was imminent, and they focused on the significance of that conviction for their everyday lives. Far more powerful at first than Darby's intricate prophetic charts was the simple expectation of Christ's return. In this most basic form, late nineteenth-century premillennialist teaching animated the lives and ministries of hundreds of thousands of evangelicals who, for many reasons, proved receptive to the view that they lived as "evening light saints" in "the shadow of the second coming."[19]

Participants noted the tendency of this "blessed hope" to transform lives. Reuben Archer Torrey, Yale-educated associate of evangelist Dwight L. Moody, for one, marked a watershed in his Christian life when he concluded that Christ's coming was near. "The blessed hope," he later reminisced, "transformed my whole idea of life; it broke the power of the world and its ambition over me."[20] The "blessed hope" radically reordered priorities: personal holiness replaced striving for worldly success and recognition.[21]

For some of its adherents, though not for all, premillennialism seemed to minimize Christian social responsibility by making social concern irrelevant.[22] It seemed to assign supreme value to private faith and individual responsibility. Torrey offered a typically blunt answer to the era's immense social challenges: "In the Return of our Lord is the perfect solution, and the only solution, of the political and social and commercial problems that now vex us."[23] Premillennialists seemed truly to long for Christ's return and to anticipate heaven in terms of the everyday act of going home.[24] One of their popular gospel songs articulated their yearnings:

> Oh, Lord Jesus, how long? How long
> E'er we shout the glad song,
> Christ returneth, Hallelujah,
> Hallelujah, Amen?[25]

It is curious that none of the forty practical consequences of the "hope" listed in an enduringly popular premillennialist manual, *Jesus Is Coming,* suggested that it should be an incentive for evangelism. That it did, nonetheless, motivate home and foreign missionary efforts is clear from the statements of many of its proponents as well as from the hymnals that help convey its popular ethos. Albert B. Simpson, founder of the Christian and Missionary Alliance, challenged his generation:

> Sound the alarm through the earth and the heavens!
> Summon the slumbering world to attend!
> Jesus is coming! The hour is impending!
> Sound the alarm to earth's uttermost end.
>
> Sound the alarm to the millions that wander
> Out in the darkness of heathendom's night!
> Tell them the King of all kingdoms is coming;
> Tell them of Jesus and send them the light.[26]

Simpson's Christian and Missionary Alliance (CMA) was among the most visible of the early American missionary agencies shaped by premillennial expectations. Born out of the evangelistic vision of this one-time Canadian Presbyterian pastor, the CMA was an interdenominational association of people who banded together to support projects at home and abroad. Created in 1887 as separate alliances, the Christian Alliance and the Missionary Alliance united in 1897 and sent out missionaries in an end-times effort to accomplish the evangelization of the world in their generation.[27] Like other premillennialists, Alliance supporters believed that their missionary efforts would not only prepare the world for judgment but also directly enable Christ's return. As Simpson put it:

> If we bring the other wandering sheep to Jesus,
> If we send the witness everywhere,
> We may hasten His long-looked-for Coming,
> And His glorious Advent may prepare.[28]

Another influential faith missions agency illustrates the extensive British influence on the spirituality of American premillennialists. The China Inland Mission (CIM) was established by J. Hudson Taylor in 1865. Nontraditional from the start, it not only served as a sending agency but it also produced literature that nurtured popular evangelical piety and greatly extended CIM influence. Led in North America by Henry Frost, the CIM marshaled evangelicals who resolved to prepare the world for judgment while they bent their efforts toward realizing a profoundly personal piety that placed the quest for a "higher Christian life" at the core of their spirituality.[29]

Turn-of-the-century popular evangelicalism, then, was receptive to the interrelated impulses of restorationism and premillennialism. Dispensationalism gained ascendancy in influential segments of evangelicalism, often promulgating negative responses to modernity, instructing believers to await miraculous escape from cataclysmic judgments, and discounting the positive accomplishments of the age to which liberals pointed as signs of progress. But occasionally other worldviews surfaced. The Boston pastor, Baptist editor, and educator A. J. Gordon, for example, commended the accomplishments of the age, but noted that evil and good advanced together. While he affirmed good in the culture, Gordon maintained that good would only triumph through Christ's return. Like Simpson, Gordon devised a restorationist eschatology in which an end-times renewal of early Christian vitality would include the exercising of apostolic power and spiritual gifts. Because they not only awaited Christ's coming but also anticipated the presence of spiritual gifts and the working of miracles in the end-times church, such premillennialists became important forerunners of Pentecostalism.

Healing

A century ago, organized sports, YMCA gymnasiums, health food stores, the expansion of the Church of Christ, Scientist, and an emphasis on "muscular Christianity" mirrored growing cultural emphases on wellness and physical fitness. The fascination for physical well-being had a religious counterpart in prayer for the healing of the sick. Prayer for the sick fit the restorationist schema: healing had played a prominent role in New Testament times and could be anticipated in the end-times restoration. Several related emphases amplified cultural influences to stimulate a renewed interest in physical healing.

First, and perhaps most visible, was an insistence that flowed from a theological premise that located healing "in the atonement" and noted as well its listing as a "gift of the Spirit."[30] While the radical evangelical world was not consistently or systematically preoccupied with theology, doctrines fascinated its inhabitants. Even as they pursued religious experiences, they quarreled lengthily and bitterly over minor points of doctrine. They churned out hundreds of thousands of pieces of literature to make the point that healing was "in the atonement." Perhaps most prominent among advocates of this view was A. J. Gordon. Second, since the Spirit's indwelling presence "quickened" believers' physical powers, healing harmonized with conceptions of the "higher Christian life."[31] Third, evangelical considerations of physical healing can be understood as a partial response to Christian Science, Unity, and other mind cure movements.[32] Evangelicals concluded that such movements thrived precisely because Christianity failed to offer hope for physical renewal.

A growing American evangelical interest in healing in the second half of the nineteenth century was informed as well by cross-cultural contacts, especially acquaintance with the efforts of a Swiss peasant, Dorothea Trudel, and a German pastor and theologian, Johann Christoph Blumhardt. Trudel offered the sick hospitality, biblical instruction, and prayer for their healing in homes she opened to them in the tiny village of Männedorf on Lake Zurich. Hers was a venture born out of her prayers for the recovery of several of her co-workers. A woman without much formal education, she drew criticism from established religious authorities who several times temporarily closed her healing homes on the charge that she practiced medicine without a license.[33]

Accounts from the ministry of Blumhardt, a Lutheran pastor in Baden-

Württemberg, Germany, also energized American expectations. After a much-publicized, prolonged, and highly irregular encounter with a member of his parish he claimed was demon-possessed, Blumhardt had perceived an emerging renewal in his congregation: attendance increased dramatically and people who had come to receive communion or absolution testified to physical healings. As a result Blumhardt left his parish, and with the assistance of the king of Württemberg, procured a resort facility known as Bad Boll, where he spent the rest of his life directing programs for people from many countries who sought both spiritual and physical renewal.[34]

Among the Americans who popularized a restorationist message that included healing, four can represent the content and application of this message that would have special significance for Pentecostalism. A. J. Gordon articulated the general message, asserting its essential orthodoxy and continuity with the early church; Albert B. Simpson explored a spirituality relating healing and the "higher Christian life"; John Alexander Dowie expounded healing as an essential component of restorationism; and Maria B. Woodworth-Etter pioneered the healing crusades that Pentecostals later imitated.

A. J. Gordon

More than a century after it first appeared, Boston Baptist pastor Adoniram Judson Gordon's influential book _The Ministry of Healing_ remains in print as a classic statement of the late nineteenth-century evangelical understanding of healing "in the atonement." Editor of a Baptist periodical, the _Watchword_, and founder of the Bible school that became Gordon College and Gordon-Conwell Theological Seminary, Gordon was a prominent associate of Dwight L. Moody and an associate editor of an influential missionary magazine, the _Missionary Review of the World_. In 1882 he wrote his book on healing.[35]

Gordon maintained that like forgiveness of sins, healing was available to anyone for the asking.[36] He regarded his day as the end-times "dispensation of the Spirit," maintaining that the Spirit's role was to "increase the knowledge of Christ," who was the Healer.[37] Assigning significance to his observation that the church had lost—at approximately the same time—its commitment to healing and its stress on the imminence of Christ's return, he argued that whenever "primitive faith" revived, the two emphases reappeared. "There is a grim irony," he wrote, "in the fact that, after death and the grave had gradually become the goal of the Christian's hope, instead of the personal coming of Christ, then we should begin to find miracles of healing alleged by means of contact with the bones of dead saints and martyrs, instead of miracles of healing through the prayer of faith offered to the living Christ."[38]

Motivated by one part of the restorationist hope, Gordon longed for a rebirth of the "primitive beauty and piety" of the Christian faith. Although he prayed for the sick privately, he did not introduce public healing services in his Boston congregation. He influenced the emerging wider interest in the subject primarily through his book, which was admitted by critics of the evangelical healing message to be "at once the most readable and the most rational presentation of the views of the Faith-Healers."[39]

Albert B. Simpson

Simpson made the "gospel of healing" a major theme of his ministry and an organizing principle of the Christian and Missionary Alliance. His views on the subject were rooted in his experience: he often recalled a healing from heart problems as a turning point in his ministry. Accepting healing as "part of Christ's glorious Gospel for a sinful and suffering world, for all who would believe and receive His word," Simpson resolved to integrate this conviction into his life and ministry, practicing and preaching healing wherever practicable.[40]

His affluent congregation, Thirteenth Street Presbyterian Church in New York City, resisted its young pastor's fascination for innovative teaching and practice. Simpson resigned and established an independent gospel tabernacle. In 1883 he dedicated a nearby Manhattan residence as the Home for Faith and Physical Healing. The next year two female associates assumed responsibility for day-to-day operations. Simpson conducted daily morning and afternoon services in a chapel, and during the first thirty months over seven hundred guests resided briefly at this faith home, while hundreds more attended services for instruction in healing.[41]

Some of Simpson's colleagues feared that his insistence on healing would lead to his advocacy of more controversial spiritual "gifts." "If you expect the healing of the sick," they cautioned, "you must also include the gift of tongues—and if the gift of tongues has ceased, so in the same way has power over disease." Simpson responded: "We cheerfully accept the severe logic. We cannot afford to give up one of the promises. . . . We believe the gift of tongues was only withdrawn from the early Church as it was abused for vain display or as it became unnecessary for practical use. It will be repeated as soon as the Church will humbly claim it for the universal diffusion of the Gospel."[42]

Rejecting the notion that faith had intrinsic curative power, Simpson shunned popular descriptors such as *faith cure* and *faith healing*. Rather, he insisted, there was a quality of health that exceeded full physical well-being, "a higher kind of life, the turning of life's waters into His heavenly wine." This life was "a very sacred thing" that gave "a peculiar sanctity to every look, tone, act and movement of the body." In this realm, one lived on the life of God and was obligated to be entirely "like Him" and "for Him." [43]

Simpson sometimes alluded to "divine health" rather than to "divine healing," asserting an integral relationship between such health and the "higher Christian life." "The power which heals the body," he observed, "usually imparts a much richer baptism of the Holy Ghost to the heart, and the retaining of this Divine health requires such constant fellowship with God . . . that the spiritual results far outweigh the temporal." [44]

John Alexander Dowie

If Simpson represented the promise that "higher Christian life" spirituality held for health, his contemporary John Alexander Dowie expounded a forthright, earthy healing gospel that had little to do with mystical piety and much to do with crusading against moral abuses, both personal and public.

An intractable but personable man, Dowie built a loyal American following around his assertion that God had restored the gift of healing to the church in his ministry. Born and educated in Scotland, Dowie spent much of his early life in Australia, where he was a Congregational pastor and a temperance activist. In 1888 he moved his family to the United States and quickly gained a reputation as an outspoken, fearless advocate of healing. In 1893 he arrived in Chicago and opened a mission opposite Buffalo Bill Cody's exhibit at the Chicago World's Fair. From these small beginnings he proceeded in the next decade to create a denomination, establish a religious community of some six thousand—Zion City, Illinois—and open mission outposts across the United States and around the world.

Dowie not only believed that his alleged gift of healing marked the beginning of an end-times restoration of spiritual gifts to the church, he also emphatically rejected all medicines and medical personnel and launched public criticism of other teachers of healing, most of whom took a far less radical stance on the use of "means."

The subject of "means," or the place of medicine in healing, proved particularly sensitive in the popular evangelical subculture. Dowie regarded all use of medicine as sinful. "God has but one way of healing," he insisted. "The Devil has a hundred so-called ways. Zion cannot go to medicine for healing. There is no fellowship between the blood of Christ and medicine." [45] Gordon and Simpson, on the other hand, discouraged

but did not denounce medical means. For them, whereas medical remedies were "limited" and "uncertain," God's provision was "complete" and
"definite."[46]

Dowie's initial efforts in Chicago evoked meager response, but early
in 1894 his situation improved. He referred to his efforts collectively as
Zion; by April Zion included a tabernacle and a large residence known
as Divine Healing Home No. 1. Late in the summer of 1894 Dowie
began publishing a weekly report of Zion's progress. Called *Leaves of
Healing*, the magazine circulated his sermons and many reports of healing; it also constituted a revealing commentary on American society,
politics, and world events. As more people identified with Zion, Dowie
added more healing homes and moved to ever-larger tabernacles. The
expansion of his work combined with his outspoken attacks on the religious establishment and Chicago's city hall to draw the attention of the
local press and provide extensive publicity. In 1896 he organized a committed band of followers into a new denomination, the Christian Catholic Church.[47]

As Dowie's vision for the restoration of the church's "primitive condition" expanded, he announced he was "Elijah the Restorer" (a reference
to the expectation that the Old Testament prophet Elijah would reappear
in the end times), declared himself an apostle, and inserted the word
apostolic into the name of his denomination.[48]

Meanwhile, Dowie purchased some sixty-five hundred acres of farm
land along Lake Michigan north of Chicago. As the twentieth century
dawned, Dowie unveiled his plans for a Christian utopia, Zion City, Illinois, to a crowd of three thousand gathered in his Chicago tabernacle for
a watch-night service. The city without "breweries or saloons, gambling
halls, houses of ill-fame, drug or tobacco shops, hospitals or doctors' offices, theaters or dance halls and secret lodges or apostate churches"
would, he promised, also exclude "hog raising, selling or handling." In
mid-July 1901 Zion was opened for settlement and the faithful began
moving in.[49]

By the turn of the century, Dowie had influenced thousands of Americans, some of whom had identified with the restorationist hopes expressed in his denomination. Many others claimed to have experienced
healings or had been convinced of the contemporary restoration of the
apostolic faith in his ranks. He offered women and African Americans
as well as white men opportunities for public roles in his organization.
His outspoken criticism of all who disagreed with him alienated many;
others were attracted by the apparent success of his message. In the
next century, many of his followers would identify with the Pentecostal
movement.

Maria B. Woodworth-Etter

The late nineteenth-century healing evangelist whose style best anticipated later Pentecostal preferences was undoubtedly Maria B. Woodworth-Etter. Born in Ohio on 22 July 1844, Woodworth-Etter's earliest religious impressions were associated with a local Disciples of Christ congregation. After her marriage she resolved to enter evangelistic ministry. Precluded from public preaching among the Disciples and discouraged by her husband, she found in a local Quaker meeting the emotional support she needed. Among the Quakers she prayed for an "anointing for service" and claimed that, in response, she was "baptized with the Holy Ghost, and fire, and power which has never left me."[50]

Satisfied that she had been spiritually energized, Woodworth-Etter began preaching and quickly achieved considerable local notoriety. She reported hundreds of conversions despite strong misgivings everywhere about a female evangelist. Her campaigns attracted reporters from newspapers across the country, who gave her free publicity. After a brief affiliation with the United Brethren in Christ, Woodworth-Etter joined the Church of God of the General Eldership, which had been founded by John Winebrenner. Her successive denominational affiliations were relatively unimportant to the story of her expanding ministry, however. In 1885 she began to pray for the sick on the assumption that all who had sufficient faith would be healed. Any who failed to find healing, then, were responsible for that failure: they either lacked faith or harbored sin. Woodworth-Etter's meetings were also known for the "trances" that became common occurrences. People would fall to the floor, apparently unconscious, only to testify later to profound spiritual experiences.

Woodworth-Etter eventually acquired a tent seating eight thousand and traveled from coast to coast preaching a popular message that made room for the emotions and offered physical as well as spiritual "victories." Such salvation/healing revivals would later play a pivotal though controversial role in the Pentecostal proclamation of healing. Woodworth-Etter (who was dismissed from the Church of God in 1904) later identified with Pentecostalism, although not with any Pentecostal denomination. Until her death in 1924 Pentecostals generally accepted and respected her as one who had anticipated their movement.

The Holy Spirit

A mounting interest in certain aspects of the person and work of the Holy Spirit formed another component in the changing kaleidoscope of restorationist millenarian fervor from which Pentecostalism emerged. Restorationists longed for energizing showers of "latter rain"; premillennialists craved personal holiness and "power for service"; advocates of healing awaited other "gifts of the Spirit"; many coveted a "higher" or "deeper" life of more intense spirituality than they observed around them. These yearnings fueled interest in a Holy Spirit who was neither abstract nor remote but constantly and personally active.

Early in the 1900s Arthur T. Pierson, a dignified and respected evangelical leader, reminisced about the past half century. A graduate of New York's Union Theological Seminary, Pierson was a pastor, editor, author, and conference speaker who was highly regarded among those who coveted a "higher Christian life." Pierson's assessment of the immediate past differed radically from that of prominent contemporaries. He ignored situations that alarmed many vocal conservatives and he disagreed with liberals who joyously affirmed the advances of modern science and the liberation of Christianity from the obscurantism of the past. His assessment was positive, and he published it under the title *Forward Movements of the Last Half Century*. First on his list of indicators of evangelical progress was "the increase of personal holiness." In spite of the crises around him, Pierson exuded confidence. In the growing contemporary interest in holiness and the Holy Spirit, he discerned the progress of God's end-times plan.[51]

Renewed interest in the Holy Spirit was expressed in many segments of contemporary Protestantism, liberal and conservative, but several contexts influenced Pentecostalism more directly than others. These included the broadly based holiness movement, which found its impulse in Wesley's teaching on Christian perfection; movements challenging Christians to experience a "higher Christian life," including proto-fundamentalist institutions and conferences where popular speakers disagreed with holiness theology but urged audiences to experience "the baptism with the Holy Spirit"; and scattered restorationist ministries, where participants anticipated the renewing showers of the "latter rain" or announced the dawning of the "evening light." These movements and ministries were not mutually exclusive; they overlapped in teaching, personalities, and, most obviously, in popular piety. Participants sang the same gospel songs, revered the same heroes and heroines of the faith, coveted intense religious experiences, subscribed to the same religious periodicals, used the same tracts, and read the same devotional literature. Despite their similar response to modernity and their shared spirituality, it is instructive to examine several representative contexts separately. They offer a sense of the different emphases that informed a growing popular radical evangelical fascination with the person and work of the Holy Spirit. Language used to describe life "in the Spirit" reveals something of the texture of life in the alternate network for which these people opted.

Wesleyan/Holiness Teaching

One source of the popular preoccupation with holiness was, of course, American Methodism. It soon spilled outward to agitate in other communions as well. Motivated by John Wesley's teaching on Christian perfection and by Charles Wesley's powerful hymns describing the life "purified by grace," generations of the Wesleys' American followers taught the present availability of "entire sanctification" through a "second definite work of grace" in which the inclination to sin would be replaced by perfect love.[52] Phoebe Palmer Knapp gave the experience popular expression in her gospel song "The Cleansing Wave":

> The cleansing stream I see, I see;
> I plunge, and oh it cleanseth me! . . .
> I rise to walk in heaven's own light
> Above the world and sin;
> With heart made pure, and garments white
> And Christ enthroned within.[53]

Advocates popularized teaching on this "second blessing" at camp meetings and brush arbors across the country. They urged it as the only "infallible safeguard against heresy," an experience with both progressive and instantaneous dimensions.[54] In a sermon preached at the Vineland, New Jersey, Holiness Camp Meeting in 1867, J. W. Horne reduced the message to simple terms: "Sanctification is a progressive work, while entire sanctification is the work of but a moment. There is a moment in which the darkness forever ceases; there is a moment in which the dying Adam is dead and the new Adam is alive; . . . there is a moment in which sanctification passes into entire sanctification."[55]

"In the condition of entire sanctification," Horne further noted, "we are enabled to devote our energies successfully to the great work of . . . strengthening the stakes of Zion at home and abroad; and to strive after the building up of saints in their most holy faith."[56] In contrast, a "state of partial sanctification" was said to "chain down" the believer's attention to personal spiritual struggles and hinder the progress of the church: "When the preacher has a consciousness of inward purity, and realizes the power of God in his heart, with what energy and success is he enabled to work!"[57]

People who pursued sanctification considered this preoccupation to be eminently practical: it proffered both purity and power and thus fostered both morality and service. They often described a facet of the experience that focused on the power of the Holy Spirit.[58] "Make, then, this consecration," a New York Methodist pastor, B. M. Adams, enjoined in 1867, "and the Holy Ghost will come upon you . . . and fill you with a power that you never had before. The nature of its influence I cannot describe; but 'Ye shall receive power after that the Holy Ghost is come upon you.'"[59] Thousands found inspiration to claim the enduring experience as they sang words by the Methodist Lelia Morris: "He will fill your heart *today* to overflowing with the Holy Ghost and power."[60] The experience was immediate, and it confirmed the believer's special relationship with God.

Physical manifestations sometimes accompanied this filling: "It makes some people boisterous in their manifestations," J. W. Horne noted, "and other people still. Some may have power that manifests itself in noise like thunder, and some silent power like the lightning."[61] Many readily identified with a popular holiness song:

> We find many people who can't understand
> Why we are so happy and free;
> We've crossed over Jordan to Canaan's fair land,
> And this is like heaven to me.
>
> So when we are happy we sing and we shout,
> Some don't understand us, I see;
> We're filled with the Spirit, there isn't a doubt;
> And this is like heaven to me.[62]

The experience not only brought spiritual power, exuberance, and freedom it also was assumed to initiate believers into a life of conscious fellowship with Christ described in rich Old Testament imagery. Like the biblical Israelites when they received the "second blessing," holiness advocates of all denominational backgrounds left struggles behind and entered the "promised land":

> 'Tis the Canaanland for our weary feet,
> With our wanderings o'er and our rest complete;
> Where we dwell with Christ in communion sweet,
> Baptized with the Holy Ghost.[63]

Those who embraced this full salvation did not attempt to rationalize their faith; they regarded it rather as a dynamic transforming experience that brought heaven into their lives. "Life wears a different face to me, since I found my Savior," they sang. "Since Christ my soul from sin set free, this world has been a heaven to me. . . . 'Tis heaven, my Jesus here to know."[64] The holiness experience, like later Pentecostalism, revolutionized individual perceptions of reality.

Songs and sermons emphasized the satisfaction the experience brought. People whose understanding of the Christian life was formed by a sense of a growing disparity between cultural values and their own priorities claimed to find in the holiness message inner "rest." Denied many of this world's pleasures and goods by circumstances and choice, they nonetheless had "true" and "abiding" riches. Among the many writings that testified to satisfaction, F. G. Burroughs's "I Have Found It" states particularly clearly the way in which holiness teaching offered an opportunity to reinterpret life. "Trials" became "conquests"; "sighs" were transformed to "praise":

> Since I came at Jesus bidding and received the
>   promised rest,
> I have found His ways most pleasant, and His paths serene
>   and blest;
> Trials have been changed to conquests, sighs are lost in
>   songs of praise;
> And all turmoil, care and conflict are transformed by
>   hope's bright rays.[65]

Seekers were assured that the experience met basic needs of companionship and assurance. "I am never lonely anymore, since the Comforter has come," believers insisted.[66] And the satisfaction could increase; the "glory never failed." This experience was not static because the faithful constantly pressed toward "higher ground" even as they yearned to go "deeper in the love of Jesus."

Those who professed the "second blessing" sometimes projected a spiritual arrogance that alienated others. In 1894 the *Journal of the Methodist Episcopal Church, South,* complained: "There has sprung up among us a party with holiness as a watchword; they have holiness associations, holiness meetings, holiness preachers, holiness evangelists and holiness property. Religious experience is represented as if it consists of only two steps. . . . The effect is to disparage the new birth, and all stages of spiritual growth from the blade to the full corn in the ear. . . . We deplore their methods in so far as they claim a monopoly on the experience, practice and advocacy of holiness."[67]

Certainly the heterodox practices that flourished under its auspices troubled thoughtful holiness spokespersons as well as observers. Holiness advocates, Methodist and others, had, in fact, proven receptive to many varieties of teaching. Their emphasis on religious experience had encouraged some to advocate a series of religious crises in the pursuit of perfection. Sallie Yancey of Greenville, South Carolina, was typical: "I was saved . . . sanctified, baptized with the Holy Ghost and fire, and received heaven's dynamite."[68] A stress on Bible study and restoration had resulted in denouncing medicine in favor of faith healing, forsaking regular employment for faith living, and distancing one's self from society to prepare for an imminent second coming. Some pursued admittedly unusual evidences of the Spirit's presence and power. And some went so far as to reject religious establishments entirely. In a book that became a handbook of "come-outism," John H. Brooks maintained that traditional churches were "too selfish, too bigoted, too far backslidden and fallen to give in . . . to a purely spiritual movement in their midst." "Holiness," he continued, "cannot be successfully propagated under sectarian conditions. . . . The time of compromise in connection with the holiness work is past."[69] Deploring those who advocated a holiness experience and yet remained "in bondage to the sects," Brooks issued a stirring call to participation in what he called the "One True Church."[70]

Around the country many radical evangelicals agreed that denominations were hopelessly backslidden and that further association with them was not only unadvisable but positively sinful.[71] Small holiness associations and missions gradually emerged, each intent on promoting a biblical experiential form of Christianity, sometimes with direct reference to the restoration of New Testament faith. The Evening Light Saints, for example, expressed the restorationist view that the "apostolic morning" of early church history had yielded to "papal night." The Reformation had produced a "cloudy afternoon." The late nineteenth century, however, was the focus of all history; it would see the restoration of primitive Christianity in "pure evening light" that would never fade.[72]

This broadly based holiness movement with its stress on religious experience and the Holy Spirit exerted influence in denominations outside the Wesleyan family and spawned countless independent congregations. And it had meaning for African Americans struggling to chart their course in post–Civil War America as well as for women who yearned to give public verbal expression to their faith.[73]

Other Evangelical Teaching

Among the radical evangelicals of all denominations who pursued experiential holiness were various prominent men and women who deemed it important to reject holiness theological categories and express their fascination for holiness and spiritual power in different categories. In practice, it often proved difficult to observe the differences among these evangelicals, but within the world of radical evangelicalism the distinctions were crucial. Coming largely from revivalistic new school backgrounds rather than from Wesleyan-rooted denominations, such people shared the sense that divine empowerment would enable personal holiness and effective evangelism. They often lacked, however, the inclination toward social holiness that was part of the heritage if no longer part of the practice of Wesleyan holiness advocates. Influenced by both millenarianism and restorationism to affirm their need for personal holiness and spiritual power, they anticipated and worked for worldwide revival. Their combination of emphases on premillennialism, faith healing, and revival extensively influenced Pentecostalism. Those who articulated these views were often identified with Bible institutes and conferences and frequently associated with one or more of Dwight L. Moody's endeavors.

Moody—whose influence permeated much of popular evangelicalism at the end of the century—used the phrase *baptism in the Holy Spirit* to describe a profound experience he claimed had altered his spiritual perception: "I cannot describe it," he insisted. "It is almost too sacred an experience to name. . . . I can only say God revealed Himself to me, and I had such an experience of His love that I had to ask Him to stay His hand."[74] Among Moody's associates, Reuben Archer Torrey became a prominent advocate of the Spirit-endued life.

Torrey perceived a lack of emphasis on the Holy Spirit in American Protestantism. He insisted that a balanced understanding of the personhood of the Holy Spirit would enrich the believer's Christian life, which he described as a "walk in the Spirit."[75]

Emphasis on the Holy Spirit prodded Torrey toward a definition of worldliness with far-reaching implications for attitudes toward leisure and entertainment. "Anyone who has really received the Holy Spirit and in whom the Holy Spirit dwells and is unhindered in His working will not want to partake of [worldly amusements]. . . . Why is it then that so many professed Christians do go after these worldly amusements? For one of two reasons: either because they have never definitely received the Holy Spirit, or because the fountain is choked."[76] A mystical dimension of ongoing "communion with God," facilitated by the understanding of the Holy Spirit as a person with whom believers could converse and interact, was something to be cherished: "How carefully we ought to walk in all things so as not to grieve Him who dwells within us," he admonished.[77]

Torrey rejected the holiness premise of two normative "works of grace" and maintained that sanctification was a progressive experience that commenced at conversion and proceeded as the believer "walked in the Spirit." Constant "victory over sin" was possible through "absolute obedience," which was the "cost" of fellowship with the Holy Spirit: "The Spirit's power may be in such fulness, that one is not conscious even of the presence of the flesh—it seems dead and gone—but it is only kept in the place of death by the Holy Spirit's power. If we try to take one step in our own strength, we fail. We must live in the Spirit and walk in the Spirit if we would have victory."[78]

This experience represented only part of the Holy Spirit's day-to-day role in the believer's life. In addition, Torrey and others taught that Christians could discover an unfailing source of spiritual power in a crisis experience called the baptism with the Holy Spirit.[79] With the encouragement of Moody, Torrey published one of a growing number of books on the baptism with the Holy Spirit in 1895.[80]

Because Torrey believed that the baptism with the Holy Spirit alone would facilitate the evangelization of the world before Christ's return, he taught that Spirit baptism was mandatory: "If I *may* be baptized with the Holy Spirit, I *must* be."[81] An ominous warning accompanied his appeal: "If I am not willing to pay the price of this Baptism, and therefore am not so baptized, I am responsible before God for all the souls that might have been saved but were not saved through me because I was not baptized with the Holy Spirit."[82]

Torrey and his contemporaries proposed no single evidence of this baptism with the Holy Spirit. Moody listed among its definite proofs a desire to "learn more about Christ," a love for the Bible, desire for spiritual knowledge and experience, and disinterested love.[83] "You shouldn't be looking for any token," he advised. "Just keep asking and waiting for power."[84]

From 1881, Moody made annual summer conferences at Northfield, Massachusetts, occasions for exploring the practical implications of the relationship between the Holy Spirit and believers. In 1881 some three hundred gathered for ten days of prayer for "revival and an outpouring of the Holy Spirit." Over the next two decades thousands of visitors to Northfield reported meetings of "thrilling character" where they received the baptism with the Holy Spirit. Moody urged them on: "Let us pray that we may be baptized with power from on high . . . that we may be always ready—ready for anything."[85] To those anticipating specific lay or ordained ministries he appealed: "Let me beg of you: Get full of the Holy Ghost. Just make up your minds you will not leave these gatherings until God fills you. Don't be afraid. Lots of people are afraid of being called fanatics. You are not good for anything until the world considers you a fanatic."[86]

Northfield Conferences incorporated other related emphases. A student conference in 1886 contributed to the formation of the student volunteer movement, which over the next few decades channeled the interests of thousands of American young people into foreign missions. As they proliferated through the 1890s, Bible institutes, too, became centers in which students were urged to experience the Spirit's immediate power and presence. Such schools and conferences attracted a wide range of participants, including women and ethnic minorities, and offered a forum for the exchange of ideas as well as facilitating networking. They also popularized the new gospel songs of Fanny Crosby, D. W. Whittle, P. P.

Bliss, Ira Sankey, Charles Gabriel, and others, some of which dealt expressly with the personal and public meaning of the end-times "outpouring" of the Holy Spirit.

In extradenominational settings across the country, then, evangelicals confidently asserted that their discovery of the dynamic role of the Holy Spirit in the lives of believers marked a new epoch—a "dawning"—in Christian history: "The long, long night is past / the morning breaks at last. . . . / The Comforter has come!"[87]

This experience-oriented message tended to obscure theological differences and to attract people of various persuasions who were less concerned with ideas than with religious experience.[88] Liberals of the period were attracted and united by the challenge to imitate the historical Jesus; radical evangelicals found a measure of unity through a focus on the Holy Spirit and an ever-present Christ. The assortment of people who advocated the "higher Christian life" illustrates how the emphasis on persons and experience penetrated doctrinal barriers. Their description "higher Christian life" was a statement about the prevalent religious situation and their dissatisfaction with the Christian life as they saw it lived around them. Drawing to some extent on the teachings of Charles Finney, who affirmed a second crisis experience of enduement and cleansing as a normal part of the Christian life and urged Christians to receive the baptism with the Holy Spirit, they extolled the potential of a "higher" (or sometimes a "deeper") Christian experience than others enjoyed. They dreamed of making the "higher" experience normative. While the practical differences among these people were often minor, their distinct approaches and methods were of enormous importance to their self-understanding.

The Presbyterian William Edwin Boardman was prominent among advocates of the possibility of an intense spirituality he considered most Christians lacked. He gave it exposure and a name with the publication of his book *The Higher Christian Life* in 1859. In the 1870s Boardman joined forces with two other popular advocates of this spirituality, Robert Pearsall Smith and Hannah Whitall Smith. The Smiths had been influenced by the Plymouth Brethren and the holiness movement to expound a Christ-centered message. "My whole horizon used to be filled with this great big Me of mine," Hannah wrote in her autobiography, "but when I got a sight of Christ as my perfect Savior, this great big Me wilted down to nothing."[89] For her, the simple message of the indwelling Christ as a present (or moment-by-moment) Savior became "the Christian's secret of a happy life."[90]

The Smiths and Boardman traveled in the United States, Britain, and western Europe, sharing the message of the availability to all believers of the constant, conscious, sin- and self-subduing inner "reign of Christ." They intersected with Europeans who were already actively pursuing a similar spirituality. They called the experience "present" salvation; "Jesus saves me now" became the core of their message as well as their theme song. Their efforts in Great Britain contributed in 1875 to the convening of the first Keswick Convention. These became annual events in which the view that holiness and spiritual power were available to all who lived a "life of overcoming" was prominent. The "secret" of this life was simple:

> Let in the Overcomer, and He will conquer thee.
> Thy broken spirit taken in sweet captivity
> Shall glory in His triumph, and share His victory.[91]

Participants accommodated Keswick teaching (which was expressed in terms of carefully nuanced, middle-class asceticism) to their needs.[92] Anglicans were joined by Baptists and Congregationalists as well as by visitors from abroad. During the last two decades of the nineteenth century, some of the most popular Anglo-American evangelical authors and speakers identified with Keswick and its fascination for an immediate sense of God's presence and power at work in their lives. F. B. Meyer, Andrew Murray, G. Campbell Morgan, J. Hudson Taylor, Arthur T. Pierson, Horatio Bonar, Andrew Bonar, Amanda Smith, and Hannah Whitall Smith were just a few. Their diverse backgrounds caused them to articulate differently the experience of full salvation that the Keswick Conventions nurtured:

> Love's resistless current sweeping all the regions
>   deep within;
> Thought and wish and senses keeping now, and every moment,
>   clean.
> Full Salvation! From the guilt and power of sin.
> Life immortal, heaven descending; Lo! my heart the Spirit's
>   shrine!
> God and man in oneness blending—Oh, what fellowship is
>   mine!
> Full Salvation! Raised in Christ to life divine.[93]

Visitors from abroad, print media, and noted American evangelicals popularized the Keswick message in the United States, and during the 1890s Moody welcomed its spokespersons to the platform of his popular Northfield Conferences. It found expression in hymns, devotional literature, "higher life" periodicals, biographies, and tracts. In civic auditoriums in major American cities as well as in tabernacles, churches, and Bible institutes, in humble missions, scattered rural churches, and home Bible studies, women and men urged Christians to "live up to their privileges" in preparation for Christ's return. Assuming that "the average Christian life [was] grievously destitute of real spiritual power and often essentially carnal," they challenged the faithful to recognize that the call to perfection was at the heart of the gospel.[94]

Another bridge between those radical evangelicals who consciously embraced Wesleyanism and those who did not was Albert B. Simpson, the founder of the Christian and Missionary Alliance.[95] Perhaps his precise differences with one side or the other were not consistently clear in his own mind. Certainly his Christ-centered message emphasized relationship over doctrine and made him an important contributor to Pentecostalism. Simpson regarded the experience of the gospel as an experience of Christ—Christ the Savior, Christ the Healer, Christ the Power, Christ the Sanctifier. Thus he was far less interested in doctrines such as healing, sanctification, and enduement with power than he was in cultivating a mystical relationship with Christ.[96]

In various popular evangelical settings, then, people awaited—and worked toward—the end-times restoration of the apostolic faith. In the relentless modernization of their culture, they saw the ominous, prophesied "signs of the times" alerting them to the fast-approaching end of human history. Their response was individualistic and highly privatized in an era when individuals seemed to be losing prestige to corporate structures. They had little or no status in the emerging urban industrial culture, but in the alternate networks they created, they affirmed in ultimate terms their worth and life's meaning. Not surprisingly, they found hopeful indicators of spiritual vigor within their ranks, but little outside. Life became a "them against us" proposition with sweeping cosmic implications. Since God was on their side, they fully expected success in their efforts to wrest individual souls from eternal damnation and to stir lethargic believers to end-times renewal. The "blessed hope" not only compelled them it also assured their triumph. They were militant and determined, compelled by a sense of destiny:

> There's a shout in the camp for the victory is coming
> O'er Satan's power;
> Through the word of the Lord we the battle are gaining
> This very hour.[97]

NOTES

1. Barney E. Warren and Andrew L. Byers, eds., *Songs of the Evening Light* (Moundsville, W. Va: Gospel Trumpet, 1897), 1.

2. John W. Welch, introduction to *The Apostolic Faith Restored*, ed. Bennet F. Lawrence (St. Louis: Gospel Publishing House, 1916), 7.

3. See Grant Wacker, "Playing for Keeps: The Primitivist Impulse in Early Pentecostalism," in *The American Quest for the Primitive Church*, ed. Richard T. Hughes (Urbana: University of Illinois Press, 1988), 196–219.

4. The term *foursquare gospel* was used during the 1920s by Aimee Semple McPherson to describe the message of her denomination, the International Church of the Foursquare Gospel. See Aimee Semple McPherson, *The Story of My Life* (Waco, Tex: Word Books, 1973). Donald Dayton, in *The Theological Roots of Pentecostalism* (Grand Rapids: Francis Asbury Press, 1987), explores the theological evolution of each of these four doctrines as they relate to twentieth-century Pentecostalism.

5. *Dictionary of Christianity in America*, s.v. "primitivism." See, for example, T. D. Bozeman, *To Live Ancient Lives: The Primitivist Dimension in New England Puritanism* (Chapel Hill: University of North Carolina Press, 1988), and Hughes, *American Quest*.

6. See, for example, E. H. Broadbent, *The Pilgrim Church* (London: Pickering and Inglis, 1931), which documents the restorationist understanding of the course of church history by tracing the fate of apostolic Christianity.

7. Lawrence, *Apostolic Faith*, 12.

8. He urged this in a long, popular treatise that his followers still circulate: John H. Brooks, *The Divine Church* (El Dorado Springs, Mo.: Witt, 1960).

9. For an introduction to this Christian Union see Charles Conn, *Like a Mighty Army Moves the Church of God* (Cleveland, Tenn.: Church of God Publishing House, 1955), 3–9.

10. For Parham's life, see James R. Goff, *Fields White unto Harvest: Charles F. Parham and the Missionary Origins of Pentecostalism* (Fayetteville: University of Arkansas Press, 1989).

11. For a fascinating account of Shiloh and the human implications of Sandford's restorationist dreams, see Shirley Nelson, *Fair, Clear, and Terrible: The Story of Shiloh* (Latham, N.Y.: British American, 1989).

12. See Grant Wacker, "Marching to Zion," *Church History* 54 (Dec. 1985): 496–511.

13. Albert B. Simpson, "The Latter Rain," *Songs of the Spirit* (New York: Christian Alliance Publishing, 1920), no. 52. By the late nineteenth century, hopes for Christian unity had, of course, begun to shape formal ecumenical efforts. The American tradition of voluntary associations—special-purpose agencies for cooperative action—was nearly as old as the republic and was used extensively for religious ends. The Evangelical Alliance, and later the Federal Council of the Churches of Christ, represented efforts toward Christian cooperation. But restorationists in the popular evangelical subculture that spawned Pentecostalism disdained ecumenism. Unable to work within established structures, they rejected them and identified with the urge, long present in the religious culture, toward biblical recreation. See Cecil M. Robeck, "Pentecostals and the Apostolic Faith: Implications for Ecumenism," *Pneuma* 9 (1987): 61–84.

14. Arthur T. Pierson, *Forward Movements of the Last Half Century* (New York: Funk and Wagnalls, 1900), 411, 409. In 1875 Dwight L. Moody had expressed the conviction that the world was "on the eve of some very great event—some very great change." He predicted that the event would either be "a great war" or "the coming of the Lord." See "Mr. Moody's Expectation of a Great War and the Second Coming of Christ," *Signs of Our Times*, 9 June 1875, 355.

15. Ethel E. Goss, *The Winds of God* (New York: Comet Press Books, 1958), 21–22.

16. See Timothy Weber, *Living in the Shadow of the Second Coming* (New York: Oxford University Press, 1979); Ernest R. Sandeen, *The Roots of Fundamentalism* (Chicago: University of Chicago Press, 1970).

17. See, for example, Charles Fox Parham, *A Voice Crying in the Wilderness* (n.p., 1910), 86; Daniel W. Kerr, "The Selfsame Thing," *Trust* 13 (Aug. 1914). For a summary of the logic, see Edith L. Blumhofer, "Restoration as Revival: Early American Pentecostalism," in *Modern Christian Revivals*, ed. Edith L. Blumhofer and Randall Balmer (Urbana: University of Illinois Press, 1993).

18. See, for example, *Presbyterian and Reformed Review* 1 (1890): 36–37; Sandeen, *Roots*, 136–39.

19. This phrase, chosen by Timothy Weber as the title for his study of American dispensationalism, conveys a sense of the practical influence this "blessed hope" had. People convinced of the likelihood of Christ's "any moment" return lived in anticipation of that event. In a real—and, they would claim, a positive—sense, it cast its glow over their lives.

An example of a prominent premillennialist who diverged from Darby's teaching was A. J. Gordon, a man whose writings deeply influenced many early Pentecostals. For an indication of the various understandings of history and prophecy that coexisted under the aegis of premillennialism, see Gordon's *Ecce Venit* (New York: Fleming H. Revell, 1889).

20. Reuben Archer Torrey, *The Return of the Lord Jesus* (Los Angeles: Grant's Publishing House, 1913), 21.

21. A popular handbook for American premillennialists listed at least forty practical consequences of the understanding that Christ's coming was near. See W. E. Blackstone, *Jesus Is Coming*, rev. ed. (New York: Fleming H. Revell, 1908). For a sense of the personal impact of such teaching, see the introductory comments by Reuben Archer Torrey and J. Wilbur Chapman.

22. On the other hand, a more positive view of the relationship between premillennialism and social reform was taken by others. See Grant Wacker, "The Holy Spirit and the Spirit of the Age in American Protestantism, 1880–1910," *Journal of American History* 72 (June 1985): 45–62.

23. Torrey, *Return of the Lord Jesus*, 7.

24. For a discussion of the terms used to express this anticipation, see Edith L. Blumhofer, *Pentecost in My Soul* (Springfield, Mo.: Gospel Publishing House, 1989), 33–37.

25. H. L. Turner, "Christ Returneth," *Hymns of Glorious Praise* (Springfield, Mo.: Gospel Publishing House, 1969), no. 138.

26. Albert B. Simpson, "Sound the Alarm," *Songs of the Spirit,* no. 115.

27. See Albert B. Simpson, *Larger Outlooks on Missionary Lands* (New York: Christian Alliance Publishing, 1893). Simpson was recognized as an innovator in publicizing missionary needs. See also Robert Niklaus, John Sawin, and Samuel Stoesz, *All for Jesus* (Harrisburg, Penn.: Christian Publications, 1986).

28. Albert B. Simpson, "Looking For and Hasting Forward," *Songs of the Spirit,* no. 123. The assumption that evangelism would hasten Christ's return was based on Matt. 24:14.

29. See Mrs. Howard Taylor, *By Faith: Henry Frost and the China Inland Mission* (Philadelphia: China Inland Mission, 1938).

30. See Charles Cullis, *Faith Cures* (Boston: Willard Tract Repository, 1879); *History of the Consumptives Home* (Boston: Willard Tract Repository, 1869); William E. Boardman, *Faith Work* (Boston: Willard Tract Repository, 1878); William E. Boardman, *The Great Physician* (Boston: Willard Tract Repository, 1881).

31. Based on Rom. 8:11. See also Raymond J. Cunningham, "From Holiness to Healing," *Church History* 43 (1974): 499–513.

32. The perception of Christian Science as an arch enemy suggests how close evangelical teaching on healing and Christian Science teaching were. When early Pentecostals listed their enemies, Christian Science usually led the list. Early Pentecostal periodicals contain many articles exposing the errors of Christian Science, suggesting that they felt especially threatened by it. Preoccupation with Christian Science waned during the 1920s, when Christian Science came to be perceived simply as one of a long list of unorthodox groups.

33. See A. J. Gordon, *The Ministry of Healing* (New York: Christian Alliance Publishing, 1882), 146ff; Charles Cullis, *Dorothea Trudel; or, The Prayer of Faith,* 3d ed. (Boston: Willard Tract Repository, 1872); Konrad Zeller, *Dorothea Trudel von Männedorf* (Stuttgart: Hanssler Verlag, 1971).

34. See Edith L. Blumhofer, "Jesus Is Victor: A Study in the Life of Johann Christoph Blumhardt," *Paraclete* 19 (Spring 1985): 1–5; Gordon, *Healing,* 158ff.

35. For how this interest fit into the larger context of Gordon's thought, see C. Allyn Russell, "Adoniram Judson Gordon," *American Baptist Quarterly* 4 (Mar. 1985): 61–89.

36. Gordon, *Healing,* 22–38. Gordon stated explicitly: "Christ's ministry was a two-fold ministry, affecting constantly the souls and the bodies of men. 'Thy sins are forgiven thee,' and 'Be whole of thy plague,' are parallel announcements of the Savior's work which are found constantly running on side by side." Ibid., 19. See also Ernest Gordon, *Adoniram Judson Gordon* (New York: Fleming H. Revell, 1896).

37. Gordon, *Healing,* 45–57.

38. Ibid., 64.

39. See, for example, Benjamin Warfield, *Counterfeit Miracles.* Warfield maintained that the neglect of "means" such as medicine and surgery was "the essence of fanaticism." Others concurred. Writing in the *Methodist Review,* George Hammell asserted: "The fanaticism of unauthorized faith consists in the misapplication of divine promises to the affairs of practical life. . . . It finds

manifestation . . . in the so-called 'faith-cure' movement." George M. Hammell, "Religion and Fanaticism," *Methodist Review* 70 (July 1888): 534.

40. Quoted in A. P. Thompson, *The Life of A. B. Simpson* (New York: Christian Alliance Publishing, 1920), 75. See also, Albert B. Simpson, "Divine Healing," *The Word, the Work, and the World*, 7 Sept. 1886, 158; Albert B. Simpson, *The Gospel of Healing* (New York: Christian Alliance Publishing, 1915).

41. "The New Berachah Home," *The Word, the Work, and the World*, 7 Sept. 1886, 186.

42. See *The Word, the Work, and the World*, 4 Oct. 1883, 172; Albert B. Simpson, *The Gospel of Healing* (New York: Christian Alliance Publishing, 1888), 83–84. The last two sentences quoted were replaced in the 1915 edition with the following: "to a greater or less extent, the gift of tongues has been continuous in the Church of Christ, and along with many counterfeits has undoubtedly been realized in the present generation."

43. Simpson, *Gospel of Healing* (1915), 37–38.

44. Ibid., 72. Simpson's followers in the Christian and Missionary Alliance never unanimously embraced his views on "divine life." For an example of continuing confusion about the teaching, see the letters under "Questions about Divine Healing," *Alliance Witness*, 4 Feb. 1987, 29.

45. John Alexander Dowie, "The Everlasting Gospel of the Kingdom of God Declared and Defended," *Leaves of Healing*, July 1899, 713.

46. Simpson, *Gospel of Healing* (1915), 183; "Inquiries and Answers," *The Word, the Work, and the World*, Nov. 1886, 339–40. Simpson, Gordon, and other evangelicals who prayed for the sick, like Dowie, affirmed the necessity of exercise and hygiene. Simpson, Gordon, and their friends Reuben Archer Torrey and Arthur T. Pierson concurred that the advances of medical science were impressive but not "omniscient or omnipotent." See Pierson, *Forward Movements*, 405. Because they did not declare medical science "a work of the Devil" and because they taught that sickness could properly be construed as chastening or discipline, Dowie unequivocally opposed them. During Torrey's tenure as superintendent of the Chicago Training Institute (later Moody Bible Institute), his daughter became critically ill with diphtheria. Torrey and his wife decided to forego medical help and pray for her recovery, and they enlisted Dowie's prayers. Dowie exploited the incident, using it to slander both Moody and Torrey. *Leaves of Healing*, 8 Apr. 1899, 457–64. Torrey's daughter lived. The Torreys had already lost one daughter to diphtheria, an incident he attributed to lack of faith and use of medicine.

47. For Dowie's life, see Wacker, "Marching to Zion"; Gordon Lindsay, *The Life of John Alexander Dowie* (Dallas: Voice of Healing, 1951); John Alexander Dowie, *Zion's Holy War against the Hosts of Hell in Chicago* (Chicago: Zion Publishing House, 1900); Gordon Lindsay, ed., *Champion of the Faith: The Sermons of John Alexander Dowie* (Dallas: Christ for the Nations, 1979).

48. Dowie's growing sense of apostolic calling is recorded in a dedicated issue of his paper *Leaves of Healing*, 24 Sept. 1904, 275. See also Edith L. Blumhofer, "The Christian Catholic Apostolic Church and the Apostolic Faith: A Study in

the 1906 Pentecostal Revival," in *Charismatic Experiences in History*, ed. Cecil M. Robeck, Jr. (Peabody, Mass.: Hendrickson, 1985), 126–46.

49. See *Leaves of Healing*, 13 Apr. 1901, 787; "The Passing of Dr. Dowie," *Word To-Day*, Apr. 1906, 359.

50. Mrs. Maria B. Woodworth-Etter, *Signs and Wonders God Wrought in the Ministry for Forty Years* (Chicago: Hammond Press, 1916), 28. This strand of pietist, holiness-oriented Quakerism in Ohio and Indiana is described more fully in Byron Lindley Osborne, *The Malone Story: The Dream of Two Quaker Young People* (Newton, Kans.: United Printing, 1970), as well as in Thomas D. Hamm, *The Transformation of American Quakerism* (Bloomington: Indiana University Press, 1988).

51. For Pierson's biography see Delavan Pierson, *Arthur T. Pierson* (New York: Fleming H. Revell, 1912), and Dana Robert, "Arthur Tappan Pierson and the Forward Movements of Late Nineteenth-Century Evangelicalism" (Ph.D. diss., Yale University, 1984).

52. For an account of the holiness movement, see Charles Edwin Jones, *Perfectionist Persuasion* (Metuchen, N.J.: Scarecrow Press, 1974). For the story of one of its primary advocates, see Charles E. White, *The Beauty of Holiness: Phoebe Palmer as Theologian, Revivalist, Feminist, and Humanitarian* (Grand Rapids, Mich.: Zondervan Publishing House, 1986).

53. "The Cleansing Wave," *The Best of All* (n.p., n.d.), no. 123.

54. G. D. Watson, *A Holiness Manual* (Dallas: Chandler Publications, n.d.), 13.

55. J. W. Horne, "Sermon," in *Penuel; or, Face to Face with God*, ed. A. McLean and J. W. Eaton (New York: W. C. Palmer, Jr., 1869), 26.

56. Ibid., 27.

57. Ibid.

58. Donald Dayton, "From Christian Perfection to the Baptism with the Holy Ghost," in *Aspects of Pentecostal-Charismatic Origins*, ed. Vinson Synan (Plainfield, N.J.: Logos International, 1975), 39–54.

59. B. M. Adams, "Sermon," in McLean and Eaton, *Penuel*, 65.

60. "Bring Your Vessels Not a Few," *Hymns of Glorious Praise*, no. 125.

61. Horne, "Sermon," 65.

62. J. E. French, "This Is like Heaven to Me," *Best of All*, no. 181.

63. Lelia Morris, "Baptized with the Holy Ghost," *Best of All*, no. 94.

64. E. E. Hewitt, "Since I Found My Savior," *Best of All*, no. 173; See also "Colin Smith's Letter" in the same issue for the relationship between Christ-centered experience and "heaven": "All Thy gifts do not suffice / Lord let Thyself be given; / Thy presence makes my paradise / And where Thou art 'tis heaven."

65. "Since I Came," *Best of All*, no. 127.

66. J. M. Kirk, "Since the Comforter Has Come," *Songs of the Evening Light*, no. 38.

67. Quoted in Vinson Synan, *The Holiness-Pentecostal Movement in the United States* (Grand Rapids, Mich.: Wm. B. Eerdmans, 1971), 50–51.

68. "Sallie Yancey's Letter," *Live Coals*, 11 Jan. 1905, 4.

69. Brooks, *Divine Church*, 271. This book popularized assumptions about the basic incompatibility of religious organizations and spiritual movements.

70. Ibid., 283.

71. It is difficult to generalize about the people who accepted "come-outist" logic, but some attempts have been made. See Carl Oblinger, *Religious Mimesis* (Evanston, Ill.: Institute for the Study of American Religion, 1973); J. Gordon Melton and Robert L. Moore, *The Cult Experience: Responding to the New Religious Pluralism* (New York: Pilgrim Press, 1982), 24.

72. William G. Schell, "Biblical Trace of the Church," *Songs of the Evening Light*, no. 20; see also R. E. Winsett, "Evening Light," *Songs of the Coming King* (Ft. Smith, Ark.: privately published, 1922), no. 124.

73. The Methodists Phoebe Palmer Knapp and Frances Willard and the Salvation Army pioneer Catherine Booth published the case for ministering women, citing the Pentecost event as the basis for women's right to preach. For a general treatment of this subject, see Barbara Brown Zikmund, "The Struggle for the Right to Preach," in *Women and Religion in America*, ed. Rosemary Ruether and Rosemary Skinner (San Francisco: Harper and Row, 1981), 1:193–214; Edith L. Blumhofer, "Evangelical Ministering Women in the Past Century," *Fides et Historia* 22, no. 1 (Winter-Spring 1989–90): 49–61; Letha Dawson Scanzoni and Susan Setta, "Women in Evangelical, Holiness, and Pentecostal Traditions," in *Women and Religion in America*, ed. Ruether and Skinner, 3:223–34; Phoebe Palmer, *The Promise of the Father* (Boston: Henry V. Degen, 1859); *Holiness Tracts Defending the Ministry of Women*, ed. Donald Dayton (New York: Garland Publishing, 1985).

74. Quoted in A. P. Fitt, *Moody Still Lives* (New York: Fleming H. Revell, 1936), 28. See also Reuben Archer Torrey, *Why God Used D. L. Moody* (New York: Fleming H. Revell, 1923).

75. Reuben Archer Torrey, *The Fundamental Doctrines of the Christian Faith* (New York: George H. Doran, 1918), 115. Ernest R. Sandeen notes the extent of this focus on the personhood of the Holy Spirit as well as on the relationship of the Holy Spirit to individuals among contemporary millenarians. See Sandeen, *Roots*, 178.

76. Reuben Archer Torrey, *The Person and Work of the Holy Spirit* (New York: Fleming H. Revell, 1910), 115.

77. Ibid., 112.

78. Reuben Archer Torrey, *What the Bible Teaches* (Chicago: Fleming H. Revell, 1898), 251.

79. Reuben Archer Torrey, *The Baptism with the Holy Spirit* (Chicago: Fleming H. Revell, 1895), 14–15; Gordon, *Ministry of the Spirit*, 67ff; Albert B. Simpson, "Principles of Christian Life and Holiness," *The Word, the Work, and the World*, Oct. 1886, 205–7.

80. Torrey, *Baptism*. Another prominent advocate of an experience he called the "filling" of the Holy Spirit was A. J. Gordon; see *Ministry of the Spirit*. For a consideration of the Pentecostal direction Gordon's work took see Russell, "Gordon."

81. Torrey, *Baptism*, 28.

82. Ibid. He urged Christian workers to "stop [their] work right where [they were] and not go on with it until [they had been] clothed with power from on high." Ibid., 24–25. Albert B. Simpson concurred: "We are not fit to represent God in the world or to do any spiritual work for Him until we receive the Holy Ghost." *The Holy Spirit; or, Power from on High* (New York: Christian Alliance Publishing, 1896), 1:82.

83. Dwight L. Moody, "Question Drawer," in *College Students at Northfield,* ed. T. J. Shanks (New York, 1888), 205.

84. Opposition emerged promptly in reviews of Torrey's and Gordon's books in denominational periodicals such as the *Presbyterian and Reformed Review* and the *Presbyterian Quarterly.* While admitting that the teaching incorporated "much that was edifying," reviewers objected that the pentecost event would not recur. Noting that Torrey inclined to some phases "of the doctrine which, in its grosser forms, is called 'the second blessing,'" reviewers suggested that Torrey's careful distinctions between his views and those of Wesleyan holiness leaders were inconsequential: his teaching produced similar results and approached the "insidious" Wesleyan error. See, for example, Talbot W. Chambers, "Review of R. A. Torrey, *The Baptism with the Holy Spirit,*" *Presbyterian and Reformed Review* 6 (Oct. 1895): 789–90; "Review of R. A. Torrey, *How to Obtain Fulness of Power,*" *Presbyterian Quarterly* 12 (Jan. 1898): 125. The *Presbyterian Quarterly* also took issue with Gordon. One reviewer noted that contemporary use of premillennial teaching made the entire system of Christian belief Christocentric with the second coming as its focal point. Gordon and others, the article correctly observed, suggested that premillennialism was "the mountaintop from which the whole landscape of the gospel" should be viewed. See D. N. McLauchlin, "Review of A. J. Gordon, *How Christ Came to Church,*" *Presbyterian Quarterly* 10 (Oct. 1896): 530.

85. Dwight L. Moody, "Enduement for Service," in *D. L. Moody at Home,* ed. T. J. Shanks (New York: Fleming H. Revell, 1886), 261.

86. Dwight L. Moody, "Consecration and Concentration," in *A College of Colleges,* ed. T. J. Shanks (New York: Fleming H. Revell, 1887), 217.

87. Frank Bottome, "The Comforter Has Come," *Hymns of Glorious Praise,* no. 118.

88. For attempts to explain this, see Wacker, "The Holy Spirit and the Spirit of the Age" and Douglas Frank, *Less Than Conquerors: How Evangelicals Entered the Twentieth Century* (Grand Rapids, Mich.: Wm. B. Eerdmans, 1986).

89. Hannah Whitall Smith, *The Unselfishness of God and How I Discovered It: A Spiritual Autobiography* (New York: Fleming H. Revell, 1903), 190.

90. Hannah Whitall Smith's book of this title, first published in 1875, remains in print as a classic statement of higher life spirituality. The spread of Keswick teaching and its cultural significance are discussed in David Bebbington, *Evangelicalism in Modern Britain: A History from the 1730s to the 1980s* (London: Unwin Hyman, 1989).

91. Freda Allen, "A Life of Overcoming," *Songs of Victory,* 3d ed. (London: Pickering and Inglis, n.d.), no. 242.

92. David Bundy, "Keswick and the Experience of Evangelical Piety," in *Modern Christian Revivals,* ed. Blumhofer and Balmer.

93. Frank Bottome, "Full Salvation," *Songs of Victory,* no. 253.

94. See Arthur T. Pierson, *The Keswick Movement in Precept and Practise* (New York: Funk and Wagnalls, 1903), and Pierson, *Forward Movements,* 32–33.

95. Albert B. Simpson, "Himself," *The Word, the Work, and the World,* Oct. 1885, 258–60. He disassociated himself from some views considered specifically Wesleyan in this widely circulated article.

96. Albert B. Simpson, "Himself," *Songs of the Spirit,* no. 24.

97. C. Austin Miles, "There's a Shout in the Camp," *Best of All,* no. 61.

CHAPTER

2

A Fresh Look at Legend and Reality,
1901–6

O N ANY GIVEN summer day in 1904 a few southeastern Kansas towns were likely to be visited by groups of fifteen to twenty young people who arrived by train and announced their presence by marching down Main Street. Attractively dressed and singing gospel songs, they carried banners that read "Apostolic Faith Movement." Upon reaching a central location, they gathered into a group and continued singing. As the curious gathered, they heard singing, testimonies, and preaching followed by an invitation to a nearby rented hall.

Those who visited the hall often encountered the magnetic personality of the founder of the Apostolic Faith Movement, Charles Fox Parham. Acclaimed as an able preacher, Parham reportedly held his audiences spellbound. He played on their emotions, handily moving them from tears to laughter. But his intent was serious: he announced the restoration of the apostolic faith, an event, he explained, of enormous eschatological import. The response he evoked in small towns in the contiguous areas of Kansas, Missouri, and Oklahoma demonstrated that he addressed effectively the felt needs of many people. His message was not profound, but the experience he advocated seemed adept at enriching his hearers. Few of the towns that he and his bands of young workers visited were the same after his departure. Wherever he went, he left behind those who believed they had been transformed by a powerful encounter with the living Christ that initiated them into the divine mysteries of God's end-times plans.

In some ways Parham seemed an unlikely religious leader. Young and frail, he had neither visible means of support nor impressive formal training. He was not an ordained minister. He had demonstrated a proclivity for innovative interpretations of Scripture that diverged sharply at times from traditional orthodoxy. Temperamentally unsuited to cooperate with established authority, Parham had broken his ties to organized religion, and, like other prophets in his religious subculture, he attracted a motley constituency. Fearless and determined, he demonstrated sensitivity to religious needs and conviction about God's intention to repeat in contemporary America the awe-inspiring phenomena of early Christianity.

One of five sons of William and Ann Parham, Charles Fox was born in Muscatine, a Mississippi River port town in eastern Iowa, on 4 June 1873. In 1883 the family moved by covered wagon to join the earliest settlers of Cheney in south-central Kansas. If, as Parham later claimed, he had little exposure to formal religious instruction or preaching during his youth in Cheney, the situation resulted from choice rather than necessity. First Methodist Church and Trinity Reformed Church had been organized by the time the Parham family arrived. St. Paul's Lutheran Church, Missouri Synod, was established nearby the next year.[1]

Late in 1885 Parham's mother died. Funeral services were conducted by C. S. Bolton, a missionary of the Church of God of the General Eldership.[2] The next year Bolton returned to Cheney to officiate at the marriage of Parham's father and Harriet Miller. A lifelong Methodist, Miller was the daughter of a pioneer northern Indiana Methodist circuit rider and was known as a devout Christian who "loved the power of old time religion."[3] She and William Parham prospered financially and opened their home for religious activities.[4] William cultivated his land, raised cattle, and later purchased a business in town. The house he constructed in Cheney in 1901 was noted in the local paper as "one of the finest private residences in the county."[5]

Charles Parham recalled conducting his first public religious services when he was fifteen. The local paper did not report them but did note his employment as a schoolteacher in nearby Norwich for the summer term of 1890.

In 1891 Parham enrolled at Southwestern Kansas College, a Methodist-affiliated school that had been established five years earlier in nearby Winfield. He attended the academy and the normal school. Registered as a student from the fall of 1891 through the spring of 1893, Parham recalled that his extensive religious work precluded satisfactory academic performance. On the other hand, he also recalled a decision not to enter the ministry but rather to become a physician.[6]

In Parham's personal religious world, events and decisions were charged with spiritual significance. When his frail health deteriorated, he concluded that God was punishing him for heeding the devil's promptings to disregard his call to preach. In a claim typical among those who shared his religious impressionism, Parham recounted that when he had reached the point of death, he "submitted," vowed to preach, and was infused with the certainty that he would be healed. A partial recovery followed. Afflicted with continued weakness, Parham "brought forcible arguments in prayer," soliciting full recovery. He later recalled an instantaneous healing, but full recovery in fact took time. Parham claimed a revelation that education would be detrimental to effective ministry, left school, and sought opportunity in the Methodist Episcopal Church, North.[7]

In mid-1893 Parham accepted an assignment as supply pastor in the Methodist congregation in Eudora, Kansas (a small town between Kansas City and Lawrence), where he served until sometime before March 1895.[8] He also preached Sunday afternoons to Methodists in nearby Linwood. His early ministry was apparently well received, although it was singularly unproductive: he reported only one convert after two years.[9] Restive under "the narrowness of sectarian churchism" and "often in conflict with the higher authorities," Parham repudiated denominational affiliation and launched an independent evangelistic ministry.[10]

Like a growing group of his contemporaries, Parham concluded that "true Bible Christianity" (which he called "the Apostolic Faith") could not be practiced in traditional settings. As an itinerant evangelist, Parham was a guest in many country homes. A man of the people, he discussed religious beliefs with his host families. Such conversation was apparently common and welcome. Kansas citizens proved receptive to his holiness orientation; the area was hospitable to various contemporary "prophets."[11]

In the small town of Tonganoxie, just west of Kansas City, Parham made friends with a Quaker, David Baker, with whom he debated doctrine. Hours of discussion led to his conclusion that the conventional understanding of hell as a place of eternal torment was unbiblical. Since eternal life "came by Jesus Christ," he maintained, only those who received Christ could live eternally; the wicked would be annihilated. Parham became an enthusiastic exponent of conditional immortality. His views on eternal life—like his opinions on other doctrines—evolved over several years. In 1902 he issued a disjointed statement asserting that the majority of humankind would receive "everlasting human life": "A promised Savior for mankind: the plan was to restore the mass of the human race to what they lost in the fall of Adam, which the unsanctified and many heathens will receive—everlasting human life. Orthodoxy would cast this entire company into an eternal burning hell; but our God is a God of love and justice, and the flames will reach those only who are utterly reprobate."[12]

On 31 December 1896, in a Friends' ceremony, Parham married Baker's granddaughter, Sarah Eleanore Thistlewaite.[13] In September 1897

their first child, Claude, was born. Shortly thereafter, Parham's health
failed, the baby took sick, and two close family friends died. In another
dramatic moment invested with spiritual significance, Parham claimed he
"found the power of God to sanctify the body from inbred disease as well
as from inbred sin."[14] "A sanctified body is as much provided for in the
atonement of Jesus as is sanctification for the soul," he would later declare.[15] Parham decided to renounce all medical help, to preach healing,
and to pray for the sick. He and his son regained strength, and the family
moved to Ottawa, Kansas, where Parham began to integrate healing into
the messages he preached in rented rooms and local schoolhouses.[16]

Parham soon moved his base of operations to Topeka, where he secured a mission and an office. In 1898 he obtained a large facility he
named Bethel Healing Home. He adopted as his theme for his ministry
"a living Christianity." Daily morning and evening prayers from 7:00 to
7:30 were supplemented by a full schedule of mission services. Sunday
mornings he conducted a holiness meeting. Sunday school followed at
2:00, with a healing service at 3:00. Sunday evenings were set aside for
evangelistic preaching. A women's Bible study on healing on Tuesdays
and Friday evening prophecy classes rounded out the schedule. Parham
emphasized "salvation by faith; healing by faith, laying on of hands and
prayer; sanctification by faith; coming (premillennial) of Christ; the baptism of the Holy Ghost and fire, which seals the bride and bestows the
gifts."[17] He published a biweekly magazine, the *Apostolic Faith,* which
clearly evidenced his growing awareness of others who shared his interests. Its title, *Apostolic Faith,* indicated his growing absorption with restorationist themes. The first issue of *Apostolic Faith* for 1900 carried a
lengthy excerpt from Albert B. Simpson's *The Gospel of Healing.* It also
advertised a pamphlet discrediting John Alexander Dowie.[18]

Parham's preference for rooting doctrine in private meditation and his
conviction that the Holy Spirit communed directly with him combined
with his impressionable nature and intransigent rejection of established
religious authority to influence his message. It is unclear when Parham
began to focus his attention on the need for an experience of baptism
with the Holy Spirit. It is evident that by 1900 he conceived of such an
experience and believed it had eschatological meaning. Further, for him
it was neither a cleansing event nor an "enduement with power for service" as he later claimed. Rather, it "sealed the bride" for "the marriage
supper of the Lamb"; only those who had been so sealed would escape the
horrors of rapidly approaching divine judgments (often called the "tribulation"). During the 1890s he believed that Spirit baptism was "the only
essential baptism," and thus for several years he did not practice water
baptism.[19]

Like his views on eternal punishment, his evolving understanding of water baptism was influenced by discussions with many people.[20] For a time, he apparently practiced immersion—first single, then triple. However, sometime in 1900, Parham became convinced of his need to "lay his teachings, creeds and doctrines at His feet and by faith in His cleansing blood trust that every error, false teaching or unscriptural thought may be cleansed."[21] As a result, he discovered that "some of the teachings we had believed to be so scriptural and some we had loved so dearly and had been the most persevering in propagating" were "wiped from his mind."[22] Among them was triple immersion. Parham began practicing single immersion using the formula "in the name of Jesus, into the name of the Father, Son and Holy Ghost."[23]

As an end-times promoter of the restoration of the apostolic faith, Parham lent his support to the contemporary quest to create a Jewish homeland, supporting Theodor Herzl and lecturing on the subject often.[24] He subscribed to Anglo-Israelism, with its inherent racism, maintaining that the Anglo-Saxon peoples were the ten lost tribes of Israel.[25] The conviction of Anglo-Saxon superiority nurtured by his eschatology corresponded neatly with racial attitudes that pervaded much of the popular culture around him. He preached a popular version of Josiah Strong's *Our Country* and Rudyard Kipling's "white man's burden."[26]

Parham operated his Topeka efforts on a "faith" basis, without visible means of support, although expenses on the property averaged $130 per month.[27] He took no offerings in services, preferring simply to pray for supply. In a pattern typical in similar ministries scattered across the country, he accepted any who shared his interest in the "full gospel," readily welcoming strangers to his home and pulpit.

During the spring of 1900 Parham left his services to visiting evangelists while he traveled to various places to explore "the latest truths restored by latter day movements."[28] After an absence of several months (during which he visited Chicago, Cleveland, New York, Maine, and Winnipeg), Parham returned to Topeka and found that he had lost most of his congregation and his facilities to the visitors. This turn of events reinforced his growing determination to embark on a new venture— opening a Bible school to promulgate and further explore his conviction that the apostolic faith was being restored to the church. In October 1900 he opened Bethel Bible School in a rented facility. Some forty people (including dependents) responded to the invitation to "all ministers and Christians who were willing to forsake all, sell what they had, give it away, and enter the school for study and prayer."[29]

Parham modeled his school on a Bible school he had visited during his recent travels. Located near Lewiston, Maine, and established in 1895 by Frank Sandford, a one-time Free Baptist pastor, the Holy Ghost and Us Bible School was part of Sandford's scheme to realize the "restoration of all things" and the kingdom of God.[30] Parham's encounter with Sandford was pivotal for the emergence of Pentecostalism; this little-known figure had anticipated much that Pentecostalism would promulgate.

After briefly attending Bates College, Sandford had been called to the pulpit of the Free Baptist Church in Great Falls, New Hampshire. As a young and promising pastor, he had been selected to visit the denomination's missionary stations around the world. But the more he achieved, the less satisfied he seemed. In 1893 he abruptly left his denomination and launched an independent evangelistic ministry. He mingled occasionally with Moody and his associates, participating at Northfield and preaching several times at Moody Bible Institute. He also visited Albert B. Simpson's outreaches in New York City and his annual camp meetings at Old Orchard Beach, Maine. In 1892 Simpson officiated at Sandford's marriage to Helen Kinney, daughter of a wealthy businessman and the first Alliance missionary to Japan. Increasingly, Sandford became convinced that his one-time mentors and colleagues failed fully to understand God's plan; he was called to do greater things than they imagined.[31]

Slowly Sandford created a congeries of ministries he called Shiloh. He constructed a seven-story tabernacle, a healing home, a children's home, a school, and a five-hundred-room dormitory. As his dreams became more radical, however, he alienated most of his friends. He subordinated his stress on evangelism to his preoccupation with the restoration of apostolic experience. Poring over the New Testament, he detected a disparity between "denominational religion" and the "apostolic primitive Christianity." Like John Alexander Dowie in Zion, Illinois, Sandford would conclude in 1901 that he was Elijah the Restorer (Mal. 4:1); he would later claim apostleship.[32]

The name of Sandford's school, the Holy Ghost and Us, indicated his intentions for its organization and operation. Founded to contend for the "whole truth" of God, the school was intentionally unconventional. "Everything gives way to the Holy Ghost's latest," one participant reported. "And it quickly becomes evident to a newcomer that the Holy Ghost does not intend that His students shall become dependent upon the routine of sleeping and eating."[33] One description of the school's early format reads as follows:

> "Curriculum" there is none: it is the Bible.
> "Faculty" there is none: it is the Holy Ghost.
> "Length [of] course" there is none: students go when the
>   Director sends them.
> This is the Holy Ghost's work. This is real teaching.
> This is supernatural.[34]

Sandford attempted to lead students "not *to* the truth, but *into* the truth": he had them read the Bible and then "pray the lessons . . . into their own hearts."[35] Classes frequently adjourned for prayer because Sandford insisted that the lessons of one passage must be "prayed in" before the next passage was considered. By 1901 Sandford would claim to have restored the one true church, which he called the Church of the Living God. On 1 and 2 October 1901 he baptized several hundred followers (among them Ambrose J. Tomlinson, later leader of a Pentecostal denomination, the Church of God, Cleveland) in what he called "the first baptism under the Restoration" and "a fresh washing to cleanse out the mixture and confusion of the past."[36] Sandford's restoration included emphases on healing, holiness, "victorious" living, and the baptism with the Holy Spirit.

As 1900 dawned, Sandford organized from among his students a group of seventy men and women to evangelize the United States.[37] He sent them out according to the biblical model, two-by-two, walking without luggage or plans until they found people who would listen. At the end of April Sandford and six of his most trusted workers left Maine, traveling by rail west to Winnipeg and then to Tacoma. Meanwhile, some of the seventy sent out in January had found response to their message in Kansas City, and two of them—Edward Doughty and Victor Barton—had won a hearing in Topeka. When Sandford and his growing number of adherents arrived by train in Kansas City to meet a group of new recruits for Shiloh, eighteen men and women, including Charles Fox Parham and several of his followers, were introduced. They boarded a train for the ride to Maine. Sandford was encouraged to believe that Shiloh would be "the rallying point for all such clusters of called-out Christians."[38]

After spending a month in Maine, Sandford, Parham, and others left for Winnipeg, where Sandford had a strong nucleus of followers. A month later, Sandford was back at Shiloh with five more recruits for his Bible school. Parham had traveled back to Topeka to organize a school of his own.

Parham's visit to Shiloh not only influenced his teaching and practice, it also made obvious his participation in a broad stream of restorationist foment in popular evangelicalism. Sandford became important to the emergence of Pentecostalism because of his direct influence on Parham, but he represents many others across North America who gathered sizable followings as they worked for an end-times restoration. Viewed separately, they seem numerically inconsequential; taken together, they reveal a strong impulse.

At Shiloh Parham saw more than a Bible school. Worship services characterized by emotional exuberance filled long hours. Participants shouted, clapped, sang spontaneously, stayed indefinitely, fought the devil (an exercise in which they shouted, waved clenched fists, and went through violent contortions, directing anger at forces unseen but purportedly present), fasted and prayed, spoke ecstatically (although Sandford later repudiated tongues speech), and preached and testified extemporaneously. The entire Shiloh community of several hundred commemorated Christ's crucifixion by fasting and praying each Thursday from 9 A.M. until 3 P.M. Parham introduced that custom in Topeka.

On 15 October the twenty-seven-year-old Parham began conducting classes at his new school. Like Sandford's, his school had only one text, the Bible, and one teacher, ostensibly the Holy Spirit (using Parham as his mouthpiece). Parham stated his goal as "utter abandonment in obedience to the commandments of Jesus, however unconventional and impractical this might seem."[39] Students lived together, combining their resources. At least one had sufficient means to purchase one hundred dollars worth of furniture for the group and seemed willing to sacrifice his farm to keep the school open.[40] Despite its seeming unity all was not harmonious at Bethel; one student later recalled that "sometimes friction and disobedience [were] manifested."[41] By the end of the year, however, students had begun to study the baptism with the Holy Spirit.

For at least eight years Parham had taught a "baptism of the Holy Ghost and Fire," which he had understood to be separate from sanctification by faith. This baptism, he maintained, "sealed the Bride and bestowed the gifts."[42] Parham believed that the bride of Christ consisted of 144,000 people taken from the church. All who craved "deliverance from the plagues and wraths of the last days" needed to be "sealed" by receiving the baptism with the Holy Spirit. The "living membership" of the bride at Christ's return would all be so baptized and by virtue of their Spirit baptism would "escape the power of the devil before this age closes."[43]

This understanding of Spirit baptism was later obscured by an emphasis on speaking in tongues and evangelism. But this stress on the necessity of Spirit baptism for assured escape from the dreaded tribulation came first and fueled Parham's determination to assert a uniform evidence for the experience. He craved assurance that he would "go up" in the rapture.

Among the students who determined late in 1900 to receive this "baptism of the Holy Ghost and Fire" was Agnes Ozman.[44] She had demonstrated a strong proclivity toward the religious individualism that made nondenominational, experientially oriented settings more congenial than traditional religious institutions. Reared a Methodist in rural Nebraska, Ozman had been active in the YMCA and had attended several faith Bible schools, assisted in city rescue missions, and absorbed the teachings of several contemporary "higher life" teachers. Thirty years old when she made her way to Topeka from Kansas City in 1900, she had no settled vocation, purpose in life, or home; she had established a pattern of wandering from place to place, pursuing some elusive spiritual reality. She had often seemed enamored of a teaching or ministry, only soon to discover an irresistible urge to move on.

Ozman later recalled that during prayer with two other women at Bethel Bible School she had spoken "three words in another tongue." "This," she noted, "was a hallowed experiment and was held in my heart as sacred; the Lord had it treasured up for each of us, and nothing was said about it until later."[45]

What happened next is not entirely clear. Ozman claimed that during the evening service on 1 January 1901 she asked Parham to lay his hands on her and pray that she would receive the "baptism of the Holy Ghost and Fire."[46] She reported that she had spoken tongues "as is recorded in Acts 19."[47]

Parham later claimed that before Ozman's tongues speech his students had unanimously agreed that the baptism with the Holy Spirit would always be evidenced by speaking in tongues (known languages, as in Acts 2). He asserted that Ozman had desired this baptism so that she could evangelize effectively on the foreign mission field. This understanding of the experience departed from his earlier eschatological approach and it does not correspond with Ozman's recollections. Following her experience, she recalled, students began "searching the Word for light" on tongues. On 1 January 1901 she did not consider tongues "the only evidence necessarily given to those who received the baptism."[48] Contrary to Parham's suggestion that consensus on the subject had already been reached, Ozman noted: "I did not expect the Holy Spirit to manifest Himself to others as He did to me."[49]

Parham asserted that Ozman spoke Chinese for three days, during which she could neither speak nor write English.[50] Ozman later corroborated this, noting that her efforts to write resulted in "automatic characters in another language."[51] She had some control over her speech, however; two separate accounts record her public prayers in English at a Topeka mission on 2 January.[52]

Within several days more than a dozen others had spoken in tongues. The discrepancies in the various accounts lend credence to the view that Parham had most likely concluded earlier that speaking in tongues was "Bible evidence" for the baptism with the Holy Spirit and that he had purposely created a setting in which others would reach the same conclusion under circumstances in which it would seem to have been "revealed."[53] He had been gripped by a need to know what the Bible meant when it described a baptism with the Holy Spirit. He admitted that for many years he had believed that Christians should possess the apostolic power miraculously to proclaim the gospel in foreign languages they had not learned. Early in January 1901 he acknowledged: "We have for long believed that the power of the Lord would be manifested in our midst, and that power would be given us to speak other languages, and that the time will come when we will be sent to go into all the nations and preach the gospel, and that the Lord will give us the power of speech to talk to the people of the various nations without having to study them in schools."[54]

Given the urgency about world evangelization that his eschatology nurtured, Parham's fascination with tongues speech to facilitate foreign missions is logical. It is interesting, however, that until he publicly advocated tongues as "Bible evidence" of Spirit baptism, he exhibited no interest in missions. Most of his efforts encouraged others to pursue dimensions of personal religious experience. His Bible school was not primarily intended to equip workers to evangelize; rather, it offered a setting in which to explore the "deeper truths" of the Christian faith. He was more fascinated with tongues as evidence of "sealing of the bride" for the rapture.

Comparison of the inconsistent accounts about Parham's introduction of tongues speech as the evidence of the baptism with the Holy Spirit yields at least one certain conclusion: he regarded this "standard" for evaluating Spirit baptism as an enhancement to his apostolic faith message. It was not an inconsequential aberration; it represented the recovery of another dimension of New Testament reality. Parham, at least, was certain that Ozman's tongues speech validated his conclusion about uniform "Bible evidence" for the baptism with the Holy Ghost and fire.[55]

Events at Bethel Bible School attracted the press and disillusioned at least one student, S. J. Riggins of Kansas City who left in disgust: "I believe the whole of them are crazy," he told reporters. "I never saw anything like it. They were racing about the room talking and gesticulating and using this strange and senseless language which they claim is the word from the most high."[56] One local paper dubbed the school "The School of Tongues" and recounted a visit during which students who had "received the gift" came into the room and performed in his presence, speaking "a few sentences in a strange and unnatural way, outlandish words of which they neither knew the meaning nor the language to which they belong. Their reason for uttering them is that the Lord inspires them."[57]

The recovery of tongues speech marked the end of Bethel Bible School. Parham attempted to convince his previous supporters, first in a series of meetings at the Academy of Music in Kansas City, then back in

Topeka, then in a rented theater in Lawrence, Kansas. In Lawrence he and some twenty associates reported initial success: "Large numbers came to the meetings, and many were saved. The sick were healed and a good number of believers received the baptism of the Holy Spirit."[58]

Despite this heartening beginning, committed supporters were few, and within several months Parham's ministry had disintegrated. His former students abandoned him, some in disillusionment, others to pursue their own interests. One group, including Agnes Ozman, left for Shiloh, Maine. They traveled as far as Kansas City, when, they claimed, their "lack of the presence of God" and their "powerlessness" convinced them that they had followed "a voice which was not the Lord's."[59]

For several years, Parham struggled to establish a base from which to proclaim the restoration of the apostolic faith. He suffered personal tragedy and public rejection. "Both the pulpit and the press sought to utterly destroy our place and prestige," he later reminisced, "until my wife, her sister and myself seemed to stand alone."[60] Parham's lectures on Zionism sometimes proved vastly more popular than his stance on the gospel.[61]

The tide finally turned during the summer of 1903 when the Parhams went to El Dorado Springs, Missouri, to conduct open-air services in the popular health resort. To the many who sought the alleviation of physical suffering, Parham preached healing. His message on the physical merits of Christ's atonement brought responses that had eluded his excitement over the restoration of tongues speech.

Among those who claimed healing was Mary Arthur, wife of a prominent citizen of Galena, Kansas, where her many years of failing health were common knowledge.[62] After her return from El Dorado Springs to Galena in good health in 1903, she and her husband invited the Parham family to preach their message in Galena. Throughout the winter of 1903–4 Parham preached twice daily, first (in the absence of the pastor) in the Methodist church, then in the Arthur home, then in a tent, and finally, as inclement weather set in, in a warehouse that seated hundreds.[63] Hundreds claimed conversion, healing, and Spirit baptism. The Joplin, Missouri, *News Herald* reported in January that over one thousand had been healed and eight hundred had claimed conversion.[64] In the small mining towns of southwest Missouri and southeastern Kansas, Parham had become a sensation. He had also finally found acceptance. For the rest of his life, the region would provide his most loyal following, and for most of those years his home was near Galena in Baxter Springs, Kansas.

From his Galena meetings Parham recruited a group of devoted young co-workers who traveled in "bands" and assisted him in proclaiming the apostolic faith from town to town in southeastern Kansas. By the end of 1904 Parham reported that "many hundreds of people from Carthage, Mo. through southeastern Kansas to Miami, Okla. were now believers in the power of the faith once delivered to the saints."[65] Also in 1904 the first frame church built specifically as a Pentecostal assembly was constructed at a crossroads in the unincorporated town of Keelville, Kansas (where it still stands).

As his influence extended, Parham apparently did not emphasize unduly his innovative doctrines. Or perhaps he was already promulgating the view he later used to silence detractors: "Truly spiritual people do not quibble over tenets and points of doctrine; it is a sign of waning spirituality to do so."[66] It is also probable that most of his hearers were barely theologically literate but unfailingly pragmatic; since his message seemed to effect results, they accepted it without pausing to digest his views on eternal punishment, Anglo-Israelism, or the bride of Christ. Amid the intense emotional exuberance and the grueling physical demands of constant meetings and daily miracles, the proclamation of the "full gospel" produced results that seemed to duplicate New Testament experiences. His message evoked responses: people thought they *experienced* God. His convert Howard Goss summarized Parham's simple, central message: "Jesus, His teachings, salvation, life and the power to heal from Christ's time to the present moment . . . [and] a clean holy life of victory for all believers."[67] Contemporaries later recalled the young Parham as a "vivid, magnetic personality with superb, versatile platform ability." Acquaintances noticed his humility. Even the often-hostile press carried a story acknowledging that "Parham does not impress one as being a peculiar man. Indeed, he is a right good fellow and is earnest in his life's work."[68]

With apostolic faith assemblies (Parham shunned the designation "church") established in the principal towns surrounding Galena, Parham took twenty-four workers with him to extend the restoration movement into eastern Texas. They soon sent back reports of marked successes in the Houston area. Once again, proclaiming healing and praying for the sick proved the most effective way to find a crowd. Reporters for the *Houston Chronicle* who in August visited a short-term Bible school Parham had established claimed that miracles occurred regularly and that they heard "speaking in all tongues known to man."[69] Parham regularly issued ominous warnings to those who failed to commit themselves to his apostolic faith movement: "God," he told them, would "hold them responsible, if they do not join in this great crusade with our captain, Jesus, against sin and Satan."[70] Innovative as usual, Parham often sat on the platform dressed in Palestinian costume. Unlike many preachers with a similar holiness-oriented message, he encouraged his workers to dress stylishly and thereby to demonstrate the attractiveness of the Christian life.[71]

Early in the fall of 1905 bands of up to eight apostolic faith workers scattered from Houston to small communities in Texas, Kansas, and Oklahoma.[72] Later that year they reassembled to participate in a Bible school that ran until the spring of 1906. The weekday schedule included morning Bible study, noon shop and prison services, afternoon house-to-house visitation, and evening street meetings followed by evangelistic services of which protracted altar services were a highlight. A Methodist lay preacher since 1899, Warren Fay Carothers assisted Parham in Bible teaching.[73]

Among those influenced by Parham's ministry in Houston were several African Americans with an intense interest in holiness. One was Lucy Farrow, known as "Auntie" among Parham's workers; another was William Seymour, whose background among the Evening Light Saints probably helped make him receptive to Parham's message.[74] Seymour apparently attended some Bible school classes (some reports indicate that he sat behind a curtain). Both Parham and Seymour preached to Houston African Americans.[75] Farrow and Seymour were well known in the area's holiness missions. At one of them, Seymour met Neeley Terry, a Los Angeles resident who worshiped at a holiness mission. When Terry returned home, she encouraged the group to invite Seymour to become the mission's associate pastor. Parham had planned to send Seymour "to those of his own color" in Texas, but the new opportunity proved too alluring to Seymour.[76] Parham then tried unsuccessfully to convince Seymour to remain in Houston at least until he had experienced the baptism with the Holy Spirit.

Sometime in January 1906 Seymour left Houston for Los Angeles. Apparently he traveled via Denver, where he sought hospitality among members of the Pentecostal Union (Pillar of Fire). The group's indomitable leader, Alma White, later characterized him as a "very untidy person" who "excelled all the religious fakirs and tramps" she had ever met.[77] Shortly after Seymour's arrival in Los Angeles, his efforts, complemented by those of Lucy Farrow and J. A. Warren, in a nondescript section of the city catapulted Parham's apostolic faith message to prominence among the networks of independent missions whose leaders coveted an end-times restoration of New Testament Christianity.[78]

During their first few months in Los Angeles, the three considered themselves subject to Parham's leadership. In July 1906, for example, after three months of daily meetings in Los Angeles, Seymour requested and received credentials (or license as a minister of Parham's apostolic faith movement) from Parham.[79] But events in Seymour's Los Angeles mission quickly overshadowed Parham's work in the rural southern Midwest. Although Parham continued to have a strong following for several years—and despite his considerable success in extending the move-

ment—the focus of apostolic faith activities shifted in 1906 from his efforts to those supervised by Seymour in Los Angeles. Parham came to
resent this bitterly and responded in part with scathing denunciations of
Seymour's mission, where "big buck niggers" prayed with their arms
around whites, and where the exuberant worship represented not the
Holy Spirit but "negroisms."[80] Parham considered that, among other excesses, "noises as practiced by the Negroes of the Southland" had been
"pawned off on people all over the world as the working of the Holy
Spirit."[81]

Bitter recriminations followed. Accused of financial irregularity and
(from the fall of 1906 and especially in 1907) sexual misconduct as well
as of doctrinal aberrations, within a year Parham became an embarrass-
ment to a movement seeking to affirm its essential orthodoxy by demon-
strating continuity with New Testament Christianity.[82] He had also fallen
victim to his own restorationism: if God had sovereignly restored the
apostolic faith, then God was its leader. "There is no man at the head of
this movement," restorationists insisted. "God Himself is speaking in the
earth."[83] Parham vented his frustrations in his magazine, the *Apostolic
Faith*. Relentless attacks on emerging leaders distanced him from a movement that owed much to his vision. For while many claimed to have
spoken in tongues prior to January 1901, none made the association between tongues speech and the baptism with the Holy Spirit that Parham
had introduced. And it was that association, with the eschatological implications shaped by its restorationist context, that gave identity to the
scattered fledgling restorationist millenarian constituency that gradually
emerged as American Pentecostalism.

Azusa Street

The new hub of apostolic faith activities was a once-abandoned building in the heart of Los Angeles that admirably suited Seymour's needs. Its
distance from residential areas assured freedom from complaints about
noise, and its utter simplicity made the setting conducive to the informality and spontaneity these antichurchly worshipers coveted. Before he
moved his meetings to the facility at 312 Azusa Street, Seymour and
several of his followers had spoken in tongues, and word of his restoration
message had spread through the city's independent missions, sparking interest and controversy.

At first at Azusa Street blacks and whites mingled as they sought spiritual renewal. Some had been convinced in the house meetings that preceded the opening of the mission that "God was working mightily." Frank
Bartleman, one who persistently sought out "movements of the Spirit,"

manifested the antiorganizational bias typical among independent restorationists. He regarded Seymour's small company as having become the focal point of God's contemporary dealings with humanity: "Evidently the Lord had found the little company at last, outside as always, through whom he could have right of way. There was not a mission in the country where this could be done. All were in the hands of men. The Spirit could not work."[84]

On 18 April the *Los Angeles Times* noted the progress of the meetings under a revealing headline: "Weird Babel of Tongues; New Sect of Fanatics Is Breaking Loose; Wild Scene Last Night on Azusa Street." The next day coverage of the San Francisco earthquake displaced such local stories, but the meetings continued with new appeal. The San Francisco earthquake, mission participants maintained, was an act of God's judgment. The natural disaster intensified spiritual concern. "Many are saying that God has given the message that he is going to shake Los Angeles with an earthquake," a bulletin in the mission's magazine, the *Apostolic Faith*, reported. "First, there will be a revival to give all an opportunity to be saved. The revival is now in progress."[85] Seymour and his followers interpreted the world around them according to this sense of their own roles as players in history's final act.

In 1906 Los Angeles was in a period of rapid growth because many settlers had recently arrived from the Midwest. Like other highly mobile populations, its citizens often sought community in religious affiliation. At least a third of the residents held church membership, but official statistics fail to account for the many who participated in newer sectarian groups.[86] Various holiness organizations as well as independent missions had successfully established themselves in the city.[87]

In addition to small holiness missions, a congregation formed by Joseph Smale known as the New Testament Church figures prominently in the story of the apostolic faith in Los Angeles. Smale, formerly pastor of the city's First Baptist Church, advertised his church as "a fellowship for evangelical preaching and teaching and Pentecostal life and service" and anticipated a revival similar to that which had recently swept Wales. Smale's response to the Welsh revival is representative of the reactions of many American evangelicals who saw in Wales an event that they believe confirmed the restoration in their day of New Testament experience.

Books and religious periodicals circulated eyewitness accounts and evaluations of the Welsh revival by noted evangelicals. In several important ways the revival contributed to the specific context from which Pentecostalism emerged. First, it directly challenged believers to obey "promptings" of the Holy Spirit and it modeled obedience in such unusual ways as unstructured services with opportunity for all to express their spontaneous worship and conviction. Second, it was presented as an end-times Pentecost, or the "first showers of the latter rain." Third, it helped make familiar the religious language Pentecostals later found meaningful and it gave that language specific experiential connotations just as the apostolic faith movement gained wider notice. The British Keswick leader Evan Hopkins summarized the revival's challenge: "Let believers be as one before God—in unity of life and love—in oneness of purpose and desire—and then the Holy Ghost, who is present, will put forth his power; God's children will be filled with the Spirit, and the unconverted will be saved."[88]

Spokespersons for the Welsh revival understood it as the end-times fulfillment of Joel 2:28: "And it shall come to pass . . . that I will pour out my spirit upon all flesh." The revival seemed to ignore the well-established methodology of revivals. Spontaneity and apparent disorder replaced promotion, scheduling, regular preaching, financial planning, and systematic evangelistic outreach. No one knew for certain who—if anyone—would preach at any service. The revival "anticipated the preacher," the *Times* reported. "The people met and poured out their souls in prayer and praise for hours before the preacher came, if he came at all."[89] Nor could anyone predict where the revival would break out. The degree of unity that its various expressions shared was due largely to the itinerant ministry of people like the young coal miner Evan Roberts.

Roberts understood the revival as the prelude to a worldwide awakening. "The world will be swept by His Spirit as by a rushing, mighty wind," he prophesied. The "great lesson" to be learned was "obedience to the voice of the Holy Spirit."[90] Noted evangelical expositor G. Campbell Morgan concurred: "It is Pentecost continued without a single moment's doubt. . . . The meetings are absolutely without order, characterized from the first to the last by the orderliness of the Spirit of God."[91]

An unusual phenomenon that received considerable press was the use of classical Welsh by "ordinary farm servants, common plough boys and practically unlettered youths."[92] Various explanations were forthcoming, but many participants preferred to believe they had been part of a supernatural event. Prominent British journalist W. T. Stead agreed. Editor of the British *Review of Reviews*, Stead sat in fascination, watching "what they call the influence of the power of the Spirit playing over the crowded congregation as an eddying wind plays over the surface of a pond."[93] "They say it is the Spirit of God," he wrote. "Those who have not witnessed it may call it what they will. I am inclined to agree with those on the spot."[94]

Such reports attracted Americans who longed for revival. Events seemed to validate the preferences of those who had severed their ties to traditional religious organizations. G. Campbell Morgan voiced their sentiments: "I am not at all sure that God is not rebuking our over-organization. . . . [God is saying] see what I can do without the things you are depending on; see what I can do in answer to a praying people; see what I can do through the simplest who are ready to fall in line and depend wholly and absolutely on me."[95]

Among the curious who made their way to Wales was Joseph Smale. Returning home convinced that the long anticipated end-times awakening had at last begun, Smale inaugurated daily prayer for revival in his First Baptist Church. After nearly four months, objections to his preoccupation with revival forced his resignation. He responded by creating the New Testament Church, and when the apostolic faith movement arrived in Los Angeles, it seemed to some of his members to be the answer to their prayers.

As word of the meetings at Azusa Street spread through the religious press, hundreds chose to investigate. The *Apostolic Faith*, a four-page monthly circulated without charge to publicize the movement, reported in September 1906 that "meetings begin about ten o'clock in the morning and can hardly stop before ten or twelve at night, and sometimes two or three in the morning, because so many are seeking, and some are slain under the power of God." In time, Smale and other leaders of local missions visited Azusa Street to find their members.[96] They found them singing without musical accompaniment gospel songs such as "The Comforter Has Come" and "Under the Blood"; they found some speaking in tongues and others praying for sanctification or healings; still others simply reveled in the intensity of spiritual release that the setting offered.[97]

Participants at Azusa Street who later devoted their lives to extending the Pentecostal movement treasured their memories of the humble mission where they alleged that fervor, intensity, and a pervasive sense of the divine immediacy charged the atmosphere. In the local popular evangelical subculture, the mission gained a reputation as a place to come for healing. Those who could not come sent handkerchiefs to be "blessed."[98] The expectation was simple: "The mission people never take medicine. They do not want it. They have taken Jesus for their healer, and He always heals."[99]

Like Parham, Seymour emphasized repentance, restitution, sanctification, healing, Spirit baptism as "a gift of power upon the sanctified life," and the imminent return of Christ. Apparently, a remarkable percentage of the Spirit-baptized claimed a divine call to a foreign country. Like those who evangelized at home, they went out "in faith." In September 1906 Seymour reiterated his commitment to Parham's stance on "faith living," noting that "a dozen or more Christian workers" assisted him, "having been called of God from other lines of employment to devote their time in praying with the sick, preaching, working with souls at the altar, etc. We believe in the faith line for Christian workers, and no collections are taken."[100]

Participants in the mission believed that Spirit baptism prodded the faithful into unity with other believers by initiating them into a New Testament experience in which believers were simply "Christians." Like Parham, Seymour claimed to stand for nothing new; rather, he proclaimed "the restoration of the faith once delivered unto the saints." This implicit indictment of accepted religious institutions (which presumably had failed to retain "the faith once delivered") manifested itself in many ways. "We are not fighting men or churches," Seymour maintained, "but seeking to displace dead forms and creeds and wild fanaticisms with living, practical Christianity. 'Love, Faith, Unity' are our watchwords, and 'Victory through the Atoning Blood' our battle cry."[101]

The pervasive sense that God was using them as part of His specific end-times plan excited and awed them. "Los Angeles seems to be the place, and this the time, in the mind of God, for the restoration of the church to her former place and power," Bartleman reflected. "The fullness of time seems to have come for the church's complete restoration."[102] Their mandate was evangelism: "When the Holy Ghost fell on the one hundred and twenty, it was in the morning of the dispensation of the Holy Ghost. Today we are living down in the evening of the dispensation of the Holy Ghost. And as it was in the morning, so it shall be in the evening. This is the last evangelistic call of the day."[103]

Countless messages in tongues were interpreted to proclaim the imminence of Christ's return. "Awake! Awake!" they pleaded. "There is but time to dress and be ready, for the cry will soon go forth, 'The Bridegroom cometh.'"[104] The baptism with the Holy Spirit was understood to be inextricably related to end-times evangelistic service. "The gift of languages is given with the commission, 'Go ye into all the world and preach the gospel to every creature,'" the *Apostolic Faith* noted. Even signing could be supernaturally enabled: "The Lord has given languages to the unlearned—Greek, Latin, Hebrew, French, German, Italian, Chinese, Japanese, Zulu and languages of Africa, Hindu and Bengali and dialects of India, Chippewa and other languages of the Indians, Esquimaux, the deaf mute language, and in fact the Holy Ghost speaks all the languages of the world through his children."[105]

The mission paper solemnly noted as well that "the Lord [had] given the gift of writing in unknown languages," "the gift of playing on instruments," as well as gifts of singing with "new voices" and translating "old songs into new tongues."[106]

For several years the meetings at Azusa Street alternated between periods of growth and decline. Other area missions sometimes rivaled Azusa Street in claims to power and miracles. At times, fiercely independent "seekers" who had never been able to work harmoniously with others bemoaned the "apostatizing" of Azusa Street and separated from Seymour. Bartleman claimed, for example, that the mission had "failed God" by hanging a sign outside identifying it as an apostolic faith mission. To him, the sign signaled that "the work had become one more rival party and body, along with the other churches and sects of the city."[107] Discovering a call "to go deeper than anything [he] had at this time attained to," Bartleman began his own meetings in a mission at Eighth and Maple streets. The withdrawal of several members from the New Testament Church resulted in the creation of the Upper Room Mission under the leadership of Elmer Fisher, to which, Bartleman reported, most of the white participants at Azusa Street eventually made their way.[108]

From the fall of 1906, then, operating out of various local missions, the movement extended its influence and claimed thousands of adherents. Five years after Parham's Topeka experience, it was estimated that some thirteen thousand had spoken in tongues and, further, that those who rejected the restoration message "backslid" and "lost the experience" they had. "Those who are older in this movement are stronger, and greater signs and wonders are following them," participants boasted.[109]

Responding to an invitation from Seymour, Parham arrived in Los Angeles late in October 1906 from Zion City, Illinois, where he was in the midst of one of his most influential revivals. Parham was appalled by the worship style and the interracial character of the services. He later claimed he had observed "manifestations of the flesh, spiritualistic controls . . . people practicing hypnotism at the altar over candidates seeking the baptism."[110] Complaining about the absence of speech in known foreign languages, Parham insisted that "seekers" at Azusa Street did not receive an authentic baptism in the Holy Spirit. He lamented that his work was being "brought into ridicule" by "fanatics" who accepted "chattering, jabbering, wind-sucking and jerking fits" as evidence of Spirit baptism.[111] He left disillusioned, charging that "counterfeit Pentecost" had been birthed at Azusa Street.[112]

Despite such rejection from within and much ridicule from without, by the end of 1900 hundreds concurred with Bartleman's view that the Azusa Street Mission was "holy ground." They came to inquire, often stayed to pray, then left to proclaim the restoration of the apostolic faith across the country and around the world. The view of history outlined at the mission generated excitement and purpose and appealed to those whose religious preferences or social situations made them uncomfortable in conventional churches. The conviction that Azusa Street participants were the heart of God's end-times dealings with humanity helped them reinterpret their lives in ways that transformed the meaning of worldly rejection, cultural disintegration, and personal disappointment. They considered who they were from the perspective of participation in a divine plan, and in so doing, they discovered a sense of purpose, dignity, and identity. Disdaining the study of the past, they devoted themselves to understanding the history of the future and the apocalyptic meaning of their religious movement.

Most of what they said had been said before, but the survival, expansion, and modification of the restorationist vision that characterized Azusa Street in 1906 deserve attention, for they helped mobilize a powerful religious movement. Shaped by adherents' social experiences as they encountered modernity, Pentecostalism offered what many ordinary people apparently craved—a glorious future and the ability to cope and even to triumph over adversity here and now.

NOTES

1. Norma Souders (Souders Historical Farm Museum, Cheney, Kans.) to the author, 3 Oct. 1987. Much work remains to be done in sorting out the details in the accounts Parham and his family wrote about his life. Most Pentecostals have accepted his story without question, but a search for documentation indicates that Parham's account is unreliable at important points. The fullest story published by the family is Sarah Parham, *The Life of Charles Fox Parham*, 3d ed. (Birmingham, Ala.: Commercial Printing, 1977), 5.

2. The obituary in the *Cheney Journal*, 19 Dec. 1885, provides the first indication of a relationship between the Parham family and the Church of God of the General Eldership. Bolton came from a distance to participate in Parham family events. He later worked with another Church of God evangelist, Maria B. Woodworth-Etter, and he later settled into the pastorate of the Topeka Church of God that had been formed out of her meetings. The spirituality of this group, as well as some of the "demonstrations of power" that marked its revivals, later characterized Parham's meetings. The inclinations toward holiness themes and charismatic experience in the Church of God undoubtedly contributed to Parham's frame of reference. For his part, Parham attributed his views directly to the Bible and the Holy Spirit. His accounts convey the sense that no parts of the apostolic faith were mediated through others. Bolton's ministry can be traced in C. H. Forney, *History of the Churches of God in the U. S. of North America* (Findlay, Ohio: Churches of God, 1914).

3. See "Mrs. Harriet Parham Was a Wife and Mother of Devotion," *Cheney Sentinel*, clipping in Charles Fox Parham Papers, Assemblies of God Archives, Springfield, Mo. (hereafter AGA).

4. See, for example, *Cheney Blade*, 11 Jan. 1889.

5. *Cheney Sentinel*, 30 May 1901.

6. Parham's account is not fully substantiated by college records. He reported that he had entered the college at the age of sixteen, which would have been in 1889. See Parham, *Parham*, 5. The school year at Southwestern College ran from September to June. Even this brief schooling was interrupted by Parham's illness. The *Cheney Herald*, 19 May 1892, reported that Parham had been brought home from school, suffering from inflammatory rheumatism. Apparently, though, Parham had insufficient preparation for enrollment in the college. Ralph W. Decker, Jr. (Registrar), to the author, 11 Dec. 1986.

7. Charles Fox Parham, *A Voice Crying in the Wilderness*, 3d ed. (Baxter Springs, Kans.: privately published, n.d.), 11–19.

8. *Cheney Herald*, 20 June 1893.

9. William E. Connally, *History of Kansas State and People* (Chicago: American Historical Society, 1928), 3:1324.

10. Parham, *Voice*, 19. Parham was never a candidate for ordination in the Methodist church. He served, rather, under a provision for qualified lay persons to obtain preaching licenses for supply preaching in a local church. Such licensing, however, did not confer ministerial status. He was not listed in the Kansas Methodist Conference records as either a probationer or a candidate for ordination.

11. See, for example, Charles B. Driscoll, "Major Prophets of Holy Kansas," *American Mercury* 8 (May 1926): 18–26, which is a Mencken-like recital of religious excesses in Kansas.

12. Parham, *Voice*, 138.

13. This date is given in Parham's biography. See Parham, *Parham*, 29. Sarah Parham's obituary (published by the family in their own paper) gives the date of her marriage as 29 Dec. 1895. The *Cheney Sentinel* reported on 17 Dec. 1896 that Parham would be married on 31 Dec. See *Apostolic Faith*, Jan.-Feb. 1938, 3. Sarah Parham's name is also in question. In the January 1900 issue of the *Apostolic Faith*, Parham referred to her as Eleanore Sarah Parham. Later references are to Sarah Eleanore Parham. The *Cheney Sentinel* listed her as S. Eleanor Thistlewaite. These are two of the minor inaccuracies in a story punctuated with inconsistencies.

14. Charles Fox Parham, "The Sources of Disease," *Apostolic Faith*, Aug. 1912, 2.

15. Ibid., 3.

16. Parham, *Parham*, 31–34. It is difficult to document Parham's awareness of other contemporary teachers of healing. On this as on other subjects, Parham attributed his religious insights to the immediate knowledge from the Holy Spirit. Within two years, it is evident that he knew several prominent advocates of healing at least by reputation.

17. *Apostolic Faith*, 1 Jan. 1900, 1.

18. Ibid. His advertising of a negative statement about Dowie is interesting since later in the year he visited Dowie's Zion as part of his quest to discover contemporary teachers of apostolic views on the Holy Spirit.

19. Parham, *Voice*, 21.

20. He never admitted advocating or practicing infant baptism. This may simply be another part of his story that he preferred to forget. It is unlikely that he supplied a Methodist congregation for two years without participating in infant baptism or baptism by sprinkling or pouring.

21. Charles Fox Parham, "Baptism," *Apostolic Faith*, Oct. 1912, 5. This is a reprint of a portion of his *Voice Crying in the Wilderness* (1902). This indicates the probable influence of Frank Sandford, who led his congregation at Shiloh in Maine in a service of consecration and rebaptized them to wash away the baggage of the past. See Shirley Nelson, *Fair, Clear, and Terrible: The Story of Shiloh* (Latham, N.Y.: British American, 1989), 162–63.

22. Parham, "Baptism," 5.

23. This formula would be important among restorationists Parham influenced. A major division among Pentecostals occurred over restoring the New Testament baptismal formula. Parham reasoned that since the Father and the Holy Ghost had neither died nor been resurrected, one could not be "buried by baptism" in their names. Parham, "Baptism," 4–5.

24. Parham, *Voice*, 101–18. For a sense of evangelical response to Herzl, see the obituary published in *Living Truths*, Aug. 1904, 466–68.

25. Parham, *Voice*, 91–108.

26. One early Parham follower claimed Parham taught African Americans could not be part of the "bride of Christ." This meant they were excluded from the rapture. K. Brower, "Origin of the Apostolic Faith Movement on the Pacific Coast," *Apostolic Faith* (Goose Creek, Tex.), May 1921, 6.

27. See the report from the *Topeka Daily Journal*, reprinted in *Apostolic Faith*, 1 Jan. 1900, 7.

28. Parham, *Parham*, 48.

29. Ibid., 51.

30. For Sandford's spiritual pilgrimage to this point, see Frank Sandford, *Seven Years with God* (1900; reprint, Mt. Vernon, N.H.: Kingdom Press, 1957).

31. Sandford recorded that "none of his counselors went all the way with the Sermon on the Mount" and registered his frustration with "what they didn't say" about "victorious" living. See Frank S. Murray, *The Sublimity of Faith: The Life and Work of Frank W. Sandford* (Amherst, N.H.: Kingdom Press, 1981), 155. In addition to Murray's hagiography, two serious critical accounts of Sanford's life and work are William Hiss, "Shiloh: Frank W. Sandford and the Kingdom: 1893–1948" (Ph.D. diss., Tufts University, 1978), and Nelson, *Fair, Clear, and Terrible*.

32. Such claims were not unusual in this popular evangelical subculture. Parham reported in 1912: "I have met eight or ten Elijahs, all the major prophets and some of the minor ones, Adam, God, David, at least fifty claiming to be Jesus, about thirty of the two witnesses (both male and female), all the twelve apostles, the fifth angel, three who were the Devil, eight who were the virgin Mary." *Apostolic Faith*, Sept. 1912, 12. See Driscoll, "Major Prophets" for accounts of some of these.

33. Quoted in Murray, *Sublimity*, 162.

34. Ibid.

35. Ibid., 157.

36. Ibid., 288–89. For a description of this event in the context, see Nelson, *Fair, Clear, and Terrible*, 162–63.

37. There are remarkable similarities between Sandford and Dowie. Dowie, too, had bands of "seventies" who evangelized by twos. Their activities were often reported in *Leaves of Healing*. See also Nelson, *Fair, Clear, and Terrible*, 134, 137.

38. Murray, *Sublimity*, 232. See also the *Topeka Daily Capital*, 6 Jan. 1901, 2; Parham, *Parham*, 48.

39. Parham, *Voice*, 32.

40. Ibid.

41. Agnes Ozman, "The First One to Speak in Tongues," *Latter Rain Evangel*, Jan. 1909, 2.

42. See description of his teachings in the ad for Bethel Divine Healing Home and Mission, *Apostolic Faith*, 1 Jan. 1900, 8.

43. Parham, *Voice*, 86–87, 75.

44. For an account of her life, see Agnes Nevada Ozman LaBerge, *What God Hath Wrought* (Chicago: Herald Publishing, n.d.).

45. Agnes Ozman, "A Witness to the First Scenes," *Apostolic Faith*, Dec.-Jan. 1912–13, 4.

46. The date is in dispute, as are many other details of the story. Pentecostals have usually accepted Parham's account uncritically, but on close examination it contains many inconsistencies. Parham later claimed he had laid hands on Ozman during the watch-night service, which had been attended by some 115 people. He attached eschatological significance to the timing of the event, claiming that just as the new century dawned, tongues speech had been restored in a setting remarkably similar to that described in Acts 2—an upper room in which some 120 people waited expectantly. Later 12 ministers, with hands uplifted, were reported to have spoken in tongues simultaneously as "cloven tongues of fire" appeared over their heads. The historian Robert Mapes Anderson rightly observed that Parham's account was simply "too pat to be true." See Anderson, *Vision of the Disinherited: The Making of American Pentecostalism* (New York: Oxford University Press, 1979), 44.

47. Ozman, "A Witness," 4. Bennet F. Lawrence, ed., *The Apostolic Faith Restored* (St. Louis: Gospel Publishing House, 1916), 52, also notes this stress on Acts 19. Given Parham's later insistence that tongues speech was *always* in known human languages, this reference to Acts 19 (which does not associate tongues speech with known languages) rather than to Acts 2 (which does) is interesting. See Acts 19:6 and Acts 2:4ff.

48. Ozman, "A Witness," 4. She continued to hold this position. See Ozman, "First One to Speak in Tongues," 2.

49. Ozman's account is quoted in full in Parham, *Parham*, 65–68. The quotation is from p. 67.

50. Parham, *Parham*, 52–53. The *Topeka Daily Capital*, 6 Jan. 1901, 2, published a specimen of the so-called "writing under the inspiration of the Holy Spirit." It is likely that the writer (whose name was given as Auswin) was Ozman.

51. LaBerge, *What God Hath Wrought*, 29.

52. Ozman in Parham, *Parham*, 67. Following her prayer in English, she claimed that she prayed in tongues in a language understood by a visiting European. This would be the first of many claims, none of which has been verified by nonparticipants or hard evidence, that speaking in tongues was a known language understood by someone present.

53. Anderson, *Vision*, 44. Parham had assigned his students the task of finding what biblical evidence was offered for evidence of the baptism with the Holy Spirit. This, Anderson posits, was to "make them believe the doctrine was not his own 'man-made' idea, but came by revelation," 56.

54. *Topeka Journal*, 7 Jan. 1901, 4. See Edith L. Blumhofer, "Restoration as Revival: Early American Pentecostalism," in *Modern Christian Revivals*, ed. Edith L. Blumhofer and Randall Balmer (Urbana: University of Illinois Press, 1993). See also 2 Cor. 1:21, 22.

55. Parham later refined his view of evidential tongues to include a clear distinction between the gift of tongues and evidential tongues, though he always held that both involved speech in known human languages. Writing in 1912 he noted: "The only point wherein we differ now from the first teaching regarding Pentecost is that neither the gift of tongues or any other of the nine gifts of the Spirit are the evidence of the baptism. If you have the gift of a tongue, you can use it as you do your English, both in speaking and understanding it. . . . Those who receive the baptism of the Holy Ghost can only speak as the Spirit gives utterance, while those who have the gift of tongues can use it at will and understand it." "Editorial," *Apostolic Faith*, Aug. 1912, 6.

56. *Topeka Daily Capital*, 6 Jan. 1901, 2.

57. *Topeka Daily Capital*, 7 Dec. 1901, 3; *Topeka Journal*, 7 Jan. 1901, 4.

58. Parham, *Parham*, 75.

59. Ozman, "A Witness," 4. Few of the students were heard from again. Ozman only acknowledged her experience of 1 Jan. 1901 after she heard reports in Omaha of the Azusa Street revival in 1906. LaBerge, *What God Hath Wrought*, 39. Between 1901 and 1906 she did not identify with the apostolic faith. Later, in a testimony published by healing evangelist Maria Woodworth-Etter after Woodworth-Etter had prayed for Ozman's healing in 1915, Ozman reminisced that she had "gotten into the flesh and was under a cloud spiritually, and was willing to lay down the baptism because of criticism and censure." Maria B. Woodworth-Etter, *A Diary of Signs and Wonders* (1916; reprint, Tulsa: Harrison House, 1980), 431–32.

60. Parham, *Parham*, 81.

61. "Restoration of Palestine," *St. Louis Daily Globe Democrat*, 2 Jan. 1904, 2. This and other clippings are in a family-owned scrapbook, part of which is available on film at the Southwestern Assemblies of God College in Waxahachie, Tex.

62. For a fuller account of Arthur's life, see Edith L. Blumhofer, *Pentecost in My Soul* (Springfield, Mo.: Gospel Publishing House, 1989), 119–30.

63. Parham's followers rented the Grand Leader Building on Maine Street, a 50-by-110-foot facility that "never accommodated the crowds." Lawrence, *Apostolic Faith*, 53.

64. Parham, *Parham*, 96; "Claim to Be Cured," *Baxter Springs News*, 7 Jan. 1904.

65. Parham, *Parham*, 102. For a participant's account of this period in Parham's life, see Ethel E. Goss, *The Winds of God* (New York: Comet Press Books, 1958).

66. Charles Fox Parham, "Hell," *Apostolic Faith*, Sept. 1912, 11.

67. Goss, *Winds of God*, 14–15.

68. Ibid., 17; quoted in Parham, *Parham*, 76.

69. "Houstonians Witness the Performance of Miracles," *Houston Chronicle*, 13 Aug. 1905.

70. Rilda Cole to Apostolic Faith Adherents, Baxter Springs, Kans., 1 Aug. 1905, Apostolic Faith Bible College Archives, Baxter Springs, Kans.

71. Goss, *Winds of God*, 69.

72. Ibid., 30ff.

73. Ibid., 34ff.

74. For Seymour, see Douglas Nelson, "For Such a Time as This: The Story of William J. Seymour and the Azusa Street Revival" (Ph.D. diss., University of Birmingham, 1981); James Tinney, "William J. Seymour: Father of Modern-day Pentecostalism," *Journal of the Interdenominational Theological Center* 4 (Fall 1979): 34–44. Despite insistence to the contrary, Parham's worldview nurtured racist assumptions that frequently surfaced. Nonetheless in 1905 African Americans attended his evangelistic services. See Rilda Cole to Apostolic Faith Adherents for the testimony of an African-American woman's healing.

75. Howard Goss, "Reminiscences," in *Apostolic Faith*, ed. Lawrence, 64.

76. Lawrence, *Apostolic Faith*, 55.

77. Alma White, *Demons and Tongues* (Zarephath, N.J.: Pillar of Fire Publications, 1919), 68–69.

78. The account in Goss, *Winds of God*, 35–36, varies at significant points. Goss, who was a student at the Houston Bible school at the time, recalled that Lucy Farrow had obtained money from Parham to travel to Los Angeles and spread his views. Her request for assistance resulted in the Bible school students' providing funds to permit William Seymour to join her. Seymour noted that three people—Farrow, Warren, and he—had been "sent by the Lord" from Houston to Los Angeles as "messengers of the full gospel." Farrow had first "brought the full Gospel" and had been "greatly used as she laid her hands on many who have received the Pentecost and the gift of tongues." By September Farrow had left Los Angeles to carry the apostolic faith message to her home city, Norfolk, Va., *Apostolic Faith*, Sept. 1906, 1; see also Brower, "Origin of the Apostolic Faith Movement on the Pacific Coast," 6.

79. See copy of letter, William J. Seymour to W. F. Carothers, 12 July 1906,

in the author's possession. Seymour specifically requested credentials so that he could qualify for clergy discount fares on the railroad. This suggests that Parham had formally registered his apostolic faith movement. When he compiled a discipline for his Los Angeles mission in 1915, Seymour disavowed the racist views Parham by then represented: "If some of our white brethren have prejudices and discriminations, we can't," he admonished. See William J. Seymour, *Doctrine and Discipline of the Azusa Street Apostolic Faith Mission of Los Angeles* (Los Angeles: privately published, 1915), 2. But Seymour later allowed explicit prejudice to surface among his followers; he reserved for "people of color" the right to be officers of his mission, limiting whites to membership. See Tinney, "Seymour," 39.

80. See Charles F. Parham, "Free Love," *Apostolic Faith*, Dec. 1912, 4.

81. "Editorial," *Apostolic Faith*, Oct. 1912, 6. As a result, Parham discouraged emotional expressions, insisting that noise evidenced resistance to the Holy Spirit. "There should be a holy enthusiasm and intensity without hysteria," he maintained. "Christianity places us in a normal state with all our faculties consecrated to decency, order and service for God, and not to consume ourselves in riotous sensations of the flesh and a sensual working up of feeling." "Editorial," *Apostolic Faith*, Oct. 1912, 6.

82. In 1907 Parham and another man were arrested in San Antonio and charged with "an unnatural act." The outcome is unclear; charges may have been dropped. See the *San Antonio Light*, 19 July 1907, 1. See also *San Antonio Light*, 23 July 1907, 7; 24 July 1907, 2. Goff's extensive notes amplify this story. See James R. Goff's *Fields White unto Harvest: Charles F. Parham and the Missionary Origins of Pentecostalism* (Fayetteville: University of Arkansas Press, 1989), 223–27. In 1916 Wilbur Glen Voliva, overseer of Dowie's legacy in Zion City, Ill., published a purported copy of a confession and affidavit sworn by Parham before I. C. Baker, district attorney, San Antonio, which reads as follows: "I hereby confess my guilt in the commission of the crime of sodomy with one J. J. Jourdan in San Antonio, TX on the 18th day of July 1907. Witness my hand in San Antonio, TX this 18th day of July 1907." This confession was purportedly witnessed by Charles Stevens, the arresting officer. See poster in AGA.

83. "A Crisis at Hand," *Household of God*, May 1909, 5.

84. Frank Bartleman, *How Pentecost Came to Los Angeles* (Los Angeles: n.p., 1925), 43.

85. *Apostolic Faith*, Sept. 1906, 1. Attempts to probe the spiritual significance of the San Francisco earthquake read like Puritan jeremiads and were common. See for example, "Earthquake Causes," *Free Methodist*, 15 May 1906, 312; "San Francisco Morals," *Free Methodist*, 22 May 1906, 329.

86. The diaries of spiritual seekers such as Frank Bartleman and Florence Crawford provide a sense of the number and variety of options Protestant missions offered. See Apostolic Faith, *The Apostolic Faith: Its Origins, Functions, and Doctrines* (Portland, Ore.: Apostolic Faith, n.d.).

87. Anderson, *Vision*, 62–63.

88. Evan Hopkins, "The Teaching of the Revival," in *The Story of the Welsh Revival Told by Eyewitnesses* (New York: Fleming H. Revell, 1905), 73.

89. *Times* (London), 13 Feb. 1905, 9d.

90. Evan Roberts, "A Message to the World," in *The Story of the Welsh Revival*, 6. See also Edith L. Blumhofer, "The Welsh Revival," *Paraclete* 20 (Summer 1986): 1–5.

91. G. Campbell Morgan, "The Lesson of the Revival," in *The Story of the Welsh Revival*, 37.

92. *Times* (London), 3 Jan. 1905, 12b.

93. W. T. Stead, "The Story of the Awakening," in *The Story of the Welsh Revival*, 64.

94. Ibid., 66.

95. Morgan, "Lesson," 50, 44.

96. Bartleman, *Pentecost*, 54.

97. Some mission leaders stayed to receive their "personal pentecosts." Smale did not. Bartleman called him "God's Moses." He had "led the people as far as the Jordan, though he himself never got across. Brother Seymour led them over." Bartleman, *Pentecost*, 62. Though agreeing that tongues speech was a contemporary possibility, Smale objected strongly to the teaching on tongues as *uniform* initial evidence of the baptism with the Holy Spirit. He also charged Bartleman with misrepresenting the divisive impact of Azusa Street on his congregation. In fact, he noted, "only about a dozen have withdrawn from the Church, and mainly such as had not been its elements of strength." Joseph Smale, "The Gift of Tongues," *Living Truth*, Jan. 1907, 40.

98. "Beginning of a World Wide Revival," *Apostolic Faith*, 1 Jan. 1907, 1.

99. Ibid.

100. *Apostolic Faith*, 1 Sept. 1906, 3.

101. "The Apostolic Faith Movement," *Apostolic Faith*, Sept. 1906, 2.

102. Bartleman, *Pentecost*, 89. At the same time, however, observers noted that events mocked pretensions to unity. Smale wrote late in 1906: "In the city there are already four hostile camps of those who unduly magnify the tongues, which prove that the tongues have not brought Pentecost to Los Angeles. When Pentecost comes we shall see the union of the Lord's people." Smale, "Gift of Tongues," 40.

103. "This Same Jesus," *Apostolic Faith*, Oct. 1906, 3.

104. *Apostolic Faith*, Oct. 1906, 1.

105. *Apostolic Faith*, Sept. 1906, 1.

106. Ibid.

107. Bartleman, *Pentecost*, 68.

108. Ibid., 84.

109. *Upper Room*, 1 June 1901, 4. Seymour noted that in the first five months about 150 had received Spirit baptism at Azusa Street. *Apostolic Faith*, Sept. 1906, 1.

110. Parham, *Parham*, 163. Smale also noted the similarity of the so-called "manifestations" to those among local spiritualists. He also reported at Azusa

Street "the imitation of animal sounds such as the dog, coyote, cat and fowl." Smale, "Gift of Tongues," 39.

111. Charles Fox Parham, "Baptism of the Holy Ghost," *Apostolic Faith*, Oct. 1912, 9.

112. Parham, "Free Love," 4; "Lest We Forget," *Apostolic Faith*, July 1912, 6.

3

A Selective Look at the Emerging
Pentecostal Network, 1906–8

O NE REASON the Azusa Street Mission succeeded in attracting
people to explore its message was that across the United States
countless clusters of people were predisposed to take seriously the notion
of millenarian restoration that constituted the essence of the apostolic
faith. Among those who had already separated from denominations, the
apostolic faith movement spread from Azusa Street, establishing itself first
in scattered settings across the country that shared its distrust of "man-
made" organizations. In responding to Pentecostalism, some of these
people demonstrated that, despite preoccupation with religious experience, participants in popular restorationist movements were not unconcerned about doctrine.

The Azusa Street version of the restoration message was embraced in
whole or in part in widely different places across the country. A brief look
at a few that became important in molding the understanding of Pentecostalism in the Assemblies of God illuminates the expectations of the
devout and their place in society. Pentecostalism extended among people
already distanced—either by choice or by chance—from the cultural
mainstream. Those who embraced Pentecostalism routinely explained
their choice in theological terms: they saw it as restoration, as full gospel.
That does not diminish its role in giving individuals identity and purpose
by focusing their understanding of society and world events around nos-
talgia for the "good old days" when America was Protestant and evangelical with pride in national mission and destiny and when the home
was the center of everyday life. It also legitimated their reluctance and
inability to address the overwhelming social evils of their own day by
offering a simple explanation for the social predicament. And it helped

root migrant people—immigrants from other nations as well as those dis-
located from families by moves from rural to urban America. But, at face
value, its primary significance lay in its ability to overwhelm human emotions, replacing despair with hope and uncertainty with assurance and an
inner sense of peace.

Zion City, Illinois

Among the first to respond with interest to reports from Azusa Street
were residents of Zion City, Illinois. Established by John Alexander
Dowie in 1901, Zion in 1906 was the hub of a worldwide network of
activities sponsored by Dowie's Christian Catholic Apostolic Church.
The city strictly regulated activities; it had but one church, a huge, frame,
seven-thousand-seat facility known as Shiloh Tabernacle, and permitted
no other religious teachers within city limits. Dowie held tightly to the
reins until financial disaster combined with rumors of Dowie's sexual immorality and his doctrinal aberrations to shatter his utopia. In 1906 the
first serious religious cleavage surfaced and some, disillusioned, sought
new religious direction. A few of these invited Charles Parham to bring
his message to Zion City.

Zion was in considerable disarray when Charles Fox Parham arrived on
20 September 1906 to proclaim the apostolic faith in the city's hotel.
Economic deprivation, social discontent, and religious turmoil had taken
their toll, but they also made Parham's visit possible.

The immediate acceptance of Parham's message seemed to attest a report in a local paper that noted his "pleasant and convincing manner that
makes his discourse almost irresistible."[1] Overflowing from a hotel room
into the halls, the services attracted hundreds during the first week. Dowie's successor, Wilbur Glenn Voliva, responded by prohibiting religious
services in the hotel and refusing Parham other facilities. Parham's home-
town newspaper reported that resistance prompted curiosity, and Parham's audience soon "numbered by the thousands."[2]

Parham accepted five separate invitations to move his preaching to
private homes. He conducted simultaneous services nightly between
seven and midnight, traveling among the homes to preach and pray.[3]
Within a month, some of the most respected citizens had spoken in
tongues.

Late in October Parham left Zion City for Azusa Street. During his
absence the services continued unabated. Voliva deprived Parham's followers of membership in the Christian Catholic Apostolic Church, an
action that brought economic and social alienation as well.

When Parham returned late in the year, the city had been placed in receivership, and he gained permission to erect a tent seating two thousand in the center of town. Later, the receiver granted the apostolic faith adherents access to Shiloh Tabernacle on weeknights and alternate Sundays. Early in 1907 Parham again left, this time to carry his message to Zion outposts in Canada and other American cities. The teaching he had introduced continued to thrive among Dowie's restorationist constituency, many of whom became prominent leaders in the emerging movement's various activities.[4] Those of Dowie's followers who identified with the apostolic faith movement concurred that this movement preserved and expanded Dowie's essential message. Shorn of its communal concerns, Dowie's stress on the full validity of New Testament Christianity for twentieth-century believers found, they would claim, its logical outcome in Pentecostalism.

The Churches of God in Christ

Early in 1907 reports from Azusa Street reached Memphis, where a loosely affiliated African-American holiness group known as the Churches of God in Christ, directed by Charles Price Jones and Charles Mason, had a strong congregation. Jones and Mason had long since agreed that all Christians should experience a baptism with the Holy Spirit. They quibbled, however, about doctrinal specifics. Jones maintained that Spirit baptism would "complete the believer in Christ" by a third work of grace. The specific object of Spirit baptism, he believed, was power for effective service.[5] Mason was less certain. He owed much to Jones, a simple, humble man devoted to a restorationist dream. Jones convinced Mason that he did not have the baptism with the Holy Spirit and that they both lacked power to heal, exorcise demons, and raise the dead (abilities Jones believed would follow Spirit baptism).[6] The two agreed that Mason and two friends would visit Azusa Street to investigate reports firsthand.[7]

Although some of what he observed on his arrival repulsed him, Mason claimed that when he heard tongues speech at Azusa Street, he "knew it was right."[8] Mason embraced the apostolic faith message, and five weeks later he and his friends returned to Memphis committed to the new movement. They found that the message had preceded them because during their absence a visitor from Azusa Street, Glenn Cook, had divided the Church of God in Christ congregation by preaching that tongues speech always evidenced authentic Spirit baptisms. Mason enthusiastically sided with those Cook had convinced. "The Spirit had taken full control of me," he later reminisced, "and everything was new to me and to all the saints. The way that He did things was all new."[9]

Jones disliked the newness. Although he readily conceded the need for a "third blessing" and had long affirmed most of what Azusa Street taught, he balked at Mason's insistence on tongues speech as "uniform initial evidence" of the much-discussed baptism. During the annual convention of the Churches of God in Christ in the summer of 1907, the two parted company. Jones disfellowshipped those who advocated tongues and changed the name of his non-Pentecostal remnant to the Church of Christ (Holiness) U.S.A.

Mason thus became the unchallenged leader of the Churches of God in Christ, a position he held until his death in 1961. Widely respected throughout American Pentecostalism by both whites and blacks, Mason exerted enormous influence. His group's membership, though predominantly African American, was interracial into the 1920s.[10] Mason incorporated his denomination, and his ministers thus received coveted clergy rail discounts and other civil recognition that eluded most Pentecostals.[11]

Southeastern Groups

Participants in several independent holiness associations and other ministries scattered across the southeast were also intrigued by reports from Los Angeles. Publications such as the *Way of Faith*, edited by J. M. Pike in Columbia, South Carolina, and *Living Waters*, edited by J. O. McClurkan in Nashville, enjoyed national circulation and offered a sense of participation in a broader movement to far-flung southern constituencies molded by an interest in holiness or a concern for restoration. The first reports from Azusa Street reached the South through such publications. Gaston Barnabas Cashwell, a minister of the Holiness Church of North Carolina, read accounts in the *Way of Faith*. "I had been preaching holiness for nine years," he later wrote, "but my soul began to hunger and thirst for the fullness of God. The Spirit led me more and more to seek my Pentecost."[12]

Cashwell decided to investigate in person. A native of rural Sampson County, North Carolina, and a Methodist Episcopal Church, South, pastor who had "come out" to identify with local holiness advocates, he left in 1906 for Azusa Street. The rail trip took six days, which he spent fasting and praying.

A middle-aged white southerner, Cashwell was at first distressed by the racial mingling at the Azusa Street mission. He overcame his reluctance sufficiently to permit Seymour to lay hands on him in prayer. After four days, he reported, "He filled me with His Spirit and love." "I am now feasting and drinking at the fountain continually and speak as the Spirit gives utterance, both in my own language and in the unknown language."[13] Cashwell returned to Dunn, North Carolina, where on 31 December 1906 he enthusiastically launched a series of meetings directed primarily toward the principal holiness groups in the area. Blacks and whites mingled at the services, curious onlookers arrived from as far away as South Carolina and Georgia, and, in the end, most of the local ministers of the Fire-Baptized Holiness Church, the Pentecostal Holiness Church, and the Free-Will Baptist Church accepted the apostolic faith message, with its stress on restoration and its focus on evidential tongues speech.[14] Cashwell sent a jubilant letter to Los Angeles reporting conversions and Spirit baptisms that stirred the small community of twenty-five hundred.

From Dunn, Cashwell toured the South. He found it necessary to resist radical holiness impulses that had taken root in some communities. Writing from Royston, Georgia, he noted: "People have been gulled here by take it by faith, reconsecrate, baptism of fire, 'dynamite' and 'lyddite' till the faith of the people is almost gone." His response was straightforward: "Get your justified experience all in good shape, then get the sanctified experience of a clean heart. Then when your faith takes hold of the promise of the Father and Son, and the Word of God . . . you can praise and bless God and the Holy Ghost will come in and praise God himself in unknown tongues."[15]

During his travels in May 1907, Cashwell preached in Memphis. Some of his hearers had ties to J. O. McClurkan's Nashville-based Pentecostal mission. As a result, two Pentecostal mission ministers, Henry G. Rodgers and Mack M. Pinson, embraced the apostolic faith. "We could scarcely wait for the message to end and the altar call to be given," they reported, "as we all sat with ears, eyes and hearts wide open drinking in every word. We must have looked like a hungry bunch."[16]

The Pentecostal mission with which Rodgers and Pinson worked had been formed in 1898 by McClurkan, a former Cumberland Presbyterian pastor. He had "claimed his second blessing" under the ministry of a veteran holiness Methodist, Beverly Carradine. In 1898 he had arrived in central Tennessee from California, gathered scattered holiness believers, and formed an association based in Nashville, intending to make Nashville "a center for the dissemination of scriptural Holiness throughout the South."[17] By 1915 the Pentecostal mission had licensed some sixteen hundred preachers, evangelists, and lay workers, many of whom had received several years of training at McClurkan's Bible school (later Trevecca College). Given the mission's uncompromising emphasis on typical holiness doctrines enhanced by a strong commitment to premillennialism, it is hardly surprising that some within its ranks accepted evidential tongues. During its 1907 and 1908 conventions, the credentials

committee considered licensing workers who spoke in tongues and indicated some support for doing so.[18] A later decision against apostolic
faith views on tongues, however, occasioned the withdrawal of tonguesspeaking participants. Pinson, Rodgers, and Nickels John Holmes left the
Pentecostal mission to assume prominent roles in various apostolic faith
enterprises.[19]

Rodgers envisioned an association to give identity to those who accepted tongues speech as the evidence of the baptism with the Holy
Spirit. He formed a loose regional fellowship, the Pentecostal Association
of the Mississippi Valley.

Later in 1907 Ambrose J. Tomlinson, leader of yet another southern
restorationist movement known as the Church of God, was associated
with Pinson in meetings in Birmingham. Amazed to hear Pinson speak
in tongues, Tomlinson, at Pinson's urging, invited Cashwell to his small
church in Cleveland, Tennessee. Throughout 1907 numerous Church of
God adherents received the baptism with the Holy Spirit, but Tomlinson
did not. Cashwell finally arrived in Cleveland in January 1908, and Tomlinson fully embraced his teaching, spoke in tongues, and brought the
constituency of the Church of God into the fledgling apostolic faith
movement.[20]

Like Parham, Tomlinson had been influenced by Sandford. He had
participated in the mass baptism that had marked a "forward move" in
Sandford's restoration. As a colporteur for the American Bible Society,
he had traveled throughout western North Carolina and eastern Tennessee, where he met a small group of restorationists who had withdrawn
from local churches and began worshiping under the leadership of Richard Spurling. They had formed the Christian Union. In 1896, during a
revival, many in this group had spoken in tongues but had assigned no
particular significance to the experience. In 1903 Tomlinson claimed a
divine communication informed him that his group was the restored
Church of God.

Also in 1908 Pinson and Rodgers visited Tomlinson in Cleveland to
discuss appropriate names for newly formed apostolic faith congregations. Their commitment to restorationist views made it imperative for
them to find "scriptural" names. Pinson and Rodgers had concluded that
"Church of God" would suit their needs and obtained Tomlinson's assurance that their use of the name would imply no relationship to his own
movement.[21]

Cashwell's travels between 1906 and 1909 won many other converts
to the emerging Pentecostal movement and left behind a trail of newly
formed Pentecostal missions. Because he addressed holiness constituencies that had already reached many of the conclusions that defined the
apostolic faith, it proved relatively easy for him to convince both minis-

ters and lay people that tongues were the biblical evidence of an experience they all affirmed in some way. Those who explicitly longed for restored New Testament norms were inclined to welcome a movement that endorsed spiritual gifts. And when the experience was forthcoming—when those who agonized in prayer for the baptism with the Holy Spirit spoke in tongues and testified to their assurance of the presence and power of the Holy Spirit in their lives—the truth of the message seemed amply evident.

The Christian and Missionary Alliance

In May 1907 leaders of the Christian and Missionary Alliance convened on the campus of the Missionary Training Institute at Nyack, New York, for their annual convention. Excitement permeated the gathering in the small town twenty-five miles north of New York City to which Albert B. Simpson had moved his home and his school. During the previous year reports from Azusa Street had encouraged numerous Alliance participants to pray for the baptism with the Holy Spirit evidenced by tongues. Alliance teaching was congenial to such an experience, and those who gathered in 1907 to transact business soon saw and felt Pentecostal fervor in their ranks.[22] One participant described events: "Meetings ran on day and night for nearly a week without human leadership, no thought of time, trains, meals, sleep, etc. The Holy Ghost did wonderfully quicken and strengthen physically all those who thus fasted and waited upon Him." Sessions focused on "agony for sin and self-life," "visions of the cross, blood, throne," and "deep whole-souled shouts of glory and praise, all testifying 'Jesus is coming soon.'" Most remarkable to some was the fact that tongues speech was interpreted, thus giving the faithful "messages from the throne direct."[23]

Those convinced in the tumult of the convention joined other Alliance men and women who had already identified with the apostolic faith. David Wesley Myland, first superintendent of the Ohio Alliance, for example, had read accounts from California and embraced the message in November 1906. Myland, a gifted musician, immediately penned a song that became a popular Pentecostal testimony:

> I'm so glad the promised Pentecost has come,
> And the Latter Rain is falling now on some;
> Pour it out in floods, Lord, on the parched ground
> 'Til it reaches all the earth around.

The Christian and Missionary Alliance shared with the apostolic faith movement understandings of Christ, the Holy Spirit, healing, and the second coming, and Simpson had written books and songs that helped popularize practical dimensions of the spirituality these teachings fostered. He had encouraged expectation of spiritual gifts and had anticipated a miraculous end-times enduement of ability to proclaim the gospel in foreign languages.

During the summer of 1907 several Alliance camp meetings were invaded by apostolic faith fervor. In Beulah Park in Cleveland, Ohio, and Rocky Springs Park in Pennsylvania, Alliance adherents—including Alliance vice-president John Salmon—spoke in tongues. People with ties to the strong Alliance branch in Indianapolis accepted apostolic faith teaching and formed an influential apostolic faith congregation.[24]

Men and women whose spiritual pilgrimage had led them to Christian and Missionary Alliance branches around the country would make vital contributions to American Pentecostalism, and Simpson's books, hymns, and missionary vision informed Pentecostal spirituality for decades.

Elim

In 1906 Rochester, New York, was home to a group of ministries collectively known as Elim. Consisting of a faith home, the Rochester Bible and Missionary Training School, and a local mission, Elim had been established in 1895 by the five daughters of a former Methodist pastor, James Duncan. Elim quickly gained a reputation in the popular evangelical subculture as a place where the practical dimensions of healing, faith, holiness, and the Second Coming were emphasized. A strong interest in missions surfaced as well, and the sisters began to publish their message in tracts and later in a monthly journal called *Trust*.

The Bible Training School opened on 2 October 1906 with fourteen regular and six part-time students and a faculty of five. The two-year course covered "Theology, or the great doctrines of the Bible; Synthesis, or an analysis of the Bible by books; Personal Work, or how to use the Bible for seekers; Ancient and Modern History, Church History, Homiletics, Exegesis, Dispensational Truth, Rhetoric and Greek, if so desired."[25] Organized on "faith lines," the school accepted students without financial resources on the assumption that teaching them "how to trust the Lord for supplies" should be part of their education.[26]

Fearing "fanaticism or the work of the enemy," the sisters responded hesitantly to the first reports from Azusa Street. After vacillating for nearly a year, they concluded "that [God] was responsible for the movement but not for everything that was in it." They decided to "trust [themselves] to God for all that was of the Spirit and to be kept from what was not of His working."[27] The sisters had anticipated a revival since reports had begun to arrive from Wales late in 1904. "When that remarkable revival broke out in Wales our hearts, like those of all Christendom, were greatly stirred. The power of God working so mightily, the absence of human machinery, the tremendous results in the salvation of souls, made us very hungry to know God in His fullness. We held special meetings for the purpose of waiting upon God in which we were greatly blessed."[28]

During Elim's annual summer convention in June 1907, the long months of prayer ended in a "manifest outpouring." Two visitors who had accepted Pentecostal teaching explained the apostolic faith message, and "almost the entire Convention became seekers at once."[29] The sisters asserted that a new dispensation had arrived; the "Latter Rain" had begun to fall; "God was doing a new thing in the earth."[30]

In at least one significant way, the sisters represented those among apostolic faith adherents who were reluctant to "label and pigeon-hole" the baptism with the Holy Spirit, "dogmatizing about what other Christians have or have not." "Many," they noted sorrowfully, "teach that no one has the Holy Spirit till they speak in tongues. The experience of God's most devoted servants throughout the centuries past disproves this statement."[31] The sisters rejected the popular distinction between evidential tongues and the gift of tongues and understood the apostolic faith movement as having dispensational significance. It had, they noted, "a preparatory bearing on the soon coming of our Lord, and is indeed the 'Latter Rain.'" After all, "Jesus [was] coming soon and [could not] translate a people from a lower plane than Pentecost."[32] Tongues speech for them was incidental. The movement was much more than the restoration of a form of speech: it was "the restoration of Pentecost . . . the lifting up of the Church to the original plane designed of God, from which they have fallen."[33]

Chicago Missions

Among the several early apostolic faith missions in Chicago, two made especially significant contributions to the larger movement. Led by strong, young, independent men, both the Stone Church and the North Avenue Mission developed national reputations as centers where charismatic gifts and Pentecostal teaching predominated.

The Stone Church

William Hamner Piper had been one of John Alexander Dowie's most prominent assistants in Zion City. After Dowie's disgrace, Piper moved to Chicago and, in December 1906, he began conducting services that attracted several hundred of Dowie's former followers. Formed as the apostolic faith message was penetrating Zion, Piper's congregation, known as the Stone Church, resisted Parham's teaching. In fact, Piper's people seemed so prejudiced against the apostolic faith that he deemed it wise "temporarily not to say very much about the Holy Spirit."[34]

Attendance reached 600, then plummeted to 125 by April 1907. "Nothing is better calculated to make a minister examine himself than a decrease in his audiences," Piper admitted. "After long days and nights of agony of spirit in earnest prayer, I was finally brought to the decision that what was claimed as the baptism in the Holy Spirit and the speaking in tongues was really of God."[35] He decided to open his pulpit to Pentecostals.

On Sunday, 30 June 1907, Piper startled his congregation with the announcement that in the evening three visitors from Zion City would expound Pentecostal teaching at the Stone Church. From the start the congregation proved receptive. After several weeks of nightly services, many members had spoken in tongues, attendance had climbed, and the church had been swept into the Pentecostal movement. Piper and his talented wife, Lydia Markley Piper, shared public ministry and began publishing a monthly magazine, the *Latter Rain Evangel*. Its editor, Anna Reiff, became one of the most influential lay women in American Pentecostalism. Because of its central location in Chicago, the church often hosted conventions and missionary rallies. In a day when many people traveling across America changed trains in Chicago, the Stone Church opened its pulpit to innumerable evangelists, missionaries, and pastors and hosted large conventions.

The North Avenue Mission

The North Avenue Mission served a different constituency. Located in an area populated primarily by immigrants, it attracted an ethnic mix.[36] Its founder and pastor, William Durham, preached salvation, sanctification, and healing. Like so many others, he firmly believed that denominations were "the greatest hindrance to the advancement of the real cause of Jesus Christ."[37]

His initial positive response in the spring of 1906 to news from Azusa Street gave way to sharp criticism of the teaching that tongues always evidenced Spirit baptism. "I understood exactly what such teaching implied and just how widely it reflected on all Christian experience, so far as the baptism in the Spirit was concerned."[38] When some of his acquaintances spoke in tongues, however, Durham began to study the apostolic faith more closely. He soon concluded that "all experiences [he] had ever seen, [his] own included, were far below the standard God lifted up in The Acts."[39] He decided to travel to Los Angeles to learn more.

Durham later recalled that he had been entranced from the moment he entered the Azusa Street Mission. Hundreds were present, yet none seemed in charge. Durham heard what participants called the "heavenly anthem": "A wave of power and glory seemed to sweep over the place, and a song broke forth in the Spirit, known in this movement as the Heavenly Anthem. It was the Spirit of God Himself. . . . I could not sing in that choir. . . . I had not received Him, who was doing the singing. I saw clearly for the first time the difference between having the influence and the presence of the Spirit with us, and having Him dwell within us in person." [40]

On 2 March 1907 Durham received the experience he had coveted. He returned to Chicago to identify his mission with the apostolic faith movement but he immediately ignited a controversy. Unlike many other apostolic faith adherents, Durham did not believe in crisis sanctification. He had been uncomfortable with the teaching before his Spirit baptism, he acknowledged, but after he returned to Chicago in March 1907 he decided to stop preaching the second blessing. [41] Silence did not suit him either, however. He began to attack the doctrine and articulated in its place what he called "the finished work of Calvary." Maintaining that "when God saves a man, He makes him clean," he insisted that "Christ [had] finished the work in our behalf." It was, therefore, illogical to believe "that we have been pardoned but that we are left full of sin" and in need of a "second work." [42]

Excoriated by holiness spokespersons, and especially by the increasingly bitter Charles Fox Parham, Durham nonetheless won a wide hearing and could cite an impressive list of converts to his views, including the most influential segment of Parham's former associates in Texas and Arkansas. [43]

The North Avenue Mission, meanwhile, achieved visibility and acclaim among midwestern adherents of the apostolic faith. Durham moved much of his work to Los Angeles in 1911, partly out of a desire to spread his views in the "cradle" of American Pentecostalism and partly because of trouble in his North Avenue Mission. Even so, he continued to exert influence in Chicago until his untimely death in 1912 at the age of thirty-nine.

The Apostolic Faith Movement in Texas and Arkansas

Parham's associates in eastern Texas continued to proclaim the apostolic faith, even as the focus of the movement shifted to Los Angeles. Parham and Carothers conducted a camp meeting in suburban Houston in August 1906 at which Lucy Farrow, fresh from the excitement at Azusa Street and on her way to spread the message to Virginia, spoke to large crowds.[44] Late in the summer of 1906 Parham imposed on his ministry the rudiments of an organization. Parham had earlier issued ministerial credentials as founder and projector of the Apostolic Faith Movement. Now he appointed Carothers general field director for the United States and Howard Goss field director for Texas, where some sixty full-time Apostolic Faith representatives evangelized.[45]

During Parham's absence in Zion City and Los Angeles, his workers opened a mission in San Antonio, where two more prominent leaders of Dowie's Christian Catholic Apostolic Church, L. C. Hall and D. C. O. Opperman, joined their ranks. Camp meetings, short-term Bible institutes, and evangelistic campaigns absorbed all of their time.

During the summer of 1907 when charges of sodomy were brought against Parham in San Antonio, the loose organization he had created was temporarily dissolved, and many evangelists "left the field."[46] They soon regrouped, however, determined to salvage as much of the Apostolic Faith Movement as they could. Shortly after renouncing Parham, they accepted an invitation to evangelize in Arkansas, where they found considerable interest. They began to refer to themselves as Pentecostals, both to disassociate from Parham and to clarify what distinguished them from others whose outlook and practices were similar. The nucleus of workers, among whom Howard Goss, L. C. Hall, D. C. O. Opperman, and A. G. Canada figured prominently, welcomed another capable worker, Eudorus N. Bell.

Bell was the forty-five-year-old bachelor pastor of a Southern Baptist church in Fort Worth when he embraced Pentecostalism. One of the best-trained men to assume leadership in early Pentecostalism, Bell had studied at Stetson University in Florida, Southern Baptist Seminary in Louisville, and the University of Chicago Divinity School.[47]

Although many of his parishioners accepted Pentecostal teaching, Bell resigned to participate in the camp meetings and Bible schools sponsored by Parham's former associates. He married a widow from Fort Worth and assumed the editorial responsibilities for the movement's magazine, the *Apostolic Faith*. In 1910, probably in response to Bell's invitation, Durham preached at a camp meeting in Malvern, Arkansas, during which he convinced participants of his "finished work" views.

These men and women had also established contact with Henry G. Rodgers. The short duration of his Pentecostal Association of the Mississippi Valley had not dampened Rodgers's enthusiasm for organizing a loose network of Pentecostal ministers. In 1908 Rodgers had set in order several churches using the name *Church of God*.[48] Rodgers had also licensed and ordained several workers for this Church of God and planned to apply for recognition by the Southern Clergy Bureau.[49]

During 1910 Rodgers met with Howard Goss and D. C. O. Opperman in Texas, and they concluded that the name Church of God identified them too closely with Tomlinson's exclusive and more thoroughly restorationist work. As a result, Rodgers and the former Apostolic Faith adherents in Texas effected a working arrangement under the name *Church of God in Christ.* Latent hostility toward organization (Goss reported that some of his colleagues considered that any organization "when committed to paper . . . was of the devil") precluded the formation of a meaningful formal structure.[50] What resulted was "mainly for the purpose of business," a "gentlemen's agreement," under which it was understood that the "untrustworthy" would be banned from "fellowship."[51]

The name *Church of God in Christ* was an expression of the restorationist quest for a biblical designation. Late in 1907 Goss had apparently visited Charles Mason of the Churches of God in Christ and received a preaching license. Goss recorded in his diary that he had obtained from Mason permission to issue ministerial credentials using the name *Churches of God in Christ* for the "white work" in Texas.[52] Although the name *Apostolic Faith Movement* remained in use for several years, *Churches of God in Christ* gained favor as a "biblical name." Camp meetings provided the best settings for scattered participants loosely identified under the heading Church of God in Christ to mingle. Whereas in May 1911 Bell's *Apostolic Faith* announced the "Sixth Annual Encampment of the Apostolic Faith Movement for Texas and the Southwest," in 1912 his *Word and Witness* announced a camp meeting of the "Churches of God in Christ of the Apostolic Faith people."[53]

In 1912 over three hundred attended the Churches of God in Christ camp meeting at Eureka Springs, Arkansas. Shortly after the camp, *Word and Witness* carried a long article about an appropriate name for the movement. In a strong endorsement of restorationism, Bell explicitly rejected the term *Apostolic Faith* because it was not a "Bible designation." "We believe," he noted, "in the Apostolic Movement not as a name for a church, but as a religious reform movement composed of all clean people who will join in our battle cry and reform slogan of Back to Christ and the apostles! Back to the faith once for all delivered to the saints! Back to the New Testament experiences!"[54] Bell proposed that local congregations join the growing ranks of "saints everywhere" who called their assemblies "Churches of God and Churches of God in Christ as we are doing. Why add to God's names Holiness church, or Pentecostal church? All should be both."[55]

Records from 1913 preserve a list of 361 ministers, at least 84 of whom were women, in association with this Church of God in Christ. They represented twenty states and five foreign countries.[56] The Church of God in Christ had a school committee, a bureau of information, and a clergy reference committee to offer advice to adherents.[57]

Operating primarily outside, or on the fringes of, established denominations, then, such tongues-speaking evangelists, male and female, lay and ordained, infiltrated independent missions, holiness associations, nondenominational and, when possible, denominational settings to proclaim the full and final restoration of New Testament Christianity in the onset of the latter rain. Their hope-filled message attracted a growing constituency held together by periodicals, traveling evangelists, and frequent camp meetings. They offered wholeness, inner peace, healing, temporal supply, and purpose as they assured all who would listen that none had fallen too low to look up and discover dignity and status as a child of God.

NOTES

1. *Waukegan Daily Gazette,* 15 Oct. 1906.

2. *Cheney Sentinel,* 5 Oct. 1906.

3. Sarah Parham, *The Life of Charles Fox Parham,* 3d ed. (Birmingham: Commercial Printing, 1977), 156–57; *Waukegan Daily Sun,* 15 Nov. 1906, reported that as many as three hundred attended a single house meeting.

4. For biographical studies of the early Pentecostal movement in Zion City and its impact on Pentecostalism worldwide see Gordon P. Gardiner, *Out of Zion . . . into All the World* (Shippensburg, Penn.: Companion Press, 1990); Edith L. Blumhofer, "The Christian Catholic Church and the Apostolic Faith: A Study in the 1906 Pentecostal Revival," in *Charismatic Experiences in History,* ed. Cecil M. Robeck (Peabody, Mass.: Hendrickson, 1986).

5. For Jones's story, see Otho Cobbins, *The Church of Christ (Holiness) U. S. A.* (New York: Vantage Press, 1966).

6. Elnora L. Lee, comp., *C. H. Mason: A Man Greatly Used of God* (Memphis, Tenn.: Women's Department, Church of God in Christ, 1967), 7–8.

7. Elsie W. Mason, *The Man: Charles Harrison Mason* (Memphis, Tenn.: Church of God in Christ, 1979), 14.

8. Lee, *Mason,* 8.

9. Quoted in Lee, *Mason,* 19.

10. Both L. P. Adams and August Feick, one of the evangelist Maria B. Woodworth-Etter's assistants at her tabernacle in Indianapolis, were associated with a white branch of the Churches of God in Christ. During the 1920s, Mason made a serious effort to formalize such a branch. See August Feick to J. W. Welch, 6 Apr. 1926, Assemblies of God Archives, Springfield, Mo. (hereafter AGA). Feick surrendered his Assemblies of God credentials to assist Mason in the endeavor.

11. By 1912 Parham claimed he had no use for incorporation and ridiculed

those who sought clergy discounts: "I would hate to give such a testimony to the world that my God was a pauper and compelled me to ride on half-fare, or confess my little faith in trusting God for full fare." *Apostolic Faith*, Sept. 1912, 9. However, six years earlier Seymour had obtained credentials from Parham in order to obtain the rail discount. Seymour to Warren Fay Carothers, July 1906, copy in the author's possession.

12. "Came Three Thousand Miles for His Pentecost," *Apostolic Faith*, Dec. 1906, 3.

13. Ibid.

14. *Apostolic Faith*, Jan. 1907, 1.

15. "Hundreds Baptized in the South," *Apostolic Faith*, Feb.-Mar., 1907, 3.

16. Quoted in James R. Goff, "The Pentecostal Catalyst to the South: G. B. Cashwell, 1906–1908," unpublished paper, AGA.

17. John T. Benson, *Pentecostal Mission* (Nashville, Tenn.: Trevecca Press, 1977), 20.

18. Pentecostal Alliance Mission Minutes, 6 Jan. 1908, AGA.

19. Holmes, who had founded a seminary, became a prominent educator in the movement. Nickels John Holmes, *Life Sketches and Sermons* (Royston, Ga.: Pentecostal Holiness Church, 1920).

20. Charles Conn, *Like a Mighty Army Moves the Church of God* (Cleveland, Tenn.: Church of God Publishing House, 1955); Ambrose J. Tomlinson, *Diary of A. J. Tomlinson*, 3 vols., ed. Homer Tomlinson (New York: Church of God, World Headquarters, 1949–55).

21. Robert Mapes Anderson's account differs from this one, which is culled from various minutes and diaries kept by Rodgers and Pinson that are in AGA. See Anderson, *Vision of the Disinherited: The Making of American Pentecostalism* (New York: Oxford University Press, 1979).

22. *Christian and Missionary Alliance*, 8 June 1907, 205.

23. A. W. Vian, "Further News from Nyack, New York," *Household of God*, Nov. 1907, 6.

24. Edith L. Blumhofer, "The Pentecostal Movement in Indianapolis," unpublished ms., AGA.

25. Elizabeth Baker, *Chronicles of a Faith Life* (Rochester, N.Y.: DuBois Press, n.d.), 117ff. See also Susan A. Duncan, *Trials and Triumphs of a Faith Life* (Rochester, N.Y.: Elim Publishing House, 1910). For a study of the faith home related to this Bible school, see Edith L. Blumhofer, "Life on 'Faith Lines': Faith Homes and Early Pentecostal Values," *Assemblies of God Heritage* 10 (Summer 1990).

26. For a student perspective on this and other practices at the school, see Marion Meloon, *Ivan Spencer: Willow in the Wind* (Plainfield, N.J.: Logos International, 1974).

27. Baker, *Chronicles*, 64.

28. Ibid., 63. Several of the sisters visited in Wales, and in 1914 and 1915 they still corresponded with Evan Roberts's brother about the Welsh religious scene. One of them also visited Pandita Ramabai in India. The number of these independent evangelicals who supported Ramabai is striking. From Moody's as-

sociates in the 1880s to Torrey's worldwide tour that coincided with the Welsh revival to early Pentecostal evangelists, Ramabai's work attracted considerable and diffuse American interest. Of special interest is Pandita Ramabai, *The Baptism of the Holy Ghost and Fire* (Kedgaon, India: Mukti Mission Press, 1906).

29. Baker, *Chronicles*, 64.

30. Ibid., 65.

31. Ibid., 127.

32. Ibid., 130.

33. Ibid.

34. Quoted in Gordon P. Gardiner, "Out of Zion . . . into All the World," *Bread of Life* 31 (Apr. 1982): 7. A brief history of the church is Lois Ephraim, *The Stone Church, 1906–1981* (Worth, Ill.: Charles E. Brinkman Publishers, 1981). The best source for the congregation's character is its monthly publication, *Latter Rain Evangel*.

35. William Piper, "Long, Weary Months of Spiritual Drought Broken by the Gracious Coming of the Holy Spirit, a Week in the Upper Room," *Latter Rain Evangel*, Oct. 1908, 3–6.

36. Immigrants and their children were well represented in early Pentecostalism. The success of the movement among Swedish Americans in some regions was noted by the *Apostolic Faith*, Apr. 1907, 2. See also Frederick Link to Robert C. Cunningham, 9 Mar. 1951, AGA, which refers to Elder Sangreen who led "the Swedish work" of the North Avenue Mission. This later separated to form the Lake View Church. Danish and Norwegians also formed separate congregations within the North Avenue Mission, as did some Italians led by a husband and wife team named Franciscone.

37. William Durham, "The Church," *Pentecostal Testimony* 2, no. 1 (n.d.), 14.

38. William Durham, "What Is the Evidence of the Baptism in the Holy Ghost?" *Pentecostal Testimony* 2, no. 1 (n.d.), 4.

39. Durham, "Evidence," 4.

40. William Durham, "Personal Testimony of Pastor Durham," *Pentecostal Testimony* 2 (n.d.), 3.

41. His failure to proclaim crisis sanctification did not immediately alienate him from others. Jennie Moore came from Azusa Street to visit his mission at 943 West North Avenue and wrote in the Jan. 1908 *Apostolic Faith* that it was "truly a blessed place—many Spirit-filled men and women and children."

42. William Durham, "The Great Battle of 1911," *Pentecostal Testimony* 2, no. 1 (n.d.), 7; "The Gospel of Christ," *Pentecostal Testimony* 2, no. 1 (n.d.), 9.

43. As Durham traveled to camp meetings and conventions, he won key individuals to his views, among whom were Pinson, Rodgers, and Howard Goss.

44. Ethel E. Goss, *The Winds of God* (New York: Comet Press Books, 1958), 56. Farrow did not stay in Virginia long. In December 1906 the *Apostolic Faith* reported that after winning some two hundred converts in Virginia, Farrow had joined a party of missionaries from Azusa Street and was on her way to Monrovia, Liberia.

45. Goss, *Winds of God*, 57.

46. Ibid., 79. But Parham associated with some of his southern followers prominently in 1908 when he was the featured speaker at an Alabama camp meeting. See announcements in *Word and Work*. Apparently there was considerable disagreement about his alleged "fall." In 1912 he seemed convinced that he was regaining the confidence of others. See editorials and reports in his *Apostolic Faith*, 1912 and 1913.

47. Eudorus N. Bell File, AGA.

48. Mack M. Pinson to J. Roswell Flower, 19 Dec. 1950, Mack M. Pinson File, AGA.

49. J. Roswell Flower to Mack M. Pinson, 4 Jan. 1950, Mack M. Pinson File. Flower quotes minutes of a meeting of the Churches of God at Slocum, Ala., on 10 Feb. 1911.

50. Goss, *Winds of God*, 163.

51. Ibid.

52. Flower to Pinson, 4 Jan. 1950.

53. At the gathering in 1911 Bell and Pinson, each of whom edited a Pentecostal paper representing one of the two major segments of this white Church of God in Christ, had decided to merge their publications. Bell's *Apostolic Faith* was absorbed into Pinson's *Word and Witness*, with Bell assuming editorial duties in addition to the pastorate of a Pentecostal church in Malvern.

54. *Word and Witness*, 20 Aug. 1912, 2; "Glory and Unity at the Eureka Springs Camp!" *Word and Witness*, 20 Aug. 1912, 1.

55. *Word and Witness*, 20 Aug. 1912, 2.

56. "Ordained Elders, Pastors, Ministers, Evangelists and Missionaries of the Churches of God in Christ with Their Stations for 1914," *Word and Witness*, 20 Dec. 1913, 4. The number of women is approximate since many ministers used their initials. It seems that women were identified by their full first names or by the titles Miss or Mrs., but it is not certain that all were so designated.

57. Ibid.

4

The Meaning and Implications of
Pentecostal Experience, 1901–13

E XPERIENCING the apostolic faith initiated people into faith communities and provided a new framework for perceiving reality. These functioned as exclusive total worlds, redefining reality, priorities, vocation, and relationships. These faith communities shaped the hopes of the people who formed the Assemblies of God in 1914. To understand the denomination's origins, it is necessary to explore the rhetoric and texture of the early Pentecostal subculture.

"This world is not my home," early Pentecostals affirmed with conviction in song, sermon, and testimony. "I am a stranger here, within a foreign land. . . . I'm here on business for my King."[1] They spoke as if Spirit baptism marked a radical disjunction in their lives, uprooting them from one culture and initiating them into another. They regarded themselves as pilgrims passing through or, to use another metaphor, as resident aliens who had no intention of being integrated into the culture around them. They found in their conception of Pentecostal experience a rationale for disinterest in contemporary society. Their attitudes toward the church and the world were rooted in both their coveted identity as pilgrims and strangers and their convictions about the imminence of Christ's return.[2]

Early Pentecostals tended to define a sphere for themselves and to use language that promoted cultural insularity. For them, spiritual conflict was constant and vivid; life was understood as "us" against "them" or, more precisely, in cosmic terms, as part of the eternal conflict between God and Satan. They ventured into the world primarily to call others out of it. Though their faith communities had no geographic boundaries, they had well-defined behavioral norms and cultural expectations; they cultivated a strong sense of community obligation, meaning, and purpose. Yet, despite people's best intentions, it gradually became apparent that the disjunction with the past was not total and that in many ways Pentecostals, like everyone else, were molded by the larger culture.

Life in the Community of Pentecostal Saints

Early Pentecostals referred to those who shared their experience as saints. The saints gathered almost daily for worship and testimony, and the schedule of virtually any Pentecostal mission illustrates how the pace of the community reminded them they were pilgrims. Meetings every weekday, five or six weeknights, and three times on Sunday left the most committed little time for diversion. The schedule took its toll on family life and may help account for rapid influx and outflow of participants, the common loss of the next generation to the movement, and frequent concern about declension. Fueled by the conviction that history and tradition were irrelevant to God's end-times intentions and certain that they could be spiritually insulated from cultural influence, they insisted that the "pure fountain" of the New Testament flowed in their midst, enabling them to revel in "days of heaven on earth."[3] "When you get that rain of the Spirit upon you," Pentecostal evangelist David Wesley Myland observed, "don't you begin the days of heaven on earth? You begin to get heavenly tongues, heavenly songs, heavenly choirs, heavenly interpretation, heavenly inspiration, heavenly fellowship; you are in the heavenlies of Jesus Christ."[4] Broadway and Hollywood seemed poor competition to heaven.

The promise of divine immediacy attracted a cross section of people— those whose lives lacked worldly comforts and compensations, recent immigrants, some working and a few middle-class Americans. People deprived of worldly status found in Pentecostal missions position and dignity as mediators of God's end-times message who, unlike the socially or economically empowered for whom they toiled, truly understood the times in which they lived. To participants, Pentecostalism did not seem disproportionately to attract the dispossessed. Status-hungry participant-observers noted with pride the worldly accomplishments of some in their ranks even as they admitted that Pentecostal experience was radically equalizing and made past achievements pale in the community of saints.

Pentecostals believed their religious experience sensitized them to spiritual realities. For them, heaven had already begun: "'Tis heaven my Jesus here to know."[5] This "life in the heavenlies" effectively sheltered them, they believed, from corrupting worldly influences, enabling them to live equipped by the Holy Spirit for forays into the world but preserved by the Spirit from the taint of worldliness. They cherished a sense of participation in a chosen community:

> Though these people may not learned be,
> Nor boast of worldly fame,
> They have all received their Pentecost
> Through faith in Jesus' name. . . .
> And I'm glad that I can say I'm one of them.[6]

Early Pentecostals eagerly anticipated effecting the renewal of vital Christian experience in the whole church through example and precept. The demonstration of the reality of the supernatural in their own lives, they believed, would attract others to their ranks. Convinced that Spirit baptism made them "living Epistles" from God to humankind, Pentecostals tended not to distinguish between the sinful and the frivolous in defining appropriate conduct for believers. They were deadly serious about nurturing their heavenly calling, and they frequently denounced as sinful a long and varied list of practices they regarded as intrusions, distractions, or poor stewardship. Wearing jewelry; drinking coffee or cola; bowling; attending theaters, dances, circuses, and ball games; using tobacco or alcohol; joining fraternal organizations; and many other such activities were deemed incompatible with the supreme purpose of being ready for Christ's anticipated return and as disruptive of the spiritual sensitivity that nurtured the presence of Christ in and among the saints. Political activism and labor unionism fell under the same stricture. After all, those who spent their days expecting to be raptured at any moment could hardly afford to be found diverting their time, resources, and energies from preparation for history's climax. They sang with anticipation: "Jesus may come today, / Glad day! / Glad day! . . . I may go home today!"[7] Their excitement was jubilant:

> Jesus is coming to earth again,
> What if it were today?
> Glory, glory! Joy to my heart 'twill bring
> Glory, glory! When we shall crown Him king.[8]

They claimed that "life in the heavenlies" created a profound distaste for worldly pursuits. "Not for all earth's golden millions would I leave this precious place, Tho' the tempter to persuade me oft has tried," they sang. Their reason? They were "safe" and "happy . . . living on the hallelujah side."[9] They coveted right priorities. In words familiar to many Protestants, they reminded themselves: "Not for ease or worldly pleasure, Nor for fame my prayer shall be."[10]

Pentecostal worship united and energized the saints. It defied simple

description, but accounts agree about at least two things. First, it absorbed one's mind and body, which were controlled by the Holy Spirit.
"All that wondrous worship and praise which overflowed my whole being
came springing up alone from the Holy Spirit within; while my whole
heart and soul constantly united with this stream of praise. No effort or
work upon my part, my work had forever ceased."[11] Second, the Holy
Spirit prompted variety: "He does not always want you to be doing the
same thing; He does not want things to run in a groove; He wants liberty
to have a diversity of operations in the Spirit."[12] "A Pentecostal meeting
where you always know what is going to happen next is backslidden," one
participant insisted.[13]

Worship burst forth spontaneously wherever the Spirit-filled congregated. "When the power of God got to building up within us, it soon
reached the level where vent had to be given to these floodtides of joy,"
Howard Goss reminisced. "At every opportunity it was instinctive to drop
to one's knees and start praying and praising."[14] Train cars, rail stations,
street corners, and home gatherings all became settings hallowed by exuberant praise, heartfelt singing, and the exercising of spiritual gifts.[15]

Intense excitement usually accompanied the initial experience of
tongues speech (which Pentecostals often called "Bible baptism" to dif-
ferentiate themselves from those who considered an experience not
marked by tongues speech to be Spirit baptism). The culmination of a
process often including repentance, restitution, sanctification, and "tarrying" (or prayerful anticipation), the baptism with the Holy Spirit was
the moment when "King Jesus took full control of their hearts."[16] Participants claimed to speak many known languages or to sing in tongues as a
response to an overwhelming, unique joy that flooded their souls. One
testimony from Clearwater, Florida, captured this sense of newness: "It
seemed as if human joys vanished. . . . This is something I never had
before. It seemed as if the whole world and the people looked a different
color. Jesus had come to me."[17]

Like a familiar refrain, those words, "Jesus has come to me," punctuated early written and spoken testimonies. Pentecostals believed their
experience "made the Lord Jesus intensely *real.*"[18] Pentecostalism was
"His fullness."[19] Leaders admonished seekers not to anticipate tongues
but to "seek Jesus." "It is not tongues," *Word and Work* maintained.
"Tongues is an evidence or a sign that He has come and subdued the
man."[20] Writing in 1910, J. Roswell Flower cautioned: "Too much stress
on tongues weakens the argument. . . . Let us not stress any gift or doctrine out of due proportion. Let us preach the Word and leave the rest
with God. When the Comforter comes, He will make Himself known,
and evidence His presence."[21] Flower voiced a further concern: an em-

phasis on tongues, he noted, would "compel us to accept all speaking in tongues as divine," when some was "purely human and other is certainly satanic."[22]

Despite an evident yearning for "old-time religion," Pentecostals always coveted the new or the fresh. Preachers were urged to be sensitive to the Holy Spirit's new message for the church. Samuel Jamieson's experience is a case in point. Jamieson had twenty-five years of experience as a Presbyterian pastor when he embraced Pentecostal teaching in 1907. In response to what he considered divine direction, he discarded his sermons to rely on the Holy Spirit: "Burn them up, and I will furnish you messages of My own choosing." He also found the Bible "practically a new book" and "preaching under the anointing" a delight.[23]

The conviction that "Jesus had come" in a vital way into their circumstances seemed to imbue participants with limitless joy and reckless courage. Joy typically found expression in enthusiastic, fast-paced "infectious" singing. Parham's associate Howard Goss appreciated the role of music in attracting converts: "Without it," he claimed, "the Pentecostal Movement could never have made the quick inroads into hearts that it did."[24] Pentecostals sang holiness songs, gospel music, and Charles Wesley's majestic descriptions of Christian experience.[25] Some of the earliest Pentecostal creativity took musical form. David Wesley Myland and Aimee Semple McPherson were among the more prominent of many who claimed to have been divinely "given" songs in tongues and interpretation that achieved a degree of popularity.[26] Within a decade, Pentecostals also began writing popular gospel songs that captured and popularized their fervent hopes. Both Thoro Harris and Garfield T. Haywood, African-American Pentecostals, won wide acclaim. Harris's "All That Thrills My Soul Is Jesus," "He's Coming Soon," "More Abundantly," and "Pentecost in My Soul" made their way into many hymnals as did Haywood's "Jesus, the Son of God" and "I See a Crimson Stream of Blood." Herbert Buffum, a former Nazarene evangelist, authored hundreds of songs both before and after embracing Pentecostalism. R. E. Winsett and Seeley Kinney became prominent Pentecostal songbook publishers.[27]

Pentecostal worship services continued indefinitely. The "anointing" to preach, prophesy, testify, or sing seemed to defy scheduling. People typically came prepared to stay. Haywood noted that his daily afternoon Bible readings and nightly services attracted many who brought their evening meal and stayed between services.[28] Even conventions to which people traveled hundreds of miles frequently anticipated no specific closing date. Pentecostals dreaded "limiting the Spirit." Their general reluctance to follow the pattern of typical Protestant services was part of their determination to assure "liberty" in the Spirit. Haywood noticed the tendency to equate even the most basic trappings of traditional worship with "quenching the Spirit." When his mission acquired a pump organ, some charged that it was "getting worldly." And "when it went from pump organ to the piano, it was becoming more worldly. And when the church had its first choir, there was such a revulsion against choirs that it was called a chorus." Even so, the chorus could not sit in a designated place or wear robes; rather, its members sat scattered throughout the congregation and "assembled around the piano when the pastor called for their services."[29]

Immersed into a world in which spiritual forces often loomed larger than tangible realities, Pentecostals frequently yielded to inclinations to neglect conventional social obligations to pursue spiritual experiences. Taking literally injunctions to love nothing more than Christ, some virtually abandoned regular family life to "follow the Lord." The movement attracted its share of adherents who disliked physical work and regarded the "faith life" as an opportunity to avoid distasteful obligations. Leaders soon found it advisable to encourage the faithful to acknowledge and fulfill family obligations. Denouncing as "false teaching" the idea that God had called married women "to do mission work, and to leave the little children at home to fare the best they can," the *Apostolic Faith* from Azusa Street was equally critical of men who abandoned their families "for the sake of the gospel": "Many precious husbands have left their wives and children at home, and their wives are working hard to support the little children, washing, ironing, scrubbing, and farming, while their husband is claiming to be doing missionary work, and saying the Lord gave him scripture regarding forsaking. They take it for granted that the Lord does not want them to be bothered with their families."[30]

Whatever their needs, Pentecostals were instructed to pray. Healing, funds, and daily direction became the subjects of intense supplication. Failure to obtain the desired object provoked self-examination. "If you are not healed," the *Apostolic Faith* editorialized, "the fault is either in you or in Jesus Christ. Which is it? Be honest with yourself and get the fault out of the way."[31]

Few significant secular events passed without comment about their prophetic import. Earthquakes, economic uncertainty, foreign affairs, political elections, and world wars were significant primarily for their place in God's prophetic calendar. Pentecostals contributed prophecies, too. With other millenarians, they anticipated that the "signs of the times" would become increasingly evident, and some had strong forebodings of dramatic judgments close to home.[32]

Pentecostalism, then, offered a frame of reference for understanding human experience and defining ultimate concern, and in significant ways

Pentecostals created for themselves a separate world in which to affirm the radical nature of the Spirit's presence in their midst. They invested speaking in tongues with a significance that made it the most obvious Pentecostal departure from others who shared their spirituality.[33] Other "spiritual gifts" were equally real to the ardent Pentecostal who also tended to reinterpret difficulties of any sort as demonic opposition— "attacks of the enemy."[34]

Participants considered themselves involved in spiritual battles through which they gained a sense of a personal participation in Christ's ultimate victory. Frequent dreams, visions, and transports mediated interpretations of the divine significance of everyday occurrences. Spiritual power sometimes took unusual turns. The published testimony of a young girl who claimed to have been "taken up two or three feet from the floor by the Holy Spirit and held there until some of the audience became frightened and put their hands on her" was followed by an attempt at explanation—"Well, the great day is just before us when the laws of gravitation shall be reversed, and we need not be shocked if God shows us a little foretaste of it occasionally in these wonderful days of the 'Latter Rain.'"[35]

In June 1909 the *Upper Room*, a Pentecostal publication from Los Angeles, printed a list of the movement's "marked features" that summarizes early Pentecostal self-understanding. Pentecostals were people who "exalted Christ and His blood," who honored the Holy Spirit and "expected His operations," and who "earnestly looked for the coming of the Lord." Missionary fervor compelled them to "pray, and give, and go as only Pentecostal people can"; they lived by "faith"; and "the spirit of praise and of worship and of prayer that is manifested in their private lives and in their meetings is phenomenal"; their "joy and liberty in the Spirit [were] very marked"; and their watchword was "Back to Pentecost."[36]

It was the Pentecostals' view of their place in history that most basically set them apart from the majority of Christians. Intrinsic to their self-understanding was a carefully articulated view of the contemporary significance of Old Testament prophecies of the "latter rain." The "days of heaven on earth" foretold in Deut. 11 were being fulfilled in their experience, they asserted. Probably the most influential statement of the Pentecostal understanding of the latter rain came from the pen of David Wesley Myland, a one-time Christian and Missionary Alliance official who became an independent Pentecostal evangelist and teacher.

In May 1909 Myland was the featured speaker at a convention sponsored by the Stone Church. His addresses, duly reported in the church's publication, the *Latter Rain Evangel*, consisted of lengthy expositions of

Old and New Testament passages to demonstrate that the Pentecostal "out-pouring" was the latter rain. They commanded wide respect among Pentecostals, who generally considered them profound in their scholarship.

Myland's approach involved "comparing scripture with scripture under the illumination of the Holy Spirit, to get its deeper sense."[37] "There are many scriptures that are not only double-barreled but triple-barreled," he noted. "They are literal, typical and prophetical; or putting it in other words, historical, spiritual and dispensational."[38] When Myland applied this hermeneutic to his search for the significance of the baptism with the Holy Spirit, he discovered that it enabled him to draw parallels between the natural course of events in Palestine and the spiritual momentum of Pentecostalism. "If it is remembered that the climate of Palestine consisted of two seasons, the wet and the dry, and that the wet season was made up of the early and latter rain, it will help you to understand this [latter rain] covenant and the present workings of God's Spirit. For just as literal early and latter rain was poured out upon Palestine, so upon the church of the first century was poured out the spiritual early rain, and upon us today is being poured out the spiritual latter rain."[39]

Myland's friend, William Hamner Piper, convinced that his generation lived "in the time when the Latter Rain truths [were] due," warmly recommended Myland's views. "Our studies in Exegesis have revealed nothing which in uniqueness and originality equals this exposition of the blessed Latter Rain truths," he noted. Insisting that "Latter Rain truths" represented another epoch in church history similar in significance to Luther's teaching on justification and Wesley's on Christian perfection, Piper urged Pentecostals to pray for a "spiritual understanding" of this all-important subject.

In fact, Myland's insights and even his language were duplicated in other publications, especially those sponsored by protofundamentalists and by the Christian and Missionary Alliance. In 1907 the Alliance's magazine, the *Christian and Missionary Alliance*, carried an editorial in which Albert B. Simpson explicitly encouraged expectation of an imminent "outpouring" of the latter rain: "We may . . . conclude that we are to expect a great outpouring of the Holy Spirit in connection with the second coming of Christ and one as much greater than the Pentecostal effusion of the Spirit as the rains of autumn were greater than the showers of spring. . . . We are in the time . . . when we may expect this latter rain."[40]

Simpson's convictions about the extent and significance of the latter rain (which he thought would include not only speech in unknown tongues but also "real missionary tongues like those of Pentecost") con-

vinced him that the Apostolic Faith Movement in all of its various expressions represented only "the sprinkling of the first drops of a mighty
rain."[41]

The term *latter rain* was commonly used in the emerging fundamentalist movement, too. Such prominent evangelicals as J. Wilbur Chapman,
James M. Gray, C. I. Scofield, and Arthur T. Pierson urged prayer for
revival with the biblical words "ask of the Lord rain in the time of the
latter rain" (Zech. 10:1). Fundamentalists charted rainfall in Palestine as
diligently as did Pentecostals but they did not expect a full recurrence of
apostolic "signs," whereas for Pentecostals the "signs" were necessary dis-
tinguishing marks of the early and latter rain.

Pentecostals heartily concurred that they had only begun to experience
the "rain." Never since Pentecost, one wrote, "until the marvelous . . .
visitations of the Spirit of God in the past three years, beginning with the
revival in Wales," had the church anywhere experienced "anything an-
swering to the promised Latter Rain."[42] Failure to "join this forward
movement of God's Spirit" would result in "terrible spiritual desolation
and uselessness." The "real place of safety" was "under the very center of
the cloudburst."[43]

Participation in the "latter rain outpouring" was marked by vigorous
rejection of "the world." Views on worldliness generally paralleled those
of contemporary holiness advocates who had demanded "separation" in
conspicuous ways. True Christianity, the faithful avowed, could never
harmonize with culture: its adherents would always be a persecuted, unpopular remnant. Yet the spirit of the age shaped Pentecostals' understanding of the Holy Spirit's presence among them, and they mirrored
their culture in significant ways.

Behavioral norms often corresponded closely with economic realities,
but Pentecostals preferred to believe that outsiders failed to comprehend
their true motivation: "The personal holiness, the purity of principle and
motive demanded of each of us was so great, comparatively speaking, that
many onlookers believed we were either insane over religion, or drunk on
some glorious dream."[44] Convinced that nothing they did would achieve
a righteous society, adherents either poured their energies into attempts
to address humanity's spiritual needs or segregated themselves and enjoyed the blessings of the deeper life. Certain that the world was about to
face judgment, they looked for ways to express their separation from its
mores. In their minds, pursuit of worldly comforts and pleasures indicated
spiritual poverty: "The truly spiritual person requires no amusement;
when He comes in He brings His own entertainment and you have a
continuous banquet. You have no desire for the amusements of the world
or of the church."[45]

Pentecostals harbored special aversions toward "church amusements." Parham's *Apostolic Faith,* like other Pentecostal magazines, often published sarcastic comments about "church sprees." The Christian Workers' Union, a band of Pentecostals near Framingham, Massachusetts, issued numerous tracts dealing with the subject. Abbie C. Morrow's writing captured the typical argument: "The sons of God should be as fearless as was the Son of God in putting away from His house everything that defiles it. Our Lord does not look with any more favor upon those in the church today who countenance fairs, festivals, dramas, and cantatas than He did upon those defilers of His temple 1900 years ago."[46] Not only was it ridiculous to "think of Peter giving a dramatic reading in the court of the temple" or to imagine Jesus "writing to the women of a certain city and asking them to get up a neck-tie social to pay His expenses to come to them," but such fund-raising ploys also "robbed the people of the privilege of giving to the Lord." Morrow did not mince her words: "Ecclesiastical amusement and money-making blight the spiritual life, influence, activity and usefulness of the church and promote almost every species of carnality and worldliness."[47]

Carnality posed a more ominous threat than worldliness. Spirit baptism "required the crucifixion of the purified natural man and the revelation of Christ in us, in the physical, affectional and mental realms."[48] While participants in the holiness movement had also been urged to "guard diligently" against exhibiting such "carnal traits" as pride or anger, Pentecostals had a more demanding obligation. "The battle," they were frequently reminded, "is not so much to keep out of sin as it is to be led by and walk in the Spirit—to keep from gliding down out of the supernatural into the natural."[49] Avoiding carnality did not merely pose a challenge: it was a matter of life and death, understood as vital to preserving the movement's meaning. Lamenting in 1910 about waning spirituality in the movement's brief history, one writer identified carnality as the cause of a "cooling of ardor, a lack of positiveness, aggressiveness." While Pentecostal meetings remained "good," "the power" no longer "fell" and persecution had waned.[50] Carnality, which represented response to the lure of satanic temptation, typically became a catchword accounting for perceived declension. Uncovering it was the challenge. That task promoted a degree of introspection that blurred distinctions between discernment and judgment and characterized the early movement; Pentecostals developed a rigorous informal theology of religious experience. Preoccupation with carnality expressed itself in many ways. One was a general concern about modesty, which differed in detail from region to region. In general, Pentecostals subscribed to the more conservative customs of regional culture. And they blamed "pride in the heart" for interest in contemporary fashions: "What greater proof have we that much of the religious profession of today is a sham than the outward ornamentation and putting on of apparel? It clearly shows we love the praise of men more than the praise of God."[51] At a time when few women had short hair or wore makeup, for example, Pentecostals made social custom virtually a matter of faith. Some sought to uproot pride by dictating plain dress or by objecting to "adornments," such as ties or jewelry. Occasionally women alleged that the Holy Spirit directly interfered with their wearing of jewelry: "A sister while under the power took the fancy pins out of her hat and threw them away. Another sister who was [Spirit] baptized, when she came to change her clothing, attempted to put on her jewelry again, but the Spirit would not let her, so she left it off."[52] "The Spirit," then, worked "in harmony with the Word, teaching His people how to dress according to the Bible."[53] Bertha Hisey credited the Holy Spirit with destroying her love of dancing. Herbert Buffum cautioned, "We cannot keep Him in our hearts . . . and indulge in theaters, etc."[54]

Even those Pentecostals who cautioned against overstressing "outward adorning" advocated plain dress as an evidence of "normal womanliness" if not of godliness. Women "must have the heavenly attire of meekness and quietness," one Pentecostal insisted. "Having lost her frivolous, superficial, worldly desires, to please the world and waste [her husband's] hard-earned money on gaieties, she now becomes normal, and assumes womanliness and love which is genuine, and which wins her to Christ."[55]

Related to such concerns was the frequent shunning of certain foods. Former Dowie followers as well as numerous holiness people followed Old Testament instructions in refusing to eat pork or pork products. Some objected to coffee, tea, and other items containing caffeine: "Dearly beloved, I want to tell you that coffee is a stimulant like unto whiskey. . . . Tea . . . will surely cause nervous trouble. . . . Now as we are to live for the glory of God, my better sense tells me I cannot glorify God in this, as it is constantly destroying God's temple."[56] Tracts with titles such as "The Great Ruination Railway" and "A Smoker's Story" detailed the evils of smoking, drinking, gambling, dancing, and general "worldly pleasures." Despite their general lack of enthusiasm for reconstructing society, Pentecostals occasionally applauded the objectives of the Women's Christian Temperance Union and welcomed prohibition.[57] To some extent restorationism sustained such ideas: early Pentecostals took literally biblical injunctions to simple dress and detachment toward material things, believing that they had new values and new goals.

This ethic of separation and the bonds of experience that forged scattered communities of saints into a religious movement nurtured profound distaste for traditional churches. Those outside the community were described as "dead" or "cold" or "lukewarm" to the things of God. Mainline churches were typically regarded as "dead denominational churches" as opposed to the lively independent missions in which Pentecostals congregated to seek God. Pentecostals studiously avoided the term *denomination* for describing their growing constituencies, preferring—even as they became increasingly intolerant and exclusive—to present themselves as participants in an end-times universal Christian renewal movement.

Pentecostal leaders, both because of their restorationism and their temperaments, then, vociferously opposed organizing their movement beyond the local level. In the Southeast, where Pentecostal teaching on Spirit baptism had been integrated into existing loose religious associations, organizational channels were in place. But elsewhere the situation was very different. William Durham warned that organization would "kill the work" because "no religious awakening . . . has ever been able to retain its spiritual life and power after man [has] organized it and gotten it under his control." Durham thought Pentecostalism needed "everything else more than it need[ed] organization."[58] Nonetheless, rudimentary forms of regional and national association emerged within a decade. And gradually some leaders asserted that only some form of accountability could save the apostolic faith from its own excesses.

Most of America's religious world ignored the Pentecostal presence. But some whose attitudes mattered greatly to Pentecostals felt compelled to respond, and their responses helped confirm and perpetuate the early Pentecostal view that the true faith could only survive on the fringes of socially respectable religion. It also sharpened the conviction that accountability through organization was essential to prevent the movement from self-destructing in fanaticism.

Some Early Responses

Several specific objections to the growing Pentecostal movement were articulated by some whom Pentecostals regarded as mentors. These objections often related to worship style, healing, or the evidence of the baptism with the Holy Spirit. The disclaimers and cautions published by several prominent evangelicals accelerated the growing disparity between Pentecostal pretensions to unity and the movement's practical sectarianism. Probably the earliest opposition focused on the Pentecostal understanding of the baptism with the Holy Spirit and came from independent holiness teachers. The biblical literacy and even theological acumen that thrived in this experience-oriented subculture made interpretations of obscure passages of Scripture major points of contention. By 1907, Albert B. Simpson and Arthur T. Pierson publicly cautioned about the movement's excesses. Somewhat later, Reuben Archer Torrey and Harry Ironside published stinging attacks. These evaluations remain significant, for opposition, both formal and popular, helped define the movement. They not only reveal perceptions of Pentecostalism but they also helped mold the attitudes of evangelicals and fundamentalists toward Pentecostalism and Pentecostals' perceptions of themselves.

Holiness Responses

Early Pentecostals were dismayed to be rejected by the Wesleyan holiness movement that had splintered from Methodism. Because many Pentecostals had participated in holiness activities and continued to affirm the necessity of the "second blessing," they understood their Pentecostal experience as continuous with their earlier spirituality. In fact, many did not immediately separate: only gradually did a discrete Pentecostal movement emerge. But Pentecostals quickly learned that prominent holiness adherents were reluctant to admit that the "second blessing" was not the baptism with the Holy Spirit. Holiness advocates objected to Pentecostal teaching as "third blessing heresy" and denied the existence of a biblical "uniform initial evidence" of Spirit baptism.

William Seymour learned in 1906 how intensely divisive such doctrinal disputes could become. Before he or anyone in his meetings in Los Angeles had spoken in tongues, he had found himself locked out of the mission in which he had proclaimed these views. Early Pentecostals recounted many stories of petty persecution and rejection by holiness advocates. Partly because Pentecostal teaching disrupted many holiness missions, holiness preachers openly accused Pentecostals of fanaticism, spiritual arrogance, and demon possession.[59]

Among the most outspoken was Alma White, founder of a radical holiness group known as the Pillar of Fire. White, who claimed to be the first (albeit self-appointed) American female bishop, nursed a personal grudge against Pentecostals for winning her estranged husband, a former Methodist minister, to their cause. In a stinging indictment that she published in 1919 under the title *Demons and Tongues*, White denounced the movement's theology and practice. Her denunciations were perhaps more outspoken than most but nonetheless represent the tone of many who repudiated Pentecostal teaching.

White objected on eschatological grounds to the identification of the Pentecostal movement with the latter rain. "This Tongues heresy," she wrote, "familiarly known . . . as the Latter Rain, is a gigantic scheme of Satan to supplant God's ancient people in the promise of the latter rain that is to come to them."[60] Her bitterness about her husband's experience found expression in her association of tongues and demons: "Had it not been for his . . . taking up with the Tongues heresy, I perhaps could never have fully understood the power of evil spirits working under a cloak of religion."[61]

White's paper, *Pillar of Fire*, carried numerous articles opposing "tongueism" well before her book was published. Claiming that "Mrs. Eddy's teaching and the present day 'Tongueism' [were] leaving spiritual death and devastation everywhere," for example, White declared that the movement that "had started with a black man" and had come "like a simoon from the African desert" was "better adapted to tropical climates where there is plenty of water to immerse the victims of this hellish power."[62]

Not all holiness polemics had such strong racial overtones, but that aside, such vehemence seemed ironic to Pentecostals who had participated in the holiness movement and were well aware of the emotionalism of Pillar of Fire worship. The evangelist Herbert Buffum recalled seeing in White's meetings "people going through every form of gymnastic exercise . . . [and] students playing leap-frog while in prayer."[63] Buffum's response to her was correspondingly direct. Referring to White's opposition, he commented: "But thank God! This turkey-buzzard vomit can not hinder the great work of God."[64]

The charge that Pentecostalism was actually a "tongues movement" and that tongues were demonic was fairly widespread among holiness advocates. When the prominent Quaker Pentecostal Levi Lupton was forced from Pentecostal leadership by adultery, for example, his disgrace elicited reflections on the movement. A Free Methodist who lived near Lupton's home in Alliance, Ohio, observed that "the tongues demon" blinded "its subjects to the truth of God's word and to the law of the land also."[65]

Others alleged that utterances in tongues when understood by foreigners or interpreted were "vile," some of "the worst things that could be said."[66] E. E. Shelhammer, a pastor in Atlanta during the Azusa Street Mission's predominance in the movement, took several members of his holiness congregation to attend one of the first Pentecostal services in the area. Insisting that people came "to obtain . . . a spectacular thing," he charged that demons conversed with him during the service. Concluding that the tongues movement "was the best counterfeit the devil had ever gotten up," Shelhammer became its outspoken foe.[67]

The respected holiness evangelist and teacher Beverly Carradine also expressed reservations. Claiming that contemporaries who pursued the "gift of tongues" exhibited a "spirit, conduct and object" in "perfect contrast" to those manifested in the Upper Room, he noted further that the "gibberish" called "tongues" only mocked the known languages spoken at

Pentecost, that tongues seekers "put a gift above the Giver," and that the Pentecostal movement lacked the results "in sweeping revival and salvation of men" that had accompanied the New Testament Pentecost.[68]

As tongues-speaking adherents of the Apostolic Faith Movement gradually appropriated the name *Pentecostal,* holiness adherents deemphasized their own Pentecostal character. The deletion of the word *Pentecostal* from the name of the Church of the Nazarene, for example, symbolized holiness advocates' unwillingness to be confused with "third blessing heretics."

The Christian and Missionary Alliance Response

As much as any other single body of American Christians, the Christian and Missionary Alliance nurtured a spirituality that made participants responsive to Pentecostal teaching. The Alliance's prolonged wrestling with issues raised by Pentecostalism reveals both the movement's appeal and its problems. Intrigued by reports of the latter rain from around the country, many Alliance people expressed an interest in Pentecostalism. Itinerant Pentecostal evangelists targeted Alliance gatherings, where they often found positive response. Records suggest that several Alliance branches became, for a time, essentially Pentecostal meetings to which people came to seek the baptism with the Holy Spirit. Although many Alliance people spoke in tongues, the experience eluded Alliance founder Albert B. Simpson, who sought a tongues experience for several years.[69]

In September 1906 the weekly Alliance publication noted "a remarkable manifestation of spiritual power" in the West (Azusa Street Mission) and urged its readers to guard against two extremes: "credulity and fanaticism" (noting that God would "not be displeased by conservative and careful" investigation) and "obdurance" ("refusing to recognize any added blessing which the Holy Spirit is bringing to His people in these last days").[70] Alliance adherents had prayed for "the outpouring of the Holy Ghost in all His fulness"; now they were enjoined to "keep . . . hearts opened to recognize the answer in whatever form it comes."[71]

Throughout the fall of 1906 Simpson reported expectancy among his people. In both the Missionary Training Institute at Nyack, New York, and the Gospel Tabernacle in Manhattan, people noticed a profound "sense of God." They came, Simpson noted, "not to hear anybody, but because God is there." The Alliance paper noted reports of similar stirrings at the Moody Bible Institute.[72] By January 1907 the paper carried several articles on tongues by a prominent Chicago Alliance minister, William T. MacArthur. Urging caution about a movement that had "brought much real blessing to many" and "possibly only fancied blessing to others," MacArthur summoned the Alliance to participate in its blessings and avoid its pitfalls.[73] Alliance publications also warned against "the tendency to seek some special gift rather than the Giver Himself."[74] Simpson reiterated his view that humankind too often evidenced a "wonder-seeking spirit" and warned that the Pentecostal movement seemed prone to encourage people to "run after some man or woman with the idea of receiving through the human instrument some wonderful gift."[75]

Late in the spring of 1907, the Alliance held its annual council at the Missionary Training Institute in Nyack, New York. Attendance was largely confined to delegates representing branches from Indianapolis to the east. Their numbers were augmented by some twenty missionaries, the institute student body of some two hundred, the faculties of the institute and the Alliance-sponsored Wilson Academy, and guests at the Alliance's nearby Berachah Home. The workers' reports convinced these "that God [was] now visiting His people in many places with a special manifestation of power" and that Alliance branches included some who had manifested an authentic gift of tongues.[76] Simpson's annual report also noted the apparent revival of the gift of tongues. The council reached a consensus that "manifestations" characterized "by the 'spirit of power and of a sane mind'" were appropriate in the Alliance; "wild excitement," however, they determined to exclude.[77]

Throughout the summer, as Pentecostal teaching radiated from several centers, some Alliance settings assumed a Pentecostal character in both worship and theology.[78] At the Beulah Park Convention in Collinwood, Ohio, for example, awed adherents reported: "God poured out His Spirit upon the people in general and upon others in particular, so that they spoke with new tongues and magnified God. The sick were healed and demons were expelled."[79] And these events were only "the earnest" of what the faithful anticipated: "It is the time of the latter rain. Jesus is coming soon. Perhaps the next convention will be in the air."[80]

Alliance men who toured the districts and attempted to establish guidelines for discriminating between excessive and authentic "manifestations" brought little criticism of what they found. Some prominent voices began to raise larger questions, however. In 1909, for example, the China missionary Robert Jaffray asked whether the Pentecostal movement actually met the biblical criteria for a spiritual outpouring. Jaffray, who had spoken in tongues in 1908 and testified the next year that "the anointing abideth," began in 1909 to caution about the subtle dangers of Pentecostal teaching.

His first objection was to the doctrine of evidential tongues. As early as 1907 Simpson had concurred in this view. The espousal of tongues as "an essential evidence of the baptism of the Holy Spirit," he had observed, had "led to division, fanaticism, confusion and almost every evil work."[81] "There is a subtle danger of attaching too much importance to supernatural utterances and interpretations of tongues," Jaffray continued, "considering that they are the very infallible Word of the Spirit of God."[82] Jaffray also noted Pentecostalism's failure to promote unity. Charging that "tongues speakers" often separated from others because they were "more holy" or constituted "a sacred, select few," Jaffray expressed disappointment in the apparent lack of practical efforts toward Christian unity. Jaffray noted as well something that few Pentecostals were as yet ready to admit: his mission had been "swept" by the renewal, and missionaries and Chinese converts had spoken in tongues. Yet the event had not "empowered for service" but had rather spawned "small select meetings" where some tried to "enjoy the blessing selfishly." In their enthusiasm for intense personal religious experience, missionaries had "backslidden" in their "missionary zeal." Jaffray considered Pentecostal experience meaningful in his personal life but disappointing on his mission station.

Jaffray had encountered the first ranks of Pentecostal missionaries, some of whom had arrived in China because they claimed to "have the tongue." These had been deceived, Jaffray chided, and their supporters were misled. Such recent arrivals had burdened regularly appointed missionaries and diverted money from the support of established missions.

For several years each annual council recorded the growing Pentecostal presence in Alliance outposts around the world. Generally favorable, the comments also consistently urged "watchfulness against counterfeits, extravagances and false teaching."[83] In 1912 the annual report observed a "marked deepening of the spiritual life of our members and an encouraging increase in their missionary zeal and liberality" wherever Pentecostal tendencies had been "wisely directed." But Alliance leaders concurred that evidential tongues represented an inaccurate view of Scripture and, by maintaining that only those who had spoken in tongues had received the Spirit, led "many sincere Christians to cast away their confidence, plunging them in perplexity and darkness, or causing them to seek after special manifestations of other than God Himself."[84]

Alliance leaders attempted to treat tongues speaking as they did several other controversial matters: "It would be wise," the report concluded, "to leave the question of 'The Latter Rain' and related doctrines, as matters of personal liberty, just as we do the question of Baptism, Church Government, and other differences of belief among the Evangelical bodies."[85] This proved insufficient, however, and on 13 April 1914 the Alliance leadership adopted an official motion:

We believe that the gift of tongues or speaking in tongues did in many cases in the apostolic church accompany or follow the Baptism of the Holy Spirit. We believe also that other supernatural and even miraculous operations on the part of the Holy Spirit through His people are competent and possible according to the sovereign will of the Holy Spirit Himself throughout the Christian age. But we hold that none of these manifestations are *essentially* connected with the Baptism of the Holy Spirit, and that the consecrated believer may receive the Spirit in His fulness without speaking in tongues or any miraculous manifestation whatever.[86]

Over several years some men and women who strongly favored evidential tongues broke their ties to Christian and Missionary Alliance branches and identified with Pentecostal missions. Because the Alliance was not yet a structured denomination and because it did not deny the validity of tongues speech, most adherents who had spoken in tongues retained their Alliance ties; Pentecostals were not forced en masse out of the Alliance. Several years after Simpson's death in 1919, however, the hostility toward tongues that characterized some local Alliance branches won the support of an Alliance leader with immense evangelical influence, Aiden Wilson Tozer. Tozer probably coined the phrase "Seek not, forbid not" that came to summarize the official Alliance position on tongues.[87] By the time he did so, tongues speech had been virtually eliminated from the Alliance.

Other Responses

Arthur T. Pierson enjoyed extensive influence among those evangelicals who used Bible institute and conference settings to promote evangelism and the higher Christian life. His spiritual pilgrimage had brought him from an influential Detroit pulpit into an evangelical network in which he espoused faith living, missions, premillennialism, the Spirit-filled life, divine healing, and baptism by immersion. Early in the twentieth century this Presbyterian leader severed his denominational ties and was baptized by immersion in Charles Spurgeon's famed Metropolitan Tabernacle in London.[88] By 1907 he was using the pages of his influential *Missionary Review of the World* to caution evangelicals about Pentecostal excesses.

Pierson's articles reveal how Pentecostalism was perceived among some who shared its basic concerns and document how extensive the movement's influence had become.[89] His earliest comments about tongues speech were part of a small notice about a European Pentecostal, Thomas

Ball Barratt, and Pentecostalism in Norway in 1906. Later, closer encounters with Pentecostals prompted careful evaluation.

Truly spiritual gifts, Pierson noted, "promot[e] peace and harmony . . . and docility of temper." The tongues movement, on the other hand, revealed a "divisive and centrifugal tendency."[90] "The Infallible Scriptures alone," he insisted, "can be our ultimate court of appeal." Nebulous religious experiences discounting "the Word" failed to meet biblical standards and were "satanic disguises and counterfeits."[91] Noting especially the impact of Pentecostal teaching on missionary zeal, Pierson admitted that tongues-speaking missionaries seemed "unusually serious and earnest." However, "side by side with revival scenes appear Satan's counterfeits, and hence a solemn awe, begotten by the conviction that this movement is one of his devices."[92]

Later in the same year, Pierson renewed his cautions. The movement had resulted in "little conversion of sinners, or edification or unification of the saints . . . in a word, few of those marks which prove the genuine working of the Spirit."[93] He claimed to have amassed considerable evidence that attested facts "too shocking to print." Pierson offered two general observations: Pentecostalism overemphasized the subjective and it was obsessed with "Holy Spirit manifestations." The first led to "morbid introspection and constant and searching self-examination," the second to the substitution of a "cult of the Spirit" for "the work of the Lord Jesus Christ."[94] In short, Pentecostals misrepresented the Holy Spirit, making the Spirit "the focus of spiritual vision" rather than "the medium for clearer, fuller vision of Christ."[95]

While Pierson admitted that his observations did not apply equally to all Pentecostals, his good friend Reuben Archer Torrey was less generous. Torrey had done as much as anyone to arouse protofundamentalists to pray for an outpouring of the Holy Spirit. Using language Pentecostals appropriated, he had affirmed the obligation of believers to pursue a baptism in the Holy Spirit, but, like many others, he emphatically rejected evidential tongues.

Torrey believed that the gift of tongues could appropriately be expected in the last days, but he was equally sure that conditions in the Pentecostal movement proved that Pentecostalism was not "of God." Like Pierson and Simpson, Torrey believed that Spirit baptism could manifest itself in many ways. His objections went further, however. Citing Parham's arrest for sodomy in San Antonio in 1907 and Levi Lupton's adultery in Ohio in 1910, he charged that Pentecostalism was "accompanied by the most grievous disorders and the grossest immoralities:"[96] "The Movement as a whole has apparently developed more immorality than any other modern movement except spiritism, to which it is so closely allied in many ways."[97]

Harry Ironside, a widely known Bible teacher who had once been part of the Salvation Army, indicted Pentecostalism by applying "the test of 1 John." He attended mission services in several parts of the country and pored over Pentecostal periodicals, looking for use of the term *Lord Jesus Christ* or the naming of God as Father. Failing to find such, he insisted that the spirit at work in the movement was unwholesome. He labeled the movement an "unpentecostal imposture" and urged his readers to "try the spirits by the only safe test—a true confession of Jesus Christ come in the flesh."[98]

Protofundamentalists objected as well to the view that healing was "in the atonement." Periodicals such as *Our Hope* regularly objected to the Pentecostal theology and method of healing. While most evangelicals agreed that physical healing was possible in their day, they denied that healing revivals had biblical precedent. And as the dispensationalism popularized in the notes of the Scofield Bible permeated segments of popular evangelicalism, objections to contemporary miracles occurred more frequently. Dispensationalists generally held that miracles had ceased with the Apostles; Pentecostalism thus could not be authentic, for its premise that New Testament gifts would mark the end-times church was false. Rejecting the latter-rain views by which Pentecostals legitimated their place in church history, dispensationalists effectively eliminated the biblical basis for Pentecostal theology. And although Pentecostals embraced most of Scofield's ideas and frequently promoted his annotated Bible, they remained irrevocably distanced from fundamentalists by their teaching on the place of spiritual gifts in the contemporary church.[99]

Within a decade, then, articulate, popular religious leaders whose inclinations seemed in many ways similar to those of Pentecostals had disclaimed Pentecostalism. Pentecostal evangelists reported various forms of popular opposition as well. On 1 June 1914, for example, L. V. Roberts, an Indianapolis pastor, participated in a tent crusade with several other workers, one of whom was a former nun who brought allegations against the Catholic Church. Instigated by a hostile mob, police interrupted Roberts's preaching and arrested him and eight assistants. The mob then burned the tent. A. B. Cox, a pastor in Cumberland, Maryland, also experienced violence. Near Alliance, Ohio, thirty young men interspersed among worshipers in a Pentecostal tent meeting threw sulfuric acid on those who went forward for prayer.[100] Petty hostilities made life difficult for outspoken Pentecostals. The evangelist Walter Higgins called one chapter of his memoirs "Rotten Egg Evangelism." Garfield T. Haywood reported that his evangelistic efforts in Indianapolis regularly attracted hecklers. Not only did "mischievous boys . . . perform many pranks" but crowded noisy services in his mission on the corner of Michigan and Minerva streets were frequently interrupted by "a brick striking against the door or a rotten egg or tomato whizzing through the transom."[101]

Meanwhile, some Pentecostals, concerned about excesses in their ranks, turned their attention toward devising a broadly based organizational framework to enable accountability, nurture faith, and express a Pentecostal worldview. Their efforts seemed sorely needed.

NOTES

1. E. T. Cassel, "The King's Business," *Hymns of Praise*, ed. E. D. Excel (Chicago: Hope Publishing, 1922), no. 196; Mrs. M. Schindler, "I'm a Pilgrim," *Gospel Hymns 1–6*, ed. Ira Sankey (Philadelphia: Bigelow and Main, 1894), no. 105.

2. 1 Pet. 2:9.

3. David Wesley Myland, *The Latter Rain Covenant* (Chicago: Evangel Publishing House, 1910).

4. Ibid.

5. C. F. Butler, "Where Jesus Is, 'Tis Heaven," *Best of All* (n.p, n.d.), no. 37.

6. I. G. Martin, "I'm Glad I'm One of Them," *Best of All*, no. 264.

7. Henry Ostrom, "Is It the Crowning Day?" *Hymns of Glorious Praise* (Springfield, Mo.: Gospel Publishing House), no. 139.

8. Ibid.

9. Johnson Oatman, "The Hallelujah Side," *Hymns of Glorious Praise*, no. 469.

10. Fanny Crosby, "Not for Ease or Worldly Pleasure," *Hymns of Glorious Praise*, no. 348.

11. Elizabeth Baker, *Chronicles of a Faith Life* (Rochester, N.Y.: DuBois Press, n.d.), 133.

12. Ibid., 65.

13. Donald Gee, *Pentecost* (Springfield, Mo.: Gospel Publishing Houses, 1932), 37.

14. Ethel E. Goss, *The Winds of God* (New York: Comet Press Books, 1958), 124.

15. Both Goss, *Winds of God*, and Sarah Parham, *The Life of Charles Fox Parham*, 3d ed. (Birmingham, Ala.: Commercial Printing, 1977), recount numerous instances of worship in such settings. Garfield T. Haywood, an African-American Indianapolis preacher, reminisced that those who attended his mission in Indianapolis in 1908 often "would board the street-car praising and blessing God on their journey home." Morris Golder, *Bishop Garfield Thomas Haywood* (Indianapolis: privately published, 1977), 32.

16. See Edith L. Blumhofer, *Pentecost in My Soul* (Springfield, Mo.: Gospel Publishing House, 1989), 18.

17. *Apostolic Faith*, Jan. 1907, 1.

18. Gee, *Pentecost*, 10.

19. Myland, *Latter Rain Pentecost*, 39.

20. Albert Weaver, "Camp Meeting, Alliance, Ohio," *Word and Work*, Aug. 1907, 215.

21. *Pentecost* 2 (Nov.-Dec. 1910): 9.

22. Ibid. See also Myland, *Latter Rain Pentecost*, 39–40.

23. Samuel Jamieson, "How a Presbyterian Minister Received the Baptism," Evangel Tract no. 657, 5.

24. Goss, *Winds of God*, 132.

25. Ibid., 131–33.

26. Issues of *Word and Work*, 1907–9, contain many songs "given" in tongues and interpretation.

27. See Blumhofer, *Pentecost in My Soul*, 17–33.

28. Golder, *Haywood*, 32.

29. Ibid., 28.

30. "Bible Teaching on Marriage and Divorce," *Apostolic Faith*, Jan. 1907, 3.

31. *Apostolic Faith*, Dec. 1906, 3.

32. Participants in the Apostolic Faith Mission in Lynn, Mass., for example, predicted that the destruction of the world would begin in 1908. Of nine people who had prophesied the imminent destruction of Boston "as a warning" of worse to follow, three were members of the Lynn congregation. Mrs. A. F. Rawson, "Apostolic Faith Mission," *Word and Work*, Feb. 1908, 49.

33. *Word and Work*, June 1907, 162, in an article called "Utility of Tongues" assigned tongues speech four "definite uses": facility in preaching the gospel in other cultures, edification of the church, self-edification, and a "sign" to non-Pentecostals. "Better have tongues than magic lanterns to draw the people," the paper urged.

34. See, for example, Elnora L. Lee, comp., *C. H. Mason: A Man Greatly Used of God* (Memphis, Tenn.: Women's Department, Churches of God in Christ, 1967), 9. When J. A. Jeter (who accompanied Charles Mason to Azusa Street) criticized the Azusa Street Mission, Mason noted that "the enemy had put into the ear of Brother Jeter to find fault," 9.

35. Addie M. Otis, "Upward Attraction," *Word and Work*, Mar. 1908, 67.

36. "Some Marked Features," *Upper Room*, June 1909, 4.

37. See Myland, *Latter Rain Covenant*, 23, for an example. On Myland, see Kevin Butcher, "The Holiness and Pentecostal Labors of David Wesley Myland, 1890–1918," (M.A. Thesis, Dallas Theological Seminary, 1983).

38. Myland, *Latter Rain Covenant*.

39. Ibid., 1.

40. "What Is Meant by the Latter Rain?" *Christian and Missionary Alliance*, 19 Oct. 1907, 38.

41. Ibid.

42. Julia Morton Plummer, "The Bridegroom Cometh," *Word and Work*, Mar. 1908, 76.

43. W. C. Stevens, "The Latter Rain," *Word and Work*, July 1908, 17.

44. Goss, *Winds of God*, 78.

45. "Testimonials from Prairie Dell," *Gold Tried in the Fire* 4 (Dec. 1910): 3.

46. Abbie C. Morrow, "Church Amusements," Christian Workers' Union Tract, no. 357 (Framingham, Mass.: Christian Workers' Union, n.d.).

47. Ibid., 3, 5, 6.

48. "Pentecostal Backsliders," *Household of God*, Mar. 1910, 13.

49. Ibid.

50. Ibid.

51. "Gospel Letter," *Word and Work*, Apr. 1908, 111.

52. *Word and Work*, Jan. 1908, 5.

53. Ibid.

54. "Testimonials from Prairie Dell," 3, 4.

55. "Wearing of Gold; Adorning the Body," *Household of God*, May 1909, 7.

56. Milton Grotz, "Eat and Drink to the Glory of God," Christian Workers' Union Tract (Framingham, Mass.: Christian Workers' Union, 1914), 2, 3.

57. "Prohibition," *Midnight Cry*, Mar. 1919, 5.

58. William Durham, "Organization," *Gospel Witness* 1 (ca. 1913): 11.

59. See for example, "The Tongues Excitement," *Free Methodist*, 6 Nov. 1906, 712.

60. Alma White, *The Story of My Life and the Pillar of Fire* (Zarephath, N.J.: Pillar of Fire, 1936), 3, 139.

61. Ibid., 116.

62. Quoted in "What They Say of Us," *Gold Tried in the Fire* 6 (Apr. 1913): 6.

63. Ibid., 116.

64. Ibid.

65. Jennie A. Jolley, comp., *As an Angel of Light; or, Bible Tongues and Holiness and Their Counterfeits* (New York: Vantage Press, 1964), 15.

66. Ibid., 15, 21.

67. E. E. Shelhammer, "Best Counterfeit," in *As an Angel of Light*, comp. Jolley, 16.

68. Beverly Carradine, *A Box of Treasure* (Chicago: Christian Witness, 1910), 83–85.

69. Albert B. Simpson, "Diary," 1906–19, Historical Collection, Nyack College, Nyack, N.Y.

70. *Christian and Missionary Alliance*, 22 Sept. 1906, 177.

71. Ibid.

72. *Christian and Missionary Alliance*, 24 Nov. 1906, 322.

73. William T. MacArthur, "The Promise of the Father and 'Speaking with Tongues' in Chicago," *Christian and Missionary Alliance*, 26 Jan. 1907, 40.

74. *Christian and Missionary Alliance*, 2 Feb. 1907, 49; see also Annual Report of President and General Superintendent of the Christian and Missionary Alliance, 1907, Alliance Collection, Assemblies of God Archives, Springfield, Mo. (hereafter AGA).

75. *Christian and Missionary Alliance,* 2 Feb. 1907.

76. *Christian and Missionary Alliance,* 8 June 1907, 205.

77. Annual Report, 1907.

78. *Word and Work,* 1907–11, indicates the degree to which Pentecostalism influenced local Alliance gatherings that never separated from the Alliance.

79. "Beulah Park Convention," *Christian and Missionary Alliance,* 14 Sept. 1907, 128.

80. Ibid.

81. Annual Report, 1907.

82. Robert Jaffray, "Speaking in Tongues," *Christian and Missionary Alliance,* 13 Mar. 1909, 395.

83. Fifteenth Annual Report of the Christian and Missionary Alliance, 10, Alliance Collection, AGA.

84. Ibid., 11.

85. Ibid., 13.

86. "Official Statement of the Board of the Christian and Missionary Alliance Setting Forth Its Position with Reference to 'Tongues' and the Baptism of the Spirit," Alliance Collection, AGA.

87. Robert Niklaus, John S. Sawin, and Samuel J. Stoesz, *All for Jesus: God at Work in the Christian and Missionary Alliance over One Hundred Years* (Camp Hill, Pa.: Christian Publications, 1986), 115.

88. For Pierson's life, see Delavan Pierson, *Arthur T. Pierson* (New York: Fleming H. Revell, 1912); Dana Robert, "Arthur Tappan Pierson and the Forward Movements of Late Nineteenth-Century Evangelicalism" (Ph.D. diss., Yale University, 1984).

89. Pierson linked it to both the Welsh Revival and Pandita Ramabai's orphanage and home for widows in India: "During the last few years, at sundry centers, notably Los Angeles, California, parts of India and China, Sweden and Wales, have recurred unusual and to some extent abnormal, manifestations, similar in character; supposed by some, and claimed by others, to be due to a supernatural gift of speaking with tongues." A. T. Pierson, "Speaking with Tongues," *Missionary Review of the World* 30 (July 1907): 487

90. Ibid., 490.

91. Ibid.

92. Ibid., 492.

93. Arthur T. Pierson, "Speaking with Tongues," *Missionary Review of the World* 30 (September 1907): 682.

94. Ibid., 684.

95. Ibid.

96. Reuben Archer Torrey, "Is the Present Tongues Movement of God?" (Los Angeles: Biola Book Room, n.d.), 4.

97. Ibid., 7. Such accusations are frequent in anti-Pentecostal literature and are directed against participants as well as leaders. In a tract entitled "Spirit Manifestations and the Gift of Tongues," the well-known British prophecy and biblical student Sir Robert Anderson detailed the "fall" of an exemplary Christian "who gave himself up unreservedly to the Spirit's guidance." "The details of

the disaster," Anderson quipped, "would gratify none save the prurient and the profane." Quoted in Louis S. Bauman, *The Tongues Movement*, rev. ed. (Winona Lake, Ind.: BMH Books, 1963), 32–33; see also Reader Harris, "The Gift of Tongues: Real or Counterfeit?" (London: S. W. Partridge, n.d.).

98. Harry Ironside, "The Apostolic Faith Missions and the So-called Second Pentecost" (New York: Louizeaux Brothers, n.d.), 15. Internal evidence suggests that the pamphlet was written in 1914 or 1915.

99. For an interesting later perspective on this, see Wilfred C. Meloon, *We've Been Robbed: Or a Dispensationalist Looks at the Baptism of the Holy Ghost* (Plainfield, N.J.: Logos International, 1971).

100. "A Dastardly Deed," *Free Methodist*, 2 July 1907, 417.

101. "Hot Times in Maryland," *Christian Evangel*, 25 July 1914, 1; *Word and Witness*, June 1914; Golder, *Haywood*, 32; Walter J. Higgins, *Pioneering in Pentecost* (privately published, 1958); Lou Ella Vaughn, *Brush Arbor Birthright* (Springfield, Mo.: Gospel Publishing House, 1986), 65.

Aimee Semple McPherson (with tambourine), choir, and orchestra at Victoria Hall Mission during her first Los Angeles meetings in December 1918. (Courtesy of the Assemblies of God Archives, Springfield, Mo.)

Charles Fox Parham and some of his devotees at the courthouse in Carthage, Missouri, in 1905. Apostolic Faith bands typically marched through the streets of Midwestern towns carrying flags and banners. (Courtesy of the Assemblies of God Archives, Springfield, Mo.)

Under the tent at an Apostolic Faith camp meeting at Brunner Tabernacle, Houston, Texas, in 1906. (Courtesy of the Assemblies of God Archives, Springfield, Mo.)

The Azusa Street Mission, Los Angeles. (Courtesy of the Assemblies of God Archives, Springfield, Mo.)

Charles Price baptizing converts at a camp meeting. (Courtesy of the Assemblies of God Archives, Springfield, Mo.)

A. J. Gordon, pastor, author, educator, and editor, whose views and piety significantly influenced Assemblies of God doctrine. (Courtesy of Gordon-Conwell Theological Seminary Archives, South Hamilton, Mass.)

David Du Plessis, affectionately known as "Mr. Pentecost" by Protestant and Catholic charismatics around the world. (Courtesy of the Assemblies of God Archives, Springfield, Mo.)

James Watt, Ronald Reagan's secretary of the interior, was an Assemblies of God layperson and is shown here addressing the Fortieth General Council in 1983. (Courtesy of the Assemblies of God Archives, Springfield, Mo.)

Thomas F. Zimmerman (*right*), longtime general superintendent of the Assemblies of God, worked closely with Billy Graham and the programs sponsored by the Billy Graham Evangelistic Association. (Courtesy of the Assemblies of God Archives, Springfield, Mo.)

Spencer Jones, pastor of Southside Tabernacle, an inner-city congregation in Chicago. (Courtesy of the Assemblies of God Archives, Springfield, Mo.)

Worshipers at Iglesia Vida Nueva en Cristo Assembly of God in Binghamton, New York. (Courtesy of the Assemblies of God Archives, Springfield, Mo.)

Two-term Missouri governor John Ashcroft, as Assemblies of God layperson, addressing the National Religious Broadcasters in 1986. (Courtesy of the Assemblies of God Archives, Springfield, Mo.)

Jimmy Swaggart wielded significant influence in the Assemblies of God, especially in its Division of Foreign Missions. He occasionally addressed the huge evening rallies scheduled at General Councils. (Courtesy of the Assemblies of God Archives, Springfield, Mo.)

Jim Bakker drew large crowds when he addressed General Council rallies like this one in Anaheim in 1983. (Courtesy of the Assemblies of God Archives, Springfield, Mo.)

CHAPTER

5

The Formative Years of the Assemblies of God, 1914–18

PENTECOSTALS talked incessantly about work and claimed their religious experience compelled them to action. "We'll work till Jesus comes, and we'll be gathered home," they sang. They exhibited a restless urge to "redeem the time" because they believed that time was short. Messages in tongues and interpretation as well as prophecies prodded them to activities. Urgency derived as well from their reading of the biblical model: New Testament Christians had maintained a relentless pace.[1] The activities in which they engaged took different forms, but most related in some way to "soul winning" or their pursuit of deeper spirituality. Without significant resources or training, but with eagerness rooted in vision and destiny, Pentecostals pioneered missions in small towns and major cities.

Their evangelism was not confined to the United States. The movement's early understanding of the latter rain and of the reason for the restoration of tongues speech contributed to a growing awareness of a missions task. And in the approach to that task, the proclivity of some to discount common sense and follow alleged leadings of the Holy Spirit made them not just curiosities but also threats to the movement's survival.

Ardent believers often based a call to foreign service on prophecy or on a language someone had told them they had spoken "under the anointing." Boasting that they "had the language of Africa" and certain that God would provide, for example, some sailed to uncertain futures in unknown lands. Without financial backing and with minimal (if any) biblical training, they traveled with the confidence that they would be supernaturally enabled to preach in foreign languages and thus facilitate the rapid evangelization of the world.

Despite their profession of utter dependence on God for their material and physical needs, missionaries of course relied on American financial support, which was not always forthcoming. Many Pentecostal pastors and editors offered to forward donated missionary funds, but they lacked accountability. Most Pentecostal publications attempted to raise support for missionaries by publishing letters recounting miracles, conversions, and needs. American adherents thrilled to the claims of men such as John G. Lake, who reportedly recruited a group of missionaries for South Africa, "prayed in" funds for their fares, and embarked. Lake had neglected the required landing fee of $125, however. He reported that in an act of faith he had stood—empty-handed—in line to pay, another passenger had handed him $200 while he waited, and the party had disembarked.[2]

Such stories heartened others to expect miracles and nurtured the tendency to deemphasize responsible action. The Azusa Street Mission encouraged would-be missionaries: "God is solving the missionary problem, sending out new-tongued missionaries on the apostolic faith line, without purse or scrip, and the Lord is going before them preparing the way."[3]

Discriminating among impressions and voices to determine which might be divine loomed as a growing problem. The Pentecostal understanding of the Bible often precluded its use as a consistent standard. "The Bible becomes a new book to those who are baptized with the Holy Ghost," adherents were informed by the Azusa Street Mission publication. "You absolutely lose your own judgment in regard to the Word of God. You eat it down without trimming or cutting, right from the mount of God."[4] A former Christian and Missionary Alliance pastor, Daniel Kerr, distinguished between systematic theology and the "spontaneous theology" that Pentecostal experience enabled: "Spontaneous theology" was "given by inspiration of God" and was to take precedence over systematic theology because it represented God directing spiritual understanding to "proceed spontaneously without labor or study from the hidden fullness of His divine nature."[5]

Traditional educational forms obviously failed to satisfy such people. Models provided by Sandford and Parham proved more appealing because they tolerated direct revelation and legitimated nontraditional expressions of religious commitment. Some Pentecostals objected even to such "faith" schools, however. William Durham maintained unequivocally that the local church was "the only place God ever provided for the training of His people for the work of the ministry."[6] He opposed schooling for the ministry on restorationist grounds: Bible schools were not "according to Scripture," nor did they have a place "in the plan of God as outlined in the New Testament."[7]

Sometimes short-term faith Bible training institutes became centers in which new revelations were promulgated. Reports of schools in which instruction was carried on in tongues and interpretation, for example, soon raised questions about the proper use of the much-celebrated spiritual gifts. Uncertain consequences in instances in which couples were instructed through purported spiritual gifts to marry disillusioned some. Careless and contradictory theological language invited misunderstanding and criticism. Adherents quarreled over alleged revelations about eternal punishment, baptism, the trinity, appropriate conduct and foods, as well as life-style. In a milieu that valued fresh revelations and sought to reform doctrine and practice on the authority of subjective experience, heterogeneity flourished. Pentecostals admitted that spiritualists and hypnotists duplicated phenomena they cited as authenticating the Holy Spirit's presence among them. The situation prompted frequent wrestling with the ancient dilemma of discerning between what was "of the flesh" and "the Spirit." Such distinctions, though virtually meaningless to outsiders, carried tremendous weight within the movement.

Teaching about marriage also frequently deviated from conventional views. With strongly worded appeals to those who pursued the distinction of being spiritual, advocates of "marital purity" extended their teaching throughout the movement. As early as January 1907 the *Apostolic Faith* found it necessary to editorialize: "It is no sin to marry. . . . There are those today in the marriage life, since they have received sanctification and some the baptism with the Holy Ghost, who have come to think that it is a sin to live as husband and wife."[8] At the other extreme were people who, though married, found their "soul mates" outside marriage. "Spiritual marriages" (deemed by some to be appropriate when spouses were spiritually incompatible) sometimes were evidenced by such material tokens as jewelry and lingerie and brought numerous Pentecostals into disrepute.

Internal disunity raised concerns about doctrine and practice. External rejection raised questions about the essence of the movement. Was it, as some had originally hoped, God's vehicle for the realization of Christian unity, God's final restoration of New Testament Christianity? Its more thoughtful friends shared the alarm of its critics over the divisiveness and confusion it seemed to foster everywhere.[9] Intransigent leaders, disinclined to make themselves accountable to anyone, strenuously insisted that Pentecostals could only fulfill their destiny in God's restorationist scheme by resisting the urge to structure their movement. A handful of tiny Pentecostal denominations confined to the Southeast were exceptions to the general opposition to organization. Hesitations about formalizing relationships were typically expressed in the religious jargon to which Pentecostals best responded. William Durham warned the organization would "kill the work" because "no religious awakening . . . has ever been able to retain its spiritual life and power after man has organized it and gotten it under his control." In Durham's view, the movement needed "everything else more than it needed organization."[10] In 1911 he commented confidently: "God is revealing His real plan to so many that they will never consent to having the present work turned into a sect."[11] The *Gospel Witness* concurred: "The Holy Spirit who . . . has carried on this glorious Pentecostal work in the earth without organization we believe is able to carry it on and control it in the future. . . . We do not believe God's people will ever again submit to human organization, and be brought back into bondage."[12]

Despite such assurances, however, some Pentecostals around the country had reached the conclusion by 1913 that the Apostolic Faith Movement could only realize its potential for end-times renewal as adherents assumed responsibility for its course. Troubled by excess yet committed to life "in the Spirit," they decided to explore the advantages of cooperating in a loosely structured network that would preserve their autonomy but also provide a forum for consideration of mutual concerns.

They did not intend to create a denomination, nor did they expect longevity for themselves or their movement. They hoped only to conserve what they understood to be the core of the Pentecostal message and to preserve the movement's sense of history and identity during a brief burst of evangelism that would culminate in Christ's soon return. On 20 December 1913 a handful of men announced a meeting to be held in April in Hot Springs, Arkansas, for those who wished to cooperate "in love and peace to push the interests of the kingdom of God."[13] They immediately faced a storm of criticism and dire predictions that anyone who attempted to organize the Pentecostal movement would "lose his power with God and his influence with men."[14]

The Organization of the General Council of the Assemblies of God

In the chilly early spring of 1914 a mixed group of male and female "workers" and "saints" convened in the old Grand Opera House on Central Avenue in Hot Springs, Arkansas, in response to advertisements that had run in Pentecostal publications since December 1913. Primarily from the Midwest but representing seventeen states and missions in Egypt and South Africa, they arrived prepared to consider proposals to facilitate cooperation for conserving the Apostolic Faith Movement.[15]

By 1914 Hot Springs had a thriving Pentecostal congregation led by thirty-year-old Howard Goss, who had embraced Pentecostalism under Parham's tutelage in 1903. Local Pentecostals had been meeting in the opera house since the fall of 1913, when evangelist Maria Woodworth-Etter had conducted several weeks of meetings there in cooperation with D. C. O. Opperman, a popular evangelist and promoter of short-term Bible institutes. Opperman secured a six-month lease on the opera house and followed the Woodworth-Etter campaign with a Bible school.[16] In April the same commodious facility accommodated participants in the General Council.

The term *general council* was taken from Acts 15. It had been used as a designation for denominational or associational meetings by some holiness groups (see, for example, *Live Coals*, the publication of the Fire Baptized Holiness Church) and became the name for the Assemblies of God governing body consisting of ministers and church delegates.

The initial call for a council had been signed by men identified with the loosely organized, predominantly white network called the Churches of God in Christ. This association had established several committees to expedite business, but these had failed to meet adequately felt needs. The men who decided to strengthen these loose ties were well known throughout much of the Pentecostal subculture. Eudorus N. Bell, former Southern Baptist pastor, led a congregation in Malvern, Arkansas, edited a monthly periodical, *Word and Witness,* and preached frequently at camp meetings and conventions; Howard Goss, converted during Parham's meetings in Galena, Kansas, in 1903, had evangelized widely in Texas and Arkansas and founded several churches; D. C. O. Opperman, one of the movement's prominent Bible teachers, had roots in Dowie's Zion and extensive visibility through his short-term Bible schools; Arch Collins, another former Southern Baptist, frequented camp meetings and had a loyal following in Texas; Mack M. Pinson, a former evangelist in the Pentecostal Mission, had ties to Pentecostals in the Southeast. These men, like other early Pentecostals, gained wide visibility by exploiting the contemporary expansion and integration of railroad lines without which their efforts would have been seriously curtailed.

Within three months, twenty-nine more well-known Pentecostals representing fourteen additional states had endorsed the Hot Springs meeting.[17] They addressed the invitation to "laymen and preachers," especially urging "all elders, pastors, ministers, evangelists and missionaries" to attend. More generally, they welcomed "all the churches of God in Christ" and "all Pentecostal or Apostolic Faith Assemblies" who shared their hopes.[18]

Despite accusations that those who issued the call were grasping for power, participants arrived in good spirits. In recognition of the economic

constraints most Pentecostals faced, the organizers scheduled the meetings to allow participants to use winter tourist rail fares and promised
those who lacked funds: "We want you to come anyhow, and if you have
not faith to get home after you are here, then we will stand with you in
trusting God for your return fare or to get out on the field."[19]

The council's agenda included the consideration of several specific
goals:

> First—We come together that we may get a better understanding of
> what God would have us teach, that we may do away with so many
> divisions, both in doctrines and in the various names under which
> our Pentecostal people are working and incorporating. Let us come
> together as in Acts 15, to study the Word, and pray with and for
> each other—unity our chief aim.

> Second—Again we come together that we [may] know how to
> conserve the work, that we may all build up and not tear down,
> both in home and foreign lands.

> Third—We come together for another reason, that we may get
> a better understanding of the needs of each foreign field and may
> know how to place our money in such a way that one mission or
> missionary shall not suffer, while another not any more worthy,
> lives in luxuries. Also that we may discourage wasting money on
> those who are running here and there accomplishing nothing,
> and may concentrate our support on those who mean business for
> our King.

> Fourth—Many of the saints have felt the need of chartering the
> churches of God in Christ, putting them on a legal basis, and thus
> obeying the laws of the land, as God says. See Rom. 13. We confess
> we have been "slothful in business" on this point, and because of
> this many assemblies have already chartered under different names
> as a local work, in both home and foreign lands. Why not charter
> under one Bible name, 2 Thess. 2:14. Thus eliminating another
> phase of division in Pentecostal work? For this purpose also let us
> come together.

> Fifth—We may also have a proposition to lay before the body for
> a general Bible Training School with a literary department for our
> people.[20]

After appointing Bell chair and a young evangelist from Indiana,
J. Roswell Flower, secretary, the council opted to limit voting rights to
men. A conference committee composed of delegates from each state
represented framed the Preamble and Resolution of Constitution. Designed to dispel hesitations about centralization and creed, the document

declared that participants were part of the "GENERAL ASSEMBLY OF GOD (which is God's organism)." It disavowed sectarian intentions as "a human organization that legislates or forms laws and articles of faith" through which to exercise "unscriptural jurisdiction" over members.[21] A statement of purpose declared:

> Be it resolved, That we recognize ourselves as a GENERAL COUNCIL of Pentecostal (Spirit Baptized) saints from local Churches of God in Christ, Assemblies of God, and various Apostolic Faith Missions and Churches, and Full Gospel Pentecostal Missions, and Assemblies of like faith in the United States of America, Canada, and Foreign Lands, whose purpose is neither to legislate laws of government, nor usurp authority over said various Assemblies of God, nor deprive them of their Scriptural and local rights and privileges, but to recognize Scriptural methods and order for worship, unity, fellowship, work and business for God, and to disapprove of all unscriptural methods, doctrines and conduct, and approve of all Scriptural truth and conduct, endeavoring to keep the unity of the Spirit in the bonds of peace, until we all come into the unity of the faith, and of the knowledge of the Son of God, unto a perfect man, unto the measure of the stature of the fullness of Christ, and to walk accordingly, as recorded in Eph. 4:17–32, and to consider the five purposes announced in the Convention Call in . . . *Word and Witness.* [22]

With considerable emotion, the council unanimously adopted the Preamble as the constitution of the General Council of the Assemblies of God.[23] Even amid the excitement, chroniclers noted that the devout carefully observed proprieties: "Such joy as is rarely seen in any religious body was manifested upon the unanimous adoption of the . . . PREAMBLE. . . . A great time of shouting, rejoicing, hand-shaking, and even hugging followed; the brethren hugging the brethren and the sisters kissing each other."[24]

Other actions of the council reveal some of the issues that agitated among early Pentecostals. The meeting opposed extreme positions on divisive questions about appropriate foods, encouraged local churches to observe Thursdays as regular days of prayer, and adopted the *Word and Witness* as its "official organ" and J. Roswell Flower's *Christian Evangel* as its weekly paper to disseminate reliable news and appropriate doctrine. It also turned its attention to the perceived need to provide institute-type training for ministry. Given the opposition recently articulated by Torrey, Ironside, Pierson, and Simpson, it seemed clear that the Bible institutes some of them had attended—places such as Moody Bible Institute, the

Bible Institute of Los Angeles, the Missionary Training Institute in
Nyack, New York—would not welcome them. They needed alternatives.

The council recommended two well-established schools: a "literary
school" run by Rueben Benjamin Chisolm near Union, Mississippi, and
the Gospel School conducted by Thomas K. Leonard in Findlay, Ohio.
Chisolm's Neshoba Holiness School (Pentecostal Faith) had originally
had ties to the holiness movement. It had been known locally since its
founding in 1908 as the Holiness Sanctification School. When its Ruskin
College–educated president had embraced Pentecostalism, his faculty
had followed suit, and Pentecostal periodicals had begun to recommend
the school.

Chisolm offered primary, academic, and collegiate courses, with theological and music training available on request. In the absence of a consolidated school system in Neshoba County, his school served the community as well as far-flung religious sympathizers. Recommended by
Pentecostals as a place for would-be preachers to obtain basic education,
the school nonetheless focused primarily on the education of children.
Chisolm also tutored college and seminary students in Greek and Latin.
An ad that appealed to the anti-urban bias of his middle America readers
appeared in Flower's *Christian Evangel,* urging parents who wanted their
children "educated in a moral country town away from the vices of the
great cities" to contact Chisolm, who offered his services for one hundred
dollars per year. Shortly after the council, Chisolm's school was destroyed
by arson instigated by local opponents of tongues speech. The entire facility was later rebuilt.

Leonard's Gospel School targeted a different constituency.[25] Geared
toward preparing pastors, it offered courses in the Bible, church history,
and English as well as a one-year home Bible study program. Soliciting
those who coveted Pentecostal experience or sought "their proper place
in the body of Christ," the school was a faith venture operated out of a
two-story brick building in the northwestern Ohio city of Findlay. Leonard advertised seven teachers and billed the school as one that made "a
specialty of the Spiritual."[26] In addition to the school, Leonard had a
local church he had long called the Assembly of God and a small printing
plant he had named Gospel Publishing House. He offered his facilities
and the printing equipment as a headquarters for the new organization.
The council gratefully accepted, and for the remaining months of 1914
the General Council of the Assemblies of God conducted its business
from Leonard's school in Findlay.

Two other issues surfaced at Hot Springs that agitated the constituency
for years: women in ministry and divorce. On ministering women, the
1914 council actions bear the unmistakable imprint of Eudorus N. Bell,

who had developed his views earlier in *Word and Witness*. This former Southern Baptist considered most women "busybodies" who tended not to settle down and accomplish anything of enduring worth. Noting that "only women of strong character and settled habits" could "open up their own stations with God's blessing," he insisted that there was "no scriptural precept or example for . . . independent leadership by women."[27] He considered that God had made males "better adapted . . . to rule and govern assemblies" and that God had wanted "to take these heavy responsibilities off [women's] shoulders."[28]

On the other hand, Bell had no objection to women as "helpers in the gospel." He objected to their authority and leadership, not to their public ministry in settings controlled by males. The records indicate no discontent among the women present. The men voted a resolution that affirmed Bell's views: Women ministers "should be permanently attached to some mission and take up some regular and systematic work for the Lord under the proper oversight of some good brother whom God has placed in charge of the work."[29] The council instructed women "to be in subjection" and not to "usurp authority over the man." Nonetheless, it authorized licenses for female evangelists and missionaries while explicitly precluding them from pastoral ministries or administrative offices involving authority over men. Later in 1914 an exception was made allowing female missionaries in foreign countries to perform "baptism, marriage, burial of the dead and the Lord's Supper when a man [was] not available for the purpose." This privilege, to be exercised only in emergencies, was carefully restricted. It was extended to female evangelists in the United States in 1922.[30]

In fact, many women preached and engaged in various forms of public ministry. An undetermined but impressive number of Assemblies of God congregations were begun by female evangelists or by women who opened their homes for prayer and Bible study. Struggling congregations that could not afford a male pastor sometimes accepted the services of a woman, relying on men only for certain functions. The Pentecostal emphasis on testimony to experience, on Spirit baptism as enduement, and on the imminence of the end shaped a setting in which women or, for that matter, children, could hardly be silenced. On the other hand, the essentially conservative social conventions that prevailed in this subculture, like those of fundamentalists, tended to restrict severely the formal roles open to women. Most women seemed content with the common language of submission and subordination that apparently reinforced biblical injunctions to a "meek and quiet spirit."

The consideration of marriage and divorce at the 1914 council set a precedent for future councils; probably no other issue has been raised so frequently over the years. The Pentecostal movement had wrestled with divorce for most of its history. Some demanded that converts whose spouses had previously been divorced separate. Some had instructed them to return to their original marriage partner. Some made participation in the local church dependent on a remarried individual's willingness to separate from his or her spouse. Others took a strict stand against divorce and remarriage but refused to interfere with situations that had developed before the individual had embraced Pentecostalism.[31]

The council urged those who had "become entangled in their marriage relations in their former lives of sin" to act according to their own conscience; it instructed local congregations not to interfere, but to "leave the matter to God." In general, it discouraged the disruption of families. The council then disapproved divorce "except for fornication or adultery" and recommended that those divorced for other reasons remain unmarried. It refused ordination to "those who have remarried and are now living in the state of matrimony, while former companions are living. Ez. 44:22–27."[32] This proved to be the only area in which the council failed to reach a unanimous decision, but the dissent was negligible. *Word and Witness* commented, "It is very remarkable that all of the hundreds present agreed, except four—only four!"[33]

When the ten-day meeting adjourned after services on Sunday, 12 April, its organizers were gratified. Existing ties had been strengthened and a legal framework had been established for the recognition of an entity that had been in existence for some time. In typical restorationist fashion, the council had refused to bind by creed, affirming simply that the Bible was its sufficient rule of faith and practice. The view of Scripture advanced by the organization's full-time chair, Eudorus N. Bell, however, should have hinted at the likelihood of future divisions: "We must keep our skylights open," Bell had admonished, "so as not to reject any new light God may throw upon the old Word. We must not fail to keep pace in life or teaching with light from heaven."[34] The fascination for the new amid the yearning for the old proved a source of tension. Before long, participants would appropriate modern tools to accomplish antimodern goals, and their talk of "old-time" and "old-fashioned" took on different meaning. The struggle between the new and the old—and the gradual displacing of the antimodern by the modern—offers a revealing way to explain the course of events in white classical Pentecostalism.

Others shared the general conviction of the Hot Springs council attendees that "more" would follow. Addressing a convention at Leonard's Gospel School in the summer of 1914, Daniel Kerr alluded to a "general belief" that "another outpouring" was necessary "to bring us to the place of real Apostolic usefulness." Kerr encouraged Pentecostals to anticipate a new wave of the latter rain that stressed healing much as tongues speech had been emphasized between 1901 and 1914. He prophesied division similar to that which Pentecostals had sparked in holiness and restorationist ranks a decade earlier since most Pentecostals would be unlikely to "take the advance step."[35] Themes of renewal and declension pervade the literature of Pentecostalism's earliest history.

Over the spring and summer of 1914, ministers and missionaries identified with the Assemblies of God. Credentials were issued to approved workers by Leonard in the East and Goss in the West. By the fall, the official list included 512 credentialed workers; 142 were female missionaries and evangelists.

One indication of the success on its own terms of the Hot Springs council was the way things proceeded as usual throughout the summer of 1914. Short-term Bible schools and the regular list of camp meetings featuring the same speakers as in other years appeared in Pentecostal periodicals. Leaders of the Assemblies of God also identified themselves as they had before. In response to the question "Who are we?" Bell stated: "We are simply New Testament Christians who have brushed aside the mental shams and hollowness of the age and in a measure gotten back to the realities of God's grace and power through the atoning blood of Christ."[36] But the two endorsed periodicals noted that several of the camp meetings had acted to confirm their loyalty to the purposes of the General Council of the Assemblies of God by forming district councils affiliated with the national organization.

Meanwhile, Bell and Flower used the printed page to convince as many as possible of the advisability of cooperation.[37] For several months they worked out of cramped quarters at Leonard's Gospel School (where they also taught). By the fall the expanding list of affiliated workers provided heartening indication that the organization had won considerable support among independent Pentecostals. Growth mandated changes, however, and the two called a second General Council for November 1914 at the Stone Church in Chicago. Bell resigned from his duties as chair, and his close friend, Arch Collins, was elected to succeed him. Both Bell and Collins viewed the leadership narrowly; each was thoroughly congregational in preference and assumed no authority that was not specifically granted. This second council recognized mature—and presumably licensed—women in attendance as "advisory members." This honorary designation did not convey the right to participate in business sessions.

The council met for two weeks and voted to move the Assemblies of God headquarters to St. Louis. From Washington, D.C., they accepted a donation of used printing machinery that, together with various purchased equipment, became the nucleus of the Gospel Publishing House. Convinced that "the very life of a movement depends upon the printed page," members authorized funds for expanded staff and facilities.

At the end of 1914 Assemblies of God leaders had reason to be pleased. Over the year about ten thousand dollars had been raised for missions—twice as much as affiliated ministers had raised in 1913. Prospects seemed bright. The troubled world situation as yet affected them little. They assumed simply that World War I meant that Christ's coming was near. Yet severe problems loomed on the horizon. At the end of October the *Christian Evangel* published "A Letter to the Pentecostal Movement from a Friend" who cautioned the optimistic membership: "You have nothing to fear from the outside forces that are arrayed against you, but everything to fear from dissensions arising from within."[38]

In the next few years internal dissension wracked the Assemblies of God and eroded its restorationist identity. Three issues posed particular problems. Each predated the formation of the Assemblies of God and each, despite stereotypes that insist Pentecostals are doctrinally unconcerned, focused on a doctrine. Assemblies of God wrestlings with each permanently influenced the broad outlines of American Pentecostalism.

The first, focusing on the "second blessing" and the practical meaning of holiness, had sparked intense controversy for several years but continued to require clarification. The second wrought the most havoc on the organization. It questioned the baptismal formula, the doctrine of the Trinity, and the understanding of the process of salvation. This "Oneness" controversy also prodded Pentecostals to probe the relationship between revelation and doctrine. The third issue forced the Assemblies of God to face the undercurrent of questioning that had long been evident about tongues speech as "uniform initial evidence" of the baptism with the Holy Spirit. These various crises played a central role in shaping the emerging denomination. They also etched the broad outlines of Pentecostalism on the landscape of American religion.

Holiness

Since delegates to the first several councils affirmed no statement of faith, the Assemblies of God embraced people whose opinions on many issues varied widely. Some matters—like abstinence from pork or foot washing—could easily be left to individual preference, but others seemed to demand clarification. The first council had been convened by people who had concluded by 1910 that, in doctrinal terms, holiness was not a "second blessing" but a process of growth and change. A significant proportion of later affiliates agreed. Eudorus N. Bell, first general superintendent of the Assemblies of God recognized, however, that when he had articulated his influential rejection of Wesleyan holiness views, William Durham had set a potentially troublesome precedent: "Not a few have tried to imitate William Durham by claiming to have something new for the people; but alas, unless God is behind the message, it is nothing."[39] Influential Assemblies of God people seemed prepared to believe that God was behind William Durham's opposition to crisis sanctification; they were less certain about other innovations.

Despite extensive support for progressive sanctification, however, many Assemblies of God adherents clung to holiness theology.[40] The presence of such people in their own ranks as well as criticism from outside seemed to obligate ministers who objected on scriptural grounds to holiness views to affirm frequently their commitment to the reality of sanctification and a life of holiness. "It has been told around and published by some that the man that does not teach the Second Work of Grace is a compromiser," Mack M. Pinson complained. "Some have gone so far as to say we have quit preaching on holiness. Bless God! The standard God Almighty holds out to you and me is HOLINESS. Glory!"[41]

Holiness Pentecostals charged Pentecostals who rejected crisis sanctification with heresy. They warned of the "danger" of spiritual power "channeled through unsanctified vessels." "People who have the Holy Ghost in an unsanctified vessel," warned Charles Parham, "find that their flesh becomes the medium through which fanaticism and wild-fire work."[42] Shortly after Durham's death in the summer of 1912, Parham published a supplement to his monthly *Apostolic Faith* in which he recounted an earlier prayer that either he or Durham (whichever was wrong on sanctification) would die. "How signally God has answered," he gloated.

The bitter infighting was duly noted by some observers. It figured, for example, in the fundamentalist Harry Ironside's published comments rejecting the Pentecostal movement.[43] For despite repeated affirmations of Christian unity, Pentecostals bickered constantly among themselves.

Both sides agreed about the dangers of neglecting holiness. It quickly became evident that Durham's followers in the Assemblies of God objected more to the extremes of holiness advocates than to the essence of the experience itself. In December 1913 Bell's *Word and Witness* carried an article entitled "The Second Blessing." Excerpted largely from writings of the respected editor of the *Way of Faith*, J. M. Pike, the article documented holiness teaching that Pike claimed would have appalled John Wesley. Pike further maintained that if Wesley "had foreseen what strained meanings would be forced into his words, he would have been more cautious."[44] Pike admitted that the term *second blessing* was not used in the New Testament, that the subject "as taught by many leading preachers and writers in the holiness movement [served] to arrest spiritual development," that being "filled with the Spirit" was different from cleansing, and that after crisis sanctification "the half has never been told" of the blessings that followed. Pike concluded by admonishing those who professed the second blessing: "Thy present possession is but the earnest. . . . There are rich effusions of the Spirit yet to be received."[45]

Bell had no problem with such sentiments. On the other hand, the doctrine as it was popularly taught seemed to him to demand response. Maintaining that the insistence that "man born of the Spirit . . . still has enough of sin in him not only to damn him, but as some put it, [to] damn the whole world" effectively "nullifie[d] the work of regeneration." He also cautioned against assuming that "there is nothing beyond or superior to" what some claimed as the experience of holiness.[46] Noting that some Pentecostals regarded tongues as the culmination of Christian experience, he prodded them to consider their error: "I honestly believe every child of God ought, from the first moment of faith, to see Christ is made unto him sanctification, to be at once baptized in water, then be filled with the Spirit and be talking in tongues in less than three days from the time he received Christ as a Savior. If the world of professing Christians were *normal* Bible Christians, truly tongues would have come in their babyhood in Christ."[47]

Efforts to avoid the extremes of both persuasions and chart a middle course on sanctification were accompanied by cautions about extremes in matters of dress. Although early Assemblies of God leaders favored a lifestyle that separated the believer in conspicuous ways from secular amusements and fashions, they deplored the tendency of some to equate "plain dress" or "poor dress" with holiness. Bell opposed the wearing of jewelry "solely for worldly adornment," but admitted: "The poor-dress gospel has been thoroughly preached before our day, and has never saved anybody yet. You may dress poorly . . . and still go to hell."[48]

When in 1916 the denomination approved an official statement on sanctification, the council found compromise wording acceptable to those of both persuasions. Rejecting much popular terminology in favor of "Bible language," the statement declared that "entire sanctification" was "the goal for all believers."[49] From its origins, then, the Assemblies of God has embraced people who have expressed their participation in the quest for holiness in different ways. The denomination affirmed that the quest was important but for the moment left its form to individual preference.

In the course of the discussion, the Assemblies of God disentangled itself further from the holiness movement and from the majority of southern Pentecostals (as well as from the other extant Pentecostal denominations) who continued to subscribe to a holiness theology. The evolution of doctrine was part of the process of discovering identity. Defining itself against the broadly based holiness movement had significant long-term results for the Assemblies of God.

Baptism and the Trinity

A more divisive issue was already agitating in Pentecostal ranks as the Assemblies of God took shape in 1914. Again, doctrinal disagreement lay at the heart of a bitter, painful struggle. And again, the struggle had implications for the future of American Pentecostalism and its relationship to other parts the American religious landscape.

The problem began almost unnoticed at a large camp meeting near Los Angeles in 1913. It mushroomed by 1915 to challenge the baptismal formula, the doctrine of the Trinity, and several other common practices. It raised basic issues about the restoration Pentecostals believed they enjoyed, and, in the end, it fundamentally altered the restorationist ethos as expressed in the Assemblies of God.

The World-Wide Apostolic Faith Camp Meeting that began on 15 April 1913 was, by any account, an impressive gathering. Meeting in Arroyo Seco near Pasadena, the gathering featured the ministry of the well-known evangelist Maria B. Woodworth-Etter. The advertisements of the camp was calculated to appeal to the Pentecostal craving for divine immediacy: it claimed divine inspiration even in the planning stages. Wherever the camp had been announced, "the Holy Ghost [had] witnessed to it."[50] R. J. Scott, a businessman from Los Angeles, had visited Woodworth-Etter's recent Dallas meetings where widely publicized conversions, Spirit baptisms, and healings occurred daily. Impressed, he had decided to invite her to Los Angeles: "Sister Etter," he discovered, "had already heard from heaven that God was going to gather His saints together in one place and deal with them, giving a unity and power that we have not yet known."[51]

Crowds thronged the meetings from the start. Mack M. Pinson estimated that about one thousand camped on the grounds while others rented nearby rooms. Prolonged, intense meetings ran constantly; frequently people preached simultaneously in different parts of the camp. Participants estimated that weeknight attendance was between fifteen hundred and two thousand, with larger crowds on Sundays. Woodworth-Etter had the primary responsibility for the plenary services.[52] Scott and his friend George Studd (brother of Moody's well-known convert C. T. Studd, who over the years was associated with various missions in the Los

Angeles area) sought to "keep the meetings on the Apostolic lines, according to the book of Acts."[53]

Woodworth-Etter estimated that she laid hands on at least two thousand people in prayer and recounted that "mighty signs and miracles"
showed "His approval of the word."[54] Pinson concurred: "The Devil is
raging, saints are shouting, and God is working," he exulted.[55] "Visions
and revelations" seemed almost commonplace; one, however, apparently
went largely unnoticed by Woodworth-Etter and the crowds. John
Schaeppe, inspired by the miracles Woodworth-Etter attributed to "the
name of Jesus," spent a night in prayer. Toward morning he had what
seemed to him a revelation of "the power of the NAME of Jesus."[56]

This revelation contributed to the emergence of a new emphasis
among those California-based Pentecostals influenced by Frank Ewart, an
Australian-Baptist-turned-Pentecostal-preacher who came to Los Angeles
via Canada. Ewart had served William Durham's Los Angeles mission as
pastor until the spring of 1913. Claiming that he then attended the Arroyo Seco camp meeting convinced that a "new move of God" was imminent, he wrote an account of the meetings that differed in significant
details from the reports published in Pentecostal papers.[57]

According to Ewart, the camp meeting's promoter, R. J. Scott, organized a baptismal service nearby and selected a Canadian visitor, R. E.
McAlister, to preach on water baptism. Ewart reported that McAlister's
casual observation that "the words Father, Son, and Holy Ghost were
never used by the early church in Christian baptism" was received with
"an inaudible shudder."[58] Although McAlister continued his sermon,
maintaining that baptism according to Matt. 28:19 was certainly valid,
he had fired Ewart's imagination. Ewart later asserted: "The shot had been
fired, and its sound was destined to be heard around the world."[59]

Ewart claimed that it was McAlister who convinced him that the three
titles, Lord, Jesus, and Christ were "counterparts to Father, Son, and
Holy Ghost and that Jesus was, in fact, THE NAME (singular) of the Father, Son and Holy Ghost." He was, of course, reviving trinitarian views
that had been excluded from the early church as heresy. The exact chro-
nology of Ewart's apprehension of this "NEW THING" (its early proponents liked to highlight their distinctive usage in full caps) is unclear;
what is certain, however, is that Ewart's fertile mind devised numerous
practical implications for his convictions. His persuasive abilities and the
fascination Pentecostals felt for new revelations assured both the survival
of the sense that something new had in fact occurred and the gradual
emergence of a series of practical implications from initially vague and
incoherent allusions.

Ewart later maintained that by 1913 he had for some time questioned traditional views of God. Convinced that the "New Thing" that had begun at the camp meeting demanded breaking former ties to launch new efforts untainted by the errors of the old, he severed his relationship to the Seventh Street Mission and opened his own, assisted by McAlister and Glenn Cook (who had once worked with Seymour). Another move brought him into association with Warren Fisher at the well-established mission known as Victoria Hall. When McAlister moved on, Garfield T. Haywood replaced him as evangelist. An African-American preacher from Indianapolis and a gifted songwriter, Haywood was widely respected.

Ewart was restless, however. He felt restricted by the more traditional attitudes of his associates—especially Fisher—from proclaiming his evolving views of the Godhead. He finally broke his ties to Victoria Hall and, with the initial assistance of its pastor, began tent meetings in the town of Belvedere. In a statement reminiscent of early Pentecostal claims, he noted that "to receive apostolic results on a full time basis," he would "have to preach the apostolic message on a full time basis."[60] To this, he dedicated his new efforts. Glenn Cook, recently returned from an eastern trip, wholeheartedly assisted him. The two purchased a baptismal tank and rebaptized each other "in Jesus' name." "Soon," Ewart reported, "the candidates for baptism in the Name of Jesus started to flock to the tent."[61] Apparently the noisy, crowded meetings became something of a local sensation. To Ewart, however, they were a "test" of the validity of his message, and events seemed to attest its truth: "the vast majority" of the rebaptized "left the tank speaking in other tongues."[62] Ewart began publishing his views in a paper he called *Meat in Due Season.* Cook, ever restless, left to proclaim this fuller restoration of the apostolic faith elsewhere.

Several issues were at stake. The most obvious centered in the baptismal formula and the significance of baptism. Ewart maintained that regardless of former baptisms, all should be rebaptized in the name of Jesus. Since Acts 2:38 read: "Repent and be baptized . . . for the remission of sins, and ye shall receive the gift of the Holy Ghost," he taught that repentance, baptism in Jesus' name, and Spirit baptism were three elements of a single conversion experience. He further came to reject orthodox language about the Trinity, claiming the identity of the Jehovah of the Old Testament with the Christ of the New.

Also at stake was the nature of the Pentecostal concept of restoration. The power of Ewart's views in attracting adherents rested in his insistence that he was recovering more of the New Testament's teaching. Until Ewart, most Pentecostals had kept the restoration well within the bounds of popular orthodoxy. Church history was dotted with the stories of similar enthusiastic groups that had come and gone. Still, as radical evangelicals, Pentecostals were religiously marginalized. Now they faced a basic challenge: what to do if the restorationist impulse moved them beyond even the porous boundaries of popular evangelicalism.

The list of Pentecostals who at first seemed inclined to move beyond was impressive. Ewart's views had been consolidating as the Assemblies of God was forming, and by 1915 it had made considerable inroads among members. Assemblies of God founders Howard Goss, D. C. O. Opperman, L. C. Hall, and Henry G. Rodgers embraced the new teaching, along with hundreds of lesser-known figures. Even Eudorus N. Bell was persuaded to accept rebaptism and to reconsider his understanding of the Godhead. Pentecostals have always been prone to take new truth seriously. Even as "oneness" teaching surfaced, Assemblies of God publications found it advisable to caution about other revelations. Especially in independent Pentecostal missions and in Assemblies of God congregations where Durham's rejection of holiness views had a firm following, there was precedent for the embracing of truth affirmed in revelations. Probably most Pentecostals shared Ewart's anticipation that the restoration would be dynamic and constantly characterized by a more powerful "apostolic" revival. Messages in tongues and interpretation regularly purported to reveal new insights; periodicals occasionally published revelations and prophecies. In this expectant, unsophisticated, fervent religious subculture, where "current" and "fresh" anointings mattered greatly, many responded to Ewart out of desire to flow with the restoration. This occasionally assumed arrogant overtones; those who failed to embrace the restoration's latest phase might well be told that their carnality or their pride prevented their understanding spiritual things or, worse, they might "miss God."[63]

The way in which this restorationist longing combined with an emphasis on Christ strengthened its appeal. Pentecostals thrilled to miracles done "in the Name of Jesus." Ewart's rhetoric maximized Christ and in so doing strengthened its appeal to people who professed a Christ-centered spirituality. Oneness songs gained enduring currency in the movement at large, especially Garfield T. Haywood's "Jesus, the Son of God" and "Down from His Glory." No Pentecostals quarreled with the message of Haywood's chorus:

> Preach in Jesus' Name, Teach in Jesus' Name
> Heal the sick in His Name;
> And always proclaim, it was Jesus' Name
> In which the power came;
> Baptize in His name, enduring the shame,
> For there is victory in Jesus' Name.[64]

David Reed has suggested a relationship between the tendency of Victorian Protestants to sentimentalize Christ and the appeal of oneness Pentecostalism. Pentecostals were not the only evangelicals whose gospel music focused on intense personal experiences and a lover-like relationship between the believer and Christ. Holiness advocate Beverly Carradine bemoaned the broader contemporary evangelical tendency to sing songs appealing to "natural affections" instead of those which stressed the "Being and attributes of God."[65] "Few of the popular gospel meeting hymn books," he noted, "are marked with any broadness as to the great subjects and doctrines of the Bible."[66] This popular Protestant proclivity to stress a sentimentalized Christ and a concomitant neglect to emphasize the Godhead was widespread and enduring in Pentecostalism.[67]

But probably most important of all was the pragmatic reality. It seemed an undeniable fact that the teaching seemed to work; it was marked, advocates claimed, by "God's approval." People testified to healing, people spoke in tongues, people claimed spiritual renewal as they embraced oneness views and submitted to rebaptism.

At the Assemblies of God headquarters J. Roswell Flower, the denomination's young office assistant and editor, concluded that given the division in leadership ranks, he should act to contain the spread of oneness views. Drawing courage from the conviction that "the crest of the wave" had passed, in language uncomfortably close to that of Ewart's party, Flower asserted that God had begun to do a "new thing" to bring about deeper unity.[68]

Such optimism proved premature, however. Throughout the summer of 1915, both *Word and Witness* and the *Weekly Evangel* addressed issues raised by Ewart's group. In restorationist fashion, both Bell and Flower claimed merely to advise by presenting scriptural views. The first sign of more general concern surfaced in an Assemblies of God presbyters meeting in St. Louis on 11 May. Disavowing any intention to legislate, the men issued a statement urging the constituency to "work these problems out on their knees before God and with the Bible in their hands."[69] "It was a profound mistake," they concurred, "to make an issue out of modern revelations and humanly coined phrases which would not be clearly justified by the unmistakable utterances of the written Word of God."[70] Most of the teaching circulated under the general designation "new issue" was not new at all, they asserted; Pentecostals were simply historically naive and mistook "rehatched teaching" for "new revelations."[71]

The statement cited as erroneous several views that generally accompanied teaching on rebaptism: references to Christ's "spiritual blood" and assertions that "Christ is the Holy Ghost" and that baptism in Jesus' name was "true Christian circumcision." They discouraged the use of wine in the communion service, a practice oneness advocates urged as conforming to the New Testament. They also denounced the view that Jesus was the name of the Father, Son, and Spirit and that this had not been revealed until Pentecost. And they emphatically denied that baptism according to Matt. 28:19 was not Christian. [72]

Despite this action, late in the summer *Word and Witness* stunned readers by announcing Eudorus N. Bell's rebaptism. [73] In an article that continued to renounce the errors the presbyters had earlier condemned, Bell confessed to "long settled doubts" about baptism. Haunted by the sense that he should be baptized by someone who had received Spirit baptism, Bell finally concluded to accept rebaptism according to the New Testament formula. Convinced that God would "refuse [him] the anointing" until he obeyed, Bell had been rebaptized by L. V. Roberts during the large (attendance reached some four thousand) Interstate Camp Meeting in Jackson, Tennessee. Another Assemblies of God founder and executive, Henry G. Rodgers, was rebaptized at the same camp. [74] Reiterating his conviction that one should not "make a hobby out of a phase of water baptism," Bell nonetheless offered the preeminent Pentecostal justification for his action: spiritual renewal, he claimed, had followed his "obedience."

The October *Word and Witness* also carried a statement issued by seven of the sixteen presbyters who had attended the Arkansas state camp meeting in Little Rock. Bell, Collins, Goss, Pinson, Welch, Rodgers, and Opperman all concurred that rebaptism should generally be discouraged and urged that adherents extend to others the "liberty to be baptized with any words" they preferred. [75] Meanwhile J. Roswell Flower had incorporated into the *Weekly Evangel* a series of articles addressing pertinent issues; Flower had also revised an article that Bell had sent into the office for publication in *Word and Witness*. [76] The article "Who Is Jesus Christ?" revealed Bell's fascination for some of Ewart's views on the Godhead. [77]

Amid growing confusion, the executives exercised their prerogative to convene a council. On Monday 4 October, following three days of prayer, delegates to the council, meeting in St. Louis, organized for business. The official roster listed 525 names; 54 were missionaries, 13 Canadians. The 76 women (in November 1914 there had been 142) had been specifically invited as advisory members; the "call" had solicited their attendance and their advice. [78]

In spite of (or perhaps because of) the unsettled situation, Chair Arch Collins was absent when the council convened for business. John Welch, selected to substitute for him, later accepted election as permanent chair. Bell terminated his editorial responsibilities, which were also assigned to Welch. [79] When Collins finally arrived, he, Haywood, Jacob Miller, and

Bell were requested to lead a general discussion on the biblical mode and formula for water baptism. Limited to thirty minutes each, the men voiced their convictions; the council allotted the remainder of the day to "free and full discussion" of the proper water baptismal formula. The next day Assistant Chair William G. Schell spoke for two hours on the baptismal practices used by the Apostolic Fathers.

Citing its intention to apply "the spirit and liberality of the Hot Springs Constitution" to the troubled situation, the council proposed a compromise:

> 1. Slight variations in the formula of baptism did not affect the validity of baptism.
>
> 2. Ministers should not urge "general rebaptizing"; rebaptism should be administered only if an individual considered prior baptism "not Christian baptism."
>
> 3. No New Testament "law" mandated the use of a certain formula.
>
> 4. Itinerant preachers should not interfere with "the proper Scriptural authorities" recognized in local congregations.
>
> 5. No "line of Christian fellowship or of ministerial fellowship" should be drawn by differences on the matter of a baptismal formula. [80]

The council further disapproved the teachings that Flower and Bell had repudiated in the *Word and Witness* and the *Weekly Evangel* throughout the summer and hoped that the new guidelines would suffice. Flower reported: "It was the general conviction that we should wait patiently for another year before arriving at a definite conclusion, allowing time for prayerful study of the Word of God." [81]

Any hope that the compromise would last quickly faded. Events continued to demonstrate the proclivity of many Pentecostals to find in purported spiritual revelations a congenial source of authority. Gradually trinitarians concurred that the situation demanded final resolution. That resolution proved painful, however, and it permanently influenced the direction of the Assemblies of God and the configuration of American Pentecostalism.

When the fourth General Council convened in a small church in St. Louis in 1916, none had as yet withdrawn from the denomination because of the "new issue." Its chief advocates—Ewart, Cook, and Haywood—though they had close ties to many within the council (Haywood had addressed the 1915 council), had never assented formally to its objectives. [82] Ewart and other oneness proponents attended and participated in the 1916 council. [83]

In an act with long-term implications that seemed to violate the restorationist Preamble adopted in 1914, a committee on resolutions introduced the Statement of Fundamental Truths. Oneness advocates accused the committee of proposing a creed to replace the Bible as the sufficient rule of faith and practice, and they were not alone. Nonetheless, on Saturday 6 October the council approved the document. It also adopted a separate resolution recommending that cooperating ministers use the words of Matt. 28:19 in their baptismal formula. These actions forced the withdrawal of oneness proponents, several of whom were denominational founders and executives, from the Assemblies of God. More than 25 percent of the ministers ultimately left. The percentage was much higher in the South, where the teaching gained rapid acceptance among Parham's earlier associates. Missionary giving plummeted.[84] A credentials committee drew up new credentials that included the "fundamental principles" and recalled all old preaching certificates.

The 1916 General Council also expedited an ongoing transition in leadership that brought men with backgrounds in the Christian and Missionary Alliance into influential leadership posts in the Assemblies of God.[85] Former Church of God in Christ leaders, on the other hand, had either left over the "new issue" or had abdicated leadership. The changing of the guard can also be assessed demographically; a higher percentage of northerners and easterners entered leadership ranks. In this separation, the Assemblies of God also began to distance itself from Pentecostals who were stubbornly independent and especially prone to new revelations. In general, those who were marginalized were more radically restorationist, imposed more restrictions on women as well as on dress, and were more inclined to pursue and nurture charismatic experience. It is perhaps significant (holiness Pentecostals at least thought it was) that all had first accepted William Durham's "new" revelation of the finished work of Calvary.

Oneness Pentecostalism has often been viewed by trinitarian Pentecostals as an aberration. Although its doctrinal distinctives distanced it from classical Pentecostalism, from another perspective its adherents must be understood as participants in the Pentecostal mainstream. If one admits the strong restorationist component at the heart of Pentecostalism's identity, oneness Pentecostals were more zealously restorationist, more doggedly congregational, and more Christ-centered—in short, in some important ways more essentially Pentecostal—than the trinitarians. Like other radical restorationists before them—Alexander Campbell or Barton Stone, for example—they found conventional Christian doctrines unduly influenced by the interpretations of councils and creeds. And their restlessness—their longing for new insights and their constant moving about from place to place—was not necessarily a desire for novelty but rather a way of expressing their continuing need to relate the human and the divine.

During the next few years, shorn of the uncertainties inherent in fluid, dynamic restorationism, the Assemblies of God grew rapidly. As measured in both numbers of workers and missionary giving the growth was substantial. General Superintendent John Welch's annual report to the fifth General Council in St. Louis in 1917 indicated a roster of 620 ministers and 73 missionaries.[86]

In the process, however, the Assemblies of God had veered sharply from some of the basic assumptions of its millenarian restorationist past. It had taken giant strides toward exclusivism and renounced people and principles that had shaped Pentecostalism's early ethos. It had also modified one of the features of a truly popular religious movement—the compelling sense of divine immediacy that anticipated revelations, transformed life to "heaven below," and made anyone a likely candidate for a divine mouthpiece. After 1916 the Pentecostal message in the Assemblies of God was considerably less fluid and much more predictable than before. Consensus had been reached about boundaries for the restoration. From then on, it would be held within the boundaries drawn by traditional evangelical doctrines.

One additional internal issue helped confirm this shift toward doctrinal definition and the curbing of individualism. It involved the formal resolution of the much-debated view that tongues speech always evidenced Spirit baptism.

The "Uniform" Evidence of Spirit Baptism

In 1918 Fred Francis Bosworth was among the best known men in the Assemblies of God. Former director of Zion City's award-winning band, Bosworth had embraced Pentecostal teaching during Parham's visit to Zion City in 1906. Shortly thereafter, Bosworth launched a career as an evangelist.[87] He suffered deprivation and persecution; in one eventful campaign he had been tarred and feathered by a mob opposed to his meetings. He became a popular speaker at camps and conventions and then established a thriving Pentecostal church in Dallas. Ardent Pentecostals across the country followed accounts of Woodworth-Etter's ministry with Bosworth in the summer and fall of 1912. Even before her arrival had drawn general attention, Bosworth had reported "a continual revival," with nightly meetings he claimed were marked by conversions, healings, and Spirit baptisms.[88]

In the course of his leadership Bosworth became troubled about popular teaching that tongues speech was uniformly the physical evidence of the baptism with the Holy Spirit. He considered that it promoted seeking a "gift" instead of the "Giver," that it tended to result in "shallow" baptisms, and that it was the source of considerable confusion. Bosworth further came to reject the distinction most Pentecostals made between evidential tongues and the gift of tongues described in 1 Cor. 12. Others had expressed similar reservations throughout the Pentecostal movement's short history.[89]

Charging that many had "NOISE without the power," Bosworth maintained that Pentecostals erred doctrinally in ways "which, if eliminated, we are certain will solve many of our difficulties, besides opening the way for . . . a much deeper work of God."[90] "After eleven years in the work on Pentecostal lines during which it has been my pleasure to see thousands receive the precious Baptism in the Holy Spirit," Bosworth claimed, "I am absolutely certain that many who receive the most powerful baptism for service do not receive the manifestation of speaking in tongues. And I am just as certain . . . that many who SEEMINGLY speak in tongues are not, nor ever have been, baptized in the Spirit."[91]

Bosworth served the Assemblies of God in executive leadership, and others gave his views serious consideration. In 1917 the Assemblies of God officially noted that questions had been raised about evidential tongues. For the moment, the regrouping denomination acted to clarify that only missionaries who accepted the "uniform initial evidence" view could receive Assemblies of God credentials.

During the summer of 1918 several prominent Assemblies of God leaders wrote articles for the *Christian Evangel* maintaining what has since become the classical Pentecostal position on tongues. By August the *Evangel* noted that in the forthcoming General Council, all of the major doctrines of the Assemblies of God would be discussed.

Meanwhile, on 24 July 1918 Fred Francis Bosworth submitted his resignation, affirming: "If I had a thousand souls, I would not be afraid to risk them all on the truth of my position that some may receive the fullest baptism in the Spirit without receiving the Gift of tongues."[92] The denomination was saved a showdown by the force of Bosworth's magnanimous spirit. Having returned his preaching license, he nonetheless traveled to Springfield, Missouri, for the General Council, where he participated in discussions and, though a nonmember, voted for the council's resolution: "Resolved, That this Council considers it a serious disagreement with the Fundamentals for any minister among us to teach contrary to our distinctive testimony that the baptism in the Holy Ghost is regularly accompanied by the initial, physical sign of speaking in other tongues, as the Spirit of God gives utterance, and that we consider it inconsistent and unscriptural for any minister to hold credentials with us who thus attacks as error our distinctive testimony."[93]

With the unanimous approval of this resolution, the Assemblies of God solidified its stance on Spirit baptism. Bosworth boarded a train for New York, where he affiliated briefly with the Christian and Missionary Alliance.[94] He later launched a career in independent healing revivalism that flowed into the midcentury salvation/healing revivals that propelled Oral Roberts and William Branham to fame.[95]

By 1918, then, Assemblies of God leaders had identified limits for the apostolic renewal; the restoration had come, but its climax—Christ's return—had been deferred. The millenarian context gradually eroded as worldly concerns overshadowed the certainty of Christ's imminent return. The old rhetoric remained, often emptied of content, as the constituency grappled with the meaning of a restoration that had spawned division and controversy even as it professed unity and generated enthusiasm and purpose. As adherents reconsidered the restoration from the perspective of people needing to relate to this world, an alternate self-perception emerged. Deemphasizing restorationism and millenarianism, they opted, rather, to perceive Pentecostalism as a "full gospel"—fundamentalism with a difference.

NOTES

1. See, for example, Frank Bartleman, *How Pentecost Came to Los Angeles* (Los Angeles: n.p., 1925), or Agnes Nevada Ozman LaBerge, *What God Hath Wrought* (Chicago: Herald Publishing, n.d.). The number and variety of their activities suggests something of the restlessness of many people who were attracted to Pentecostalism.

2. Gordon Lindsay, ed. *The John G. Lake Sermons* (Dallas: Voice of Healing Publishing, 1949), 12–13.

3. *Apostolic Faith*, Nov. 1906, 2.

4. *Apostolic Faith*, Jan. 1907, 3.

5. Daniel W. Kerr, "Spontaneous Theology," *Weekly Evangel*, 17 Apr. 1915, 3.

6. William Durham, "Bible Schools and Training Homes," *Gospel Witness* (ca. 1913): 5.

7. Ibid.

8. Charles Mason voiced similar sentiments. See "Marriage" in *C. H. Mason: A Man Greatly Used of God*, comp. Elnora L. Lee (Memphis, Tenn.: Women's Department, Churches of God in Christ, 1967), 48–50. Mason insisted that espousal of marital purity opened opportunities for "seducing spirits, working in dreams or in visions."

9. See, for example, Robert Jaffray, "Speaking in Tongues," *Christian and Missionary Alliance*, 13 Mar. 1909, 395–97.

10. William Durham, "Organization," *Gospel Witness* 1 (ca. 1913): 11.

11. William Durham, "The Church," *Pentecostal Testimony* 2, no. 1, ca. 1911, 14.

12. *Gospel Witness* 1 (ca. 1913): 11, 14.

13. *Word and Witness*, Dec. 20, 1913.

14. Durham, "Organization," 13.

15. General Council Minutes, 1914, 3, Assemblies of God Archives, Springfield, Mo. (hereafter AGA). This figure comes from the information under "conference committee," which states that the committee included one member from each state and foreign country represented. John Lake apparently represented both Pennsylvania and South Africa.

16. William B. McCafferty to J. Roswell Flower, 19 Aug. 1939, William B. McCafferty Papers, AGA.

17. *Word and Witness*, 20 Mar. 1914, 1.

18. Ibid.

19. *Word and Witness*, 20 Dec. 1913, 1.

20. Ibid. While the council was not to be limited by these items (its conveners had announced that "the scope of the meeting may be enlarged as the Lord shall lead the brethren"), they remained the underlying purpose for its eventual creation of the Assemblies of God.

21. General Council Minutes, 1914, 14.

22. Ibid.

23. Ibid., 5.

24. "General Council Special," *Word and Witness*, 20 May 1914, 1.

25. Michael G. Owen, "Preparing Students for the First Harvest," *Assemblies of God Heritage* 9 (Winter 1989–90): 5.

26. "The Gospel School," *Word and Witness*, 20 Aug. 1914, 3.

27. "Some Complaints," *Word and Witness*, 20 Jan. 1914, 2.

28. Eudorus N. Bell, "Women Elders," *Christian Evangel*, 15 Aug. 1914, 2.

29. *Word and Witness*, 20 Jan. 1914, 2.

30. This was done in response to the request of two missionaries to India, Hattie Hacker and Jennie Kirkland. Executive Presbytery Minutes, Nov. 1914, 23; Executive Presbytery Minutes, 5 July 1922, Assemblies of God Secretariat, Springfield, Mo. (hereafter AGS).

31. See, for example, Garfield T. Haywood, "The Marriage and Divorce Question in the Church" (reprint, Indianapolis: Christ Temple Publications, 1989).

32. General Council Minutes, 1914, 8.

33. "General Council Special," *Word and Witness*, 20 May 1914, 1.

34. *Word and Witness*, 20 Mar. 1914, 2.

35. *Christian Evangel*, 1 Aug. 1914, 1.

36. "For Strangers, Who Are We?" *Word and Witness*, 20 May 1914, 1.

37. See, for example, Eudorus N. Bell, "Bible Order v. Fanaticism," *Word and Witness*, 20 Mar. 1914, 2; "General Convention of Pentecostal Saints," *Word and Witness*, 20 Mar. 1914, 1; Elizabeth Sisson, "Organization of Organism,"

Latter Rain Evangel, Mar. 1914, 20–23; J. Roswell Flower, "Great November Meeting," *Christian Evangel,* 12 Sept. 1914, 1.

38. *Christian Evangel,* 24 Oct. 1914, 2.

39. See A. G. Garr, "That Yellow Book," *Word and Witness,* 20 Apr. 1914, 3.

40. Bennett F. Lawrence, ed., *The Apostolic Faith Restored* (St. Louis: Gospel Publishing House, 1916), 48ff.

41. Mack M. Pinson, Bible study notes for studies given at the Hot Springs General Council, 4, Mack M. Pinson File, AGA.

42. Charles F. Parham, "The Sources of Disease: Sanctification of Spirit Soul and Body," *Apostolic Faith,* Aug. 1912, 4. Parham charged that the emergence of "free-love," "affinity-foolism," and "soul-mating" among Pentecostals stemmed from the denial of crisis sanctification. "All the people . . . who had ever had a tinge of free-love," he fumed, "swallowed [Durham] and his teaching whole." Charles Parham, "Free-Love," *Apostolic Faith,* Dec. 1912, 5.

43. *Apostolic Faith,* supplement, Oct. 1912. Harry Ironside, "The Apostolic Faith Missions and the So-called Second Pentecost" (New York: Louizeaux Brothers, n.d.), 6.

44. J. M. Pike, "The Second Blessing," *Word and Witness,* 20 Dec. 1913, 2.

45. Ibid.

46. Eudorus N. Bell, "Questions and Answers," *Christian Evangel,* 21 Nov. 1914, 2. On the subject of sanctification, see also H. L. Lawler, "The Flesh: What Is It?" *Word and Work,* 20 Feb. 1913, 4.

47. Bell, "Questions and Answers," 2.

48. "The Dress Fad," *Word and Witness,* 20 June 1913, 2. This reluctance to espouse the holiness movement's preferences about dress, when combined with the rejection of holiness language describing sanctification, resulted in the charge that the Assemblies of God was "soft" on holiness. Frequent articles on the subject appeared in denominational publications. See, for example, "Believers in Sanctification," *Word and Work,* Oct. 1914, 3.

49. General Council Minutes, 1916, 11, AGA.

50. "World-wide Apostolic Faith Camp Meeting," *Word and Witness,* 20 Mar. 1913, 1.

51. Ibid.

52. Mack M. Pinson, "From Los Angeles World-wide Camp Meeting," *Word and Witness,* 20 May 1913, 1. The numbers varied; while Pinson reported from 75 to 100 ministers, Woodworth-Etter quoted R. J. Scott's claim that there were 200. See Maria B. Woodworth-Etter, *A Diary of Signs and Wonders* (1916; reprint, Tulsa: Harrison House, 1980), 250.

53. Pinson, "Meeting," 1.

54. Woodworth-Etter, *Signs,* 250.

55. Pinson, "Meeting," 1.

56. J. Roswell Flower, "History of the Assemblies of God," 24-A, class notes, church orientation, Central Bible College, Springfield, Mo., 1950, AGA.

57. See Frank Ewart, *The Phenomenon of Pentecost,* rev. ed. (Hazelwood, Mo.: World Aflame Press, 1975), 94ff.

58. Ibid., 106.

59. Ibid.

60. Ibid., 110.

61. Ibid., 112.

62. Ibid., 113.

63. See, for example, *Word and Witness*, May 1915, 4; A. G. Garr, "Have You Been Baptized in the Name of Jesus Christ?" *Victorious Gospel*, Spring 1915, 3.

64. Quoted in Paul D. Dugas, comp., *The Life and Writings of Elder G. T. Haywood* (Portland, Ore.: Apostolic Book Publishers, 1984), 22.

65. Beverly Carradine, *A Box of Treasure* (Chicago: Christian Witness, 1910), 175.

66. Ibid.

67. The first Assemblies of God Executive Presbytery had taken steps to prepare a Pentecostal hymnal in November of 1914. Kerr, Andrew Fraser, and Fred Francis Bosworth had been appointed to a committee to compile the book. Apparently none materialized. See Executive Presbytery Minutes, 25 Nov. 1914, 5, Assemblies of God Secretariat, Springfield, Mo. (hereafter AGS).

68. Ibid.

69. Eudorus N. Bell, "Editorial Statement," *Word and Work*, June 1915, 1.

70. Ibid.

71. Ibid.

72. See, for example, Eudorus N. Bell, "The Sad New Issue," *Word and Witness*, June 1915, 2, 3.

73. Eudorus N. Bell, "There Is Safety in Counsel," *Word and Witness*, Oct. 1915, 1.

74. Rodgers left the General Council in 1916, but initiated steps in 1921 that resulted in his return to the fellowship. See correspondence, Henry G. Rodgers File, AGS.

75. "Personal Statement," *Word and Witness*, Oct. 1915, 4.

76. See, for example, J. Roswell Flower, "The Lord's Supper," *Weekly Evangel*, 24 July 1915, 1; Eudorus N. Bell, "Jesus, the Great Life-Giving Spirit," *Weekly Evangel*, 17 July 1915, 2; Eudorus N. Bell, "Who Is Jesus Christ?" *Weekly Evangel*, 14 Aug. 1915, 1 (this also appears in *Word and Witness*, Sept. 1915, 4); Eudorus N. Bell, "To Act in the Name of Another," *Word and Witness*, May 1915, 2, was essentially a Bible study that presented what the Bible said about acting in Jesus' name. It was the first of this genre of articles that sought to address issues raised by oneness teaching.

77. Oneness advocates offered for distribution text that they claimed was the unamended version. A copy is in the AGA.

78. See *Word and Witness*, Sept. 1915, 1.

79. See *Weekly Evangel*, 16 Oct. 1915, 2.

80. General Council Minutes, 1915, 5, AGA.

81. Flower, "History," 26.

82. Flower implies that Haywood had been a member of the council. See ibid., 28.

83. Ibid., 27.

84. Flower, "History," 28.

85. Robert Mapes Anderson has argued that the oneness controversy within the Assemblies of God should be understood as a political strategy dominated by Flower to reorganize the leadership of the fellowship. See *Vision of the Disinherited: The Making of American Pentecostalism* (New York: Oxford University Press, 1979), 183ff.

86. Flower, "History," 29.

87. See, for example, Fred Francis Bosworth, "Confirming the Word by Signs Following: Jesus Saves, Heals, and Baptizes," *Latter Rain Evangel*, Dec. 1908, 7–8. This account of Bosworth's tent campaign in Plymouth, Ind., included accounts of Bernice Lee and others having spoken in tongues and having been understood by foreigners present.

88. See Bosworth's account included in Woodworth-Etter, *Signs and Wonders*, 172–75.

89. William Hamner Piper, founder of the Stone Church, for example, had not dogmatically accepted evidential tongues; neither did the numerous former Dowieites who banded together to form the Zion Faith Homes; Agnes Ozman had voiced her doubts in Piper's *Latter Rain Evangel;* even J. Roswell Flower occasionally had pointed out the tendencies of overzealous espousal of evidential tongues in his magazine *Pentecost.*

90. Fred Francis Bosworth, "Do All Speak with Tongues?" (New York: Christian Alliance Publishing, n.d.), 3.

91. Ibid., 4.

92. Fred Francis Bosworth to John Welch, 24 July 1918, AGA.

93. General Council Minutes, 1918, 8, AGA.

94. Probably the only other prominent individual who left the General Council with Bosworth was his brother, B. B. Bosworth. For a summary of the contributions of both to popular evangelical revivalism, see the obituary of the Bosworth brothers (who died less than a month apart), *Alliance Weekly*, 23 Apr. 1958, 15.

95. David Edwin Harrell, *All Things Are Possible* (Bloomington: Indiana University Press, 1976). The denomination had taken another step in its move away from the early Pentecostal ethos by insisting on conformity on evidential tongues. Many early proponents of the latter rain typology had rejected the idea of tongues as uniform evidence of Spirit baptism, proposing, rather, that tongues and other such "gifts" were "marks" of both the early and the latter rain, not "the absolute and only evidence" of the baptism with the Holy Spirit. "What Meaneth This Speaking in Tongues?" *Latter Rain Evangel* 1 (Oct. 1908): 15.

CHAPTER

6

From Pilgrims to Citizens,
1914–18

W HILE DOCTRINAL disagreements prodded the Assemblies of God
to reevaluate restorationist identity, adherents wrestled with how
to relate to the culture. In the years following 1914 they groped toward
finding appropriate ways to relate to society and the next generation. A
look at three areas reveals an evolving sense of identity. In responding to
World War I, they faced a larger question of citizenship and belonging;
in creating educational institutions, they provided what they could to
assure the continuation of their denomination while acknowledging that
its experiential essence was at risk; in channeling their energies into
missions, they affirmed their commitment to an exclusive faith that made
them responsible for "lost souls" everywhere and thus set them into a
particular relationship with the world. In each of these areas, they
grappled with the larger issue of restoration and responsibility to themselves, the future, and the world.

Like other Pentecostals, early Assemblies of God members professed
little interest in contemporary society; they had either not yet glimpsed a
broader world or had consciously turned from it. Major political, social,
and intellectual transitions had significance primarily because of how they
fit the prophetic agenda to which Pentecostals subscribed. Contemporary
human experience, they reminded one another, pointed to the imminent
"coming of the Lord," the event for which they professed to live. They
reminded themselves to resist worldly allures and live as "pilgrims and
strangers" on earth; yet, as men and women standing "on the firing line"
for God, they sometimes felt pressured to take sides on cultural issues.[1]
Discussions about World War I reveal some of the tensions that tore at
people determined to live "in the world" without being "of" it. They

reveal how far the Assemblies of God has come from its roots and illustrate the forces that modified the millenarian restorationist views that once kept them keenly aware of their alien status.

When Woodrow Wilson led the nation into war, members of the newly formed Assemblies of God were forced to address complex issues of civil obedience and military participation. The eschatological bases of Wilson's vision for America veered sharply from Pentecostal chiliasm. Early Assemblies of God attitudes toward war reveal Pentecostal identity in transition.

Like other American Protestants, Pentecostals were accustomed to religious language rich in militaristic symbols. In the familiar words of Isaac Watts, they were "soldiers of the cross" with an obligation to fight: "Sure I must fight, if I would reign."[2] And in the triumphant cadence of Lelia Morris's "Victory All the Time" they sang their encouragement to one another:

> In the midst of battle be not thou dismayed
> Though the powers of darkness 'gainst thee are arrayed;
> God thy strength is with thee, causing thee to stand
> Heaven's allied armies wait at thy command.[3]

Pentecostals considered themselves engaged in a daily conflict infinitely more momentous than any earthly struggle: Christians fought daily "in the gospel war."[4] It is hardly surprising, then, that their first response to war was expressed in cosmic terms; World War I could be understood as an extension, an outward manifestation, of the spiritual conflict in which they had been engaged all along.

Early response to the progress of the war in Europe fueled intense awareness that theirs were the end times. Dozens of Pentecostal periodicals analyzed how current events fulfilled prophecy. Amid rampant excitement about approaching cataclysm, spiritual enthusiasts uttered predictions reinforcing biblical prophecy. Although its editors carefully avoided endorsing date setting, the Assemblies of God official organ (newly renamed *Pentecostal Evangel*) published several prophecies affirming—using ecstatic utterances and crude mathematical evidence—that Christ would return during the celebration of the Jewish holidays in the late summer of 1917.[5] Pentecostals introduced an unusual piece of evidence to support their conviction that the world was engaged in a climactic struggle: a vision George Washington had purportedly experienced at Valley Forge. Citing a third-hand account from the *National Tribune* in December 1880, Pentecostals used considerable ingenuity in applying the story to buttress their claims.

Washington, the story maintained, had had a supernatural encounter in which he had seen three great crises challenging America. The third and most severe, he had been informed, would be worldwide in scope. All attempts to stay the trouble would fail; only divine assistance, in the form of the Second Coming, would rescue the world from self-destruction. From this perspective World War I was Armageddon.[6] The war, then, reinforced Pentecostal identity as latter rain people; with renewed conviction they affirmed their place in history. On 22 February 1916 the *Weekly Evangel* reminded its readers: "Don't forget these are days of special importance. Don't forget that the coming of Jesus for His Bride is to be expected daily. Don't forget that many signs and many events of the present point to the next great coming event. Don't forget the war. Don't forget that this is the time of the Latter Rain. Don't forget that the purpose of the Latter Rain is to bring in the Harvest. Don't forget that Jesus said, 'The harvest is the end of the world.' Don't forget that you must be ready."[7]

The concept of citizenship offers a useful way to explore Pentecostals' interest in the progress of events around them and their changing sense of who they were. As citizens of another kingdom, Pentecostals expressed disinterest in their culture; yet, they soon learned to move handily from operating under the pilgrim model to expressing their concerns as Christian soldiers. Those with the strongest sense of pilgrimage—of citizenship in heaven—tended to be pacifists; others, while concurring, claimed an obligation in that pilgrimage to counter evil; still others affirmed dual citizenship, identified morality with the Allied cause, and supported the war.

The issue was, at first, decidedly more pressing in Europe. In 1914 Assemblies of God adherents had been following the progress of British Pentecostalism for some time. Alexander Boddy, an Anglican vicar in Sunderland and the movement's acknowledged leader, had visited most established Pentecostal centers in North America, and his publication, *Confidence*, circulated widely in the United States, providing news of the progress of Pentecostalism in Europe. The *Christian Evangel* reprinted a series of editorials from *Confidence* in which Boddy unabashedly advocated the Allied cause. Designating Germany a "bully," he argued the need to "bring that bully to his senses in the quickest way possible."[8]

William B. McCafferty, Assemblies of God pastor and prolific writer, responded with the view that the Christian's heavenly citizenship mandated pacifism. Arguing that it was always wrong to fight either in self-defense or to defend a weaker nation that was "in the right" from a stronger oppressor, McCafferty insisted that God's word to the contemporary church was "Ye followers of the Prince of Peace, disarm yourselves."[9]

Evangel editors seemed ready to agree. In June, July, and August they published three articles by the independent Pentecostal Frank Bartleman presenting an unyielding pacifism.[10] He considered the war divine judgment on sinful humanity. Whereas few Pentecostals endorsed contemporary calls for social righteousness, Bartleman insisted that the absence of such righteousness invited judgment. His language echoed the concerns of contemporary social gospelers who called for an ethic of love and descried the absurdity of war. Maintaining that the war was the product of economic rivalry, he examined the propaganda issued copiously by both sides and labeled America's official neutrality "hypocrisy."[11]

Bartleman's attempt to apply a consistent ethic seemed, to some, to be unacceptably pro-German. Reflecting on the situation later, he complained that to be a Christian during the war "meant to be denominated 'pro-German.'"[12] Considering that the war made a travesty of Christ's injunction "Love your enemies," for example, he intoned: "It is not right to curse our enemies simply because it is popular. During the war there was little else left for a preacher to do. . . . The Gospel was scarcely allowed to be preached. One could not preach 'love your enemies.'"[13]

Bartleman believed that participation in war meant rejection of Christ: "War is contrary to the whole Spirit and teaching of Christ," he urged. "Anyone going into war is bound to lose out. Christ's kingdom is 'not of this world.'"[14] *Evangel* editor Stanley Frodsham amplified Bartleman's views of heavenly citizenship. Such citizenship mandated more than neutrality; it meant that Christians should live their lives as pilgrims and strangers in any country. Pride in nation and race was "an abomination."[15] This impatience with conflict had a restorationist bent: its advocates ardently sought to imbue their generation with both the ethic of Christ and the cultural disinterest they perceived in the early church.

The *Evangel* also carried pacifist literature written by members of the Booth-Clibborn family. Several of these grandchildren of William and Catherine Booth (founders of the Salvation Army) contributed strong pacifist statements. Samuel H. Booth-Clibborn argued against Christian participation in war in *Should a Christian Fight?: An Appeal to Christian Young Men of All Nations.* His father, Arthur Booth-Clibborn, expressed similar sentiments in *Blood against Blood,* a book distributed by Gospel Publishing House.[16]

Samuel H. Booth-Clibborn addressed his remarks specifically to other Pentecostals. In both his book and an article published in the *Evangel* just after the United States entered the war in April 1917, he argued for nonresistance. Urging those who had "nothing higher to live and die for" to fight for their countries, he reminded Christians: "We do have a better cause to live and die for."[17] For Christians, the outcome of a war made no real difference: "What does it matter under what flag you are? . . . Jesus lived all His life in a conquered country and never objected to paying the tribute of subjection to victorious Rome. If He put up with it, why can't we?"[18] Strongly denouncing "the wretched idolatry of nation-worship where parents sacrifice their young men on the bloody altars of the modern 'Moloch' of PATRIOTISM," he insisted that Christian participation in war involved dire moral and spiritual consequences for individuals as well as for nations. Christians had no alternative but pacifism.[19]

Arthur Booth-Clibborn concurred. Christians who fought were "assisting the Prince of Hell, who was a murderer from the beginning."[20] On the same note, the *Evangel* also published an unnamed English conscientious objector's avowal that Christians who "measured [their] walk by the Word of God" would not fight.[21]

As time passed and British fortunes deteriorated, *Evangel* editors used Washington's vision to demonstrate the likelihood of eventual American involvement.[22] Bartleman concurred in 1916 that events pointed toward America's entry into the war; he regarded it as satanically inspired. "Satan seems . . . to be preparing the way for killing here," he wrote in 1916. "For two years our daily papers have been full of killing. Conscience is getting seared. A selfish spirit, refusing the voice of God, is predominating. God must give a rebellious people the sword."[23]

Honest efforts to address the ethical issues raised by war were—as they have always been—controversial. Pacifism became unpopular and dangerous as war enthusiasm swept the country and the Sedition Act enumerated harsh penalties for a wide range of dissent.

It had become evident, too, that Assemblies of God adherents did not uniformly embrace pacifism. Though pilgrims, they were also patriots. Responses to Bartleman accused him of sympathy for Germany and resulted in an editorial disclaimer that urged readers to neutrality. Meanwhile, the *Evangel* editor encouraged young men preparing for war: "We are all very proud of our soldiers and our sailors, and of all those who have so nobly responded to their country's call to arms." The challenge was not so much militarism as recognition, on the part of those involved, that they might face an imminent "call into eternity." Evangelism among soldiers was encouraged: some local congregations opened ongoing evangelistic efforts at military bases.

Meanwhile, the *Evangel* increasingly mirrored the diversity of its readers. While Eudorus N. Bell argued that it was "spiritually unsafe" for Pentecostals to join the army, he admitted that there were some "bright Pentecostal lights" among European soldiers. More traditional than some of his colleagues on subjects such as war and women in minis-

try, this southerner believed that two factors made military service acceptable: a draft law or the necessity to defend "mothers, wives and children." He was also convinced that the defeat of Germany would "benefit
righteousness."

After the United States declared war in April 1917, Assemblies of God
executives adopted a resolution on military service. In keeping with the
denomination's objective of cooperative fellowship, the resolution was
not primarily an effort to deal theologically with the problem of Christian
participation in war but rather was framed to secure "the privilege of
exemption from military service." At the same time, however, editors
insisted that those adherents who "felt free to do so" could certainly take
up arms.

The resolution, dated 28 April 1917, was accompanied by a letter
signed by Stanley Frodsham, who had already made his own pacifist views
evident. The resolution made some startling claims: Scriptures such as
"follow peace with all men," "resist not evil," "thou shalt not kill," or
"love your enemies" had "always been accepted and interpreted by our
churches as prohibiting Christians from shedding blood or taking human
life."[24] "As a body," Assemblies of God adherents, then, could not
"conscientiously participate in war and armed resistance which involves
the actual destruction of human life."[25] Frodsham, serving as general
secretary for the denomination, noted further that the principles of the
General Council "were in opposition to war from its very beginning."
The introduction of the matter in the *Evangel* tied Pentecostals to the
historic peace churches: "From the very beginning, the movement has
been characterized by Quaker principles. The laws of the Kingdom, laid
down by our elder brother, Jesus Christ, in His Sermon on the Mount,
have been unqualifiedly adopted, consequently the movement has found
itself opposed to the spilling of blood of any man, or of offering resistance to any aggression. Every branch of the movement, whether in the
United States, Canada, Great Britain or Germany, has held to this
principle."[26]

This resolution, framed by several of the denomination's executives
(during the brief period when Bell was excluded from their ranks) and
approved by its governing bodies, the Executive and General Presbyteries, ignored the militaristic strain expressed in Boddy's early defense of
the war, implied a Pentecostal consensus by speaking for "all sections of
the Pentecostal Movement," and maintained that Pentecostalism was "a
monolithic whole" in its nonresistance.[27]

Later issues of the *Evangel* urged young men to fulfill their obligation
to register with local draft boards. Pressure during the war years encour-

aged some independents who had avoided affiliation with the Assemblies of God to seek credentials. One such was William I. Evans, a young pastor in New Jersey. Like many other early Pentecostals, Evans had had strong reservations about organization. He led an independent mission until the draft law made it advisable for him to affiliate with a registered religious group. He needed an organization through which to affirm his conscientious objection; the alternative was imprisonment. When the war ended, however, Evans considered that he had compromised. He returned his Assemblies of God license and resumed independent ministry.[28]

At the 1917 General Council Arch Collins informed participants that the Texas District Council of the Assemblies of God had decided to cancel the credentials of any minister who spoke against the government. The General Council "agreed that such radicals do not represent this General Council."[29] Two models of Pentecostal attitudes toward culture were in tension: pacifism with an unyielding commitment to the Christian's heavenly citizenship and a "Christian soldier" model that identified fighting for America with being on God's side. Texas Pentecostals clearly did not wholeheartedly share fellow Texan William B. McCafferty's commitment to heavenly citizenship.[30]

Certainly Bell did not. The 24 August 1918 issue of the *Evangel* carried Bell's advice that Assemblies of God adherents should destroy the tract form of one of Bartleman's pacifistic *Evangel* articles, "Present Day Condition." Later that year, with the war drawing to a close, Bell found the courage to express more fully his own nonpacifist views. From his perspective, participation in war was not sinful. Hatred, however, was. If one kept personal hatred out of one's heart, "he was not a murderer when he obeyed his country in executing just punishment on the criminal Hun."[31]

The espousal of voluntary conscientious objection satisfied many on both sides of the larger issue and avoided addressing the tougher question of appropriate Christian response to war, patriotism, and citizenship. Only a few persisted in the sense that the movement "lost something" when it veered from pacifism.[32]

Changing views in the Assemblies of God were part of a profound move in American Pentecostalism at large. Robert Mapes Anderson has traced the shift in Pentecostal rhetoric after World War I from challenging the social system to buttressing it.[33] R. Laurence Moore has noted that in the same years, Pentecostalism's early egalitarian innovations were suppressed. "Premillennial condemnations of patriotism in Pentecostal journals," he wrote, "gave way to reproductions of the American flag."[34]

By World War II, the denomination had no qualms about participation, and by the 1990s, the identification of Pentecostalism with the American way of life was virtually complete.

During World War I, however, Pentecostals were still exploring the complications of the restorationist life-style they professed to embrace. The war exposed ambiguity about identity. If that of noncitizens—of pilgrims and strangers—suited some, others found the battling soldier serving God and country more congenial and more American. Two decades later, when the nation again stood at the brink of war, few would admit the "sinfulness" of strong national loyalties; most would opt—with considerable pride—to serve their country. No longer as certain that the end was near—and with a growing stake in American economic and social policies—they opted to act out their concerns for life in this world rather than to wrestle with the practical meaning of citizenship in a heavenly kingdom that had puzzled their predecessors. Not until 1989, with debate swirling around abortion, would the denomination again come close to officially approving civil disobedience.

It is perhaps noteworthy that World War I turned some Assemblies of God leaders to studying historical precedents for a decision about participation. During the same years, they invoked historical precedent for excluding oneness Pentecostals as unorthodox. These instances represent a significant break from restorationist thinking that makes the New Testament all sufficient. By moving leaders toward a consideration of history, these issues had a farther-reaching impact on the Assemblies of God than was generally recognized. It is no coincidence that the same period saw efforts to establish long-term institutions, an activity that paralleled the grudging acknowledgment of greater respect for historical tradition as well as expressed a sense of obligation to the future.

Building Institutions

Interest in the creation of educational institutions that would indoctrinate students and pass on Pentecostal faith indicated recognition of the possibility that Pentecostals might have to face an indefinite, earthly, worldly future. At first virtually no one had considered formal training for ministry essential or even advisable; time was too short to invest in education. Many men and women achieved their goals without it, and some of the constituency explicitly opposed it. But those who brought into the Assemblies of God memories of training in fundamentalist Bible institutes or denominational seminaries eventually concluded that they had an obligation to create similar environments for their movement's future leaders. Hostility toward Pentecostals in most established schools seemed to exclude the option of working within existing structures.

The training these Pentecostals decided to provide was similar to that offered in the growing number of fundamentalist Bible institutes: it set out to proclaim a point of view and to locate where those who differed were in error. A fear of the unknown and a worldview that made evangelism more important than learning occasioned rejection of the liberal arts.[35]

As Assemblies of God districts were organized around the country, several districts cooperated to support Bible institutes, but Assemblies of God executives determined to work toward the creation of a school owned and operated by the entire denomination. Late in the summer of 1922 they opened Central Bible Institute (CBI) in the headquarters city of Springfield, Missouri. Assemblies of God executives sat on its board of directors and began framing the policies that would eventually shape a denominational education program. In 1923 they decided to make CBI the model for all schools endorsed by the Assemblies of God; in 1925 the General Council meeting in Eureka Springs, Arkansas, gave the denomination representation on all recognized regional Bible institute boards of directors.

Despite the virtual lack of academic requirements at Assemblies of God Bible institutes, some who desired training could not do the work. The persuasion that training should be made available to all who felt called to ministry shaped admissions policies and occasioned the offering of one-year preparatory programs. Denominational executives recruited prominent pastors to the faculty of CBI and encouraged them to prepare textbooks providing a Pentecostal perspective on evangelical doctrine and mission. These men had attended various Bible institutes and seminaries before embracing Pentecostalism and prodded the denomination to standardize curricula and establish three-year programs. For the moment, however, most students obtained only the most rudimentary training. Others, either unconvinced about the need for education (the denomination's leaders found it necessary to reiterate urging about training) or unable to afford even its modest cost, failed to complete their programs.

Assemblies of God leaders tended to stereotype American higher education as unacceptably secular and unashamedly materialistic. They expressed strong support for sheltering Assemblies of God youth in academic schools where Christianity and patriotism would inform the curriculum. Given meager resources during the depressed 1930s leaders did no more than express sympathy with the concept of Christian day schools, however. Not until the resurgence of fundamentalism in the 1970s would significant numbers of Assemblies of God congregations have the resources to provide an alternative to the alleged secular humanism of the public schools. Serious discussion focused first on denominationally funded higher education.

In 1929 a denominational report proposed:

> On account of the worldliness of many of our High Schools and Colleges and their antagonistic attitude for the most part to the Pentecostal message, there is a growing need of academic schools of our faith in different parts of our country to provide education without contamination of worldly and anti-Christian influences. We believe that our fellowship should look with favor upon the establishment of such schools, and should look forward to the time, if the Lord tarry, when we may have somewhere an institution of college grade, where the most complete and thorough education can be obtained under Pentecostal auspices."[36]

This recommendation, appended to six suggestions for the improvement of Bible schools, expressed concerns similar to those that helped shape parochial school systems, Catholic and Protestant, across the country. But resources and consensus were lacking, and debate and discussion went on inconclusively for two decades.

Meanwhile, denominational executives monitored a growing number of regional schools using standards established for CBI which was, in a sense, the denomination's flagship Bible institute. Scattered around the country, operated with Assemblies of God money and personnel, were Glad Tidings Bible Institute, San Francisco; Southern California Bible College, Pasadena; Southwestern Bible Institute, Enid, Oklahoma; North Central Bible Institute, Minneapolis; Shield of Faith Bible School, Amarillo, Texas; Northwest Bible Institute, Seattle; Great Lakes Bible Institute, Zion, Illinois; Peniel Bible Institute, Stanton, Kentucky; and Eastern Bible Institute, Green Lane, Pennsylvania. In 1931 the denomination's Committee on Bible Schools urged that prospective ministers be encouraged to attend Bible school, that a uniform policy for endorsement of schools be adopted, and that an educational commission be formed. Recognizing an enduring lack of consensus on the advisability of even rudimentary Bible school education, they begged Assemblies of God pastors to give "whole-hearted interest and cooperation." For those who either could not or would not attend Bible institutes, during the 1930s the schools began offering correspondence classes.

Deep divisions about Bible institutes and "literary education" plagued the denomination through this period. In part the debate symbolized theological and identity crises. On theological grounds, some opposed the standardization of training because they believed classroom learning inevitably "quenched the Spirit." A deeper and largely unarticulated issue faced them too. People who had perceived themselves as "pilgrims" were finding it necessary to act like "citizens." Those who had anticipated an imminent rapture were growing old in this world while a second genera-tion of Assemblies of God adherents was coming of age; their needs and expectations were different. Institutionalization seemed to some to jeop-ardize the denomination's dynamic and identity. Only reluctantly would they admit the need to provide for a worldly future. Their hope to restore the New Testament faith in a whirlwind of activity culminating in their "rapture" had eroded; they groped for something to take its place without finding willingness to relinquish it entirely.

In 1937 the denomination carried the institutionalizing process for-ward by creating the Department of Education and Home Missions and providing for a full-time, salaried director. Even as its administration for-malized, however, education in the Assemblies of God lacked a unifying philosophy. Most Assemblies of God educators had had little formal training themselves. They accepted uncritically generalizations that often stereotyped other cultural and religious traditions. Despite their regular invocations of the Spirit as the source of truth, some who believed Pen-tecostals should be "Spirit-taught, led and filled" distrusted them. Edu-cators nonetheless called for a "united vision for the future perpetuation of the great Pentecostal message. We must pass this heritage on to our youth that they may go forth in the power of the Spirit."[37] Some dreamed of a day when the Assemblies of God would produce its own texts and realize uniform standards for faculty and students.

This sense of a need to equip the next generation heralded a subtle shift in self-perception. For the moment, leaders hoped to balance two concepts that were fundamentally in tension: on the one hand, commit-ment to the imminent return of Christ; on the other, the need to assure preservation of the movement's message, which was essentially a message of experience rather than doctrine. But they faced an insurmountable obstacle: they could formalize the message but they could not induce ex-perience. By the 1930s the recognition that education was at the core of the church's task was finding broader support. It conflicted directly with the restorationist expectations that had shaped early Pentecostalism. "The great Pentecostal message" was no longer couched in terms of res-toration; rather, it heralded the availability and power of a "full gospel" for the twentieth-century church.

Some set out to use Bible institutes not only to indoctrinate but also to preserve early Pentecostal preferences about plain dress by imposing them on the next generation of leaders—students. In 1939 two former holiness Methodists, J. Narver Gortner and Robert A. Brown, wrote a resolution about female dress that was adopted by the General Council:

> Be it resolved by this General Council that we condemn such un-scriptural conduct as the donning of male attire, or the wearing of shorts or slacks, on the part of the lady students in any of our Bible Schools, while attending picnics, going on hikes, or on any occa-sion on which they may appear in public; that we brand such con-duct as being, in our opinion, essentially worldly; and that we place ourselves on record as opposing all trends and tendencies that ap-pear to break down, or blot out, or make less outstanding, the line of demarcation between the holy and the unholy, the sacred and the profane; and that we recommend that the standard in dress es-tablished by Central Bible Institute be the recognized standard for all our Bible Schools, and that a failure to conform thereto shall subject the school thus failing to censure or disapproval.[38]

Dress standards at Bible institutes were recommended as standards for the constituency at large, too. Already prior to 1939 female students had been forbidden "bobbing and undue waving of the hair, use of such cos-metics as tend to change the color of the complexion, plucking of the eyebrows, and the painting of the fingernails."[39] These resolutions dif-fered significantly in tone from early Assemblies of God reluctance to endorse the "plain dress" gospel. To be sure, they probably summarized how most Assemblies of God men and women felt on the subject, as well as how Americans of similar social location thought, but, more impor-tant, enumerating them evidenced the institutionalizing process at work. Conformity in both doctrine and life-style was becoming increasingly im-portant in this once loosely structured denomination. What it meant to be Pentecostal was evolving, almost without notice.

Missions

Convinced that evangelism was one of the basic reasons for the resto-ration of the apostolic faith, early Assemblies of God adherents devoted their meager resources to spreading their message. They felt called to responsibility for the salvation of everyone, everywhere. They developed Gospel Publishing House primarily to facilitate evangelism. From 1914 the publishing house issued magazines that raised money for missions and reported the extension of the Pentecostal movement around the world. In 1917 Gospel Publishing House consolidated these magazines to create the *Weekly Evangel,* predecessor of the *Pentecostal Evangel.* With a current weekly circulation approaching three hundred thousand, the *Pentecostal Evangel* has become one of the most circulated religious weeklies in the United States. The publishing house also issued tracts and carried books and Bibles. Its personnel probably influenced the general perception and the effectiveness of the denomination's endeavors more profoundly than did other denominational leaders.

Assemblies of God leaders considered the *Pentecostal Evangel* "at the base of all the work of God in the General Council."[40] It "kept missionary enthusiasm at a boiling point."[41] In 1919 the average *Evangel* reader contributed $5 per year to foreign missions. Bell considered soliciting new *Evangel* subscribers an essential part of the missionary task; five thousand new subscribers promised at least $25,000 more for missions.[42] By 1925, when missions were fully separated from Gospel Publishing House and placed under the supervision of a full-time director, missionary giving had increased to over $177,000.

Missions interest had several sources: millenarianism, with its focus on preparing the world for Christ's imminent return; a desire to hasten Christ's return, based on a literal understanding of Matt. 24:14 ("This gospel of the kingdom shall be preached in all the world for a witness unto all nations; and then shall the end come"); the conviction that the "latter rain" had been prophesied to "all flesh"; and restorationism, which stressed the example of the early church and the end-times character of the Pentecostal revival.

After 1906 missionaries from Europe and North America carried the Pentecostal message around the world. Their earliest efforts were often among missionaries who then spread Pentecostal views to an ever-enlarging constituency. Concentrations of missionaries in China and India made these countries the focus of early Pentecostal efforts, and in both countries missionaries under appointment with various evangelical faith missionary societies as well as some under denominational boards embraced Pentecostalism. Some remained under board appointment; others were forced to choose between advocacy of Pentecostal experience and continued affiliation with their sending agencies; and still others chose independent efforts as the "biblical way" to evangelize. In 1908, for example, Susan Easton was in India as a missionary of the Women's Union Missionary Society. She accepted Pentecostalism and instituted "tarrying meetings" (meetings during which people awaited Spirit baptism) in the WUMS mission in Calcutta. The mission's board objected that her interest in tongues speech and healing violated the society's commitment to noncontroversial evangelical views and issued an ultimatum. Easton resigned; a colleague who shared her views submitted. Easton returned to the United States, gained visibility within the Assemblies of God, and returned to India under Assemblies of God appointment.

Others chose a similar course. W. W. Simpson had been with the first party of American missionaries to evangelize on the Tibetan border. Sent by the Christian and Missionary Alliance, he was also given the choice of muting his Pentecostal tendencies and remaining on his thriving mission station. He, too, opted to sever ties to his sending agency, returned home to publicize his needs among Pentecostals, and accepted an Assemblies of God appointment to China in 1916.

Unlike many other Pentecostal associations (an article in the *Evangel* estimated that some forty distinct groups existed by 1916) in which missionary goals tended to be general, the Assemblies of God early enumerated specific goals. It intended to generate missionary fervor at home, establish guidelines to assist candidates to gain denomination endorsement, and assure that missionaries obtained adequate support. At the same time, leaders hoped to encourage coordination and cooperation among missionaries already on the field.

Implementing this vision took time. The 1919 General Council named J. Roswell Flower the denomination's first missionary secretary. Flower, who had already served the denomination as general secretary and as a pastor, regarded as his task the "recognition of the Pauls and Barnabases" and the "elimination of the John Marks who would likely lose heart and come back before they should."[43] Deciding how to assign undesignated funds proved challenging; Flower noted that fully two-thirds of Assemblies of God missionaries qualified for any funds submitted for "the neediest missionary."[44]

Flower's approach captured the pervasive, sometimes unacknowledged, persuasion that somehow Pentecostals were called to do something different from other missions agencies. Restorationist dreams (though modified by the 1920s) sustained the sense that the Assemblies of God had been charged with a solemn and distinctive mandate, a mandate that legitimated its missionary efforts and distinguished them. "Pentecostal missionaries," Flower insisted, "have a holy calling. They cannot follow the methods of non-Pentecostals who have gone before, neither can they bend their efforts in building up charitable institutions, hospitals and schools. Pentecostal missionaries have a Pentecostal commission—to be witnesses in Jerusalem, in Judea, and to the uttermost parts of the earth. Witnesses!"[45] Executive Presbyter Daniel Kerr concurred: "It is not wise to construct much machinery. We have enough! What we need is a lubricant—oil from heaven."[46]

Missionaries quickly discovered the advantages of "machinery," however. In Egypt, Lillian Trasher channeled her efforts through an orphanage. In North India and parts of Africa, Assemblies of God missionaries established leper colonies. Gradually some missionaries overcame fears that efforts to meet human needs through traditional channels were inherently inferior to direct evangelistic outreach. By 1925, when a change in executive leadership acknowledged the growth of the Assemblies of God foreign missions program, Flower had reason to be pleased. With one missionary for every five stateside pastors, the Assemblies of God had established a missionary presence in China, India, several parts of Africa, and scattered parts of Central and South America and the Middle East. Working under a philosophy of "establishing self-supporting native churches in each field," the foreign missions department also coordinated efforts to extend missionary interest at home.[47]

The mid-1920s were no exception to the persistent Pentecostal tendency to sense that "the whole structure of civilization" was threatened by unprecedented cultural change. Optimistically and naively, they proclaimed native religions obviously inadequate to meet the crisis.[48] To their way of thinking, Pentecostal Christianity was "the only adequate force." Their words implied that the task of rapid evangelism could—and should—be easy. Though reports often noted the "victories" Pentecostals anticipated, missionaries learned through hardship the inevitability of conflict and the loneliness of rejection. Often criticized by their contemporaries for disdaining and undermining native cultures or for working to impose Western customs on their converts through education, some missionaries (perhaps unintentionally) also made vital contributions to indigenous movements striving to disown colonial allegiances.[49]

Reports of progress abroad were tempered by the fact that in some years as many as half of American Assemblies of God congregations contributed nothing to foreign missions. For those who insisted that Pentecostalism was rooted in a compulsion to end-times evangelism, this fact raised questions about the widely accepted opinion that foreign missions was at the core of the denomination's reason for being.

Assemblies of God missions prospered especially after 1927 when Noel Perkin arrived in Springfield, Missouri, to take charge. A native of London, Perkin was reared in the Wesleyan Methodist Church and embraced Pentecostalism as a young man in Canada. After a brief stint as a missionary in Argentina, Perkin arrived at the Elim Bible Training School in Rochester, New York, in 1921 to "seek God's mind" and assist in the ministry at Elim Tabernacle. He married a graduate of the Bible school, Ora Blanchard, and filled several pastorates in upstate New York before moving to Missouri, where he headed the denomination's mushrooming missionary efforts until 1959.

Both Flower and Perkin sought ties with established missionary agencies. Such associations were vivid reminders of the continuing struggle for identity. Although many local preachers with only the most rudimentary education stirred their congregations with a Pentecostal version of separatist fundamentalist diatribe, at another level the Assemblies of God included those who recognized the advantages of association, formal and informal, with non-Pentecostals. The conviction that Pentecostalism should energize and unify the Christian world resurfaced occasionally, but it remained troubling. Assemblies of God leaders generally seemed convinced that they needed to work on their own, writing their own textbooks, publishing their own devotional materials, and providing their own tracts. Missionary reports often conveyed the impression that Assemblies of God missionaries were the only missionaries in areas that had had a large missionary population for decades. But missionary work tended, in the end, to promote a degree of ecumenism abroad that eluded the sending churches. Before long, Perkin recognized that the Assemblies of God could best use its resources by concentrating them in areas that lacked an evangelical witness rather than by attempting to "Pentecostalize" existing Christian communions abroad.

Far more women than men served as Assemblies of God missionaries before World War II. This was true of American foreign missions in general. In 1931 Perkin cited the findings of "competent authorities" who had surveyed Assemblies of God missions and advised him that "the work of the General Council of the Assemblies of God depends too much on women workers." Noting gratitude to the women who "filled the gap" (implying that men were rejecting their responsibility and that women were temporarily supplying the need), he encouraged men and married couples to seek missionary appointment.[50]

Concerns voiced during the prosperous twenties continued to be heard during the depressed thirties; missionary finances would be more than adequate if every member contributed. In 1933 Perkin estimated that five cents per member per week would "restore our missionary giving to its highest level of the past."[51] Six cents would enable "advanced missionary effort." Yet missionary funds came from a mere 30 percent of adherents; the rest gave "almost nothing."

Such statistics changed little. Nor did the basic question was the Assemblies of God essentially an evangelistic agency, rooted in a distinctive understanding of an "enduement with power for service?" Far fewer than half of the affiliated congregations seemed to agree. The statistics revealed a fundamental disagreement among adherents about the practical meaning of Spirit baptism. The growing presence of second- and third-generation Assemblies of God adherents compounded the problem. Among this constituency, at least, a Pentecostal was no longer necessarily one who had had an experience, but rather one who believed specific doctrines.

Waning restorationism and muted apocalypticism in the second generation both indicated and contributed to a changing perception of culture. As right belief replaced right experience in marking a Pentecostal, Assemblies of God adherents sensed more affinity with fundamentalists.

The Assemblies of God and Fundamentalism

Until the 1940s the Assemblies of God, like other Pentecostal denominations, was relatively isolated from other Christian groups. In general, its adherents rejected institutional affiliation and practical cooperation with non-Pentecostals. For that matter, Pentecostals had little contact with one another. Several factors made distance from others necessary and attractive.

First, early Pentecostals ardently believed that they had a more accurate perception of New Testament Christianity than others. They spurned "cold," "dead" churches and accused them of ignoring the Holy Spirit. Second, an important ingredient in the early Pentecostal psyche had been the cultivation of a sense of alienation from the culture. Sermons, songs, and published admonitions reminded Pentecostals that they lived in perpetual spiritual conflict. The enemy, real or imagined, played an important role in shaping their identity. If physical persecution waned, spiritual conflict continued. And nowhere was that conflict more intense than with "unbelievers" in the church. Modernists, fundamentalists, holiness advocates, and ordinary members of traditional churches had many dissimilarities, but they all rejected the Pentecostal message. At any given time one or all of them fulfilled the role of enemies against whom Pentecostals flexed their spiritual muscles. Third, the splintering of Pentecostalism complicated the picture, highlighting internal disarray. In its opposition to institutional authority, Pentecostalism had nurtured a strong individualism; in its appeal to the authority of the Holy Spirit as Revealer and Illuminator, it had assured the persistence of new insights that often shattered old loyalties and spawned new sects.

In spite of frequent claims that Pentecostals were forced by the ill will of others to form their own denominations, clearly early Pentecostals found that rejection by other religious groups confirmed for them the truth of their message. Isolation was not entirely imposed on them: it was carefully cultivated and served an important social function.

Before World War II, the Assemblies of God was by far the largest and most widely dispersed Pentecostal denomination, and few of its leaders believed that cooperative efforts could strengthen their movement and extend their influence in the culture. Some Assemblies of God ministers nonetheless cooperated extensively with non-Pentecostals in local evangelistic efforts. The causes espoused by fundamentalists seemed to coincide in meaningful ways with Assemblies of God denominational interests and to offer as well an opportunity for declaring Pentecostal sympathies with doctrinal "fundamentals."

The question of whether they were fundamentalists did not preoccupy early Assemblies of God leaders; they simply assumed they were. It had significant implications, however, for some cherished Pentecostal assumptions as well as for non-Pentecostal definitions of *fundamentalist* and *evangelical.* Were Pentecostal distinctives optional or did they constitute an essential part of Christian experience? Many Pentecostals maintained that Pentecostal doctrines were essential to full Christian experience, some held that tongues speech was necessary for salvation, and many more believed Spirit baptism a prerequisite for the rapture. Promoters of cooperation with others seemed to say that Pentecostal views were optional benefits, not essential to salvation. For their part, could fundamentalists properly acknowledge those who upheld the importance of experiences the dispensationalist hermeneutic dismissed?

Assemblies of God adherents wavered as well on the subject of dispensationalism. The *Pentecostal Evangel* usually promoted the Scofield Reference Bible, although occasionally the executives voted to exclude advertisements for this popular dispensationalist Bible from Gospel Publishing House materials. Assemblies of God adherents in fact affirmed most of Scofield's system but claimed their dispensationalism was "dispensationalism with a difference": the Pentecostal version of the latter rain supported end-times events that popular fundamentalist dispensationalism relegated to the apostolic age.

Pentecostals did not seek—nor were they offered—affiliation in the voluntary associations through which fundamentalists often operated. Confrontations with modernists honed fundamentalists' sensitivity to "error" and made toleration of Pentecostal aberrations unlikely. Assemblies of God adherents nonetheless identified with fundamentalist views on the verbal inspiration of Scripture and other "fundamentals" and shared their prophetic fascination for current events.

In 1928 the Assemblies of God found itself (with other Pentecostals and with modernism) the target of the World's Christian Fundamentals Association, one of the agencies through which fundamentalists offered one another support. As the resolution by the association stated: "Be it Resolved, That this convention go on record as unreservedly opposed to

Modern Pentecostalism, including the speaking in unknown tongues, and
the fanatical healing known as general healing in the atonement, and the
perpetuation of the miraculous sign-healing of Jesus and His apostles,
wherein they claim the only reason the church cannot perform these miracles is because of unbelief."[52]

Pentecostal Evangel editor Stanley Frodsham reported this action in the
paper under the heading "Disfellowshipped!" Claiming that the resolution "disfellowshipped a great company of us who believe in all the fundamentals of the faith as much as they themselves do," Frodsham ex-
horted Assemblies of God adherents to "love these Fundamentalists."[53]
"We are Fundamentalists to a man," the *Evangel* had insisted earlier.
Closer analysis of the fundamentalist resolution yields an interesting
point. The convention adopted all resolutions unanimously except the
one on the tongues' movement. William Bell Riley, the association's
president, spoke for just four short of a majority when he argued that the
association should not react to the tongues' movement at all since adherents of the movement did not oppose the inspiration of Scripture, the
deity of Christ, or other points in the association's profession. In Riley's
view, fundamentalists had sufficient work before them: opposing infi-
delity, not "chasing down and bringing to judgment fanatics."[54]

Frodsham's list of the "fundamentals" to which Assemblies of God adherents subscribed coincided with similar lists authored by fundamentalists. Further, Assemblies of God adherents shared the antipathy toward
modernism that motivated fundamentalists. Assemblies of God leaders by
the thirties inclined toward the view that Pentecostals were essentially
fundamentalists energized by an experience called the baptism with the
Holy Spirit. Like fundamentalists, they supported diverse ministries
headed by charismatic individuals: Charles Fuller and the "Old-Fashioned
Revival Hour"; Walter Maier and the "Lutheran Hour"; and Uldine
Utley, Gerald Winrod, and J. Elwin Wright and the New England Fellowship. This direction signaled an emerging inclination to acknowledge
that while all Christians should experience "Pentecostal fullness," that
"fullness" was not essential to the faith. While the Assemblies of God
affirmed the power of the apostolic faith in the present age, as civility
moderated its earlier exclusivism, it acknowledged affinities with those
who disagreed on issues once deemed critical. Those who attempted to
locate the Assemblies of God in a broader context did not fully succeed
either within or outside the denomination in the thirties. Their quest,
however, accelerated the move away from other segments of American
Pentecostalism and assured the responsiveness of this fast-growing denomination to overtures from non-Pentecostals in the future.

NOTES

1. Robert Mapes Anderson provides a provocative discussion of Pentecostals and society in *Vision of the Disinherited: The Making of American Pentecostalism* (New York: Oxford University Press, 1979), 195–222.

2. Six stanzas of this old hymn were included as number 121 in *The Best of All,* a hymnal used widely in early Assemblies of God congregations.

3. *Best of All,* no. 5.

4. Lelia Morris, "On the Firing Line," *Best of All,* no. 3.

5. See especially Mrs. Clarence Shreffler's letter, published on 21 Apr. 1917, 4; "The Great War and the Speedy Return of Our Lord: Light on the Present Crisis," *Weekly Evangel,* 10 Apr. 1917, 3. The same issue cited H. Grattan Guinness, *Light for the Last Days* (London: Hodder and Stoughton, 1893), to the effect that those living in 1917 would "have reached one of the most important, perhaps the most momentous of these terminal years of crisis." For Washington's vision, see the *Weekly Evangel,* 25 Mar. 1916, 5, 8, 9.

6. The "vision" was printed in tract form, entitled "General Washington's Vision," and circulated by the Christian Workers' Union in Framingham, Mass.

7. *Weekly Evangel,* 22 Feb. 1916, 6. As the war ended without the anticipated climax of Christ's return, Bell and Frodsham signed an appeal issued through the *Christian Evangel* for readers to join in two days of prayer (3 and 4 Nov. 1918) to "invite Jesus, our heavenly Bridegroom, to return." Still convinced that "it was time" for Jesus to come, the two encouraged what was probably the last official effort in the Assemblies of God to make the conviction that many Pentecostals had shared a reality.

8. *Christian Evangel,* 12 Dec. 1914, 1.

9. William B. McCafferty, "Shall Christians Go to War?" *Christian Evangel,* 16 Jan. 1915, 1.

10. "Present Day Conditions," *Christian Evangel,* 5 June 1915, 1; "The European War," *Christian Evangel,* 10 July 1915, 1; "What Will the Harvest Be?" 7 Aug. 1915, 1, 2. For a thorough consideration of Bartleman's views on war and other social issues, see Cecil M. Robeck's introduction to Frank Bartleman, *Witness to Pentecost* (New York: Garland Publishing, 1985).

11. Other Pentecostals shared Bartleman's conviction that the war was economically motivated. The 29 Apr. 1916 issue of the *Weekly Evangel* published a poem by George T. Sisler entitled "War Profits:"

> So you to whom people have granted great power
> Make boast of the work you have done,
> In hurling poor men at other men's throats,
> With a longing to kill and to burn?
> Know ye not that these men you have fired with hate,
> With a hunger and thirst for strife
> Will at last stand with you there where all shall bow down
> To a mighty omnipotent Christ?

Then what doth it profit? this question so old,
Yet with meaning and force still new
Is asked of you now as you stand with the power
And the wealth you have gained about you.
When you know that those men—filled with anger and hate—
Whom you spurred on with your greed and lust,
Must with you finally stand at the judgment bar
And be judged by a God who is just?

12. Frank Bartleman, "War and the Christian," 4, Assemblies of God Archives, Springfield, Mo. (hereafter AGA).

13. Ibid.

14. Ibid.

15. Stanley Frodsham, "Our Heavenly Citizenship," *Weekly Evangel*, 11 Sept. 1915, 3. See also Howard N. Kenyon, "A Social History of the Assemblies of God: Race Relations, Women and Ministry, and Attitudes toward War" (Ph.D. diss., Baylor University, 1987).

16. It is significant that the Booth-Clibborns and Bartleman chose during the war to side with oneness Pentecostals, among whom the radical restorationist vision of the early movement survived longer.

17. Samuel H. Booth-Clibborn, *Should a Christian Fight?* (Swengal, Pa.: Bible Truth Depot, n.d.), 39.

18. Ibid., 38.

19. Ibid., 39–40; see also Samuel H. Booth-Clibborn, "The Christian and War," *Weekly Evangel*, 28 Apr. 1917, 5; 19 May 1917, 4, 5.

20. *Weekly Evangel*, 21 Apr. 1917, 2.

21. *Weekly Evangel*, 28 Apr. 1917, 7.

22. *Weekly Evangel*, 25 Mar. 1916, 5, 8, 9.

23. Frank Bartleman, "In the Last Days," *Word and Work*, Sept. 1916, 393.

24. *Weekly Evangel*, 4 Aug. 1917, 6, 7.

25. Ibid.

26. "The Pentecostal Movement and the Conscription Law," *Weekly Evangel*, 4 Aug. 1917, 6, 7.

27. Roger Robins, "Attitudes toward War and Peace in the Assemblies of God," unpublished ms., 31, AGA. See also Jay Beaman, "Pentecostal Pacifism: The Origin, Development, and Rejection of Pacific Belief among Pentecostals" (M.Div. Thesis, North American Baptist Seminary, 1982); Murray Dempster, "Reassessing the Moral Rhetoric of Early American Pentecostal Pacifism," *Crux* 26 (Mar. 1990): 23–36.

28. William I. Evans File, AGA.

29. General Council Minutes, 1917, 18, AGA.

30. Dispensationalists divided along similar lines, with a small faction, dominated by Plymouth Brethren views, opting for pacifism. See Ernest R. Sandeen, *The Roots of Fundamentalism* (Chicago: University of Chicago Press, 1970). Assemblies of God publications carried articles by non-Pentecostal prophecy teach-

ers who shared their sense of the eschatological import of the war. See, for example, C. I. Scofield, "The War in the Light of Prophecy," *Weekly Evangel,* 28 Oct. 1916, 6, 7; citation from H. Grattan Guinness in "Signs in the Heavens Above," *Weekly Evangel,* 10 Apr. 1917, 3; Mrs. Reader Harris, "Nearing the End of the Pentecostal Age," *Weekly Evangel,* 15 July 1916, 7, 9.

31. "Questions and Answers," *Weekly Evangel,* 19 Oct. 1918, 5.

32. In his retirement, Ernest Williams, reflecting on the contrast in Assemblies of God attitudes toward the two world wars, expressed this sentiment to the author in an interview in Springfield, Mo., 18 June 1976.

33. Anderson, *Vision of the Disinherited,* 222.

34. R. Laurence Moore, *Religious Outsiders and the Making of Americans* (New York: Oxford University Press, 1986), 143.

35. For a look at Bible colleges that includes consideration of early Assemblies of God schools, see Virginia Lieson Brereton, *Training God's Army: The American Bible School, 1880–1940* (Bloomington: Indiana University Press, 1990).

36. General Council Minutes, 1929, 83, AGA.

37. General Council Minutes, 1937, 105, AGA.

38. General Council Minutes, 1939, 61–62, AGA.

39. Proposed amendment to resolution "Regarding Worldliness," General Presbytery Minutes, 1935, copy in author's possession.

40. General Council Minutes, 1919, 11, AGA.

41. Ibid.

42. Ibid.

43. Quoted in Noel Perkin, "Our First Five Years," *Pentecostal Evangel,* 25 Oct. 1964, 14.

44. Quoted in Noel Perkin, "Highlights of the 20s (1920–24)," *Pentecostal Evangel,* 29 Nov. 1964, 17.

45. Ibid., 18.

46. Ibid.

47. General Council Minutes, 1925, 47, AGA.

48. Pentecostals shared this sense of impending cataclysm with fundamentalists. Rooted largely in their Darbyite dispensationalism, it discounted the positive accomplishments of the era (which liberals hailed as progress) and proclaimed imminent judgment.

49. See, for example, Lamin Sanneh, "Christian Missions and the Western Guilt Complex," *Christian Century,* 8 Apr. 1987, 330–34.

50. General Council Minutes, 1931, 58, AGA.

51. General Council Minutes, 1933, 59, AGA.

52. "Resolutions and Reports," *Christian Fundamentalist* 1 (June 1928): 9.

53. *Pentecostal Evangel,* 18 Aug. 1928, 7.

54. "Resolutions and Reports," *Christian Fundamentalist* 1 (June 1928): 6.

7

Evangelism and Women's Roles, 1918–40

T HE ABOVE WORDS offer one simple explanation for Assemblies of God growth: everyone was summoned to evangelize. Cultural realities predisposed some to accept the announcement of restoration. The most effective church extension occurred at the grass-roots level, assisted by swelling ranks of people who professed to be specially called and devoted their full time to the task. From 1918 both the ministerial and the missionary lists increased regularly. By 1925 there were 1,155 credentialed ministers in the United States and 235 missionaries represented the constituency abroad. By 1941 4,159 ministers, including 394 missionaries, worked among a growing worldwide membership; in 1991 over 11,000 ministers and more than 1,600 missionaries whose efforts were complemented by thousands of national workers abroad served an international constituency approaching 23 million, with about 2.2 million in the United States.

While Pentecostals generally joined the chorus of criticism of shifting cultural standards in the 1920s, they nonetheless imbibed much of the fast-paced spirit that marked the prosperous decade. In a celebrity-driven culture, they celebrated the achievements of their own list of superstars—evangelists such as Aimee Semple McPherson and Charles Price. Camp meetings, where emotional displays rivaled those of the nineteenth century, were an important gathering place for the faithful. Taking such popular figures as Billy Sunday for their example, Pentecostal preachers vigorously denounced modernity, especially as manifested in bewildering new patterns of social behavior. Yet their determination to spread their message influenced them to appropriate the most modern technology to serve avowedly antimodern ends. Pragmatists first and last, they seemed willing to do what was necessary to achieve their goals. The best known and most controversial Pentecostal preacher of the period, Aimee Semple McPherson, was heralded by the secular press as a consummate entertainer whose career was made possible by precisely those modern social realities most Pentecostals thought they rejected.

The notoriety often attached to Aimee Semple McPherson's name came later. When she affiliated with the Assemblies of God in 1919, the twenty-nine-year-old evangelist had already earned a reputation as an innovative, energetic, effective preacher. Born Aimee Kennedy in Ontario, Canada, 9 October 1890, McPherson embraced Pentecostalism in 1907 and married the evangelist, Robert James Semple, who had converted her. After she was ordained at the North Avenue Mission in Chicago, the two sailed as missionaries to China. Three months after their arrival Robert died in Hong Kong; the next month (September 1910), their daughter, Roberta, was born. Early in 1911 Aimee returned to the United States; on 28 February 1912 she married Harold McPherson. A son, Rolf, was born to them in March 1913.

Restless in the confines of her marriage and home, McPherson rediscovered her call to preach. In 1915 she left her husband, taking her children to her father's home in Ingersoll, Ontario. That year she gradually entered the world of itinerant evangelism. When her husband joined her and promised to assist her ministry, her future seemed promising. From 1916 to 1918 the McPhersons traveled up and down the East Coast, conducting huge tent crusades in which she preached the full gospel and practiced faith healing. Everywhere she went tumult followed. Dramatic and unpredictable, she proved exceptionally adept at transfixing her audiences as she recounted a simple, unsophisticated gospel message. When asked about her doctrine during her meetings in Philadelphia in 1918, she quipped: "We have no doctrine. We believe in real repentance."[1] While the content of her preaching was ordinary, however, her delivery was not. Crowds thronged to hear her emotion-packed illustrated sermons; they also saw purported spiritual gifts in operation. In 1917 McPherson began to publish *Bridal Call,* a monthly magazine she edited both to communicate her message and to report events in her meetings. From Maine to Florida she gained a public hearing for Pentecostalism, and wherever she went she strengthened the visibility and the prospects of struggling Pentecostal missions.

In 1918 McPherson, separated from her husband (they would divorce in 1921), took her two children and her mother on a transcontinental preaching tour that ended in Los Angeles. During the next five years she crisscrossed the United States eight times, conducting about forty revival crusades in tents, theaters, and municipal auditoriums in large cities such as Philadelphia, Washington, D.C., St. Louis, and Denver.[2] Her Denver meetings, in which some twelve thousand people crammed the Coliseum nightly for a month, were publicized across the nation. Wherever she went, her sensational preaching and dramatic results won her acclaim and notoriety. In 1920 she preached to the Assemblies of God General Council. (The first, and one of only three women, ever to have done so.) A 1922 visit to Australia lent an international flavor to her endeavors.[3]

By the time she opened her permanent headquarters, Angelus Temple, in Los Angeles on 1 January 1923, McPherson had established a broad support base. Although she received considerable help from other Pentecostals, her own converts provided the principal funds and the incentive for constructing her commodious church. Her Los Angeles audiences, consisting primarily of recent arrivals from the Midwest, regularly filled her 5,300-seat auditorium to capacity long before scheduled services began. She never advertised meetings at Angelus Temple: the facility could not have accommodated the crowds. She filled a grueling schedule, with nightly meetings, including regular healing services, Thursday night baptismal services, prayer gatherings, youth outreaches, and three preaching services every Sunday. She boasted that the lights never went out at Angelus Temple.

Meanwhile, however, this popular, flamboyant evangelist discovered growing hesitations about her relationship with the Assemblies of God. Lurking in the background was uneasiness about ministering women; her success forced some to confront their reservations about women in the pulpit. Objections by Assemblies of God leaders to her construction of Angelus Temple (allegedly diverting funds that could have been better employed among the denomination's 234 "starving" missionaries) were part of a more general uneasiness. McPherson courted and thrived on publicity that eluded most other Pentecostals. Heralded as one who provided "the best show of all" in a city renowned for its show business, McPherson gave transplanted, entertainment-starved, working-class people a rich sampling of theatrical skill. At a time when Pentecostals shunned theaters, McPherson offered an appealing substitute. When she defended her actions to Assemblies of God executives in 1922, she asserted: "Assemblies have been built up and your work established more than I believe you realize. All this adding not only numerically and spiritually but financially for the work at home and in foreign fields."[4]

By 1922, however, the dimensions of McPherson's work and the long-held views of some, especially in the Southern California District, about appropriate roles for women combined to accelerate her withdrawal from the Assemblies of God. In January 1922 she returned her ministerial credentials. Over the next decade McPherson's troubled private life occasioned relief that she had withdrawn when she had. Divorced from Harold McPherson in 1921, she was accused of an affair with an employee in 1926. Banner headlines in the nation's most respected newspapers tracked her alleged kidnapping in 1926, a scenario many believed she concocted to cover her affair. In 1931, despite long-held views against divorce and remarriage, she married David Hutton. They divorced the next year, beset by rumors and charges brought against Hutton for breach of promise. Financial problems dogged McPherson too, when she briefly contracted with producers and realtors for several ill-fated projects.

McPherson did not merely serve as a focus around which contention swirled, however. In addition to the support her early campaigns lent to local Pentecostal congregations, her ministry in the 1920s gave the Assemblies of God some of its most talented young ministers. McPherson's tumultuous campaign, using a seven-thousand-seat tent provided by San Jose's First Baptist Church in 1922, is a case in point. Invited by the congregation's pastor, D. E. Towner, as part of a ploy to attract crowds and raise needed finances, McPherson managed to convert Towner and then to conduct a campaign that transformed not only his congregation but the lives of thousands who packed the tent erected to accommodate the masses. Among those who "got the hallelujahs" was the staid Oxford-educated pastor of Lodi's prosperous First Congregational Church, Charles Price. From 1922, when he launched a career in independent healing evangelism, Price enjoyed enormous growing popularity in the Assemblies of God. A featured speaker at district conventions and camp meetings, Price published a monthly paper, *Golden Grain,* and influenced thousands of Assemblies of God adherents to anticipate increasingly intense and "powerful" evidences of ongoing restoration. Price's personal life, however, did not thrive as his public career did. Little is known of his wife, who played no active role in her husband's career. They divorced in the late 1920s and she remarried. The Price evangelistic team usually included his daughters and his pianist, with whom it was several times alleged Price was having an affair.[5]

While much of what national visibility Pentecostalism achieved in the twenties focused on McPherson, numerous evangelists and pastors emerged within the Assemblies of God who would deeply influence local constituencies. At the popular level, after McPherson, Raymond T. Richey undoubtedly had the strongest national support. Born in Illinois on 4 September 1893, Richey had been reared in a home charged with healing and restorationist expectations. After his father, Eli, claimed healing from cancer, he moved his family from their Illinois farm to Dowie's utopia in nearby Zion. Raymond later left for Texas, where he claimed healing of an acute eye disease and was converted in 1911.

He began preaching at the Gospel Tabernacle in Houston, Texas, as an assistant to his father, who had recently arrived to mobilize a dwindling membership.[6] Four of Eli's eight children helped him turn things around. During World War I, Raymond branched out to create the United Prayer and Workers' League, a voluntary association to distribute literature to service members and coordinate their activities. Disqualified from military service because of poor health, by the end of the war he was desperately ill with tuberculosis. In September 1919 he announced his second healing and launched a career in healing evangelism.

It began inauspiciously in Hattiesburg, Mississippi, when a scheduled evangelist, Warren Collins, failed to arrive. Richey filled his commitments, and on the third night he announced he would pray for the sick. Several claimed healings, the next day's newspaper carried the story, and the hall was crammed nightly for the next two weeks.[7] As his popularity grew, Richey's audiences filled churches, tents, civic auditoriums, and tabernacles around the country. His marriage to a divorced woman forced his withdrawal from the Assemblies of God in 1921, but his efforts continued to mushroom. Undoubtedly his success influenced the course of later events. Assemblies of God leaders accepted Richey's wife's application for recognition of her first marriage as annulled, clearing the way for Richey's reinstatement. By the midthirties he was back in the denomination, active not only in nationwide evangelism but also in a thriving Houston church, Evangelistic Tabernacle, and in Southern Bible School, which he founded in the church.[8]

A popular new face on the denomination's evangelistic circuit in the thirties was Edith Mae Pennington. Born Edith Patterson in Pine Bluff, Arkansas, she had won a national beauty contest in 1921. She promptly gave up teaching school and accepted an offer to tour the country. She hired a business manager, J. B. Pennington, and accepted engagements in cities around the nation, finally arriving in Hollywood, where she attempted unsuccessfully to launch a career in acting. She married Pennington and moved eventually to Oklahoma City.

There in 1925 she noticed a Pentecostal Holiness church with a large sign proclaiming "Jesus Saves." The following Sunday she and her husband began attending services in the small, white, frame building. After several weeks she had an emotional conversion experience as a result of which, she insisted, she was "delivered" from desires to wear jewelry and attend theaters. The couple moved to Birmingham, Alabama, where Pennington entered the ministry.

In 1928, back in her native Pine Bluff, Arkansas, she became the assistant pastor of a newly formed Assemblies of God congregation. Her national evangelistic efforts began in 1930. She quickly discovered that

Pentecostals—who preached lengthy sermons about the sinfulness of movies, theater attendance, beauty contests, contemporary fashions, and jewelry—thrilled to her emotion-packed sermons alleging the emptiness of "worldly" living. They readily responded to invitations to hear one who had actually tasted a life-style they disavowed. Wherever she went, she was billed as a "beauty queen" and a "former actress" rather than simply as a preacher. Subtle psychological factors were clearly at work; perhaps relinquishing the stage for the pulpit did not involve much reorientation. And wherever she traveled, crowds thronged to hear her and Assemblies of God adherents claimed renewal. Pennington's husband did not share her enthusiasm for either the evangelistic circuit or, later, the pastorate. They divorced early in the 1930s.[9]

Such people preached a simple message that promised immediate positive results, and in the depression years, they rallied Assemblies of God adherents to spread their message of hope amid social despair. Amid cultural upheaval, they persuaded people of the validity of the familiar "old time religion," complete with camp meetings, brush arbors, and revival tabernacles. Despite oft-repeated opposition to divorce and remarriage, Assemblies of God constituents tolerated the vagaries of the people whose preaching touched their emotions and brightened their lives. They seemed willing to excuse flaws or rationalize behavior, to give the benefit of the doubt, despite the harsh, unyielding language in which their leaders denounced sin.

Evangelism and increasingly focused home missions programs helped extend Assemblies of God congregations into every state. The growth in numbers of adherents, workers, and missionaries suggests only part of the story, however. In many places, Assemblies of God adherents became accustomed to the petty hostility of other Christians who either misunderstood them or who perhaps understood Pentecostals better than Pentecostals understood themselves.

Some Pentecostals also looked askance at the growth and institutionalization in the Assemblies of God. The denomination, wrote John G. Lake, one of its founders, was commendably efficient, but it was most emphatically not Pentecostal: "Every little man is doing the best he can on a big job." But the movement had "drifted clear away from a true scriptural Pentecost ideal"; the Assemblies of God was "becoming more and more a little bigoted denomination." "The spirit of denominationalism in the Assemblies of God," Lake lamented, "is probably narrower than even in the old churches from which Pentecostals have been escaping . . . so that as a power to bless mankind . . . it does not seem to me they are worth considering."[10]

Reports of grass-roots renewal persisted side by side with such expressions of concern about declension. By 1941 a movement that had thrived on the preaching of itinerant evangelists such as Richey, Price, and Pennington lamented the evident "dying interest" in evangelism. Richey and Pennington settled into pastorates; McPherson and Price died in the mid-forties and no new recruits filled the vacancies.[11] A transformation was, in fact, in process, but it would be years before its full implications would become apparent.[12]

In later years, adherents would recall the twenties and thirties as the "good old days" when emotion-charged testimonies and unchecked shouts of praise contributed to ecstatic services and sustained fervor. Separation from the world was perhaps less conspicuous than participants in that era would later recall, for in eschewing divorce, drinking, smoking, contemporary fashions, mixed bathing, makeup, or bobbed hair, Assemblies of God adherents affirmed a life-style shared by millions of other American Protestants. Yet their frequent references to things spiritual did not preclude the devising of ways to embrace some of the new things their culture offered. Hesitantly but certainly, they admitted that movies could be used for their own ends; that radio offered a medium for evangelism (Aimee Semple McPherson began broadcasting over one of the nation's first church-owned radio stations, KFSG, in Los Angeles in 1924); in short, that the world's new technology had much for them to appropriate.

In 1929 the Assemblies of God elected Ernest Williams to lead the denomination. For the next twenty years he presided over its most rapid growth and its most harmonious era. A California native, Williams had embraced Pentecostalism and received his ministerial credentials at the hallowed Azusa Street Mission. Williams brought to the headquarters in Springfield a reputation for integrity and spirituality that reassured those confused by the denomination's changing identity.

During Williams's tenure, formalized Christian education programs revealed changing perceptions of restoration. Slowly but surely, hesitations about the formalization of church training in Sunday schools and the utilization of such helps as quarterlies and visual aids gave way to their use. Gospel Publishing House expanded its line of materials graded for small children; growing interest in vacation Bible schools resulted by 1941 in the creation of a three-year cycle of materials suitable for this outreach.

The growing interest in Sunday schools (as well as in other aspects of Christian education) resulted in part from the emergence of a forceful advocate, Ralph Riggs. Born 16 June 1895 in Coal Creek, Tennessee, Riggs had spent most of his boyhood in Meridian, Mississippi. After attending the Rochester Bible Training School in Rochester, New York, Riggs served as a pastor in Syracuse. In 1920 he sailed for South Africa as a missionary. There he married Lillian Merian, a missionary already in the field. Six years later they returned to the States, and in 1928 they moved to Springfield. Riggs's book, *A Successful Sunday School,* together with another by Myer Pearlman (one of the denomination's best-known Bible teachers) entitled *Successful Sunday School Teaching,* greatly facilitated the Assemblies of God Sunday school efforts by establishing goals and training workers. [13]

In part because of its concerted efforts, in part because its message appealed directly to basic human needs for happiness, confidence, and companionship in troubled times, the Assemblies of God grew rapidly during the depression. The ministerial roll swelled by 285 percent, the number of churches increased 321 percent, and membership gained 290 percent between 1927 and 1941. At least 2,080 Sunday schools were started between 1937 and 1939 alone. [14]

The prominence of women in the growing membership as well as the visibility of female evangelists and Sunday School workers made the subject of women in ministry cogent in the Assemblies of God during the thirties. In 1935 the Assemblies of God acted to define women's ministry sphere.

The status of women had been ambiguous throughout the brief American Pentecostal past. On the one hand, the broader context in which the Pentecostal movement thrived tended to support female gospel workers. Anti-denominationalism, free church polity, emphases on the Holy Spirit and the end times, and a preference for voluntary associations nurtured many forms of women's public witness. On the other hand, however, were an emphasis on the biblical model and the preferences of dominant Pentecostal male leaders, several of whom had backgrounds in traditions that had long silenced women.

> As the Holy Ghost takes sway and control, women rise in place, position and power. . . . In these days of promise, these "latter days," there is an overturning, an awakening, an enlargement of vision. Woman under the anointing and imbuing of the Holy Ghost is to be a great factor in the . . . work of these latter days. . . . Every woman should receive and honor the Holy Ghost, as He is the Great Emancipator, and the blessed Equalizer, and as He controls, He brings in the equality of the sexes, the brotherhood of man, the sisterhood of woman, the unity of the race, His own Motherhood, the brotherhood of Jesus, and the Fatherhood of God. [15]

These words by Stephen Merritt, a wealthy turn-of-the-century New York City undertaker who traveled widely to address gatherings of believers yearning for the "higher Christian life," were reprinted in 1916 in the

Midnight Cry, a magazine published by a growing Assemblies of God congregation in midtown Manhattan. They capture the sentiments of many
turn-of-the-century evangelicals and the promise some Pentecostal
women thought their movement offered them.

Those Pentecostal women who felt called to forms of ministry that
involved "priestly functions," however, soon clashed with the strong reservations prominent Pentecostal leaders had expressed about the equality
of the sexes in ministry at least since the Azusa Street days in 1906. Even
as they celebrated women's calling, these men, including Azusa Street
leader William Seymour, narrowed their sphere:

> Before Pentecost, the woman could only go into the "court of the
> women," and not into the inner court. The anointing oil was never
> poured on a woman's head but only on the heads of kings, prophets
> and priests. But when our Lord poured out Pentecost, He brought
> all those faithful women with the other disciples. . . . All the
> women received the . . . oil of the Holy Ghost and were able to
> preach the same as men. . . . The woman is the weaker vessel and
> represents the tenderness of Christ, while the man represents the
> firmness of Christ. They both were coworkers in Eden and both fell
> into sin; so they both have to come together and work in the Gos-
> pel. No woman that has the Spirit of Jesus wants to usurp authority
> over the man. The more God uses you in the Spirit, the more
> humbled and meek and tender you are and the more filled with the
> blessed Holy Spirit.[16]

Encouraging women "in their work" also had a self-serving dimension
for men: "encourage the woman . . . and God will honor and bless us as
never before."[17] Decidedly more restrictive than Seymour's blend of ad-
mission and restriction were the opinions of some who more directly participated in forming the Assemblies of God.

Warren Fay Carothers, a Methodist-turned-Pentecostal who led the
Apostolic Faith Movement in Texas and served briefly as an Assemblies
of God executive, demonstrated how the calling to participate in the
Holy Spirit–prompted end-times restoration of New Testament Christianity could limit women's utterance. In a book on church government
published in 1909, Carothers introduced his consideration of women's
place in the church with nine New Testament verses that instructed
women to silence and submission. He then alleged that man's prerogative
was rooted in creation: "Man is especially made in the image and likeness
of God, and is therefore by right the sovereign of all creation. It is man's
prerogative to rule in all things."[18] God had made a distinction between
male and female spheres that to Carothers's mind was best preserved "in

the chivalrous Southland." "Nothing," he insisted, "is more heavenly than the sincere observance of this distinction . . . and nothing more of a monstrosity than modern efforts to obliterate and disregard the differences between the sexes."[19]

Pondering the widely advocated right of women to prophesy, Carothers insisted that prophecy properly meant only "preaching under direct inspiration from the Holy Spirit." Such preaching, he noted, did not involve the intellect. Persons functioned simply as channels, and in the absence of intellectual engagement, women exercised no authority while prophesying. Because of this, prophecy was appropriate for anyone, even children.[20] And if women seemed "anointed," the place to "test their call" was not at the anointing but in the Scriptures, which forbade women to instruct men.

Pentecostal women sometimes agreed—at least in theory. The five sisters who ran a congeries of ministries in Rochester, New York, known collectively as Elim identified their efforts with the Pentecostal movement in 1907 and soon decided to construct a tabernacle to house their growing congregation. Curiously, however, the five—who had reputations as "vessels" through whom the Holy Spirit spoke—opposed women pastors. They dealt with their uneasiness in a typical Pentecostal fashion. First, they prayed for a male pastor. When no satisfactory male presented himself, they claimed divine instruction to proceed without a pastor. Invoking the Holy Spirit as pastor, they conducted preaching and prayer services. They organized a male board of deacons to officiate at communion. Confining themselves to "anointed utterance" in the services, they proceeded until they secured a male pastor. The implication for the students at their Bible institute, many of whom affiliated with the Assemblies of God, was clear: local congregations needed male leadership for all but prophetic functions. Outside the church, however, these women taught, edited, evangelized, and administrated. Those were long-established, appropriate "women's spheres."

Assemblies of God members, male and female, who objected to women in leadership asserted that they did not belittle women. One-time Southern Baptist Eudorus N. Bell, for example, insisted that God had chosen not to burden women with the heavy responsibilities of leadership. He had given them a higher calling. Bell often used the pages of the *Pentecostal Evangel* to instruct the constituency about appropriate restrictions on women. Given the variety of circumstances that encouraged willing females—ranging from claims of spiritual authority to a shortage of workers to the large plurality of women in the movement—Bell occasionally found it necessary to justify the status quo.

If God "granted women the privilege . . . in His sovereignty," if He "set His seal" on her leadership by "granting her souls," and if she had the ability to "build up the assembly in the Lord and in peace," how then could "the brethren" oppose her temporary service? Even given charismatic enduement, however, Bell simply could not conceive of a woman pastor on more than a supply basis. Neither "female rights" nor "New Testament command or example" established her place as pastor. Rather, in the absence of men, women might temporarily "fill in." But "if she is wise," he continued, "she will push the man." The right person for congregational and administrative leadership, every time, was a man: after all, God had "specially designed" the ministry for "strong shoulders." Women might substitute for men who "failed God." In such cases, they were God's "second best," and among people constantly enjoined to know and experience "God's best," the "second best" had little appeal. To Bell, Paul's instructions seemed straightforward: in response to a reader's question, Bell insisted Paul "meant what he said. . . . The squabbles in the church, the disputing and disorder, men should handle it."[21]

The Assemblies of God set its course with the statement in 1914 that Gal. 3:28 ("In Christ there is neither male nor female"), a passage often used in support of ministering women, meant rather that "in the matter of salvation, the lines of sex are blotted out." Citing 1 Tim. 2, it affirmed that women were to be in subjection to men, but it acknowledged their call to prophesy and to be "helpers in the Gospel."[22] Women were licensed as evangelists but not as pastors and were unqualified to receive much-coveted clergy discounts on the railroads. One issue of the *Evangel* instructed "the brethren" to submit applications for railroad discounts; it urged women simply to trust God for full fare.

Female evangelists could not vote at denominational meetings until 1920. Opposition to women's service as regular pastors was reiterated regularly until 1935, when, apparently with little discussion, women were granted ordination as elders (or pastors). The 1935 resolution merits a close look, however, for it perpetuated reservations in significant ways, asserting first of all "a difference between the ministry of men and of women in the church."[23] To qualify for ordination as pastors, women were required to be "matured and not less than 25 years of age" and to have a developed and generally acceptable "ministry of the Word." Similar wording was not deemed necessary for men, about whom such characteristics could presumably be assumed. In addition, women could "administer the ordinances of the church when such acts [were] necessary."[24]

Suspicions about women's moral influence had deepened in the twenties as flappers came to symbolize the "new woman" of the post–World War I era. Denunciations of the "new woman" were as much part of the era as the fads that occasioned them. "The prevailing flapper and child

Prodigy Evangelism prove the effeminacy of our present ministry," bristled independent Pentecostal evangelist Frank Bartleman. "Effeminate men follow a female ministry too largely through a spirit of fleshly attraction to the opposite sex."[25] "Next to every good woman is a deep chasm," warned the Assemblies of God teacher Peter C. Nelson, founder of Southwestern Bible Institute in Enid, Oklahoma, "and alas, many have already fallen into it."[26]

During the same years, a gradual process of institutional, emotional, and spiritual segregation effectively restricted growing numbers of women. In the Assemblies of God as in similar groups, an auxiliary women's organization marshaled the talents of the denomination's women into traditionally acceptable spheres and the women enthusiastically followed. Several women evangelists gained national followings in the Assemblies of God between the world wars, but they functioned as evangelists in settings generally controlled by male leaders, an arrangement with which many Pentecostals had always been comfortable. And their message was often oriented either toward the "deeper life" or toward storytelling and sentiment. This is not to deny their power, but their ministries did not violate the traditional "women's sphere."

Despite public rhetoric urging female submission and Christianity's masculine attributes, Assemblies of God women continued to serve and to find fulfillment in service. As missionaries, editors, teachers, evangelists, and sometimes as pastors, they implemented their calls in ways women had used for decades. Women enjoyed extensive cultural authority, then, and much grass-roots Pentecostal activity depended on their prodigious efforts. But institutional segregation and public pronouncements usually channeled women's aspirations into the "women's sphere." It is true that after 1935 that sphere for Assemblies of God women was potentially somewhat broader than the sphere for other Pentecostal women. Most Pentecostal denominations continued explicitly to deny women the right to serve as pastors. But additional burdens placed on women seeking ordination as Assemblies of God pastors made it apparent that the ethic of domesticity thrived in the Assemblies of God. As time passed it also became clearer that it thrived among the denomination's women as well as among its men.

Most Assemblies of God women and men understood the relationship between males and females hierarchically. In addition, for Pentecostals, tensions in the restorationist legacy complicated the issue. Women's calling tended to be channeled by both social expectations and biblical injunctions.

The issues raised by restorationism were complex. On the one hand, the restorationist reading of the New Testament backed the appeal for new power in the Holy Spirit. Early Pentecostals took metaphors such as latter rain with restorationist seriousness and thus challenged accepted practices and traditions, including appropriate roles for women. On the other hand, restorationists noticed the apparently overwhelming preponderance of texts that narrowed woman's sphere. The liberationist and the patriarchal exegesis, then, were rooted in ambiguities in the restorationist reading of Scripture, for taking everything in the New Testament literally gives us both daughters speaking their visions and women keeping silence.

The post–World War II era was marked by a broad cultural reorientation as woman's role as homemaker appeared to lose much of its moral significance. Pentecostals, like other Americans, had long regarded marriage as having social utility and divorce as having grave social implications. But amid the shifting values of the postwar era, personal fulfillment replaced social utility as the purpose of marriage, and the traditional notions of social order long advocated by Pentecostals seemed out of touch with reality.[27]

New terms entered a renewed discussion of "the woman question" as a yearning for order amid growing cultural disorder surfaced. The extent of the appeal of a hierarchical paradigm for understanding male and female relationships is readily apparent in the spate of marriage advice literature that has issued since World War II from evangelical presses and has been promoted by the Assemblies of God. Tim and Beverly LaHaye, Bill Gothard, Larry Christensen, and Elisabeth Elliot are the better known of a host of advocates for the view that women's subordinate status is rooted not in the fall, but in creation itself.

In the context of a broadly based call for evangelical social awareness in the 1970s, some evangelical women organized the Evangelical Women's Caucus. The formation of Christians for Biblical Equality in 1989 and its call for the affirmation of ministering women in 1990 drew more Assemblies of God support than the Evangelical Women's Caucus. But assent came from individuals who tended to be scholars in non-Pentecostal institutions, not from denominational leaders.

The situation in the Assemblies of God—which, after fifty-four years of ordaining women had only about three hundred women pastors among more than eleven thousand in 1989—reveals why ordination is an inadequate issue through which to address the roles women may play in the church. For women, ordination does not translate into equal access to positions of leadership traditionally available to the clergy. In fact, granting women ordination can make it "harder for women to lay claim to their own vocation, because the most obvious charge of discrimination is eliminated."[28] Assemblies of God leaders are usually ordained ministers who are elected to administrative posts. In theory, ordination gives women and men equal access to all levels of leadership, but no woman has ever seriously contended for elective or appointive offices within the Assemblies of God structure.

The Assemblies of God has shown little or no interest in the larger question of the social dimensions of Pentecostalism, a consideration with significant implications for women. Women's place has also never been examined with reference to the larger question of the place of the laity in local congregations. Some Assemblies of God congregations exclude women from church boards even as women pursue ordination. Meaningful institutional gains for women would seem to be integrally related to an understanding of their identity as Christian believers interacting with other members in local congregations.

These are not simply women's issues, and perhaps that helps account for a reluctance to address them. They have implications for men, too. Issues swirling around the central question of the place of women in Pentecostal ministry have agitated in the constituency since the Assemblies of God was formed in 1914. They continue to challenge the Assemblies of God to come to terms with the gospel and the culture. Since the thirties, no women evangelists have had national appeal in the denomination, and most of the handful of prominent female pastors who once exerted influence have died. Women played a pivotal role in planting the denomination across the country and around the world despite considerable ambiguity about proprieties and frequent outright hostility. The continuing struggle of some for affirmation as full partners with men in leadership at all levels is part of the legacy of restorationist ambiguity and the complex interplay between faith and culture. The contentment and fulfillment of many more who either resist or are indifferent to change, on the other hand, attests to the essentially conservative temperaments of a constituency once challenged to radical equality by a restorationist dream.

NOTES

1. "Old-fashioned Methodism Outdone at Pentecostal Camp Meeting," *Philadelphia Public Ledger*, 16 Aug. 1918, 16.

2. Aimee Semple McPherson, *This Is That* (Los Angeles: Bridal Call Publishing, 1921), 149ff.

3. Several autobiographical accounts give her view of her expanding efforts. The most recent is Aimee Semple McPherson, *The Story of My Life* (Waco, Tex.: Word Books, 1973). The first, *This Is That,* was published in 1921 and contains sermons, testimonies, and pictures of her meetings.

4. Aimee Semple McPherson to John Welch and Eudorus N. Bell, 28 Mar.

1922, Aimee Semple McPherson File, Assemblies of God Secretariat, Springfield, Mo. (hereafter AGS).

5. See Charles Price, *The Story of My Life* (Pasadena: privately published, 1935).

6. Eloise M. Richey, *What God Hath Wrought in the Life of Raymond T. Richey* (Houston: United Prayer and Workers' League, n.d.), 30–31.

7. See *Hattiesburg American*, 16 Oct. 1920, 8; 18 Oct. 1920, 8; 21 Oct. 1920, 7; 25 Oct. 1920, 8; 26 Oct. 1920, 8; 27 Oct. 1920, 8; 30 Oct. 1920, 8; 1 Nov. 1920, 8; 2 Nov. 1920, 8; 3 Nov. 1920, 8; 5 Nov. 1920, 8; 8 Nov. 1920, 8.

8. This school was one of three that merged in 1943 to create Southwestern Assemblies of God College in Waxahachie, Tex.

9. For her story, see "From the Footlights to the Light of the Cross; or, From Movieland to Canaanland," *Full Gospel Messenger*, June 1931, 2, 3, 8. In 1931, for example, after seven weeks, her campaign in the nation's capital—sponsored by the Full Gospel Tabernacle (Harry Collier, pastor)—continued unabated; meetings had to be moved to larger facilities. Pennington preached every night except Saturdays and also found time to conduct children's services in the afternoon. Ibid.

10. John G. Lake to Charles Fox Parham, 24 Mar. 1927, Assemblies of God Archives, Springfield, Mo. (hereafter AGA). Warren Fay Carothers shared these sentiments. His sympathy with Lake can be understood best by a comparison of his 1909 book, *Church Government*, with the situation in the Assemblies of God in the twenties. See also Carothers's letter of resignation, 10 Apr. 1923, Warren Fay Carothers File, AGS.

11. General Council Minutes, 1941, 66, AGA.

12. See General Council Minutes, 1927, AGA. Apart from the transformation, in 1927, the Assemblies of God adopted a constitution and by-laws, thus completing an important phase in the organizational development of the Assemblies of God.

13. In 1935 the General Council approved a resolution to use all the means at its disposal to encourage the constituency to develop local Sunday Schools "in spirituality, efficiency and numbers." General Council Minutes, 1935, 97, AGA.

14. These statistics, given in the General Council Minutes, recorded only the numbers actually reported. Accurate figures have been notoriously difficult to discover since a substantial percentage of congregations failed to report in any given year.

15. Stephen Merritt, "Women," *Midnight Cry*, 6 Mar. 1919, 5.

16. William Seymour, "Who May Prophesy?" *Apostolic Faith*, Jan. 1908, 2.

17. Ibid.

18. Warren Fay Carothers, *Church Government* (Houston: J. V. Dealy, 1909), 43ff.

19. Ibid., 44.

20. Ibid., 47.

21. Eudorus N. Bell, "Questions and Answers," *Weekly Evangel*, 22 July 1916, 8.

22. General Council Minutes, 1914, 7, AGA.

23. General Council Minutes, 1935, 21. The passage of the 1935 resolution without comment was probably a reaction to a strongly worded resolution opposing women pastors passed in 1931. That resolution had been sharply criticized by some, and the general secretary, James R. Evans, had noted that some congregations had women pastors because they could not afford to pay a man. Disagreement on this issue was evidently strong between 1931 and 1935. See correspondence in Ethel Musick File, AGS.

24. General Council Minutes, 1935, 21.

25. Frank Bartleman, "Flapper Evangelism—Fashion's Fools Headed for Hell," Los Angeles, privately published tract, 2.

26. Peter C. Nelson, "Are Women Still under Paul's Restrictions?" unpublished class notes, 1931, Peter C. Nelson File, AGA.

27. Margaret Bendroth, "The Search for 'Women's Role' in American Evangelicalism, 1930–1980," in *Evangelicalism and Modern America*, ed. George Marsden (Grand Rapids, Mich.: Wm. B. Eerdmans, 1984), 130.

28. Sara Maitland, *A Map of the New Country: Women and Christianity* (Boston: Routledge and Kegan Paul, 1983), 103.

8

Relating to Evangelicalism and Fundamentalism, 1940–48

DURING World War II, the Assemblies of God identified formally with the vision for American religion and culture articulated by a consolidating group of fundamentalists who called themselves "new evangelicals." Distraught over the course of events in mainline denominations and fragmentation in fundamentalist ranks, a new generation of fundamentalists determined to establish channels to facilitate common action in their separatist subculture. Their agenda was predicated on cultural as well as religious assumptions, and they invited all who shared these to join them for cooperative evangelism.

Separatism

During the 1930s separatism had loomed ever larger in a growing fundamentalist debate about appropriate response to the course of events in mainline denominations. Since the twenties the Northern (later American) Baptist Convention and the Presbyterian Church in the U.S.A. had been embroiled in controversy as fundamentalists unsuccessfully attempted to gain ascendancy and force doctrinal uniformity. Separatist fundamentalists countered by forming their own churches and denominations. Cultural hope waned as they seemed to be losing on many fronts. Anticipation of Christ's return seemed the only cultural solution and personal solace.

Independent churches proliferated as aggressive leaders called the faithful out of "unholy alliances" with mainline denominations. Although they often failed to exert extensive denominational influence, fundamentalists formed networks that significantly influenced extradenominational

Protestantism. Periodicals, Bible institutes, Bible conferences and camps, broadcasts, and revival campaigns all served the fundamentalist cause. In these settings, dispensationalism, with its emphasis on prophecy and the end-times calendar, flourished. Like cultural changes, modernism was viewed by separatists as a "sign of the times." The faithful remnant could never transform culture, nor could they win worldly approval; they could do little more than pray for Christ's speedy return and provide alternative institutions for education and worship. Though some sought to save the nation by advocating temperance, anticommunism, patriotism, or anti-Catholicism, they knew the battle would not be won.[1]

By the late thirties a growing cleavage over separatism revealed deep tensions within fundamentalism. An emerging generation of leaders recognized that internal disagreements accounted in part for the movement's lack of cultural force. Because they believed deeply that the contemporary fundamentalist disarray did not express "the inherent genius of the great evangelical tradition," they determined not to abandon fundamentalism but to recover its dynamic.[2]

George Marsden has pointed out that those who emerged as leaders disliked separatism and the cultural implications of thoroughgoing dispensationalism.[3] Led by men like Harold John Ockenga and J. Elwin Wright, they were influenced as well by conservative Presbyterian theology as represented at Princeton Theological Seminary by J. Gresham Machen. Their historical roots were not in Old School confessionalism, however, but rather in eighteenth- and nineteenth-century New Light and New School revivalism.[4] They thus represented a heritage with deep cultural roots that helped their cause appeal to Baptists, Presbyterians, and moderate dispensationalists.[5]

Marsden has also described a fundamentalist paradox: sometimes fundamentalists regarded themselves as the defenders or conservers of true Christianity; sometimes they saw themselves as cultural outsiders.[6] As defenders, fundamentalists often overlooked traditions that shared their view of scripture but not their evangelical Calvinist heritage.[7] Lutherans, Disciples of Christ, Wesleyans, and Pentecostals, for example, held convictions about scripture and doctrine that made them sympathetic with many fundamentalist goals. They formed a growing segment of the American evangelical subculture, but they were not accepted by fundamentalists.

In 1940 several young fundamentalist men decided to act on plans they had contemplated for some time. Primarily pastors and editors, they also tended to be associated with one or another of the nondenominational voluntary associations through which fundamentalism exerted a wide—though often overlooked—influence on the American scene.

As leader of the New England Fellowship, J. Elwin Wright had toured the country extensively during the thirties, building a wide support base among conservative evangelicals, fundamentalists, and others for inter-denominational evangelistic efforts. From 1939 he used such opportunities explicitly to encourage evangelical cooperation through a national evangelical front. His friend Ralph T. Davis of the Africa Inland Mission followed up such personal contacts with correspondence. Late in 1940 Davis probed the attitudes of several leading fundamentalist Bible school presidents. J. Davis Adams of the Philadelphia School of the Bible, Howard Ferrin of Providence Bible Institute, Will Houghton of Moody Bible Institute, and Louis Talbot of the Bible Institute of Los Angeles responded favorably to his suggestions about rallying conservatives for united action.[8]

In lectures, sermons, and correspondence during 1940 and 1941, Wright and Davis shared with evangelicals around the country their fears about liberal Protestant encroachments on basic American liberties. "Insidious forces are at work against us," Davis wrote, "and we question whether we are awake to the probable consequences of their activities." For them, modernism had assumed a specific threatening institutional form that made a visible target—the Federal Council of Churches of Christ. This agency, established in 1908 to promote cooperation among America's Protestant denominations, had become, fundamentalists charged, nothing less than a front for those conspiring to subvert fundamentalists' civil and religious liberties.

Davis's correspondence alleged that the majority of America's Protestants deplored the theology of the Federal Council's leaders; he specifically objected to the cultural influence the Federal Council exerted as the widely accepted "voice" of American Protestantism. He warned his contacts that as long as evangelicals remained "divided into so many larger and smaller groups with but little point of contact," they could not hope to counter Federal Council conspiracies.

Assured of the support of some key Bible institute presidents, Davis, J. Elwin Wright, and Harold John Ockenga (energetic pastor of Boston's historic Park Street Church) invited others who shared their vision to convene at Moody Bible Institute in Chicago. The meeting in October 1941, chaired by Moody's president, Will Houghton, had the endorsement of some of the most popular nationally known conservative evangelicals—V. Raymond Edman, president of nearby Wheaton College; Walter Maier, radio preacher on the "Lutheran Hour"; Lewis Sperry Chafer, president of Dallas Theological Seminary; and Charles Fuller, founder of a popular radio broadcast, the "Old Fashioned Revival Hour." Present with these were Carl McIntire, H. McAllister Griffiths, and Harold

Laird, separatist Presbyterians who represented the Bible Presbyterian Church. Like Davis, Wright, and Ockenga, they had dreamed for some time of uniting fundamentalists. They had, in fact, already begun. One month earlier they had launched the American Council of Christian Churches.[9]

The formation of the American Council immediately prior to the Chicago meeting raised doubts in some minds about the proper course to pursue: should those gathered in Chicago urge others to unite with this organization or should they explore possibilities further?[10] It soon became apparent that prudence mandated distancing themselves from the American Council. McIntire had arrived in Chicago prepared to join forces with others on his terms; whereas most participants intended to discuss strategies for cooperation, he had brought nonnegotiable battle plans.

The immediate issue centered in the Federal Council of Churches of Christ; McIntire urged an all-out attack on the Federal Council and insisted that congregations desiring affiliation with a united evangelical front should repudiate all ties to denominations represented by it.[11] The majority, however, disavowed confrontation and opted rather to offer simply to represent those who did not wish the Federal Council to speak for them. Participants also decided to avoid terms such as *modernist* and *fundamentalist*; they would soon adopt the label *new evangelicals.*[12]

Outvoted on these basic issues, McIntire vowed to proceed on his own. He understood this to involve delineating clearly the "pagan evils" of the Federal Council, insisting on doctrinal orthodoxy, and upholding separation as a critical test of faith.[13] Each issue of his periodical, the *Christian Beacon*, faithfully exposed the "heresies" of the new evangelicals as well as those of Protestant liberals.

Accounts of what happened at the Chicago meeting vary, but it is clear that McIntire and Ockenga—both as individuals and as representatives of opposing views about fundamentalism and American religious institutions—came to a parting of the ways. From 1941 Ockenga probably best represented those who disavowed separatism and called for united evangelical action. McIntire headed an increasingly vocal separatist council that made antipathy not only toward the Federal Council but also toward nonseparatist conservatives requisite for membership. Ironically, the attempt to overcome separatism fostered separation.

The formation of the American Council had already elicited prompt response from several fronts. While the editor of the *Lutheran Witness* (Lutheran Church, Missouri Synod) cheered McIntire on, the *Christian Century* labeled his charges against the Federal Council "unprovable and preposterous."[14] "It takes more than a desire to capture free radio time to divide the churches or to start the great revival which the sponsors of this movement declare they want," the editor noted.[15] The *Church Times* agreed: "The sickening news that a group of little men who have been notorious disturbers of the peace and unity in the Christian churches have set up a so-called American Council of Churches" would "make the enemies of religion rejoice."[16] For McIntire, such comments proved him right and fueled his determination.

Meanwhile, those who stayed at the Chicago planning meeting formed a temporary committee, named Ralph T. Davis chair, and issued a call to another planning session for April 1942 in St. Louis.

A Forum for United Action

The call described the dream of cooperation that had been partially implemented in J. Elwin Wright's New England Fellowship; the Congo Protestant Council, an interdenominational council of missions in the Belgian Congo, also served as an institutional model. The new evangelicals proposed to create a voluntary association that would uphold the "traditionally accepted evangelical position."[17] They envisioned as potential "fields for cooperative endeavor" issues pertaining to the separation of church and state, religious radio broadcasting, public relations, evangelism, foreign missions, Christian education, and local evangelical cooperation. The Assemblies of God, the Church of God (Cleveland), and several holiness denominations were invited to participate. Assemblies of God general secretary J. Roswell Flower was one of 147 religious leaders who in 1941 accepted the invitation to sign the call to St. Louis.

In these early steps to implement their plans for united action, these new evangelicals revealed a willingness to move beyond typical fundamentalist boundaries. The invitation to selected holiness and Pentecostal groups acknowledged what some Assemblies of God leaders had said all along: fundamentalist ideas permeated these constituencies. In fact, many Assemblies of God leaders traced their spiritual heritage to the people George M. Marsden has identified as the precursors of fundamentalism. The fundamentalists who envisioned this new organization, then, broadened their scope sufficiently to enable cooperation among those whose histories overlapped. They ultimately failed, however, to create a forum in which evangelicals who expressed (or interpreted) their faith differently (like Missouri Synod Lutherans) felt able to participate.[18]

Some 150 religious leaders gathered in St. Louis on 7 April 1942. As J. Elwin Wright stood before the group to deliver his opening remarks, he had cause for satisfaction. The prospects seemed good for unprecedented cooperation among a broader fundamentalist constituency. In his audience sat delegates from denominations that had purposely avoided one another for decades. Wright urged them to "speak out with courage against apostasy and apostate movements" while at the same time being "wise and gracious enough to recognize that there are differences of doctrine among Bible believing members of the church of Jesus Christ upon which there is little hope that we will see eye to eye."[19] Pentecostal "distinctives," it followed, were nonessential "differences of doctrine." This was a major acknowledgment indeed, one that neither side would have made earlier and that many on both sides resented.

The delegates elected Harold John Ockenga president of a newly constituted evangelical agency, the National Association of Evangelicals for United Action (NAE). Delegates also learned (to the surprise of some) that fears that "I, only I remain a prophet" were groundless.[20] Pledges of financial support came from congregations, denominations, voluntary associations, and individuals. (A constitutional convention would complete the organizational process in May 1943.) When the Assemblies of God delegation returned to Springfield on 9 April 1942, they had embraced the vision of strength through unity.

Implementing United Action

Several concerns predominated during the first years of attempted cooperation. First, organizers hoped to broaden the base of support. Early expectations that independent Bible institutes and voluntary associations as well as major denominations would commit themselves to NAE objectives were soon frustrated. Especially disappointing was the failure to attract major southern denominations. While many Baptist and independent congregations affiliated, the larger cooperating denominations tended to be of holiness or Pentecostal origin: the Free Methodist Church, Church of God (Cleveland), the Assemblies of God. Bible institute leaders, some fundamentalist voluntary associations, and independent religious publishers, though initially cooperative, soon largely faded from the scene, probably because they could not afford to align themselves closely with one side in the ongoing dispute over separatism and compromise.[21]

A second concern centered on the recognition that this attempt to foster united evangelical action had revealed how deeply divided conservatives were. McIntire was not alone in stridently opposing the NAE; William Bell Riley (whom NAE organizers later honored as the "grand old man" of fundamentalism) responded bitterly to the St. Louis meeting. In an article entitled "The Fatal Weakness of Fundamentalism," Riley charged Ockenga and McIntire with promoting division to slake their thirst for power. "So it goes," he bemoaned. "The army of the Lord has not enough regiments to make room for would-be officers. I saw that years ago and joined the privates. . . . Fundamentalism would prosper more if fighters increased and officials diminished."[22]

The *Sunday School Times* also attacked the NAE for not enjoining separation.[23] Ernest Gordon, son of Baptist pastor and editor A. J. Gordon, commended McIntire's attacks on the Federal Council, calling it "the extensive approximation to Unitarianism which goes under the name of Modernism." Gordon's descriptions of the Federal Council were nearly as charged as McIntire's: "The FCC is to American Protestantism what the snake entanglements were to Laocoon and his sons. The Holy Spirit is forgotten and a veritable mania for organization has taken its place."[24]

An overview of the literature of the rival conservative associations reveals several significant features of the growing fundamentalist rift. In spite of widely aired disagreements, the similarities between the American Council and the National Association of Evangelicals were more striking than the differences; the agencies shared fully an understanding of the nature and function of the Federal Council of Churches, which motivated their actions (and which Federal Council representatives claimed was a "misunderstanding").[25] The two groups also shared deeply rooted anti-Catholic prejudices, strong anticommunism, and reverent patriotism (features evident as well among liberal Protestants of the period).[26] Their disagreement over the Federal Council was one of method rather than of substance, and McIntire exploited it. In his report to the NAE board of administration in 1943, field secretary J. Elwin Wright noted sadly (expressing sentiments he would reiterate often): "The American Council of Christian Churches is working against us in every way they can. They are a foe that is wily, astute, and will do everything they can to wreck the movement."[27]

Differences in conservative theological priorities became apparent as well. Not surprisingly, some who shared Ockenga's fundamentalist heritage found cooperation with Arminian holiness and Pentecostal denominations distasteful. During the first year, serious disagreements jeopardized the association's existence. And it rather quickly became apparent that, in McIntire's view, separation from any form of doctrinal error—modernist or Pentecostal—had become essential. The NAE was wrong, not only because it apparently tolerated the Federal Council but also because it embraced Pentecostal and holiness congregations and denominations.

Although the participation of Pentecostals did not prompt debate among NAE founders (Wright had solicited Pentecostal participation in his New England Fellowship and invited it in the NAE), it troubled some fundamentalists and some Pentecostals.[28] In 1944, for example, Donald Grey Barnhouse, pastor of Philadelphia's Tenth Street Presbyterian Church (and, for the moment, an NAE supporter), called on the annual NAE convention to solicit old-line denominational participation to counterbalance Pentecostal influence. Barnhouse unequivocally declared that the NAE could not be a meaningful force unless it was controlled by well-established denominations. (He suggested Southern Presbyterians, Southern Baptists, and United Presbyterians.) If they failed to gain control within five years, he warned, the NAE would be just "one more movement to bury." Leadership by "the little fringes on the fringe" simply would not work.[29]

Although Ockenga personally had little empathy with Pentecostals, he did insist that they be recognized as evangelicals.[30] And he argued for his convictions with special eloquence when fundamentalists were his antagonist. McIntire grouped holiness and Pentecostal advocates together and insisted their theology was "a subtle, disruptive, pernicious thing" and that their movement "was a work of darkness whose disorder is known to all."[31] He declared his readiness to affiliate his American Council with the NAE if the NAE met two conditions: took an "organizational position" against the Federal Council and "got rid of the radical Holiness, tongues groups."[32] With his offer spurned on both counts, he continued his attacks on the NAE.

Criticisms of Pentecostal participation were not entirely one-sided, however. Not all Pentecostals regarded the NAE as either a vehicle for their own legitimation or a means of extending their influence; some adherents declared Assemblies of God involvement a fundamental betrayal of their own identity. Robert Brown, influential pastor of New York City's large Glad Tidings Tabernacle, for example, did not mince his words. Brown believed Pentecostalism (or any revival movement) could only thrive if it distanced itself from traditional organized religion. Commenting on the NAE he declared: "This association is not Pentecostal and many of their speakers who are listed for a convention . . . not only do not favor Pentecost, but speak against it. This [cooperating with the NAE] is what I call putting the grave clothes again on Lazarus, while the Scripture says: 'Come out from among them, and be ye separate, saith the Lord, and touch not the unclean thing; and I will receive you and will be a Father unto you, and ye shall be my sons and daughters, saith the Lord Almighty.'"[33]

Such disharmony seemed at times to jeopardize the ambitious tasks new evangelical leaders had placed on their agenda. They hoped to appoint evangelical chaplains and to clarify the rights of evangelicals to radio time. They supported the efforts of other voluntary associations—like the National Fellowship for Spiritual Awakening, which sought to promote revival, or the National Commission for Christian Leadership, which mobilized lay people in breakfast groups and campus ministries—and they worked to alert Americans to court decisions relating to such division of church and state issues as released time for religious instruction and public subsidies for Catholic schools.

The NAE and American Culture

All of this was woven together in Harold John Ockenga's grand vision for American culture. It combined his ardent anti-Catholicism and his hope for a Christian (i.e., Protestant) America as the basic components of a renewed Christian culture. Ockenga warned conservative Christians of the growing political menace of a "Roman Catholic machine." Americans, he charged, were blissfully unaware of the dangerous philosophy promulgated by Monsignor Fulton J. Sheen, popular speaker on "The Catholic Hour." Sheen's views, he warned, might well "involve a change in American culture almost as fundamental as that of Joseph Stalin."[34] He challenged American evangelicals to respond by "reaffirming the Reformation." He called his constituency to defensive warfare: enemies (Catholicism, communism, modernism) were marching. Charging growing political interference by the Catholic Church, he claimed to note deference toward Catholicism in such varied settings as the entertainment industry and pamphlets distributed to the military.[35]

In his NAE leadership role, Ockenga imbued his following with a broad sense of American destiny with deep roots in his Presbyterian heritage and expressed their sentiments for them. It is hardly a coincidence that Assemblies of God views on war and country that differed radically from the World War I period coalesced at about the same time the denomination affiliated with the NAE. In many ways, Ockenga expressed and influenced Assemblies of God opinions about American culture. After all, some Assemblies of God leaders had considered America a chosen nation all along; and, in the grim days after Pearl Harbor, a call to patriotic destiny offered meaning in suffering. In a presidential address to the NAE constitutional convention in 1943, Ockenga challenged:

> I believe that the United States of America has been assigned a destiny comparable to that of ancient Israel which was favored, preserved, endowed, guided and used by God. Historically, God has prepared this nation with a vast and united country, with a popu-

lation drawn from innumerable blood streams, with a wealth which is unequaled, with an ideological strength drawn from the traditions of classical and radical philosophy but with a government held accountable to law, as no government except Israel has ever been, and with an enlightenment in the minds of the average citizen which is the climax of social development.[36]

The nation, Ockenga continued, was at a crossroads; the "kingdom of hell" was "at hand." If evangelical religion were not revived, a return to the "Dark Ages of heathendom" threatened. In fact, the force of "heathendom" was powerfully at work in America, he warned. Yet he offered more hope than did separatist dispensationalists. After its chastening in World War II America would emerge with renewed seriousness about government, religion, and morals; the "present indifference to God" would yield to the triumph of evangelical faith if only his hearers would dedicate themselves to the contemporary realization of their historic American evangelical heritage.[37]

Such sentiments coincided neatly with Assemblies of God leaders' confidence in America's destiny under God. Well-publicized confrontations between Catholics and Protestants in South America as well as events at home also seemed to lend credence to Ockenga's anti-Catholicism.[38]

Ockenga called for Christians to become intellectual leaders. The church, he declared, had to produce "thinkers" who "stood for Christ" to lead a new generation. He urged as well that Christians assume prominent places in business and above all that they commit themselves to discovering a "new power in personal life."[39]

Many of the 613 delegates responded favorably, among them numerous Assemblies of God participants. Southern California District superintendent Ben Hardin (who admitted coming with "many questions and mental reservations") was surprised that no one "shed a wild gourd into the pottage on doctrinal matters." The evangelist Raymond T. Richey found the sessions "deeply spiritual and constructive."[40] More important, J. Roswell Flower gained a place on the executive committee, (as did J. H. Walker, general overseer of the Church of God [Cleveland]).

In the complex evangelical network, then, the Assemblies of God identified with the evangelicals. Like many Assemblies of God leaders, these were white males with a fundamentalist heritage. Although they sympathized with NAE objectives, however, Assemblies of God leaders could not formally affiliate with the NAE without General Council action. In September 1943 the General Council authorized denominational application for NAE membership and financial support for the cooperative agency.[41] The application received favorable action by the NAE later the same month.[42] The Assemblies of God had officially become part of an evangelical coalition dedicated to assuring evangelicals a voice in the public arena.

The National Religious Broadcasters

Much of the NAE's impatience with the Federal Council revolved around issues pertaining to radio broadcasting. During the 1940s radio networks offered free time to Protestants, Catholics, and Jews, and network managers looked to the Federal Council (as the most visible "voice" of Protestantism) to provide Protestant programs. The Federal Council included over twenty-five denominations and claimed to speak for some 36 million Protestants. Harry Emerson Fosdick, speaker on the "National Vespers Hour," was probably its best-known radio voice.

Like the Federal Council, Fosdick (pastor, author, professor at Union Theological Seminary, radio speaker) had become a symbol of what conservatives considered was wrong with American Protestantism. Fosdick's magnetic personality, his confident message (assuring his generation that scientific advances did not destroy Christianity's timeless truth), his wistful hope for moral progress, and his yearning for certainties amid changing realities evoked widespread response.[43] He addressed the felt needs of millions of Americans.

To fundamentalists, however, Fosdick symbolized the evils of modernism. Even the more irenic among them could not admit without reservation that Fosdick was, in fact, a Christian. Yet he was probably America's most popular Protestant preacher, and he was closely identified with the Federal Council.[44] His participation seemed to conservatives to validate J. Elwin Wright's contention that the Federal Council was "hopelessly heretical" and "committed to the destruction of the evangelical faith."[45]

NAE organizers especially disliked two situations. The first was that powerful American agencies assumed that the Federal Council (and thus Fosdick) adequately represented a majority of American Protestants. Given long-held fundamentalist expectations of an end-times world church, the Federal Council (like the emerging World Council of Churches), seemed especially threatening.[46] Although this had implications for other matters (like the appointment of military and institutional chaplains), it seemed most immediately to jeopardize evangelical access to broadcast media.

Leaders of the American Council and the NAE repeatedly challenged the Federal Council's right to be the "voice" of Protestantism, claiming that Federal Council statistics were misleading and that at least half of

America's Protestants were evangelicals. "Fundamentalists," William Bell Riley insisted, "constitute not less than five-sixths of the Evangelical Church membership. The Federal Council's claim of 20,000,000 associates in unfaith is an egregious lie; and they know it."[47] Fundamentalists quarreled among themselves about numbers, too: McIntire asserted in 1944 that his American Council spoke for some 750,000. The NAE countered that he had no more than 150,000 followers.[48]

When NAE leaders addressed questions about free air time to the networks, they learned that organizations representing constituencies of 4 to 5 million could anticipate free time slots. Meanwhile, they accused McIntire (who gained free time on the Blue Network [ABC] late in 1943) of grossly misrepresenting his constituency to do so.[49]

The question of free time raised less serious immediate problems than did more specific patterns of local behavior. Free time could be obtained once evangelicals truly united; lack of free time seemed intolerable mostly because it was based on the assumption that speakers for the Federal Council adequately represented American Protestants. Keeping paid broadcasts on the air posed a second and more serious challenge.

This challenge came from local stations, and NAE publicists exploited it in desperate attempts to help raise their budget. The Federal Council, they believed, had helped persuade the CBS and NBC radio networks to exclude paid religious broadcasts and to grant free time to the major faiths. Since denominations affiliated with the Federal Council represented a majority of American Protestants, Federal Council leaders had successfully argued their right to the Protestant segment of free air time. By 1941 the Federal Council was part of an interfaith coalition lobbying the Mutual Broadcasting System and the National Association of Broadcasters to exclude paid religious broadcasting.

NAE publicity urged pastors to support the association in order to protect their congregations from the alleged hostility of local mainline churches. Mainline Protestants (abetted by the Federal Council), the NAE warned, might well complain to station managers about evangelical church-sponsored local programming. Station managers would most likely respond by putting fundamentalists off the air.[50] NAE publications also alleged that liberal Protestants and Catholics would be likely to conspire with local authorities against conservative congregations seeking building permits.

Some of the earliest conveners of the NAE were radio broadcasters. Among the most outspoken was William Ward Ayer, pastor of New York City's Calvary Baptist Church. Ayer had a dual concern. He wanted first to pressure the Federal Communications Commission to encourage stations to air local religious programs and to find ways to assure the rights

of broadcasters to purchase time. He found the common practice of stations granting several free slots and then refusing to sell time for additional religious broadcasts unacceptable. Ayer's second dream was to for-
mulate ethical standards for religious broadcasters.[51]

These were, in fact, timely concerns. Much of what Ayer wanted in a
code of ethics resembled recommendations circulated to religious radio
broadcasters by the National Conference of Christians and Jews. That
agency encouraged broadcasters not to attack other faiths, but rather to
affirm their own; not to appeal for funds on the air or to charge for religious objects; to address broadcasts to a cross section of the potential
audience, not to a selected group. Liberals and conservatives agreed that
the world war was stimulating a "reawakening" of religious interests, and
advocates of the major religious traditions, liberal as well as conservative,
hoped to use radio time to kindle a national revival.

The Assemblies of God followed these events closely. The group as yet
had no official radio broadcast, but many of its local churches purchased
radio time.[52] It had, however, authorized radio outreach in 1933. Ten
years later (just as the Assemblies of God became part of the NAE), a
General Presbytery committee began to consider national network broadcasting. A radio department was organized at the headquarters in 1945,
and in 1946 the denomination began releasing a fifteen-minute broadcast,
"Sermons in Song." The name was changed to "Revivaltime" in 1950,
and in 1953 the Executive Presbytery appointed a full-time speaker,
C. M. Ward, for a half-hour paid broadcast over the ABC network. The
"Revivaltime" broadcast, since 1978 under the leadership of pastor-
evangelist Dan Betzer, remains a vital denominational outreach. It is carried on over 550 stations in more than 100 countries.

Assemblies of God adherents shared evangelical suspicions of a Federal
Council–engineered conspiracy to deprive them of a hearing, and—as
they organized their own radio outreach—they readily cooperated with
NAE efforts to address the situation. Some 150 religious broadcasters met
during the second annual NAE convention in April 1944 and organized
the National Religious Broadcasters (NRB). Later that year, the new voluntary association adopted a constitution, developed a code of ethics, and
elected officers. Thomas F. Zimmerman, an Assemblies of God pastor in
Granite City, Illinois, served on the first executive committee.[53]

Meanwhile, as the NAE gained visibility it was occasionally offered
free time on one or another of the networks.[54] In June 1944 the Blue
Network sponsored NAE weekly broadcasts over which Ayer, Barnhouse,
and Stephen Paine, president of Houghton College, spoke. Through the
NRB as well as in other ways, evangelicals monitored congressional bills
that affected religious broadcasting. In 1944 at the suggestion of Walter

Maier of the "Lutheran Hour," for example, they lobbied to assure that the communications act then under consideration would subject religious broadcasters only to such restrictions as applied to all broadcasters.[55] Believing as they did that "broadcasting the gospel [was] an evangelical duty," they considered themselves engaged in a vital task.[56]

Within a few years the situation changed. Free time for religious broadcasting became a thing of the past, their access to paid air time seemed assured, and other issues absorbed the energies of the NRB. The timing, evangelicals believed, was no coincidence: their efforts had succeeded. In its first few years, it seemed to those evangelicals supportive of the NAE and the NRB that they had taken long strides toward effecting their desired ends. They no longer felt powerless; they had begun the campaign to recapture cultural influence.

Although the NAE and related agencies never achieved the degree of evangelical unity and thus the influence the founders had envisioned, they did comprise a diverse segment of American evangelicals. Perhaps the new evangelicals had overestimated either the percentage of committed conservatives in American denominations or impatience in the rank and file with the Federal Council. Most likely many ordinary lay people had little experience with the issues being targeted. Some undoubtedly concurred with Federal Council leaders who maintained that the attack on the Federal Council was rooted in a basic misunderstanding of its position. In general, Federal Council representatives refused to be drawn into controversy. "We have," noted Samuel Cavert, Federal Council general secretary, "too weighty a responsibility to justify our dissipating our energies in argument with other Christians."[57] And occasional contacts of NAE representatives with Federal Council personnel in fact tended to demonstrate the shared commitment of both groups to evangelism.

Certainly NAE organizers had exposed the fierce individualism that thrived in fundamentalism. Strong independent leaders—like John R. Rice and Bob Jones—cooperated for a while, then chose separatism. Many fundamentalists not only failed to join, they maintained a steady barrage of criticism. As an association, the NAE failed in its primary goal: it never directly won the support of the millions of evangelicals it maintained constituted the majority of American Protestants.

The Assemblies of God (one of the NAE's key financial contributors) formally reevaluated its commitment to the NAE during the late forties. Some pastors, citing tension on the local level, tried to discourage continued denominational participation.[58] Strong feeling that Pentecostals necessarily compromised their distinctiveness whenever they cooperated with non-Pentecostals continued to agitate the Assemblies of God for the next several decades. Considerable confusion (aided by McIntire's allegations) about NAE-affiliated congregations belonging to denominations represented by the Federal Council prompted misunderstanding. An Illinois pastor wrote to the headquarters urging clarification: "Some of my people are unduly alarmed, in as much as they think we as the General Council of the Assemblies of God have joined the Federal Council of Churches. Some of our folk are converted Lutherans and utterly opposed to that organization and threaten to leave the Council if we have joined."[59]

Undoubtedly some Assemblies of God pastors supported the NAE with dubious motives. Some clearly hoped to persuade NAE adherents to accept Pentecostalism. Carl McIntire bluntly accused them of being "hopeful" that the gift of tongues would "come on all."[60] And McIntire was partly right, as a sampling of correspondence between Assemblies of God ministers and the denomination's general secretary indicates. An enthusiastic description of an NAE regional meeting in Baltimore in 1942, for example, began with the following report of progress: "Dr. Gordon Brownville of Tremont Temple sounds Pentecostal. I heard him say, 'Praise the Lord, Amen.'"[61]

Reconsiderations about cooperation with new evangelicals were part of a broader unsettlement in the Assemblies of God during the late forties. For some, denominational loyalty took apparent precedence over the common experience of opposition to modernism. In a period of transition, they clung to the past. But with increasing frequency those who were committed to cooperation gained national office and built on the foundation J. Roswell Flower had ably laid.

On the other side, things were also changing. Most conspicuously, the immediate "enemy," the Federal Council of Churches, was superseded by the National Council of Churches of Christ as well as by the World Council of Churches. NAE representatives hoped that in the transition from the Federal Council to the National Council, "a more Biblical viewpoint, a more evangelistic program, a more democratic organizational structure and a united front for Christianity in America might emerge."[62] Disappointed when Federal Council members failed to invite their participation or to call union prayer meetings, conservatives castigated the National Council as a "superchurch" that threatened to destroy "individual freedom of thought and action."[63]

As noted, NAE-affiliated congregations and denominations not only affirmed several "fundamentals" they also shared some basic convictions about America. Their perception of history, culture, and enemies united them perhaps as strongly as their theological views. A sense of having been forced to surrender cultural leadership to an unacceptable party (or of having been arbitrarily excluded from such leadership) haunted them and made some willing to minimize issues that had historically been divisive.

Although the Federal Council and the Roman Catholic Church were the primary institutional targets of evangelical criticism, cultural patterns also alarmed the new evangelicals. America needed to return to its roots; these evangelicals echoed the call for a Christian America. They urged a return to a "Christian Sabbath," called for moral reform (including the removal—by executive order—of beer from army camps "to preserve the moral fiber of the cream of America's manhood"), and urged education reform.[64] Educators, they warned, were "poisoning America with communistic teaching." In response they proposed a Christian university and called for evangelical intellectuals who could produce a "new literature," a "new Bible history abreast of recent archeology," a monthly magazine, evangelical "reading rooms," and an evangelical apologetic.[65] "The main attack on Christianity has begun," they declared. The world war was but a prelude. "Hosts of antichristian armies and powers are in motion. Whole nations are again on the march towards heathendom and idolatry."[66]

Cataclysmic events did not mean despair. The horrors of war raised their expectations of revival. They had hope, confidence in the moral fiber of a nation that needed purging but would emerge strong. The NAE organized local chapters through which it sponsored evangelistic outreaches. It identified, too, with other agencies working toward revival: the National Fellowship for Spiritual Awakening, formed in 1946 to coordinate prayer and efforts for revival in Washington, D.C. (which, its promoters were convinced, would spread around the world); Christ for America, led by Horace F. Dean, an early supporter of the NAE; and the National Commission for Christian Leadership (which had begun in 1935 in Seattle). At the same time, Americans in general became more interested in religion. Through its participation in the NAE, then, the Assemblies of God recommitted itself to revitalize America and evangelize the world. When, in 1949, the new evangelicals discovered a prophet for the anticipated national revival in Billy Graham, they dared to believe the awakening had begun.[67]

In identifying with the new evangelicals, Assemblies of God leaders acted on the assumption that they were evangelicals energized by a spiritual experience, who shared both a meaningful evangelical past and a vision for the future. Some adherents disagreed, and later leaders would attempt to reemphasize Pentecostal "distinctives," but for the moment,

at midcentury the Assemblies of God found its new identification congenial. That it could easily do so demonstrated how far it had moved from
the radical millenarian restorationism in which it had been born.

The Assemblies of God and Other Pentecostals

Their experience in the National Association of Evangelicals encouraged participating Pentecostal denominations to create a forum for
American Pentecostals, who remained badly fragmented. In May 1948
representatives of eight white trinitarian Pentecostal denominations
met in Chicago after the annual NAE convention to discuss ongoing
association.

In August the group met again, this time with representatives of four
more Pentecostal denominations. They appointed a committee, chaired
by Flower, to frame a constitution for a convention they scheduled in Des
Moines, Iowa, for October. When nearly two hundred delegates assembled on 26 October, they proceeded quickly and amicably through
their business and gave structure to the Pentecostal Fellowship of North
America (PFNA). J. Roswell Flower was chosen the first secretary of the
PFNA. A rising Pentecostal star, Oral Roberts, addressed the new association's evening rally.

The PFNA resembled the NAE in its statement of faith and its constitution. Its purposes were to coordinate common efforts, to express the
fundamental unity of "Spirit-baptized believers," and to facilitate evangelism. Assemblies of God leaders responded favorably to the PFNA, and
the 1949 General Council approved Assemblies of God membership. Serious misgivings soon surfaced, however, revealing the persistence of
sharp divisions among Pentecostals over holiness, sanctification, and
worldliness.[68]

Promoters of the PFNA won their case, however, and the Assemblies
of God over the years has made substantial financial and leadership contributions to the PFNA. The PFNA has not succeeded in effecting full
classical Pentecostal cooperation, however. Affiliated denominations remain white and trinitarian, while large segments of American Pentecostalism are black, Hispanic, and nontrinitarian. The PFNA represented,
rather, the segment of American Pentecostalism that disclaimed the full
implications of its restorationist past in favor of affirming evangelical
identity.

The Pentecostal World Conference

Whereas American Pentecostal denominations developed with little
reference to one another, European Pentecostals shared contact from the

beginning. Regular conferences contributed to the solidarity and growth of independent movements in several northern European countries until World War I. In 1921 contact through occasional conferences resumed. Several men, notably England's Donald Gee and Sweden's Lewi Pethrus, enjoyed popularity in the movement as a whole. Both were also well known in the United States.

European and American Pentecostals gathered in Zurich in May 1947 to organize the Pentecostal World Conference. Misgivings among Pentecostals with strong congregationalist sympathies (especially Scandinavians) at first jeopardized the experiment. At the second meeting in Paris in 1949, however, delegates were persuaded that the conference would respect member groups' autonomy and organizational preferences. Since 1949 conferences have met triennially and have included a growing number of participants from both classical and charismatic Pentecostalism. They continue, however, to retain a trinitarian cast. Several recent meetings in the Far East, including one of the most recent in Singapore in October 1989, have affirmed the extent and much of the pluralism of the Pentecostal movement worldwide.

The Assemblies of God participated from the beginning in the Pentecostal World Conferences, and through it J. Roswell Flower, Ernest Williams, and especially Thomas F. Zimmerman decisively influenced the course of the worldwide movement.

By 1950, then, the Assemblies of God had not only discovered advantages in cooperation but it had also assumed leadership roles in each of the cooperative associations it had helped organize. Over time, each of them helped reassure Assemblies of God adherents about other Pentecostals and evangelicals,˙ and through them, the dream of a Christian America was added as a competitor to the restorationist vision.

Events during World War II forced acknowledgment of the declining role of restorationist thought and facilitated a new sense of identity that further separated the Assemblies of God from many Pentecostal groups. It offered influence in American public life. But it soon evoked a challenge from within as at the popular level some attempted to reassert an older Pentecostal identity and others determined to promulgate Pentecostal distinctiveness through mass evangelism.

NOTES

1. There were ties in the twenties and thirties between some Pentecostals and right-wing politicians such as Gerald Winrod and Gerald L. K. Smith. See Charles Fox Parham Papers, Apostolic Faith Bible College, Baxter Springs, Kans.

2. See, for example, Carl Henry, "Has Fundamentalism Lost Its Social Con-

science?" *United Evangelical Action,* 1 June 1947, 3, 5. Henry argued that fundamentalists—including those active in such ecumenical efforts as the National Association of Evangelicals for United Action or the American Council—desperately needed to couple their resistance of liberal Protestant agencies (which were devoted to "attacking social ills") with a "forceful assault on social evils in a distinctly supernaturalistic framework."

3. George M. Marsden, *Reforming Fundamentalism* (Grand Rapids, Mich.: Wm. B. Eerdmans, 1987), 6.

4. Ibid.; George M. Marsden, *The Evangelical Mind and the New School Presbyterian Experience* (New Haven: Yale University Press, 1970).

5. Marsden, *Reforming Fundamentalism,* 6.

6. George M. Marsden, *Fundamentalism and American Culture* (New York: Oxford University Press, 1980), 6–7. R. Laurence Moore discusses this at length in his *Religious Outsiders and the Making of Americans* (New York: Oxford University Press, 1986).

7. Joel Carpenter, "The Fundamentalist Leaven and the Rise of an Evangelical United Front," in *The Evangelical Tradition in America,* ed. Leonard I. Sweet (Macon, Ga.: Mercer University Press, 1984), 267.

8. Ralph T. Davis letter, 11 Dec. 1940, Herbert J. Taylor Papers, Box 14, File 27, Collection 20, Billy Graham Center Archives (hereafter HJT Papers).

9. Carl McIntire, "Editorial," *Christian Beacon,* 17 Dec. 1942, 1.

10. Assemblies of God leaders noted the similarities in the early stages of the two plans and responded to an invitation from Davis and Wright to participate in their association with the information that the American Council seemed to be doing the same thing. Flower intimated that McIntire's associate, H. McAllister Griffiths, had led Assemblies of God leaders to believe that no objections would be raised on doctrinal grounds to Assemblies of God participation in the American Council. See J. Roswell Flower to Ralph T. Davis, 3 Dec. 1941; J. Roswell Flower to R. L. Decker, 27 Oct. 1949, National Association of Evangelicals for United Action Collection, Assemblies of God Archives, Springfield, Mo. (hereafter NAE Collection and AGA).

11. This attitude later figured in McIntire's attack on the Assemblies of God. He repudiated Pentecostal doctrine and accused the Assemblies of God of deceptive cooperation with the Federal Council.

12. For this story see Joel Carpenter, "Revive Us Again: Alienation, Hope, and the Resurgence of Fundamentalism, 1930–1950," in *Transforming Faith: The Sacred and Secular in Modern American History,* ed. M. L. Bradbury and James B. Gilbert (New York: Greenwood Press, 1989), 105–26.

13. Thomas R. Birch, the editor of the *Presbyterian Guardian,* listed these three areas of disagreement as reasons for the "stormy session" at Chicago and for continued charges that United Evangelical Action sponsors were "compromisers." *Presbyterian Guardian,* 25 Mar. 1942. It seems apparent that the American Council was ready to accept Pentecostals. If McIntire could have consolidated the others in support of his program he would by all indications have been as tolerant as the new evangelicals toward Pentecostalism and holiness people. Hav-

ing failed in Chicago, within a year he began criticizing the others for accepting Pentecostals.

14. *Lutheran Witness*, 25 Nov. 1941, 395; *Christian Century*, 1 Oct. 1941, 19.

15. *Christian Century*, 1 Oct. 1941, 19.

16. *Church Times*, 27 Sept. 1941, 19.

17. Ralph T. Davis, letter of invitation to St. Louis, Box 65, File 16, Collection 20, HJT Papers.

18. See Carpenter, "Fundamentalist Leaven," 261.

19. Manuscript copy of Wright's opening remarks, 5, Box 65, File 20, Collection 20, HJT Papers.

20. Ben Hardin's comment is printed in his letter in "United We Stand: NAE Constitutional Convention Report," 58, Box 65, File 20, Collection 20, HJT Papers.

21. Prolonged bickering discouraged some (like InterVarsity or independent Bible institutes) from maintaining early ties to the NAE. R. L. Decker to Howard J. Taylor, 29 Feb. 1948, Box 66, File 14, Collection 20, HJT Papers. Conservative voluntary associations needed support from the broadest possible constituencies. Aligning with one side or the other could have dire financial consequences.

22. William Bell Riley, "The Fatal Weakness of Fundamentalism," *World-Wide Temple Evangelist*, 19 June 1942, 1, 6. See also William Bell Riley, "National Association of Evangelicals for United Action," *Pilot*, Nov. 1942, 53, 54.

23. See especially an editorial by Philip E. Howard, "St. Louis Convention," *Sunday School Times* 84, no. 25 (20 June 1942): 493–94, 498–99. See also "Four Significant Organizations," *Sunday School Times* 85, no. 29 (17 July 1943): 573, 574, 578, 587, 588.

24. Ernest Gordon, "Ecclesiastical Octopus," *United Evangelical Action*, 15 Nov. 1948, 7. Another Baptist, Robert Ketcham, edited the *Baptist Bulletin*, the organ of the General Association of Regular Baptist Churches, in which he denounced the NAE. See, for example, "Facing the Facts," in the Nov. 1942 issue. Some of his editorials—such as "Shadow of the Federal Council"—were reprinted in pamphlet form. See also "Why the General Association of Regular Baptists Declared Itself in Fellowship with the American Council of Christian Churches (Rather Than the Widely-publicized National Association of Evangelicals for United Action)," undated article clipped from *Baptist Bulletin*, NAE Collection, AGA.

25. Samuel McCrea Cavert to Bishop Leslie R. Marston, 20 Apr. 1945, Federal Council of Churches File, AGA.

26. A random selection of titles from *United Evangelical Action* evidences these views. On communism: "Enemy of Religion," 15 Nov. 1947, 8; Daniel A. Reed, "Facts about Communism and Communists," 1 June 1948, 5–6. On Catholicism (much of this pertained to church and state questions): Glenwood Blackmore, "How Rome Seized an Ohio Public School System," 1 June 1947, 4ff; James Murch, "Threat to Liberty," 1 Mar. 1947, 12–13; Glenwood Blackmore, "Is Roman Catholicism Broad and Tolerant?" 1 June 1948, 7ff; William Ward Ayer,

"Romanism's Pied Piper: A Gospel-eye View of the Roman Catholic Church's Top Propagandist—Msgr. Fulton J. Sheen," 15 Aug. 1948, 3ff. On patriotism: Samuel E. Boyle, "Jesus Christ and the American Tradition," 15 Sept. 1947, 3ff; S. Richey Kamm, "The Christian and His Civic Responsibility," 15 May 1947, 3ff; V. Raymond Edman, "New Lamps for Old?" 1 Oct. 1947, 3ff., strongly implies that the desirable "old lamps" can be equated with traditional American values. Of the many derogatory comments about the designs of Federal Council leaders, Glenwood Blackmore, "It Can Happen Here!" 15 Mar. 1947, 7–8, is typical.

A sampling of liberal views on these subjects can be gained by an overview of *Christian Century* or the *Federal Council Bulletin*.

27. Minutes, Board of Administration, 21 Sept. 1943, 7, Box 65, File 18, Collection 20, HJT Papers.

28. There was considerable discussion in the NAE executive committee over admitting the International Church of the Foursquare Gospel, not primarily because the denomination was Pentecostal but because of controversy surrounding its founder, Aimee Semple McPherson. The ICFG ultimately was accepted. It is important to note, however, that the vast majority of American Pentecostal groups (numbering well over 250) neither sought nor were offered NAE membership. That was confined to longer-established, larger, white denominations. Of the many Pentecostal groups in existence in 1942, only the Assemblies of God and the Church of God (Cleveland) gained immediate prominence within the new organization.

29. "Ockenga Disavows Barnhouse's Speech at N.A.E. Convention," *Christian Beacon*, 27 Apr. 1944, 1. Apparently Barnhouse found his audience somewhat sympathetic: he found it necessary to "rebuke" those who shouted "Amen." Carl McIntire reported much "waving of hands around in the air" during prayer and claimed that during the NAE meeting a holiness advocate sought to convince him of sinless perfection and a Pentecostal tried to "sell him" on tongues. He charged that holiness and Pentecostal delegates had "well organized ground plans" and hoped to "pentecostalize" the NAE. See W. O. H. Garman, "Analysis of National Association Convention and Constituency," *Christian Beacon*, 27 Apr. 1944, 2. Both Barnhouse and McIntire accurately gauged the potential situation. Before long, the Assemblies of God became (and it has remained) by far the largest affiliate of the NAE.

30. He and Wright apparently did so despite Flower's frequently repeated offers to defer to non-Pentecostal leadership. "We wish to assure you that the Assemblies of God desire no great prominence in this movement, although we are interested in its success. . . . We recognize that this association has done a new thing in the earth by the recognition of groups formerly excluded from "Fundamentalist" associations. . . . If the publicizing of these groups will hinder other good evangelicals from uniting with the movement, then our advice would be that no prominence be given to them, but that they be kept in the background." J. Roswell Flower to Harold John Ockenga, May 1943, NAE Collection.

31. Carl McIntire, "Analysis of National Association Convention and Constituency," *Christian Beacon*, 27 Apr. 1944, 2.

32. Ibid.

33. Robert Brown, "Hindrances to the Work of God," *Glad Tidings Herald*, May 1944, 2.

34. News release, 3 May 1944, Box 65, File 21, Collection 20, HJT Papers.

35. Ibid.

36. "United We Stand," 10.

37. Ibid.

38. Evangelicals were not the only Protestants to voice such sentiments. Both the *Christian Century* and the *Federal Council Bulletin* published misgivings about Roman Catholic intentions and dreamed of a righteous America.

39. "United We Stand," 10.

40. Ibid., 58.

41. General Council Minutes, 1943, 8, AGA.

42. Minutes, Board of Administration of the National Association of Evangelicals for United Action, 21 Sept. 1943, 3, Box 65, File 20, Collection 20, HJT Papers.

43. Harry Emerson Fosdick's *The Living of These Days: An Autobiography* (New York: Harper and Brothers, 1959) remains an eloquent account of his aspirations and accomplishments. For a thorough assessment, see Robert Moats Miller, *Harry Emerson Fosdick: Preacher, Pastor, Prophet* (New York: Oxford University Press, 1985).

44. See, for example, Ernest Gordon, "Ecclesiastical Octopus: Evangelism without an Evangel," *United Evangelical Action*, 1 Nov. 1948, 5–8, which includes a long segment entitled "The Radio and the FCC." Gordon alleges that Fosdick's ideas coincided with Nazi theology. That *United Evangelical Action* would publish Gordon's allegations indicates how close the NAE and the American Council actually were in these years.

45. In a statement "Why I Joined the National Association of Evangelicals," Michigan Baptist pastor H. H. Savage included these quotes from J. Elwin Wright's *Death in the Pot: An Appraisal of the Federal Council of the Churches of Christ in America* (Boston: Fellowship Press, 1944).

In spite of such protestations about the Federal Council, it is striking to note similarities in the concerns of NAE and Federal Council proponents. In addition to shared anti-Catholicism, anticommunism, and strong patriotism, both groups urged prayer and preparation for revival, encouraged evangelism, and urged morality in government and in public affairs.

46. It is interesting that though much popular fundamentalist thought anticipated a world church and world government, these fundamentalists chose not to acquiesce in the "inevitable" but rather to challenge it.

47. Riley, "Fatal Weakness," 1.

48. J. Elwin Wright to NAE Board of Administration, 8 Jan. 1944, Box 65, File 25, Collection 20, HJT Papers.

49. Ibid.

50. See sample letter to pastors of churches whose denominations are affiliated, Box 65, File 21, Collection 20, HJT Papers.

51. Minutes of the Executive Committee of the NAE, 7 Dec. 1942, 11, HJT Papers.

52. Under the farsighted leadership of R. J. Craig, Glad Tidings in San Francisco organized its own radio station in 1925. See R. J. Craig File, AGA.

53. Over the years Zimmerman has played an important role on the executive committee of the National Religious Broadcasters. He has served it and the NAE as president. As of 1990 he attended every one of the forty-seven annual National Religious Broadcasters conventions.

54. See, for example, *United Evangelical Action*, 1 May 1948, 5; 15 Sept. 1948, 5.

55. Minutes, Executive Committee of the National Association of Evangelicals for United Action, 14 June 1944, 2, Box 65, File 23, Collection 20, HJT Papers.

56. See William Ward Ayer in *United Evangelical Action*, 1 June 1943, 17.

57. Samuel Cavert to Leslie R. Marston, 20 Apr. 1945, NAE Collection.

58. General Presbytery Minutes, 1949, 6; see also J. Roswell Flower to R. L. Decker, 29 Sept. 1949, J. Roswell Flower Papers, AGA.

59. R. D. Shaw to J. Roswell Flower, 13 June 1944, J. Roswell Flower Papers.

60. *Christian Beacon*, 27 Apr. 1944, 2.

61. Alexander Clattenburg to J. Roswell Flower, 2 Oct. 1942, J. Roswell Flower Papers.

62. James DeForest Murch, "The Proposed National Council of Churches," *United Evangelical Action*, 1 Oct. 1946, 6.

63. Ibid., 7.

64. See, for example, J. Alvin Orr in *United Evangelical Action*, 1 June 1943, 1. *United Evangelical Action* is the best source for a sense of the cultural issues that perturbed these evangelicals.

65. *United Evangelical Action*, Jan. 1944, 3; Wilbur Smith, "The Urgent Need for a New Evangelical," NAE Report, 1946, 42–48, Box 66, File 4, Collection 20, HJT Papers.

66. *United Evangelical Action*, 10 Sept. 1943, 2.

67. Carpenter, "Revive Us Again," 115.

68. "Report of Committee on Pentecostal Fellowship of North America," General Presbytery Minutes, 1949, Assemblies of God Secretariat, Springfield, Mo.

9

Disturbing Claims of New Restorations, 1948–60

O N 13 February 1949 nearly five thousand people crammed the facilities of Bethesda Missionary Temple, an Assemblies of God church in Detroit. Some seventeen hundred more were turned away. The occasion was the dedication of the congregation's new three-thousand-seat auditorium. But the event was much more than a ceremony because the crowd was charged with excitement about a new restoration.[1] The word was out: the latter rain had begun to fall, and the New Testament faith was being restored. A participant exulted: "At last it is here! Had I not seen it with my own eyes and felt the witness in my own heart, I might have been skeptical, but it's real! Hallelujah! What am I talking about?—THE LATTER RAIN OUTPOURING! We've dreamed about it, prayed about it and hoped to see it. Now the showers are falling and spreading rapidly."[2]

Some of the same people had said precisely the same things forty years earlier. The language evoked American Pentecostalism's earliest history; nearly five decades after Charles Fox Parham announced the restoration, second- and third-generation Pentecostals yearned anew for tangible evidence that they were God's end-times people. Discouraged by waning spiritual fervor and the relentless institutionalization and professionalization of North American Pentecostalism, they viewed their early history as having merely set the stage for a greater event and opted once again to believe that in their day, the restoration of apostolic power would be realized.

They discovered—as their forebears had—that emphasis on the latter rain and restoration involved implicit and explicit indictment of their fellow believers. And it revived themes, language, and experiential expectations that had long since faded from general Pentecostal use. Since theirs was the *full* restoration, it followed that early Pentecostalism had been a partial restoration.

It is noteworthy that the latter rain movement of the late 1940s directed its criticisms of the status quo almost exclusively at other Pentecostals. Unlike the first generation of Pentecostals who hoped to influence Protestantism generally, latter rain advocates felt it necessary to demonstrate why turn-of-the-century Pentecostalism was not the prophesied end-times restoration. Theirs was a remnant mentality. They knew they were outsiders, even in relation to other outsiders, and they consciously cultivated that recognition. Though they occasionally hinted that their message would someday engage the larger religious world, for the moment they focused on their own movement.

Bethesda Missionary Temple attracted many who hoped for a dynamic intrusion of the divine into their lives. Its popular pastor, Myrtle Beall, was recognized as a leader among those who believed that the turn-of-the-century Pentecostal revival had been the "early rain" and that in the 1940s the true "latter rain" was falling. But Beall had accepted such views from others. The events that made her congregation a center of latter rain expectations had been set in motion in a tiny hamlet in Saskatchewan late in the fall of 1947.

The Restoration and the Latter Rain

George and Ernest Hawtin and Percy Hunt had fallen into disrepute with their denomination, the Pentecostal Assemblies of Canada (the Canadian parallel organization to the Assemblies of God) in 1947. They had left under pressure and launched an independent Bible school in North Battleford, Saskatchewan. The Bible school was an extension of the efforts that Herrick Holt, a minister of the International Church of the Foursquare Gospel, had already established in the town. Some of the students from the Pentecostal Assemblies of Canada's Bible school in Saskatoon (which George Hawtin had founded twelve years earlier) had joined the men to form the nucleus of the student body.

The school routine resembled that of early Pentecostal Bible schools. Students and staff spent much time in prayer, setting aside prolonged periods for fasting, until by early February 1948 they believed they had entered a "new order" of spiritual experience. Ushered in by prophetic announcement, the "new order" focused on prophecy and the exercise of spiritual gifts. Surveying the organized Pentecostal movement from the vantage point of disinherited participants, Hawtin, Hunt, and Holt found departures from early Pentecostal practice and expectations rampant.

They launched a stern critique of Pentecostalism and announced a new and more powerful revival.

Although their personal problems with Pentecostal denominational leaders undoubtedly influenced them, they were not alone in perceiving a fundamental shift in the direction of North American Pentecostalism, a shift they attributed largely to organization. Others had expressed similar reservations over the years. Much of what advocates of the new order declared had basic similarities to teaching at Ivan Spencer's Elim, a faith Bible school in Hornell, New York; it also shared in significant ways the emphases of Seeley Kinney and Max Wood Moorhead, longtime independent Pentecostal evangelists and writers who, by the thirties, were prominently associated with Elim.[3] Its antidenominationalism (which took the form of advocacy of radical congregationalism) was identical to that of the Scandinavian Pentecostals who organized the Independent Assemblies of God in Chicago.

If the Hawtins' predispositions could be traced among other Pentecostals, the continuity of their message with the views of early Pentecostals assured them both a hearing and opposition. Advocates of the new order rediscovered William Durham, whose name remained familiar as the precipitator of one of the most divisive controversies in Pentecostal history, that over the nature of sanctification. Pentecostals who agreed with Durham's views on sanctification had read him selectively. They had usually disregarded his uncompromising hostility toward organization and formal education. Durham's views on these and other subjects indicted the course North American Pentecostalism in general, and the Assemblies of God in particular, had taken. Advocates of the new order found Durham's most dire predictions of declension fulfilled in the Pentecostal denominations they attacked.

There was precedent, too, for the eschatological thrust of new order advocates. Daniel Kerr, for example, noting a declining focus on healing as early as 1914, had heralded a coming dispensation in which healing would have the prominence accorded to tongues at the turn of the century. As Pentecostal groups had organized and charismatic fervor had waned in some places—or was largely confined to revival campaigns and camp meetings—voices had been raised to assert that the turn-of-the-century Apostolic Faith Movement had been only the beginning of a restoration whose more copious latter rains were yet to come.

Some bewailed the movement's declension, then, regularly reminding adherents of the characteristics of the early revival. Others, on a more positive note, encouraged the faithful to expect more miracles and more fervor in the future. While many Pentecostals looked contentedly on their growing, stabilizing movement, a few here and there, uncom-

fortable with acculturation, sought to fill a prophetic role and keep restorationist expectations current. In so doing, they recalled a radically
separatist part of their Pentecostal heritage most Pentecostals had gladly
neglected. As outsiders calling a movement to task, however, they helped
reveal dimensions of Pentecostal self-understanding that had seldom been
so clearly targeted.

The New Order Message

Those who participated in the meetings at North Battleford in which
the post–World War II restoration occurred described in glowing terms
the intense, highly charged context in which the end-times church was
set in order. Through prophecies, tongues, and interpretation of tongues,
prophets instructed individuals to fill designated offices in the church.
The laying on of hands was used as an act of initiation. Reports of new
dimensions of worship, gifts of healing, slayings in the Spirit, and calls to
a "deeper" life struck responsive chords in the hearts of thousands of Pentecostals in western Canada and then in the United States. The yearning
for a contemporary recurrence of apostolic power seemed intense; like
their Pentecostal forebears, some dreaded "missing God."

As in early Pentecostalism, a wide range of teaching and practice
emerged in the ranks of new order advocates. While some views (like
transubstantiation—or "rightly discerning the Lord's body") were admittedly extreme and not widely disseminated, both doctrine and polity were
reconsidered from the perspective of the deeper spirituality that was advocated. Two basic issues loomed especially large as the Hawtins and
Hunt disseminated news of the restoration; one focused on church government, the other on spiritual gifts.

Since radical restorationists led the discussion, it was filled with appeals to the New Testament. Advocates of the new order insisted that
the New Testament mandated strict congregationalism. To prove that
this had Pentecostal antecedents, they invoked William Durham's long-
ignored tract entitled "Organization." Their rejection of organization became one of the main points of controversy with the existing Pentecostal
movement, most of which was by then clearly divided into numerous
denominations.

New order spokespersons found themselves in agreement as well with
several articles that Joseph Mattson-Boze had published in the June 1944
issue of the *Herald of Faith,* the official publication of a largely Scandinavian denomination known as the Independent Assemblies of God. These
asserted that the "Biblical way" called for sovereign local congregations
"founded on the Word of God" and "filled with His Spirit."[4] Pentecostal

denominations, it followed, were rooted not in faith, but in unbelief: "People are not awake that God was able to take care of his own business. Like Uzzah of old, they stretched forth their own hands to help God and like Israel of old they cried for a king, to be like the rest of the people. God never wanted it that way."[5] Pentecostal denominations—and the Assemblies of God in particular—had emerged either because no wise "masterbuilder" (1 Cor. 3:10) had been available or because his advice was ignored.

By 1949 the controversy had exploded, and George Hawtin found it advisable to systematize his thoughts on the church. In a book entitled *Church Government,* he maintained that "all sects and denominations from Paul's day till now exist because of Man's carnality."[6] Rooted in humankind's "unscriptural fence building," denominations effectively excluded "new wine" and "greater light." They stagnated—and then actively opposed a "true work of God."

Hawtin believed that much of the problem was rooted in unwillingness to recognize the validity of the ministry of apostles and prophets. If each congregation adopted full congregational sovereignty and did so with spiritual rather than ambitious intentions, true unity among "full gospel" believers would inevitably follow. Local churches, whose members presumably included apostles, prophets, teachers, evangelists, and pastors, should set apart their own workers, commission their own missionaries, and discipline their own members, all the while maintaining a cooperative attitude toward other local congregations.[7] To Hawtin, this not only made sense, it conformed to the biblical model.

The emphasis on congregational responsibilities and the concomitant attack on organization frequently seemed directed at the Assemblies of God. The Assemblies of God—in Canada and the United States—was the largest, most affluent, powerful, and visible Pentecostal group. It was also the denomination with which many of the prophets and apostles of the revival had once identified.

A second primary focus of the new order was on spiritual gifts. At first this emphasized discovering those within local congregations who could exercise the nine spiritual gifts listed in 1 Cor. 12. Before long, however, other gifts were added to the list, and people found themselves singled out as recipients of such purported gifts as journalism, cartooning, mercy, and giving.[8]

The act of discerning gifts seemed simple. One participant described how it was exercised daily during a week of prayer at Detroit's Bethesda Missionary Temple: "During the day men of God, who have been called to various offices by the Lord, as they feel led by the Spirit, call out of the congregation folks whose hearts have been made ready, lay hands upon them and set them apart for God. This laying on of hands is accompanied by various prophecies relative to their ministry and gifts of the Spirit that God has bestowed upon them."[9] In practical terms, this seemed to discount Assemblies of God ordination by district presbyteries because such laying on of hands involved no prophetic designation of the ministry and gifts the ordinand should exercise. Those whose gifts had been prophetically assured—lay or ordained—then, constituted a higher order within local congregations and exercised their gifts as local circumstances warranted.

The elevation of prophets and apostles obviously made way for strong individuals to exercise and abuse authority. And it allowed some to give the "Spoken Word" equality with scripture. "There could be no greater error," denominational leaders warned. "Such prophets commence by saying, 'I, the Lord thy God, say unto thee.'"[10] Predictive prophecy, Assemblies of God general secretary J. Roswell Flower cautioned, had "resulted in untold disaster wherever it had been given free course."[11] The new order was nothing new, Flower cautioned. The ground had been covered before, with lessons learned through costly mistakes. Now a new generation seemed to want to begin again.

In fact, some new order advocates apparently intended to outdo the earlier generation. They assured people that they would be spirited into Russia, or other closed countries, for example, where they would be supernaturally enabled to preach the gospel in local dialects before being spirited back to safety.[12] A couple in their midfifties was instructed through prophecy to embark for China. As soon as their feet touched Chinese soil, they were promised, they would both gain ability to speak in "all the Chinese dialects" and the wife's total deafness would be healed.[13]

The Canadian evangelist R. E. McAlister reported that a pastor's wife had been given a gift of administration, while her husband had been granted the gift of obedience: "He was to ask his wife what he should preach and do accordingly."[14] More significant than the variations on the prophetic theme (all of which had occurred frequently in early Pentecostalism), however, was probably the reemphasis on another subject that had preoccupied some Pentecostals—"the manifestation of the sons of God."

Derived from a phrase in Rom. 8:18–23, the "manifestation of the sons of God" focused on the notion that a privileged few, whom new order advocates designated "overcomers," would receive "redemption bodies" in this life. "Eternal life" really meant eternal physical life (a thought that had intrigued Charles Fox Parham early in his ministry). Those who "pressed through" to receive it—the "manifest" sons of

God—would never die.[15] These, then, constituted a select group within the church.

Max Wood Moorhead, Seeley Kinney, and Ivan Spencer all thought they were "manifest sons of God." Moorhead preached frequently and fervently on "victory over death." When he died on 2 May 1937 Spencer hailed him as one who had "embraced the truth," though he had not experienced it.[16] The restoration, Spencer noted, came "by stages"; he believed the "manifest sons of God" were part of God's final stage. In 1970 Spencer, in deteriorating health, was forced to admit that "translation" had eluded him, too, and he was deeply agitated. "Standing for the truth as you see it," his daughter reminded him, "is as acceptable to Him as the act of your translation."[17]

A rereading of the New Testament with a stress on contemporary restoration, then, led to a harsh indictment of contemporary Pentecostalism and to an emphasis on congregational polity, spiritual gifts, and supernatural phenomena. The movement urged days of prayer and fasting, and even its detractors admitted that new order services often had "a very fine spiritual atmosphere."[18] It is not surprising that some thought the new order a powerful manifestation and continuation of early Pentecostal power. New order churches tended to operate on schedules that most Pentecostal congregations had long abandoned but that had once been typical of the movement at large—a weekly schedule including nightly meetings, days of prayer, morning Bible studies, and three Sunday services was not uncommon. Nor is it surprising that these two streams within Pentecostalism collided: new order themes had been latent throughout Pentecostal history, and they clashed—as they always had—with dominant views. Pentecostals in organized denominations naturally took offense at what they regarded to be the primary effort of new order advocates—"the dividing and breaking up of organized work."[19] And they were probably correct; the new order considered the denominations the symbol, if not the cause, of the spiritual stagnation they claimed was rife in Pentecostalism. New order advocates reintroduced views that would explode and be developed within the charismatic movement a generation later. Tensions in the forties laid the groundwork for later controversies.

The New Order of the Latter Rain in the United States

Bethesda Missionary Temple in Detroit became a center of new order teaching after Myrtle Beall traveled to Canada to examine the restoration firsthand. Beall, a high school graduate with seven years of experience in evangelistic efforts before she received Assemblies of God credentials in

1937, maintained a grueling schedule and built a sizable congregation in Detroit before she identified with the restoration movement. In addition to shepherding her congregation she extended her influence via three daily weekday radio broadcasts.[20]

Beall affirmed unequivocally: "This is the hour of Restoration."[21] Her facilities became a center for days of prayer, the exercising of spiritual gifts, and the setting apart of Christian workers. New order sympathies generated new networks that transcended prior loyalties. For example, Beall's sermons were printed in the *Elim Pentecostal Herald,* the organ of the Elim Missionary Assemblies in Hornell, New York, as well as in the *Voice of Faith,* a latter rain publication from Memphis, Tennessee. For Beall, the new network replaced the Assemblies of God in priority.

The new order leaders in Canada designated three apostles for the United States who they believed understood "the fundamentals" of the latter rain outpouring. They were A. W. Rasmussen (Tacoma, Washington) of the Independent Assemblies of God and two Assemblies of God ministers, D. Bruzelius (Monroe, Wisconsin) and Elvar Blomberg (Hibbing, Minnesota).[22]

The Assemblies of God and the New Order

Many factors helped shape the Assemblies of God response to the restoration teaching. Not least was the new order's explicit indictment of the "old Pentecost" that had shaped their movement. "This is not the old whoop, shout, and jump Pentecost," new order advocates boasted of their revival, "but a fresh revelation of God's Word and an entirely different moving of God's Spirit. Don't try to make this outpouring fit in with preconceived ideas of what the LATTER RAIN OUTPOURING should be like. Other denominations tried to do that with Pentecost in 1906 and missed the 'day of His visitation.' "[23]

In the spring of 1949, Assemblies of God general superintendent Ernest Williams resolved to meet the growing demand for response to issues raised by the revival by writing two articles for the *Pentecostal Evangel,* "Are We Pentecostal?" and "Spiritual Gifts." These appeared on 9 and 16 April. On 20 April the denomination sent its ministers a six-page ministers' letter, outlining the disagreements between the denomination and the new order and explaining the denomination's stance on prophecy. These actions responded to growing numbers of letters questioning views promulgated from several cities, through networks linked to Detroit and Canada. Strong centers of new order teaching had been formed in Detroit; St. Louis; Memphis; Oklahoma City; Beaumont, Texas; Tacoma, Washington; and Portland, Oregon, and the movement had outspoken leaders in many small towns, especially in the upper Midwest.

In 1949 the General Council, meeting in Seattle amid increasing controversy over the new order, specifically disapproved three practices: imparting, identifying, bestowing, or confirming gifts by the laying on of hands and prophecy; the teaching that the church was built on the foundation of present-day apostles and prophets; and advocacy of confessing sins and problems to people who then pronounced deliverance or absolution.[24]

During the late forties, then, the felt needs of large numbers of Pentecostals for spiritual vitality made them receptive to a modified form of the early Pentecostal message. This reinforced their outsider identity and reinvigorated the sense of conflict with everyone outside the remnant through which they met their needs for status and meaning. If the world in general and their denominations in particular did not confer it, they created contexts in which to find it. Presented as God's "restoring early Church power to the last minute Church," the New Order of the Latter Rain promised vitality and blessing. Often criticized by the Assemblies of God for fostering a "martyr spirit" and nurturing spiritual arrogance and exclusiveness, the new order nonetheless survived and influenced the course of other movements with which the Assemblies of God—and other classical Pentecostals—have interacted in the past forty years. The two most prominent of these have been the salvation/healing revival and the charismatic movement.

The Salvation/Healing Revival

In 1955 the Assemblies of God evangelist Asa Alonzo Allen announced an ambitious plan, "The Billion Souls Crusade." The "miracle ministries" of Allen, T. L. Osborn, Velmer Gardner, and Gordon Lindsay were poised, Allen reported, to conduct a crusade that would "bring JESUS BACK." They billed it as "the greatest thing that has ever been announced."[25]

"A billion souls for Christ," the Assemblies of God minister Gordon Lindsay mused. "There are a billion souls in this world ready to hear the Gospel if it is preached with the signs following."[26] The "signs" would surely make the difference. Lindsay launched an appeal for finances for a series of crusades designed to "take the secrets that God has given us and move forward in the only plan that will save the world from . . . horrible catastrophe."[27]

Lindsay played a central role in channeling a growing popular religious fascination with the miraculous and making it a financially feasible reli-

gious venture. He and others like him appealed not just to people within
Pentecostal denominations; their activities also helped reveal the dimensions of the nondenominational Pentecostal movement and contributed
to the growth and visibility of independent Pentecostalism. Convinced
that their message of the spiritual and physical benefits of faith offered
the world its final opportunity for redemption, salvation/healing revivalists (many of whom were Assemblies of God ministers) gained visibility
by preaching simple, emotion-packed sermons to huge audiences that
crowded into tents to hear prophecies and witness miracles. The setting
encouraged relaxing the rules by which most Americans typically worshiped. Warmth, rhythm, and shouts pervaded the atmosphere, which
was also hospitable to spiritual gifts. Crowds identified with the overstate-
ments and the exaggerated criticisms that punctuated the messages. But
the highlight of such gatherings was usually the time allotted for prayer
for the sick. In a faith-charged setting, charismatic leaders whose magnetic personalities charmed their audiences claimed to exercise gifts that
brought physical—and sometimes temporal—benefits to believers.

William Branham and Oral Roberts were two of the most prominent
representatives of this revival, but scores of lesser-known men and women
also carried its message.[28] That message was shaped by Pentecostal expectations and found a generous response among members of various Pentecostal denominations. But the effort was part of a much broader hope that
revival would sweep America. The late 1940s and early 1950s saw the
proliferation of evangelistic outreaches across America as such efforts as
Youth for Christ rallies, Billy Graham crusades, and religious radio broadcasts sought to promote religious awakening.

Although the "Billion Souls Crusade" faded from the headlines as its
promoters became sidetracked by other issues, it initially conveyed admirably what a growing group of Pentecostal evangelists set out to accomplish. Convinced that miracles would attract the masses and that Pentecostal experience was "endowment with power," they set out to preach
the present possibility of deliverance from sin and sickness. Their message
was cast in end-times rhetoric and generally stressed increasingly miraculous claims. They tended to charge that the Pentecostal movement had
strayed from its heritage; they thus played on sentimental memories of
the "good old days" and the yearning for the new and the fresh that
evoked response among Pentecostal people who were often bewildered by
their movement's changing character.

In general, promoters of the salvation/healing movement came from
lower-class backgrounds. They spoke the language of the people and identified with the physical and economic hardship many in their audiences
experienced. Once they had established a support network, they often

made increasingly radical claims.[29] For example, late in the fall of 1955 Asa Alonzo Allen pitched his tent in Los Angeles. Allen's magazine gave a glowing description of the ensuing meetings:

> Many had declared that never before had they seen the Spirit of God manifested in such a miraculous way. People had received heal-ing while sitting in their seats. . . . Tumors disappeared as those so afflicted stood before [Allen]. Blind eyes came open at the touch of his hand, even without prayer. Scores of people had already leaped from wheel chairs. People who had been carried in on their death beds had arisen from their beds and carried them out of the meeting. There was no question that the miracle working power of God had been in operation from the start.[30]

As the excitement mounted, a woman stood to prophesy. The hushed crowd heard her announce that God would do "a new thing" within three days. (The promise of a "new thing" was historically well calculated to capture Pentecostal attention: it was evidence some needed of God's im-mediacy and reassurance of participation in his contemporary plan.) All who believed would see "miracle oil" flowing from their hands. This oil would bring responsibility. Believers were charged to lay their oil-exuding hands on the sick with the promise that the blind, deaf, and lame would be healed.[31]

The next day participants began to claim that oil flowed from their hands, and the afflicted came themselves or sent handkerchiefs in expec-tation of healing. The meetings continued for weeks. Allen drew up a statement that twenty-four ministers (some of whom represented local Assemblies of God churches) signed, attesting that they had seen the oil.[32] Countless varieties of such claims surfaced in other ministries, too.

While the revivalists welcomed such signs as conclusive evidence of God's activity through them, their interests also included a more typical premillennialist fascination with current events and signs in the heavens. In April 1954 the *Voice of Healing* magazine, organ of the largest associa-tion of salvation/healing revivalists, published a cover story entitled "The Mystery of the Flying Saucers—in the Light of the Bible." Testimonies to many varieties of divine intervention in commonplace circumstances vied for space in such magazines with glowing reports of the revival's progress, testimonies of healings, and explanations of current events.

In an effort to make the revival more credible by promoting account-ability, Gordon Lindsay became its promoter and made an enormous con-tribution to it. He proved adept at working with people of various reli-gious affiliations and contributed his business sense and literary skills to the movement's progress.

In April 1948, while working as campaign manager for healing revivalist William Branham, Lindsay began to publish the *Voice of Healing*, a
monthly magazine, to publicize the revival. When Branham withdrew
temporarily from ministry, Lindsay's magazine featured the meetings of
William Freeman, an evangelist linked to the New Order of the Latter
Rain. At the end of one year Lindsay had a circulation of thirty thousand,
which was rapidly growing.

In December 1949 Lindsay organized a convention of healing revivalists in Dallas. It featured two men whose ministries dated from early Assemblies of God history, Fred Francis Bosworth and Raymond T. Richey.
In addition to these mentors of the new generation, Lindsay featured
several with emerging ministries, some of whom were Assemblies of God
evangelists: O. L. Jaggers, Gayle Jackson, Velmer Gardner, and Clifton
Erickson.[33]

The next year some one thousand evangelists gathered at the Voice of
Healing Convention. The movement was growing rapidly; from a risky
venture that had absorbed most of Lindsay's personal savings, it had become an impressive popular religious movement. In Lindsay's mind, then,
the Voice of Healing was two things: it was a loose, voluntary association
of salvation/healing revivalists, male and female, who agreed to abide by
certain regulations, and it was a monthly magazine that featured testimonies drawn from many revival campaigns and publicity about upcom-
ing meetings. Listing in the *Voice of Healing* implied the evangelist's willingness to follow the association's rules; the magazine advertised only
those evangelists with proven ministries.[34] The conventions helped demonstrate the movement's magnitude and its diversity. They offered inspi-
rational rallies and small workshops, and participation on the program
was a coveted honor.

Healing evangelists received considerable press coverage, which
brought notoriety. Among the most popular of the evangelists was the
Assemblies of God's Jack Coe. Ordained to the ministry in 1944, Coe
renounced a rough life-style to travel the revival circuit. Crowds loved
his blunt, forthright language; his defiance of ministerial dignity; his bold
faith. Always ready for the "hardest" cases, he seemed to court publicity.
Outspoken in his opposition to medicine, Coe insisted on the supreme
adequacy of faith.

In February 1956 Coe was in Miami, in the midst of a forty-four-day
campaign that at first drew capacity crowds of six thousand, when he was
charged with practicing medicine without a license. The trial brought to
Florida some of the most prominent leaders of the revival to testify in
Coe's defense. Charges were dismissed.[35] Early the next year, Coe's death
in a hospital of polio shocked his following. Forty-seven years old, he had

denounced the use of medicine by his followers, but his family had turned to physicians in his illness. The various institutions through which he had conducted his ministry continued, but without him, their visibility waned.

During his heyday, Jack Coe had been dismissed from the Assemblies of God. A contentious man, he had failed to honor Voice of Healing guidelines and had disagreed bitterly and publicly with denominational leaders. Fiercely independent and naturally zealous for his own efforts, he had consciously sought to undermine the denomination's credibility among those who participated in the revival. The brevity of Coe's leadership has obscured his popularity; during the early fifties he was a force with which others had to reckon, especially as he rapidly gained the popular support necessary to withdraw from Lindsay's umbrella organization.

Another member of the original nucleus of the Voice of Healing, Asa Alonzo Allen, also held Assemblies of God credentials. Late in 1955 Allen was arrested in Knoxville for driving while intoxicated. The evidence gathered by Knoxville police was conclusive. Allen chose to label the incident "persecution," was incensed that others would believe the incident had occurred, and refused to abide by a recommendation that, until the matter was settled, he refrain from preaching.[36]

Both the Coe and Allen cases brought the Assemblies of God unprecedented media attention. Not only the secular press but also the magazines spawned by the revival (which circulated by the scores of thousands—in 1958 Coe's *Herald of Healing* had a circulation of three hundred thousand) aired the controversies between the evangelists and their denomination.[37]

The Coe and Allen cases were the most publicized of several that demanded denominational attention during the height of the salvation/healing revival in the fifties. They forced the Assemblies of God to respond to issues raised by the revival. Coe and Allen were major figures among the evangelists, preaching in tents (Coe claimed his was the world's largest) and on a growing number of radio stations. They published their own monthly magazines and built sizable organizations. They lived in a world in which miracles and intense spiritual experiences were commonplace, in which prophecies and conflicts with evil forces were part of everyday life. It is hardly surprising that, from their viewpoint, average churches were "dead" and denominational organizations were hopelessly politicized.

Discussions in the denomination's governing body, the General Presbytery, in September 1953 resulted in the adoption of several motions recommending a renewed emphasis on the teaching and practice of "scriptural truths" of healing and "deliverance from sin, sickness and satanic forces."[38] They disapproved fund-raising methods and reports of attendance and healing that were open to challenge and endorsed the preparation of a series of articles for the *Pentecostal Evangel* on divine healing, the baptism with the Holy Spirit, and prophecy.[39] They noted with concern that the excitement and extravagance of salvation/healing crusades tended to make people dissatisfied with local congregations and pastors.

During the early fifties Lindsay's influence as coordinator and promoter of the revival waned, and the restraint he had urged through the Voice of Healing virtually disappeared. Open confrontations between denominational officials and independently minded Assemblies of God evangelists publicized bitter recriminations. The Texas district, in which some of the more controversial healing evangelists held credentials, was especially hard pressed. No longer compelled by their need for legitimation to accept Lindsay's restrictions, evangelists who set up their own organizations increasingly defied Assemblies of God precedent and structure.

Although many denominational leaders had reservations about the healing revival, large numbers of adherents did not. Their willingness to support financially the projects of the revivalists made the movement possible and took support from denominational projects and local church programs.

During the fifties healing evangelists undertook large-scale overseas efforts, claiming divine inspiration for the use of salvation/healing campaigns and "signs and wonders" in overseas evangelism. Issues of the *Voice of Healing* as well as magazines representing individual ministries publicized reports of immense crusades abroad. Some evangelists enjoyed considerably more success abroad than at home, notably Tommy Hicks (whose 1954 crusade in Argentina was described by David Edwin Harrell, Jr., as "perhaps the most famous single meeting in the history of the revival") and T. L. Osborn.[40] In 1967 Lindsay symbolized his changed focus by renaming the *Voice of Healing Christ for the Nations*. Just as *Voice of Healing* was much more than a publication, so *Christ for the Nations* came to describe a growing network of efforts, including a large charismatic Bible school in Dallas that continues to operate under that name.

While Pentecostal missionaries at first welcomed the mass meetings, the fund-raising practices they generated (compounded by their general lack of financial accountability) and their emphasis on national workers soon complicated the picture. Concerns about related issues supported the definite trend among executive leaders to distance the Assemblies of God from the salvation/healing revival.

In 1965 fund-raising techniques related to institutions and causes spawned by the salvation/healing revival resulted in the adoption by the General Council of Criteria for Independent Corporations. These criteria

ultimately forced Gordon Lindsay (who had remained an Assemblies of
God minister in good standing throughout the tumultuous years of the
revival) to choose between the Assemblies of God and the various independent efforts to which he had devoted most of his life. Not surprisingly,
he withdrew. His Dallas-based efforts did not suffer. With his talented
wife, Freda, he identified increasingly with neo-Pentecostalism; expanded
his native church program, his production of native literature, his teaching tapes (some two thousand of which he supplied to charismatic prayer
groups monthly); and devoted himself to the operation of his school and
thirty-acre headquarters complex in Dallas. When he died suddenly on
1 April 1973, Lindsay had gained widespread recognition for his varied
abilities. Perhaps most significantly, he left a sizable body of literature in
which he chronicled and explained the revival. His passing marked the
end of an era. His experience reached through denominational affiliation
back to participation with some of Pentecostalism's earliest leaders and
forward into charismatic settings. He had known the revival's founders
and their successors. Although he had failed to contain their efforts, he
had succeeded in retaining his own reputation for integrity.

By the time Lindsay died, the revival was no longer so prominent. Its
character changed somewhat, as leaders aged and died and tents gave way
to televangelism. In a sense, deliverance evangelism never died; rather,
it remade itself into the electronic church.[41]

The boundaries of the post–World War II salvation/healing revival are
difficult to chart, for it overlapped in significant ways with other movements in American evangelicalism. And it served multiple purposes. Not
only did it reveal the persistence of fiercely independent prophetic leadership within Pentecostalism it also demonstrated that hundreds of thousands of Americans willingly identified with charismatic figures accountable to no one. Perhaps it did challenge an increasingly institutionalized
movement to renew its stress on the miraculous. Certainly it also proved
that the rhetoric and claims of the first-generation Pentecostal revival still
struck responsive chords in both Pentecostal and non-Pentecostal souls.

It thrived at least in part because the claims of its leaders made sense
to their contemporaries. Many Protestants anticipated revival and believed that the horrors of war had inclined people toward religion. Americans were proving responsive to the assurance of people such as Norman
Vincent Peale, whose book, *The Power of Positive Thinking,* became a
best-seller in 1952. The seeds of later "positive confession" teaching that
meshed Pentecostal religion and the American dream were clearly evident among some of the healers. Kenneth Hagin, whose charismatic leadership and Rhema Bible Institute (Tulsa) have become symbolic of the
view that a Christian commitment should effect health and prosperity,

was an Assemblies of God minister who identified prominently with the salvation/healing revival from its inception. The evolution of such thought—with its implications for fund-raising—is most readily traceable in the ministry of Oral Roberts. [42]

The healing revival was perceived as a call to "old-time religion" under old-fashioned gospel tents in an era in which science and modernity seemed to renew their challenge to evangelical faith. It was presented as essentially American—as opposed to "godless communism"—in an era in which the cold war gave religious commitment patriotic as well as spiritual overtones (and it was linked, through some of its personalities, to right-wing politics). It unashamedly avowed the presence of the supernatural to transform human existence. It exposed thousands of people for the first time to settings in which Pentecostal worship and spiritual gifts were commonplace. Reports of miracles and the aura of tent revivals attracted people who would not have entered a Pentecostal church. Out of it came associations that promoted and influenced the emerging charismatic movement—like the Full Gospel Business Men's Fellowship International. It was also a business venture of major proportions that packaged and marketed the gospel in ways that fundamentally altered its message. If its rhetoric claimed that its primary goals were religious, its practices seemed at times to belie that claim. Even as its religious features were unitive, its frankly entrepreneurial cast became divisive.

In reemphasizing experience, the salvation/healing revival downplayed doctrinal differences, first among Pentecostals, then among Christians. By the seventies, for example, Pentecostal evangelist Kathryn Kuhlman had become a well-known charismatic leader whose efforts readily embraced Catholics and Protestants of all varieties. Especially after it became evident that no Pentecostal denomination would identify with the revival, many salvation/healing evangelists forsook Pentecostal denominations (either willingly or under duress) and stressed the essential unity of all who shared charismatic experience. Links among the various healing ministries, especially in support of specific associations or gatherings, were not uncommon.

Independent Pentecostals who had historically rejected organization of their movement and charismatics who forsook denominations in which they no longer felt at home (or who chose to remain in denominations and to identify as well with charismatic networks) together constituted an increasingly visible and vocal segment of American Pentecostalism. Some who had been alienated from Pentecostal denominations over the New Order of the Latter Rain readily accepted the premises about faith and miracles that salvation/healing revivalists urged and identified with nondenominational Pentecostalism.

The salvation/healing revival, then, gave rise to many of the assumptions that operated later in charismatic circles. It contributed, as well, to the reservations Pentecostal denominational leaders expressed about the charismatic movement. The connections are most visible in the careers of men and women such as Oral Roberts, Gordon and Freda Lindsay, and Kathryn Kuhlman.

Taken together, the New Order of the Latter Rain and the salvation/healing revival revealed the dimensions of a large segment of Pentecostalism that had opted historically for nonorganization. They demonstrated as well the continuing appeal of restorationist and end-times concepts and the ambiguity of classical Pentecostals about their denominations. On the one hand, the conviction that denominations had betrayed the movement's essence was widespread; on the other, the recognition that they served a vital purpose persisted.

Despite attempts by denominational leaders to label them aberrations, the New Order of the Latter Rain and the salvation/healing revival revealed the continuing fascination of American Pentecostals for the themes that dominated Pentecostalism's early history. They served further as reminders of the inadequacy of definitions of American Pentecostalism that focus on its denominations and ignore the vitality and direction of its independent sector. They highlighted ambiguities about independence and organization as well as the considerable gap between leadership and constituency.

NOTES

1. Unsigned letter addressed to the Guardians of Our Heritage, 28 Feb. 1949, Latter Rain Collection, Assemblies of God Archives, Springfield, Mo. (hereafter LRC and AGA).

2. Ibid.

3. Moorhead, a former missionary to India, accepted Pentecostal views in 1906 and became an itinerant independent preacher, teacher, and author. After spending some time in England during World War I (where his objections to the war fervor of England patriots resulted in his imprisonment as a German spy) he taught at Beulah Heights and other schools before identifying with Spencer's efforts. See his obituary, *Elim Pentecostal Herald*, May 1937, 7.

4. Mattson-Boze, "Too Big to Bag," *Herald of Faith*, June 1944, New Order of the Latter Rain Collection (hereafter NOLRC), AGA.

5. Ibid.

6. George Hawtin, *Church Government* (Los Angeles: Fox Printing, 1949), 8.

7. Ibid., especially chaps. 3 and 5.

8. R. E. McAlister, "Apostles—True or False," *Truth Advocate* 1 (May 1949): 20.

9. Letter to Guardians of Our Heritage. The AGA has transcriptions of various prophecies by the Hawtins and Myrtle Beall instructing the recipients about their gifts and callings.

10. R. E. McAlister, "Prophets—True or False," *Truth Advocate* 1 (May 1949): 6.

11. Assemblies of God Ministers' Letter, 20 Apr. 1949, 4, Assemblies of God Archives, Springfield, Mo. (hereafter AGA).

12. R. E. McAlister to Ernest Williams, 23 Apr. 1949, NOLRC.

13. Ibid.

14. R. E. McAlister, "The Restitution of All Things," *Truth Advocate* 1 (May 1949): 20.

15. R. E. McAlister, "What Is Meant by the Manifestation of the Sons of God?" *Truth Advocate* 1 (Aug. 1949): 11.

16. Ivan Spencer, "In Memoriam," *Elim Pentecostal Herald*, May 1937, 6.

17. Quoted in Marion Meloon, *Ivan Spencer: Willow in the Wind* (Plainfield, N.J.: Logos International, 1974), 224.

18. C. B. Smith (General Superintendent of the Pentecostal Assemblies of Canada) to F. J. Lindquist, 7 Dec. 1948, NOC.

19. Ibid.

20. Myrtle Beall File, Assemblies of God Secretariat, Springfield, Mo. (hereafter AGS).

21. Ralph E. Northrup, "Belief of the Latter Rain People," NOC.

22. See *Herald of Faith* 25 (July 1950): 3. As time passed, the dominant male leaders had serious reservations about women's participation in apostolic roles. It seems evident that Beall exercised more authority in discerning and bestowing gifts than her male counterparts thought appropriate.

23. Unsigned letter addressed to Guardians of Our Heritage, 1 Mar. 1949, NOLRC.

24. "Report of the Committee on the New Order of the Latter Rain," General Presbytery Minutes, 1949, AGS.

25. "A Last Minute Word from A. A. Allen," *Voice of Healing*, special ed., 1955, 2.

26. Gordon Lindsay, "A Billion Souls for Christ," *Voice of Healing*, special ed., 1955, 10.

27. Ibid.

28. For the story of the revival, see David Edwin Harrell, Jr., *All Things Are Possible* (Bloomington: Indiana University Press, 1975); David Edwin Harrell, Jr., *Oral Roberts: An American Life* (Bloomington: Indiana University Press, 1985).

29. Eve Simson, in *The Faith Healer* (St. Louis: Concordia Publishing, 1977), analyzes their social backgrounds.

30. "The Miracle of the Outpoured Oil," *Miracle Magazine*, Jan. 1956, 2.

31. Ibid., 3.

32. Ibid., 4.

33. Harrell, *All Things Are Possible*, 55.

34. Ibid., 56.

35. *Jack Coe's International Healing Magazine*, May 1956, 22, 23; Harrell, *All Things Are Possible*, 62.

36. Asa Alonzo Allen, "My Final Answer to the General Council of the Assemblies of God," *Miracle Magazine*, May 1956, 4; R. W. Schambach, "Has A. A. Allen Been Persecuted?" *Miracle Magazine*, May 1956, 5.

37. Severe internal criticism came in the sixties from a balanced, respected Pentecostal leader, Granville H. Montgomery. Montgomery had edited the *Pentecostal Holiness Advocate*, the official publication of the Pentecostal Holiness Church, for many years. He joined Oral Roberts's team, then left Roberts in 1961 and identified with Jack Coe's efforts, led by his widow, Juanita. In 1962 Montgomery published a series of articles he entitled "Enemies of the Cross" in which he castigated major revivalists and the Pentecostal denominations which, he claimed, had forced the revivalists to extremes. Harrell rightly summarized the force of Montgomery's critique: it was at once "the protest of a sympathetic insider" and that of a "true believer." *All Things Are Possible*, 141.

38. General Presbytery Minutes, 1952, 14, AGS.

39. Ibid., 15.

40. Harrell, *All Things Are Possible*, 79.

41. For the story of recent related themes, see Bruce Barron, *The Health and Wealth Gospel* (Downers Grove, Ill.: InterVarsity Press, 1987).

42. See Harrell, *Roberts*, 460–62.

10

Changing Perspectives on Renewal
and Unity, 1952–75

E ARLY Pentecostals had talked much about Christian unity. Early in its history, the Assemblies of God welcomed like-minded people of all affiliations and understood Pentecostalism as end-times renewal for the whole church. Pentecostals understood one of the primary purposes of the restoration to be unity. By midcentury, however, unity had assumed specific overtones, and a series of events illustrated how far the Assemblies of God had moved from the early Pentecostal vision. Its interaction with ecumenical leaders and the charismatic renewal shows that despite continuities with an earlier rhetoric of unity, the denomination shared the fundamentalist and new evangelical distrust of mainstream Protestantism. Yet its protestations about its loyalty to widely shared evangelical doctrines did not necessarily assure its welcome among these non-Pentecostal conservatives. From 1960 the denomination worked out new ways in which to express its identity and further modified its restorationist millenarian self-understanding.

When Dennis Bennett, rector of St. Mark's Church in Van Nuys, California, resigned his parish under pressure early in 1960, his predicament attracted media attention. On 4 July 1960 *Newsweek* carried a story about the controversial rector's recent spiritual pilgrimage, which focused on tongues speech and other "gifts of the Spirit" that had surfaced in his experience and among his congregation.[1] Considered "proper" for Pentecostals, such speech proved "strange and troublesome indeed" for a well-educated, upper middle-class, suburban Protestant Episcopal parish.[2] And, more troubling, what occurred was not an isolated event: Bennett and some seventy members of his congregation were part of a growing network of local ministers and laypeople in the diocese who had spoken in tongues since late in 1959. An electronics wholesaler turned Congregationalist minister turned Anglo-Catholic Episcopalian, Bennett had emerged as the acknowledged leader of this enthusiastic group that had determined to nurture a Pentecostal witness from within the historic denomination.[3]

When Bennett attempted to explain and defend the practice of tongues speech before his congregation, one of his curates took off his vestments and resigned during the service and church officers demanded Bennett's resignation. Bennett complied, but at the same time refused to renounce the priesthood and urged his supporters to remain in the church. A few months later he accepted reassignment to a struggling, nearly bankrupt parish, St. Luke's in Olympia, Washington. Within a year, nearly one hundred communicants of St. Luke's had spoken in tongues, and the congregation had outgrown its building. By the midseventies some two thousand people worshipped weekly at St. Luke's and Bennett had become the symbol of a movement that had spread throughout the world.[4]

Classical Pentecostal Bridges to Charismatic Renewal

Stories in *Newsweek* and *Time* played an important role in giving a general growing interest in the Holy Spirit national visibility. The interest manifested itself in two separate but interrelated arenas: the charismatic renewal in some mainstream Protestant denominations and Roman Catholicism and the ecumenical movement. The events the media covered in 1960 helped mark a new phase in American religious awareness of charismatic Christianity. They became part of the stream of events that made Pentecostalism the largest twentieth-century Christian movement. While scholars may debate whether the charismatic movement was spawned primarily by classical Pentecostalism or if it was an indigenous development in mainstream Protestantism and Catholicism, it is evident that several trends within classical Pentecostalism helped forge ties between the two movements. For over a decade at least three developments had generated expectations and occasioned events and institutions that helped make some Pentecostals hospitable toward the emergence of Pentecostal forms of religious experience in non-Pentecostal churches.

First, the latter-rain movement, despite its elitist message, energized expectations that helped mold the perceptions of some who later became charismatic leaders. Second, the salvation/healing revival introduced masses of non-Pentecostals to the Pentecostal ethos and created a variety of nondenominational agencies and institutions that helped sustain and channel interest in charismatic worship and spiritual gifts. Third, the remarkable activities of David Du Plessis, an Assemblies of God pastor and international Pentecostal leader, gave Pentecostalism visibility, first among ecumenical leaders of mainstream denominations and then in Roman Catholicism.

Each of these created substantial friction within Pentecostal denominations such as the Assemblies of God. Each thrived, however, partly because it claimed to recapture something that had been central to early Pentecostal perceptions of the movement's meaning and mission. Each insisted that Pentecostalism was essentially a renewal movement that should not be confined to specific denominations; its purpose, rather, was to empower the entire church and enable the church to realize its essential unity in Christ.

Each of the three also emphasized the conviction that the extent and intensity of Pentecostal witness should constantly increase. Resisting the tendency to locate Pentecostalism's golden age in the past, they maintained that it was in the present and future. The New Order of the Latter Rain leader George Hawtin described a "wonderful deliverance from the terrible bondage of the Babylon of the denominational system" as he substituted "present truth" for "past truth."[5] The healing evangelist Asa Alonzo Allen used the slogan "miracles today"; he and his Voice of Healing colleagues proclaimed a worldwide revival.[6] They emphasized divine activity in their day rather than wistful hopes for a return to prior power. In so doing, they legitimated their ministries in the familiar way of placing themselves at the center of God's end-times plan, but they looked forward rather than backward for restoration. Jack Coe, despite his feisty reputation, expressed a hope many healing evangelists shared: "I'm only interested in bringing the body of Christ into the unity of the Spirit, with love in their hearts for one another."[7]

Most prominent healing evangelists had broken their ties to denominations by the midfifties. Their interdenominational appeal clearly targeted a broad audience without urging new denominational loyalties. "Doctrine," Coe insisted, "is not the basis of fellowship among Christians. The basis of fellowship is the blood of the Lord Jesus Christ."[8] Coe foresaw a day when Pentecostal phenomena would sweep through the Christian church without respect to denomination or creed: "Soon the wilderness is going to be made rivers of water and the desert places are going to spring forth . . . and you old 'dry hides' are going to get into this thing too!"[9]

Both advocates of the Latter Rain and salvation/healing evangelists explicitly coveted early Christian fervor and power. While they found more evidence of such fervor in American Pentecostal history than among their contemporaries, they believed they were heralds of "God's second call," a "call" that would find readier response among traditional Protestants than among Pentecostals who believed the restoration had already come.[10] Their own circumstances contributed to such convictions, of course. Criticized by Pentecostal denominational leaders, the Pentecostal prophets of God's contemporary "new move" were forced to develop an emphasis on progressive restoration and Christian unity in order to build and expand independent ministries.

Themes of unity resonated as well with a growing trend among Pentecostal denominations toward associational agencies like the National Association of Evangelicals and the Pentecostal World Conference. The British Pentecostal editor Donald Gee (who had wide influence in the American Assemblies of God) noted that such associations eased friction and strengthened common testimony. Gee observed, however, that Pentecostals who rejected denominational organization for independent ministries only superficially imitated primitive Christians.[11] Rather, they evaded "the stern necessity of serving our own generation."[12] A similar concern "to serve the present age" had motivated denominational federations such as the Federal Council of Churches of Christ. Gee's vision for unity was remarkably similar to that of both the Federal Council and the World Council of Churches: he urged "unity of obedience to Christ as Lord," unity that he described—with typical Pentecostal individualism—as a "personal matter." "My ultimate unity," Gee maintained, "is with my brother, irrespective of whether we belong to the same or different, outward communions. We do not come together to 'make' unity, for it already exists by the grace of God. . . . Its test is mutual acceptance of the Lordship of Jesus Christ."[13]

While many Assemblies of God adherents agreed in theory, in practice increasingly stringent denominational requirements and popular triumphalist rhetoric made it difficult to realize the vision the talk of unity projected. Two prominent Pentecostals, Oral Roberts and Demos Shakarian, a wealthy Californian, sought to give it institutional expression in 1951 when they created the Full Gospel Business Men's Fellowship International (FGBMFI). Focusing on business and professional men, the FGBMFI offered neutral forums in which people from many denominations could explore their common faith. It was apparently widely influential in cultivating a grass-roots charismatic ecumenical outlook. Local chapters organized social meetings in which those interested in Pentecostal experience as well as tongues-speaking members of non-Pentecostal denominations mingled with adherents of Pentecostal churches. Offering neutral turf, such meetings provided more respectable settings than did humble Pentecostal churches and were among the few places in which classical Pentecostals and charismatics mingled. Since the FGBMFI was not con-

trolled by a Pentecostal denomination, its programs promoted no specific church affiliation. From 1953 the FGBMFI extended its influence
with a monthly publication, *Full Gospel Business Men's Voice*. Filled
with accounts of members of mainline denominations who had spoken
in tongues, the magazine was widely distributed outside of Pentecostal
denominations.

Many Assemblies of God adherents shared the excitement and vision
that prompted efforts like the FGBMFI. While some pastors and leaders welcomed efforts to witness Spirit baptism in mainline denominations
without raising divisive doctrinal differences, however, others were deeply
concerned. The Assemblies of God by this time understood Spirit baptism
in the context of a baptistic evangelical theology. Some local pastors also
resented the time and money their well-to-do business members devoted
to the FGBMFI. And the FGBMFI ultimately conflicted as well with Assemblies of God Men's Ministries, which were denominationally focused.

Puzzled by apparent inconsistencies, Assemblies of God adherents
struggled with the meaning and extent of the term *unity*. By the 1950s
Pentecostal denominations emphasized specific doctrines and practices as
biblical requisites for Spirit baptism. Assemblies of God adherents, for
example, generally anticipated that Spirit baptism evidenced by tongues
would follow a crisis conversion experience and baptism by immersion.
When people who claimed charismatic experiences failed to leave liturgical churches, to reject infant baptism and be rebaptized, to turn from
sacramental theologies, and to renounce life-styles that permitted long-
held Pentecostal taboos—dancing, smoking, drinking, bowling—they
raised uncomfortable questions. Was shared experience of the Holy Spirit
a sufficient basis for unity? Or would true unity necessarily begin with
doctrinal agreement and shared behavioral norms? If the charismatic experience of Spirit baptism was authentic, were the classical Pentecostals
wrong? Was their separatist life-style necessary?

Renewal and Ecumenism: David Du Plessis

For members of the Assemblies of God, such questions were raised
most forcibly by a South African immigrant, David J. Du Plessis, in whose
career the two issues of renewal and ecumenism became inextricably in-
tertwined.[14] Du Plessis had joined the Pentecostal movement in 1918 and
had been secretary of his denomination, the Apostolic Faith Movement
(South Africa). With Donald Gee, he promoted communication among
isolated Pentecostal groups throughout the thirties and assisted in running
the first Pentecostal World Conference in 1947. As secretary of the Pentecostal World Conference, Du Plessis was widely recognized for his

gentle, persuasive spirit. Late in the forties he and his wife, Anna, migrated to the United States, where he soon obtained Assemblies of God preaching credentials and accepted a small congregation, Stamford Gospel Tabernacle, in Stamford, Connecticut. He continued to serve the Pentecostal World Conference and to exert influence well beyond his congregation.

Du Plessis shared with Donald Gee the simple persuasion that true Christian unity came through acknowledgment of Christ as Lord. When the ongoing broader Protestant quest for unity in submission to the Lordship of Christ issued in the formation of the World Council of Churches in 1948, a deluge of Pentecostal and evangelical protests drawing on prophetic images of "superchurches" and "the beast" followed. Du Plessis, however, resisted the logic. In typical Pentecostal fashion, he later recalled, he "began to pray earnestly about His purposes."[15]

Before long, he claimed divine instructions to visit World Council leaders and witness to his Pentecostal experience. Arriving at the council's New York City offices unannounced, he was surprised to be warmly welcomed. He spent the entire day in conversation with the staff, explaining "things that I thought they did not want to hear."[16] His visit began a lifelong association with mainline denominational leaders that was marked by mutual respect.

In 1952 Du Plessis accepted an invitation to participate in the International Missionary Council's extended sessions in Willingen, West Germany. The meetings brought together some two hundred representatives (many of whom were prominent in the growing ecumenical movement) from forty-five countries to consider the church's missionary obligation; as a group they strongly endorsed a basic Christian commitment to evangelistic witness.[17] During the ten-day conference Du Plessis responded to several questions in plenary sessions and to requests for personal interviews from over half the delegates.[18]

By 1954 when the World Council of Churches met for its second assembly in Evanston, Illinois, Du Plessis was a familiar figure in ecumenical ranks. Prominent leaders such as John Mackay, president of Princeton Theological Seminary, and Visser 't Hooft, secretary of the World Council of Churches, urged him to mingle freely with delegates, talking about Pentecostal experience. Du Plessis was elated when he discovered widespread interest in his testimony among church leaders and academics, but he soon discovered that he was "without honor in his own country."[19]

Like others in the National Association of Evangelicals, most Assemblies of God adherents misunderstood and mistrusted the ecumenical movement.[20] Many in the denomination had long been fascinated by predictive prophecy. Major religious and political developments invariably

invited prophetic speculation. Heightened in the forties by events in Israel and the world war's presentation of a roster of likely candidates for
the Antichrist, this attempt to make current events fit the prophecies of
Ezekiel and Daniel found expression in such common evangelistic tools
as dispensational charts. Assigning ecumenism prophetic import, then,
they considered that it heralded the prophesied world church; they also
rejected its stress on unity as predicated on false assumptions. This despite
disavowals by leading American proponents of the ecumenical movement
during the fifties of an attempt to unite denominations: "The idea of a
world church ecclesiastically united has not found explicit or even vague
expression in this movement," editor Charles Clayton Morrison wrote in
the *Christian Century* in 1954.[21] Nonetheless, evangelicals generally preferred to believe that the prophesied world church would soon emerge
through the World Council of Churches. Du Plessis's involvement, then,
represented a fundamental betrayal of Pentecostal principle because he
associated with heralds of the "scarlet woman" and compromised truth in
favor of experience.

Du Plessis understood this attitude: he had once shared it fully. Recounting his growing ecumenical involvement during the fifties, he later
reminisced: "I could remember days when I had wished I could have set
my eyes upon such men to denounce their theology and pray the judgment of God upon them for what I considered their heresies and false
doctrines."[22] Du Plessis, ever a champion of religious experience, claimed
his attitude had been transformed by "a warm glow" of the Holy Spirit
that filled him with love for the mainstream church leaders whom so
many of his fellow Pentecostals distrusted.

Not only did Du Plessis engage in suspect ecumenical activities, he
further alienated his peers by joining those who voiced concern from
within about the waning vitality of American Pentecostalism. During the
forties the *Pentecostal Evangel* published articles alleging that despite its
growth, much of the movement had departed from its early practices.[23]
Du Plessis heartily concurred and prescribed a remedy in a widely distributed tract, "God Has No Grandsons."

Noting that "today the sons and grandsons of Pentecostal pioneers are
teaching in Sunday Schools and holding all kinds of offices in the local
churches without ever having had a real baptism in the Spirit," Du Plessis
warned that "the waves of Pentecostal power and revival are receding
fast. There is danger that in another generation we may have a Pentecostal Movement without Pentecost—that is, without the experience, just
like other revivals which still emphasize some or other truth but never
experience it. Revivals crystalize into societies and establish churches
when the 'grandsons' take over. But *God has no grandsons.*"[24] From his

perspective, only a divinely inspired renewal of experience could reverse the situation. He anticipated God's activity rather than human success in recovering apostolic power. "God," he maintained "wants to repeat what He did in the first Christian Church in every generation."[25] He envisioned successive restorations of experience, rather than one all-encompassing end-times return to New Testament norms.

The World Council of Churches and the End Times

Du Plessis, then, challenged Pentecostal denominations on at least two fronts: he raised questions of identity that were rooted in long-nurtured suppositions and he deplored the movement's status quo. His activities helped force the Assemblies of God to make explicit some long-held assumptions about the burgeoning ecumenical movement. As noted, by 1948 when the World Council of Churches was formed in Amsterdam, most Assemblies of God leaders had fully identified with the new evangelicalism of the National Association of Evangelicals. Like others in that association, they transferred their dislike of the Federal Council of Churches to the World Council and later to the National Council of Churches, reserving their deepest disdain for American proponents of ecumenism.

From time to time the *Pentecostal Evangel*, like *United Evangelical Action* and other evangelical periodicals, noted the progress of worldwide ecumenism. The World Council, for the most part, the *Evangel* alleged, represented denominations that were "spiritually cold and formal."[26] In pursuing Christian unity, moreover, they coveted something they would never gain, something that should not be sought, but maintained, since all true Christians possessed it.[27] Those who sought unity through ecumenism, it followed, could not be described as "true" Christians.

Such views underscored the more basic contention that ecumenical leaders sought to create a "superchurch," a concept that evoked both horror and excitement in evangelical minds. (In the postwar period this was fed, as well, by general American fears of rising communism.) Dire predictions of end-times judgment accompanied warnings about religious unity. "The fact that so many churches may be in a mood to unite may be one of the most significant signs of the times," the *Evangel* noted. "Could it be that the steps now being taken are leading to the unholy and illegitimate pseudo-church which we believe is mentioned in Bible prophecy?"[28] Such observations, however, encouraged the faithful to await with renewed expectancy the soon return of Christ.

Pentecostals also disliked the kind of Catholic church they thought ecumenism promoted. Disregarding the possibility that all denominations (including their own) might well include both saints and sinners, they deplored any ecclesiastical structure in which regenerate and unregenerate mingled. Such settings, they noted, had historically been "the enemy of the prophetic type of Christianity."[29] Charging that the same liberals and modernists who had dominated the Federal Council had emerged as the American presence in the World Council, Assemblies of God spokespersons insisted that the organization would inevitably "water down the gospel testimony" and "compromise with worldliness."[30] But it was not only theological liberalism that repelled them; they foresaw, rather, the ultimate unfolding of a new religion focusing in the worship of the Antichrist. The *Evangel* quoted with approval the words of the prominent evangelical leader Wilbur Smith: "Christians need well beware of all this talk about a world church. A world church . . . will become a perfect agency for the accomplishment of Antichrist's purpose."[31]

When in 1948 the World Council issued a statement of Christian faith that evangelicals were forced to admit was "sound" (the statement forcefully affirmed the virgin birth, substitutionary atonement, physical resurrection, and future return of Christ), the intensity of evangelical antipathy toward the ecumenical movement was laid bare. Nothing the mainstream denominations did, it seemed, could be right in the eyes of some evangelical and fundamentalist constituencies. J. Elwin Wright spoke for the Assemblies of God as well as for the National Association of Evangelicals when he alleged that those who signed the World Council statement of faith were liars guilty of gross hypocrisy, "wolves in sheep's clothing."[32]

Pentecostal concern about a "superchurch" was part of a broader rejection of federation as a "sign of the times." They assumed that consolidation would mark every aspect of human organization in the end times. At midcentury the *Pentecostal Evangel* editorialized about the "weeds" that were being "gathered and bundled" in contemporary America: "In industry, a corporations bundle; in labor, a trade-unions bundle; in international politics, NATO and the United Nations; and in religion, ecumenical federations." "Our Lord," the *Evangel* solemnly warned, "said that the bundling would be for the burning."[33]

Such reflections marked the grim years of Soviet aggression in Eastern Europe and conflict in Korea. The "signs of the times" seemed evident everywhere, and considerable speculation about the end times characterized evangelicals who awaited judgment but also worked for revival and joyously anticipated their own release in Christ's triumphant return.

Coming as they did amid such prophetic speculation, Du Plessis's activities were suspect from the start. In the same years that the *Pentecostal Evangel* warned readers against the ecumenical movement, Du Plessis won the confidence of growing numbers of ecumenical stalwarts who came to relish their contact with an "insider" when official relations were impossible. Since Du Plessis was an acknowledged leader in the worldwide Pentecostal community, it is not surprising that some on both sides as well as in the secular media considered that he acted in an official capacity in his dealings with ecumenical organizations. Especially after 1959 when Dennis Bennett's activities captured media attention, the press tended to identify Du Plessis as "a leader of 10 million Pentecostal church members throughout the world."[34]

Carl McIntire predictably entered the fray with an article in his *Christian Beacon* entitled "Are the Pentecostalists Also to Be Duped?"[35] Calling Du Plessis a "world leader of the Pentecostal churches," McIntire vehemently denounced the "ecumenical apostasy" with which he claimed Du Plessis sought to associate Pentecostalism. McIntire vented his wrath on the movement as a whole. Charging that the most recent World Pentecostal Conference (which had met in Jerusalem in May 1961) had failed to denounce three Third World Pentecostal denominations that had affiliated with the World Council of Churches, McIntire noted that the Assemblies of God general superintendent Thomas F. Zimmerman, featured speaker on Pentecost Sunday, was also president of the National Association of Evangelicals. Zimmerman's presence symbolized for McIntire the NAE's inexcusable compromise on ecumenism. By failing to repudiate those Third World Pentecostals with ecumenical sympathies, then, McIntire charged, Pentecostals assisted "the church of the Antichrist, the one great world church, the coming ecumenical Babylon."[36]

Meanwhile, complaints from Assemblies of God pastors and adherents resulted in denominational action against Du Plessis. While denominational leaders readily admitted that they had no quarrel with Du Plessis's "testimony for Pentecost," they cited criticisms of his advocacy of the ecumenical movement and objected to the use of the influence and name of the Assemblies of God "as tools for compromise."[37] The Executive Presbytery requested Du Plessis to make three promises, which revealed much about contemporary Assemblies of God attitudes toward the religious culture. Given the perspectives of the men in leadership and the prophetic fascinations of their constituency, the requests seemed reasonable. They would, however, have ended Du Plessis's decade-long involvement in a movement that would soon explode as charismatic experience erupted in Roman Catholicism.

First, Du Plessis was requested to avoid "making disparaging remarks or reflecting on the position of the Assemblies of God" in his discussions with World Council leaders. Second, he was asked not to "pose, officially or unofficially, as spokesman for the Assemblies of God." Third, he was asked not to invite others to accompany him to National Council or World Council meetings.[38] Not surprisingly, Du Plessis and the Executive Presbytery failed to reach agreement, and Du Plessis was invited to withdraw from the denomination.[39] His departure was indisputably under pressure. As his influence in the ecumenical movement increased, Du Plessis remained a member of an Assemblies of God congregation in Oakland, California. Shortly after Du Plessis lost his preaching credentials, the rapid expansion of the charismatic movement changed the focus of Assemblies of God concern from ecumenical issues to charismatic phenomena. For the next two decades the Assemblies of God wrestled with issues raised by the charismatic movement, many of which had roots in independent Pentecostalism and the ecumenical movement. The restoration of Du Plessis's credentials in 1980 signaled the mellowing among some adherents of attitudes that had ostracized Du Plessis even as he had gained wide acclaim outside the constituency.

In 1962 after Du Plessis submitted his Assemblies of God credentials under duress, in an action that probably reflected grass-roots sentiment, the General Presbytery formalized the denomination's long-standing opposition to ecumenism. Noting that the ecumenical movement was both a "sign of the times" and "contrary to the real Biblical doctrine of spiritual unity in the Church of Jesus Christ," the presbyters opposed "ecumenicity based on organic and organizational unity" and the formation of a "World Super Church" that, they speculated, would "probably culminate in the Scarlet Woman or Religious Babylon of Revelation."[40] They recommended that Assemblies of God ministers and congregations refrain from promoting the ecumenical movement or any of its organizations. An amendment permitting Assemblies of God ministers to participate on a local level in interdenominational activities and to offer "Pentecostal witness" freely was added to the original resolution, perhaps indicating a measure of support for Du Plessis's accomplishments. It also tacitly acknowledged that many Assemblies of God ministers already participated in such local interdenominational forums through ministerial alliances.

The Problem of Pentecostal Identity

Du Plessis's plight in his denomination symbolized, at least in part, the persistence of two perceptions of Pentecostal identity in tension. By 1961 Assemblies of God leaders were firmly committed to the evangelical consensus of the National Association of Evangelicals. They shared fully the anticommunism, anti-Catholicism, and antiecumenism of other NAE members. Disturbed by cultural trends toward federation and international organizations, they shared as well Senator Joseph McCarthy's absorption with communist conspiracy. When the Methodist bishop G. Bromley Oxnam (a principal figure in the ecumenical movement) was called before the McCarthy hearings, evangelical suspicions about ecumenism seemed confirmed. Oxnam, who had been chosen American Protestantism's "man of the year" in 1944, had been president of the Federal Council of Churches and replaced Fosdick during the postwar years as the symbol of what evangelicals deemed wrong with traditional Protestantism and ecumenical efforts.[41]

Du Plessis, on the other hand, classified Pentecostalism as a distinct form of Christianity. "There are three main streams of Christianity," he noted. "They are Roman Catholicism, which emphasizes structure of the church; Protestantism, with its emphasis on doctrine; and Pentecostalism, which accents the Holy Spirit."[42] A similar observation made in 1958 by Du Plessis's friend Henry Pitney Van Dusen had received wide publicity. In an article in *Life* magazine entitled "The Third Force in Christendom," Van Dusen had noted the contemporary vitality of several groups of religious "outsiders," especially Churches of Christ, Pentecostals, Adventists, and Jehovah's Witnesses. Citing impressive growth statistics, Van Dusen noted among mainstream Christians "a chastened readiness to investigate the secrets of [this] mighty sweep, especially to learn if it may not have important, neglected elements in a full and true Christian witness."[43]

Van Dusen listed several reasons for the third force's growing appeal:

Its groups preach a direct biblical message readily understood. They commonly promise an immediate, life-transforming experience of the living-God-in-Christ which is far more significant to many individuals than the version of it normally found in conventional churches. They directly approach people—and do not wait for them to come to church. They have great spiritual ardor, which is sometimes but by no means always excessively emotional. They shepherd their converts in an intimate, sustaining group-fellowship: a feature of every vital Christian renewal since the Holy Spirit descended on the Disciples at the first Pentecost. They place a strong emphasis on the Holy Spirit—so neglected by many traditional Christians— as the immediate, potent presence of God both in each human soul and in the Christian fellowship. Above all, they expect their followers to practice an active, untiring, seven-day-a-week Christianity.[44]

The perception of Pentecostalism as a third force enabled ecumenical leaders to link the movement's focus on the Holy Spirit with their own ecumenical objectives without disrupting their participation in historic Christian communions. Du Plessis shared their views, which few evan-

gelicals or Pentecostals attempted to understand. Van Dusen put it suc-
cinctly: "A correct understanding of the Holy Spirit is the crucial issue in
the Doctrine of the Church. And it is a commonplace among students of
the divisions of Christendom that the differences which divide Christians
into separated Churches all center in their divergent Doctrines of the
Church."[45] From this perspective, the Holy Spirit was the "point of contact" through whose presence and activity the fundamental oneness of all
believers could be acknowledged.

A major source of tension over issues raised by this growing Protestant
interest in ecumenism and the Holy Spirit had been nurtured in the Assemblies of God by songs, sermons, literature, and testimonies throughout
the movement's history. These celebrated the believer's passage from
"dead," "cold" denominations into a movement that proclaimed the
"full gospel." Recalling his youth in an Assemblies of God congregation,
for example, Cecil M. Robeck, Jr., of Fuller Theological Seminary has
written:

> One would think by the way we Pentecostals assessed the spirituality
> of the "other Christians" that we used a thermometer. Trium-
> phantly we lumped the "others" together in groups, ranging by de-
> grees from "dead" (Catholics and "liberals"), to "cold" (mostly
> mainliners), to "lukewarm" (evangelicals and holiness folk), to "on-
> fire" (us). . . . Lots of these pastors had "D. D.s" after their names.
> That usually meant, I was told, that they couldn't be trusted. They
> were "false shepherds," "broken cisterns," "whited sepulchres," or,
> an early favorite, "Dumb Dogs," who had graduated from theologi-
> cal "cemeteries."[46]

More than a hint of triumphalism pervaded the literature and assured
the persistence of such stereotypes. Pentecostals typically neither attended other churches nor read the people they fervently denounced.
After 1941 they were deeply influenced by the leadership of the NAE,
people who influenced Assemblies of God attitudes at least as extensively
as the Assemblies of God influenced theirs. Du Plessis discovered the
inadequacy of the stereotypes and rejected them with a winsomeness that
won him wide acclaim, and his actions helped mitigate stereotypes of
Pentecostals as well. Just as Pentecostals had heard and believed stories
about other segments of the church (and about church history), so
mainline Protestants and Roman Catholics had preconceptions about
Pentecostals they never bothered to test. They simply passed them on,
with the net result that they often "bore false witness against their
neighbors."[47]

Protestants in general and Pentecostals in particular harbored deep sus-

picions about Roman Catholic intrigue, fed at midcentury by Paul Blanshard's *American Freedom and Catholic Power.* [48] When Du Plessis joined
ecumenical leaders at Vatican II and then took every opportunity to proclaim his message to Catholic audiences, he defied long-held assumptions
about the nature, design, and prophetic role of Roman Catholicism.

Shortly before, during the campaign for the 1960 presidential election,
Assemblies of God anti-Catholicism had become unusually focused. [49] Not
only did the denomination's converts from Catholicism at home and
abroad preserve the anti-Catholic diatribe but in 1960 the *Pentecostal
Evangel* carried an article by the denomination's newly elected gen-
eral superintendent, Thomas F. Zimmerman, explaining why a Catholic
(John F. Kennedy) should not be president. Kennedy was not named.
The accent was not on policies but on religion:

> So strong is the influence of the President of the United States
> that he could begin a major tide in the direction of a Roman Catho-
> lic controlled and directed America through his appointments if he
> so desired. The question is, would he do so? The answer is a clear,
> simple and short, "Yes."
>
> Every Roman Catholic is completely under the control of his
> church, mind, soul and body. . . . A Roman Catholic cannot make
> a decision on any level which runs counter to the thinking and
> expressed policy of Papal authority. In other words, under threat of
> excommunication, every Catholic is bound by Rome.
>
> We must not now let down the guard and lose our time-honored
> and sacred position by giving the highest position in the land to the
> Roman Catholic Church. But, to avoid doing so, we must take a
> positive stand both in conversation with others and at the polls in
> November. It is not sufficient to hope and pray, for faith without
> works is dead. [50]

Such explicit political advice seldom found its way into the pages of
the *Pentecostal Evangel* unless politics raised issues that touched vital religious nerves. Culturally rooted distrust of Catholicism certainly marked
most Pentecostals as it did many other Protestants in the fifties and early
sixties. The Assemblies of God General Presbytery endorsed Zimmerman's views and recommended their wide circulation. Though the presbyters' news release disclaimed "religious bias," it charged the Catholic
Church with "bigotry," citing its stance on papal infallibility. [51]

By 1960 generations of Pentecostals had passed along stories about
other traditions that had become, in a real sense, Pentecostal "habits of
the heart." Since, to some extent, the ecumenical and charismatic movements were at first perceived as related (especially given the influence of

David Du Plessis in each), opposition to ecumenism influenced reservations about charismatics. And suspicions about the nature and ultimate
purpose of Catholicism assured distrust of Vatican II and the charismatic
renewal that emerged in Roman Catholicism in the midsixties.

In spite of reservations, on the local level some Assemblies of God
churches were deeply influenced by the charismatic movement as it
spread in local congregations of all types. In an era of cultural and political unrest that was marked by challenges to established institutions, charismatics reveled in religious experiences that seemed to infuse their traditions and liturgies with vitality. Their preference for spontaneity and
informality ultimately influenced traditions that theoretically opposed
charismatic teaching. The widespread use of Scripture choruses and new
forms of worship music as well as widespread clapping and raising of hands
in worship are but a few obvious examples of their enduring effect. Although the movement's impact on the Assemblies of God is difficult to
measure, several generalizations can be made.

First, the charismatic movement, with its enthusiastic witness to the
Spirit's activity in contemporary life, stimulated some Pentecostals to re-
discover their experiential heritage. Third- and fourth-generation birthright participants in the Assemblies of God were challenged to seek renewal and to abandon themselves to experiences in the Spirit. At the
same time, contact with charismatic believers encouraged trends already
evident toward more participation in worldly pursuits. Charismatics did
not generally exhibit the radical behavioral changes that had routinely
been urged on Pentecostals. In some places these seemed inextricably
linked to doctrine. Charismatics, on the other hand, danced, drank,
smoked, attended theaters, bowled, swam at public pools and beaches,
owned television sets, dressed fashionably, and generally failed to embrace the taboos that had long helped reinforce Pentecostal identity as
"peculiar people." Yet they spoke in tongues and exercised spiritual gifts
more frequently than did many Pentecostals. The shifting of the boundaries that have defined acceptable behavior for Assemblies of God adherents in recent years cannot be attributed to any single cause. Certainly,
however, the charismatic movement played a role that should not be
overlooked.

The charismatic movement not only brought new visibility to older
classical Pentecostalism it also enhanced the membership of Pentecostal
denominations as some left historic denominations for the less-formal
worship settings of Pentecostal congregations. Deep cultural and theological differences typically distinguished new members from long-standing
adherents. The charismatic movement also spawned a wide variety of
independent institutions and greatly enhanced the strength of indepen-

dent Pentecostalism. It generated its own devotional literature and sup-ported Bible schools and evangelistic efforts that superficially, at least, resembled early Pentecostal efforts in their stress on charismatic phe-nomena and faith. They sometimes rediscovered long-forgotten early Pentecostal "prophets" such as E. W. Kenyon, Smith Wigglesworth, and Maria B. Woodworth-Etter. And they facilitated the emergence of pros-perity evangelism, which urges believers to claim their rights to health, wealth, and worldly success. Assemblies of God leaders have deplored the "humanistic" and "materialistic" orientation of prosperity evangelism, but it has nonetheless infiltrated their ranks as have many other trends that ebb and flow in independent settings influenced by the charismatic renewal.[52] Pentecostals who disagreed with the Assemblies of God or did not wish to conform to its requirements found in the independent Pen-tecostal sector as invigorated by the charismatic renewal opportunities for innovative endeavors.

For many reasons, then, Assemblies of God leaders were cautious about endorsing the multifaceted charismatic renewal. In 1972, under increasing pressure, they declared their desire to identify the Assemblies of God with "what God is doing in the world today": "The winds of the Spirit are blowing freely outside the normally recognized Pentecostal bodies. . . . The Assemblies of God does not place approval on that which is manifestly not scriptural in doctrine or conduct, but neither do we categorically condemn everything that does not totally . . . conform to our standards. It is important to find our way on a scriptural path, avoid-ing extremes of an ecumenism that compromises scriptural principles and an exclusivism that excludes true Christianity."[53]

Meanwhile, to meet the need for a forum where Pentecostals and char-ismatics of all persuasions could reflect on the movement's development and meaning, several scholars created the Society for Pentecostal Studies (SPS) in 1971. An independent scholarly society, the SPS has promoted annual conferences in which scholars working in the Pentecostal and charismatic traditions bring their various perspectives to focus on issues of mutual concern. Not surprisingly, until his death in 1987, David Du Plessis was a regular participant.

Assemblies of God positions on ecumenism and charismatic renewal have been influenced by many factors. A denomination with many mem-bers who had been dissatisfied in other denominations naturally nurtured stereotypes that few bothered to verify. And with millions of members and hundreds of missionaries keenly aware of physical persecution in the recent past at Catholic instigation in Latin America and elsewhere, the Assemblies of God could not easily endorse Catholic charismatic renewal.[54]

Prophetic speculation gave form and content to much of the antiecu-
menical diatribe as well. And it is significant that in the postwar years as
many evangelicals participated wholeheartedly in the "communist watch"
of the McCarthy era, communism and ecumenism seemed inextricably
linked. Participation in the NAE also reinforced Assemblies of God pre-
dilections about ecumenism and charismatic renewal.

By the post–World War II years most if not all of the American, white,
trinitarian, Pentecostal denominations had shed the movement's early
restorationist stress on unity. Their reluctance to embrace it failed to
check the spread of charismatic renewal in the Christian world. Assemblies of God leaders found it much simpler to identify with evangelicals
than they did to embrace charismatics. And the difficulties have intensified as denominational charismatic renewal has been complemented by
the dramatic growth of independent ministries that exploit modern technology to promote a wide variety of emphases on worship, practice, and
life-style. Their language is often brash and abrasive and some focus on
little-emphasized elements in the Pentecostal heritage—the prophetic
word and spiritual warfare. (The book that stimulated much of the contemporary so-called "Third Wave" preoccupation with spiritual warfare,
This Present Darkness, was written by Frank Peretti, an Assemblies of God
minister's son.) In an interview with *Christianity Today* in the mideighties, General Superintendent G. Raymond Carlson acknowledged the
charismatic contribution but called for balance in a statement that aptly
summarizes the consensus of Assemblies of God leaders: "I'm grateful for
what the charismatic movement has brought with regard to celebration. . . . We need more than celebration. We always need that balance
of the Word and the Spirit. You need to anchor solidly in the Word."[55]

The remarkable growth and continued vitality of charismatic renewal
movements helped reveal how thoroughly denominationalized classical
Pentecostalism had become. Evangelical priorities seemed solidly en-
trenched. But the sense of "third force" potential survived as well, sustaining a tension that holds potential for future reflection on Pentecostal
identity.

NOTES

1. "Rector and a Rumpus," *Newsweek,* 4 July 1960, 77. See also "Speaking in
Tongues," *Time,* 15 Aug. 1960, 53, 55.
2. "Rector and a Rumpus," 77.
3. Bennett did not permit charismatic intrusions in formal worship services,
but added prayer and fellowship meetings to the schedule. In this he duplicated

the Anglican vicar Alexander Boddy's stance early in Pentecostalism's European history. Boddy's Anglican parish was the early focus of English Pentecostalism, but it remained thoroughly Anglican in its stated schedule. See announcements and accounts Boddy published in his magazine *Confidence*, 1909–14.

4. Dennis Bennett, *Nine O'Clock in the Morning* (Plainfield, N.J.: Logos International, 1970).

5. George Hawtin to Wayne Warner, 15 Dec. 1987, 2–3, Assemblies of God Archives, Springfield, Mo. (hereafter AGA).

6. "Miracles Today Is on the Air," *Miracle Magazine*, Dec. 1955, 2; "World Wide Revival," *Voice of Healing*, Jan. 1951, 5.

7. Jack Coe, *Apostles and Prophets . . . in the Church Today?* (Dallas: Herald of Healing, 1954), 3.

8. Ibid., 4.

9. Ibid., 12.

10. Ibid., 30.

11. Donald Gee, "Possible Pentecostal Unity," *Voice of Healing*, Jan. 1951, 3.

12. Ibid.

13. Ibid., 7.

14. For his biography, see David Du Plessis, *A Man Called Mr. Pentecost* (Plainfield, N.J.: Logos International, 1977).

15. David Du Plessis, *The Spirit Bade Me Go* (Plainfield, N.J.: Logos International, 1970), 13.

16. Ibid., 14.

17. Charles W. Forman, "The Church under the Cross," *Christian Century*, 13 Aug. 1952, 923–24.

18. Du Plessis, *The Spirit*, 15.

19. Ibid.

20. They reconsidered their understanding of early World Council activities after its third assembly in New Delhi in December 1961, noting that before New Delhi the World Council gave a stronger evangelical testimony than did the National Council. From 1961 their opposition to early World Council efforts was mitigated by their sense that 1961 was a watershed that had somehow allowed radical political, social, and religious agendas to take control. See, for example, G. Aiken Taylor, "New Delhi—Afterwards," *United Evangelical Action*, Feb. 1962, 7–9; George Ford, "Ecumenicity: A Threat to Christian Unity," *United Evangelical Action*, May 1962, 8–11.

21. Charles Clayton Morrison, "Protestants in the World Council of Churches," *Christian Century*, 23 June 1954, 760.

22. Du Plessis, *The Spirit*, 16.

23. See, for example, Stanley Frodsham, "The Tarrying Meeting," *Pentecostal Evangel*, 19 May 1945, 4–5, which mourned the "discarding" of tarrying meetings and urged their revival. "The Early Days of Pentecost," *Pentecostal Evangel*, 11 Aug. 1945, 2–3, reprinted a lengthy article from the *Upper Room* (1909) with the comment: "It is a very easy thing to drift away from the simplicity that characterized the Pentecostal Movement in its early days." "Utter Dependence on

the Holy Spirit," *Pentecostal Evangel,* 20 Oct. 1945, 5, noted: "It is not a flattering commentary on our spiritual state that so few members of our assemblies gather for prolonged seasons of prayer. Nor is it complimentary to have such small quarters for the places of prayer." P. C. Nelson, "Shall We Surrender the Fort?" *Pentecostal Evangel,* 3 Nov. 1945, 1, 12, noted declining emphasis on divine healing.

24. Du Plessis, *The Spirit,* 67.

25. Ibid., 64.

26. "A World Council of Churches," *Pentecostal Evangel,* 20 Nov. 1948, 15.

27. "Church Union," *Pentecostal Evangel,* 27 Nov. 1948, 15.

28. "To Create a Superchurch?" *Pentecostal Evangel,* 10 Dec. 1949, 9.

29. Ibid., 8.

30. Ibid.

31. Quoted in "The 'World Church' Movement," *Pentecostal Evangel,* 26 Mar. 1949, 10.

32. "The World Council of Churches," *Pentecostal Evangel,* 4 Feb. 1950, 9.

33. "Unity—False and True," *Pentecostal Evangel,* 17 Dec. 1950, 2.

34. See, for example, "Pentecostal Leader Sees 'Awakening,'" *Seattle Post-Intelligencer,* 1 Feb. 1969, 33.

35. *Christian Beacon,* 15 June 1961, 8.

36. Ibid.

37. General Presbytery Minutes, 31 Aug. 1962, 39, Assemblies of God Secretariat, Springfield, Mo. (hereafter AGS).

38. Ibid., 39–40.

39. Du Plessis refused to withdraw. He received a letter from the denomination's general secretary informing him that he was no longer a minister. Bartlett Peterson to David Du Plessis, David Du Plessis File, AGS.

40. General Presbytery Minutes, 31 Aug. 1962, 40, AGS.

41. See "No Pentecost," *Time,* 13 Sept. 1948, 51–53.

42. Quoted in "Visiting Cleric Sees Move to Christian Unity," from the *Seattle Times,* 1 Feb. 1969, 2, David Du Plessis File.

43. "The Third Force in Christendom," *Life,* 9 June 1958, 124.

44. Ibid., 122.

45. Henry Pitney Van Dusen, *Spirit, Son, and Father* (New York: Charles Scribner's Sons, 1958), 84.

46. Cecil M. Robeck, Jr., "Growing Up Pentecostal," *Theology News and Notes,* Mar. 1988, 5.

47. Ibid., 6.

48. Paul Blanshard, *American Freedom and Catholic Power* (Boston: Beacon Press, 1951).

49. Zimmerman's article expressed sentiments that had been published in the NAE's *United Evangelical Action* since the likelihood of a Kennedy nomination became apparent in 1958. See, for example, Don Hillis, "If We Elect a Roman Catholic as President," 15 Mar. 1958, 3–4; Don Hillis, "Will Rome Rule the World," Apr. 1959, 3, 6–7; George L. Ford, "A Catholic President: How Free

from Church Control?" May 1960, 5–7, 13. After Kennedy won, the NAE urged a strategy to assure continued religious freedom in Clyde Taylor and George Ford, "A Protestant Strategy for the Sixties," Dec. 1960, 5–7, 16.

50. Thomas F. Zimmerman, "A Protest against Electing a Roman Catholic President," General Presbytery Minutes, 1960, Exhibit P, 3–4, AGS. This was published in the *Evangel* on 18 Sept. 1960.

51. News release, 2 Sept. 1960, included in General Presbytery Minutes, 1960.

52. Harold B. Smith, "America's Pentecostals: Where They Are Going," *Christianity Today*, 16 Oct. 1987, 28.

53. Executive Presbytery, "Charismatic Study Report," *Advance*, Nov. 1972, 3.

54. Persecution by Catholics left a wide variety of Protestants outraged. See, for example, *Christian Century*, 16 June 1954, on Catholic persecution of Protestants in Columbia.

55. Quoted in Smith, "America's Pentecostals," 28.

11

Survival and Adaptation in the Modern Era, 1960–89

S ANDWICHED among articles on medical mysteries, the scientist Carl
Sagan, and discipline in the U.S. Marine Corps in the summer 1982
issue of the *Saturday Evening Post* was a profile of the Assemblies of God
by Edwin Plowman. In conversations with adherents across the country,
Plowman had probed the denomination's ethos and thought he discovered a disparity between popular perceptions of Pentecostals and realities
in the Assemblies of God. "Tongues speaking," he commented, was not
"a consuming issue." Rather, according to Plowman, Assemblies of God
adherents differed little from other evangelicals; "Love for God" and "intense desire that others might come to know and love Him, too" coupled
with "rock-ribbed belief in the authority of the Bible" were the elements
uniting the denomination's constituency.

Plowman also called attention to the denomination's considerable diversity, averring that there was no such thing as "a 'typical' U. S. Assemblies of God congregation." Such diversity had in fact characterized the
Assemblies of God throughout its history. In recent decades the denomination's rapid growth, augmented by interest in Pentecostalism generated
by the charismatic renewal and by the rise of Pentecostal media stars,
politicians, and megachurches, has given visibility to the widely different
styles of worship and life that coexist under the Assemblies of God name.
An examination of several areas of denominational life suggests the continuities and discontinuities between the Assemblies of God at seventy-
five years of age and its restorationist heritage.

Mission

The denomination's dramatic expansion in the seventies and eighties
followed a period of slowed growth in the fifties and sixties. At the 1959

General Council in San Antonio, several longtime national leaders were replaced by younger men. With the change in leadership came an opportunity to reassess denominational priorities. The new Assemblies of God general superintendent, Thomas F. Zimmerman, decided to reinvigorate the commitment to evangelism. A bridge-builder to other Christian communions, Zimmerman was also closely associated with the growing number of evangelistic efforts orchestrated by evangelicals through voluntary associations. Even as he concurred with the denomination's historic commitment to aggressive foreign missions, he determined to refocus energies to address the North American setting.

Several thousand people met for the Council on Evangelism in St. Louis in 1968 to consider reasons and remedies for lagging growth. They defined a newly focused threefold denominational purpose: evangelism, worship, nurture. The Assemblies of God existed primarily as "an agency of God for evangelizing the world," the St. Louis meeting affirmed. Also important were its purpose to be "a corporate body in which man may worship God" and its resolve to be "a channel of God's purpose to build a body of saints being perfected in the image of His Son."[1]

The council also affirmed the continuity of the Assemblies of God with "the New Testament apostolic pattern," citing as evidence the denomination's teaching on Spirit baptism, which was observed to have three primary purposes: evangelism ("with accompanying supernatural signs"); worship (to which it was said to add a "necessary" dimension); and expression of spiritual fruit, gifts, and ministries ("as in New Testament times").[2] This conceded a far narrower view of the apostolic pattern than had energized the denomination's earlier years and was a significant shift from early perceptions of what the "New Testament apostolic pattern" had called for. In 1968 the doctrine of tongues speech as uniform initial evidence of Spirit baptism constituted proof that the denomination conformed to the apostolic pattern. Once that doctrine had been a minor component in a thoroughgoing restorationist worldview.

During the sixties Assemblies of God leaders made several other far-reaching decisions. They disavowed ecumenism and distanced the denomination officially from the first phase of the charismatic renewal, stances symbolized by the dismissal of David Du Plessis; they expanded the Statement of Fundamental Truths to conform to that of the National Association of Evangelicals (in 1961), thus completing a significant phase in the formal evangelicalizing of the denomination; they ignored much of the social disarray in the nation as well as the burgeoning charismatic renewal; and they defined traditional expository evangelism as their primary goal. In a sense, they attempted to recommit the denomination to cultural alienation. Yet at the same time tension between historic cultural alienation and a growing interest in creating Christian parallels to the secular culture became apparent. This interest led to thriving networks of thousands of Christian day schools, Christian educators in public schools, opposition to abortion, legislation that addressed family issues, and an aggressive, pro-Israel American foreign policy. Among the diverse results have been the election of John Ashcroft, member of the Assemblies of God, as Missouri governor; the appointment by Ronald Reagan of James Watt, another lay member, as secretary of the interior; and the dream of Jim and Tammy Faye Bakker to preside over a Christian amusement park, a Christian dinner theater, and a Christian cosmetics and fashion empire.

In the post-Eisenhower years, the Assemblies of God, like all American denominations, operated in a context of bewildering change characterized by cultural disarray, social ferment, an apparent crisis in historic denominations, the alienation of the young from the churches, and the public emergence of evangelicalism. Part of the trauma of the time was the emerging sense of moral pluralism that differed from the denominational pluralism to which Americans were accustomed. Out of the perceived breakdown of core values emerged a more publicly active evangelicalism. Assemblies of God mobilization to the task of evangelism can be accurately evaluated only from the perspective of the larger context of the era.

While institutional and organizational directions are easy to chart, the denomination's character and diversity are not as readily clarified. Even as ongoing efforts at the denomination's headquarters sought to cultivate certain emphases and attitudes, the constituency's well-being at the popular level was more closely tied to the perceptions and activities of local pastors, evangelists, and lay leaders who molded adherents' views on public issues.

One reason for apparent rapid growth in the Assemblies of God in the eighties had less to do with the overwhelmingly white constituency's response to the mandate to evangelize the unchurched than with the steady growth of a sometimes overlooked sector within the Assemblies of God— its Hispanic outreaches.

Hispanic Growth

Assemblies of God efforts among Spanish-speaking Americans is as old as the denomination and has been the most successful ethnic-directed effort the denomination has pursued. In motion as the denomination organized, these activities saw sustained growth; without its Hispanic constituency (which comprised nearly 15 percent of American membership) the denomination could not have claimed the growth rate that for several years in the eighties made it America's fastest-growing denomination.

Since early Pentecostalism had strong clusters of congregations in southern California and Texas, it is hardly surprising that its earliest adherents included Hispanics. Mexican Americans had participated in the Pentecostal movement at least since its Azusa Street days, and some who affiliated with the Assemblies of God at its inception in 1914 were already actively evangelizing in Mexican communities from Texas to southern California. Organized efforts among Spanish-speaking Americans began after Henry C. Ball, a young Methodist, embraced Pentecostalism and was ordained by the Assemblies of God in 1915. The next year, he organized a Hispanic congregation among migrant Mexican farmhands in Kingsville, Texas, that became a center from which he launched a broader outreach. Converts became lay workers, spreading the message among cotton pickers and local migrant co-workers. Ball selected the most promising members of his fledgling congregation and sent them to pioneer in far-flung Texas communities.[3]

Steady calls for more workers resulted in the introduction of programs and literature to train Hispanic converts for leadership. Ball and Alice Luce, a former British missionary to India who devoted the second half of her life to Spanish-speaking Americans, organized Bible institutes in Texas and California; prepared Spanish correspondence courses; published a Spanish gospel hymnal; and provided the periodicals, tracts, and other literature that facilitated the communication of the message.[4]

In January 1918 Ball's successful efforts among Hispanics were acknowledged by the Texas–New Mexico District of the Assemblies of God when the district explicitly sanctioned his efforts and commissioned him to organize Assemblies of God congregations among Spanish-speaking people everywhere. He married Sunshine Marshall in June 1918, and the two devoted their time to evangelism. The Hispanic ministers with whom the Balls and Alice Luce worked elected Ball the first superintendent of the Latin American District when the Hispanic outreach became independent of the denomination's Foreign Missions Department in 1929.[5]

The Latin American District grew rapidly. At first focusing especially in the southwest from Texas to California, efforts among Spanish-speaking Americans soon spread to the East Coast as well. By the post–World War II era Hispanics formed a growing percentage of the Assemblies of God constituency, and the Latin American districts of the Assemblies of God together constituted the largest Protestant presence among Hispanics in the United States.[6] In 1988, the seventieth anniversary of the formalizing of Assemblies of God efforts among Hispanics, statistics revealed the appeal the Assemblies of God has had among Spanish-speaking North Americans. From 7 ministers, 6 churches, and 100 members in 1918, the

Assemblies of God Spanish-speaking districts together had grown to embrace 164,105 adherents in 1,217 churches. The constituency was served by 2,517 ordained and licensed ministers and constituted some 15 percent of the total American Assemblies of God membership.

Gospel Publishing House and the denomination's Life publishing in Miami (the largest North American publisher of Spanish religious materials) continue today to provide Sunday school and other literature in Spanish. Berean College, the denomination's accredited nontraditional college, still offers Spanish correspondence courses.

Also early in its history, the Assemblies of God focused attention on major European population groups and organized networks of foreign-language-speaking congregations (German, Hungarian, Polish, Ukrainian, and so forth). As European groups assimilated and failed to be replenished by significant new immigration, these churches were absorbed into the geographic districts of which they were part. While acculturation resulted in the decline of European segments, Asian immigration challenged the denomination to consider forming Asian-directed outreaches.

Recognizing the growing Korean presence across America, in 1981 Assemblies of God leaders looked favorably on the creation of a Korean district. At the time, there were approximately 47 ministers serving 60 organized Korean Assemblies of God churches with some 7,000 members. These became the nucleus of the Fifty-seventh District Council of the Assemblies of God. The rapid influx of Korean immigrants in the eighties shaped this district's challenge. In 1988 this district was coordinating the efforts of over 260 ministers in some 100 churches with over 14,000 members.

African Americans

While Hispanic, European, and Korean minorities posed no special problems for the Assemblies of God, the history of the denomination's relationship with African Americans has been uneasy from the start.

Presuppositions of white American Pentecostals about black Americans derived from many sources. Assemblies of God adherents mirrored the racial attitudes of other white Americans of similar social class and educational background. With the exception of its efforts among Hispanic Americans (which until 1929 were considered foreign missions), the denomination had historically been predominantly Anglo. The constituencies that united to create it were, too. Though they claimed to revere black Pentecostals such as Charles Mason, Thoro Harris, and Garfield T. Haywood, most white Pentecostals did so at a distance. At first heavily southern, and frequently led nationally by men of southern birth, the denomination failed to attract a sizable African-American membership. During the denomination's early years, the name of only one African-American minister appeared briefly on its roster—that of E. S. Thomas, a pastor from Binghamton, New York, whose name was followed by the designation "(colored)." I. S. and Mattie Neeley, African-American missionaries to Liberia before 1914, affiliated briefly with the Assemblies of God for further service in Liberia.

Before World War II, there is scattered evidence of the presence of a few African-American men who held Assemblies of God preaching licenses especially in the northeast (where a prominent white pastor, Robert A. Brown, encouraged them). In general, a few African-American men (and, from 1922 to 1935, at least one talented African-American woman, Cornelia Jones Robertson) acquired district preaching licenses; a few (mostly in New York and on the West Coast, including Robertson) were ordained. Most districts, however, hesitated to ordain them, alleging the difficulties inherent in the national visibility that might follow. For ordination, it was recommended that they look to the Assemblies of God "sister organization," the predominantly African-American Church of God in Christ.[7] During the forties a suggestion that the Assemblies of God create a "Colored Branch" was introduced several times but met with little general enthusiasm. In his report to the General Presbytery in 1949, General Secretary J. Roswell Flower commented: "If anything is to be done for the colored people, it would seem that someone must get a burden for some type of evangelistic or philanthropic work and devote themselves to it."[8] Discussions about evangelizing African Americans became more frequent during the fifties. A committee on race relations, appointed by the 1956 General Presbytery, prepared a report entitled "Segregation vs. Integration." The appointment of the committee was intended to counter allegations that the denomination was ignoring the problem, which was of growing national concern. At a denominational meeting in Oklahoma City, after discussing issues raised by the civil rights movement, leaders expunged all of their actions from the minutes. "We could not afford to go on record as favoring integration," General Superintendent Ralph Riggs later recalled, "neither did we want it to be known that we were in favor of segregation."[9] (In other comments, Riggs noted that integration could be "disastrous"; Flower cautioned that integration might well result in the loss of white members.[10]) The solution seemed obvious: "a convenient and deliberate approach" would be to appoint a study commission. "Our answer to those who challenged us," Riggs maintained, "would simply be that we have a commission appointed to study the problem."[11]

Interest in the subject was stimulated by the aggressive civil rights

stance of the Truman administration, the emerging civil rights movement, and the 1954 unanimous Supreme Court ruling against "separate
but equal" public schools. These had elicited responses from northern
mainline Protestant bureaucracies—though not necessarily equally from
their constituencies. In February 1956 the *Reader's Digest* published an
article entitled "The Churches Repent" that chronicled official mainline
church response to moral questions raised by the predicament of African
Americans. Some Assemblies of God adherents who read the article questioned their denomination's official stance on civil rights.[12] General Superintendent Ralph Riggs's response to one such inquiry clarified again
the leadership's dilemma. Riggs, a native of Mississippi and a former missionary to South Africa, noted that the General Presbytery had discussed
creating a separate branch and attempting to integrate the constituency.[13]
The subject had intentionally been considered in the smaller General
Presbytery and excluded from general discussion on the floor of the General Council. Riggs reported: "We did not feel free to create a Colored
Branch for this would be condoning segregation and even creating segregation when this is not felt the right thing to do at the present time. On
the other hand, the intense social conflict, particularly in the deep South,
makes it unwise to introduce integration at the present time. For these
reasons we felt that it would be best for us to mark time at the moment
until the matter had developed further in the public consciousness and
practice."[14]

This willingness to await cultural accommodation to the concept of
integration and then to bring the Assemblies of God into line characterized the denomination's leaders in the Eisenhower years. Although Riggs
assured others that "we are thoroughly alert as to the trend of the times
and also what our Christian duty in this regard is," he and his colleagues
sensed no compulsion to perform such "duty" until they were certain that
other factors inclined the constituency to acquiesce.[15]

Also in the Eisenhower years, Assemblies of God leaders attempted to
counter charges that they had "excluded blacks from the great commission" by forging stronger ties to the Church of God in Christ. Such contact was facilitated by personal acquaintances made at the Pentecostal
World Conference, one of the few associations in which black and white
Pentecostals mingled. Charles Mason (whom Ralph Riggs routinely addressed in correspondence as "Venerable Father") and others welcomed
Riggs and Flower to the Church of God in Christ's National Convocation
in Memphis in 1955; for several years the two denominations discussed a
potential business relationship (that never materialized). The aging Mason sent a representative to the 1957 General Council; Ralph Riggs and
Thomas F. Zimmerman represented the Assemblies of God at the fiftieth

anniversary convocation of the Church of God in Christ, also in 1957. But such contacts failed to issue in long-term cooperation.

Meanwhile, in the Northwest and in New York, a few African-American men were quietly ordained by Assemblies of God districts.[16] In 1958 a request from the Northern California–Nevada District about receiving an African-American church into membership and ordaining its pastor opened the question for renewed discussion in the General Presbytery.[17] A committee once again considered a "colored fellowship," this time recommending that it be supervised by the National Home Missions Department.[18] Concern about possible involvement "in the present agitation regarding racial problems prevalent in society at large" resulted in the tabling of the committee's report.[19] Meanwhile, denominational leaders routinely ignored pleas from the National Association for the Advancement of Colored People urging the religious community to support financially their quest for civil rights.[20]

As growing numbers of African colonies gained independence, some missionaries became anxious about their welcome abroad. In a letter to *Christianity Today* an Assemblies of God missionary, after commenting on Americans who refused to integrate their own churches but willingly evangelized in Africa, noted the likelihood that African leaders would "look into the parent body of missions in that country and see if in the home churches segregation is practiced."[21] Bringing this sentiment to the attention of the denomination's new general superintendent, Thomas F. Zimmerman, the missionary John Garlock noted a condition that apparently some assumed to be true in the American Assemblies of God: "If it is true that Negro students are not welcome at Central Bible Institute (unless they come from overseas); if it is true that most of our districts are reluctant to ordain Negro ministers; if it is true that in many districts local congregations would be unwilling to accept Negroes into membership, our missionary work overseas may become a great deal more difficult than it is now."[22]

In June 1963 Zimmerman and Bartlett Petersen, Assemblies of God general secretary, participated in a White House conference on civil rights at which John F. Kennedy and Attorney General Robert Kennedy urged religious leaders to cultivate a climate of understanding. President Kennedy's announcement that discussion would continue under the auspices of National Council of Churches leadership prompted the departure of about a third of the two hundred discussants. Among those who left were Zimmerman and Petersen.

But the tide was slowly beginning to turn. Ending years of hesitation and responding to the accelerating civil rights movement, the 1965 General Council adopted a resolution affirming civil rights:

RESOLVED, That we reaffirm our belief in the teachings of Christ including His emphasis upon the inherent worth and intrinsic value of every man, regardless of race, class, creed, or color and we urge all our constituency to discourage unfair and discriminatory practices wherever they exist; and, be it further

RESOLVED, That we believe those in authority in political, social and particularly in evangelical groups, have a moral responsibility toward the creation of those situations which will provide equal rights and opportunities for every individual. [23]

The resolution was prefaced with the statement that "the teachings of Christ are violated by discriminatory practices against racial minorities" and the insistence that Christian conversion "breaks down prejudice and causes justice to prevail." [24] By the seventies the sentiments of the resolution were beginning to be implemented in a few places as renewed denominational focus on inner-city evangelism, prompted in part by the exodus of urban Assemblies of God congregations to the suburbs as well as by the emergence in the denomination of a handful of talented young African Americans with a vision for inner-city renewal, resulted in several thriving racially integrated urban efforts. [25] In 1989 at its seventy-fifth anniversary celebration, the Assemblies of God formally acknowledged racism as a sin, explicitly naming as sin hatred of Jews and Arabs as well as of Africans. [26]

Other Cultural Issues

As the Vietnam war accelerated social upheaval in the late sixties, the Assemblies of God General Presbytery responded in part by adopting a social statement in August 1968. [27] The socially conservative document repudiated "devised confrontations between those alienated" as well as the view (that seemed popular on some college campuses) that "revolution is the key to social progress." [28] "Community-betterment projects and legislative actions on social improvement" at best could only alleviate symptoms of the fundamental human problem—sin. The church's most significant social contribution would always be preaching "the Biblical gospel of the Lord Jesus Christ." [29] This document and the actions of the St. Louis Council on Evangelism in the same year are revealing. In a period of intense cultural disarray, the Assemblies of God rejected the agenda of the era's social activists and opted anew for traditional evangelism that addressed spiritual needs rather than the full complement of human experience. The Assemblies of God did not cooperate in the emergence of socially concerned evangelicalism over the next few years.

Instead, its accommodation to the values of middle America became more apparent; relaxed standards for social behavior became easier to rationalize even as insensitivity toward the social crisis dominated official statements. Motivated by the conviction that the conversion experience offered humankind's only hope, the Assemblies of God endorsed an "old time" message; at the same time it exploited modern technology, a modernized idiom for Pentecostal experience, and a life-style that endorsed the American way of life.

Assemblies of God leaders and constituents have tended to opt for conservative stances (justifying them as biblical stances) on major social questions as well as on domestic and foreign policy issues (Vietnam, the Grenada invasion, the Iran-Contra Affair, and so forth). Increasingly its members took their cues from the emerging Christian parallel to the secular popular culture, which enabled them to be "of the world" but not "in" it. Several of a series of "position papers" released by the leadership during recent decades have reiterated the denomination's long-standing opposition to abortion, homosexuality, alcohol, and gambling. While the Assemblies of God has no official statement on the women's movement, it is easy to document anxiety in responses to issues raised by secular and evangelical feminists.

In 1978 an instructor at the denomination's Evangel College reported to Zimmerman her concern about trends among women students: "More and more we are hearing of young ministers' wives who do not have a complete dedication to God and to their husband's calling," she lamented.[30] Such women tended to opt for "independent careers in the secular world." Liberation movements, especially those urging biblical feminism, she noted, presented a growing challenge.[31]

Several Assemblies of God executives' wives attended an Evangelical Women's Caucus at Fuller Theological Seminary in Pasadena, where their fears that evangelical feminism jeopardized life as they knew it seemed justified. In an address entitled "Women and the Evangelical Movement," Faith Sand, a Protestant missionary to Brazil, urged her audience to acknowledge how thoroughly cultural biases influenced their perception and communication of the gospel. Sand noted various inconsistencies in evangelical use of Scripture. It is instructive to note which of her statements seemed most threatening to the Assemblies of God women: an indictment of "our worship of capitalism"; a call to boycott religious institutions that gave only lip service to women's rights; and an insistence that "women's liberation portends the end of evangelical chauvinism."[32]

While it is evident that some leaders sensed in the women's movement a serious threat to traditional social institutions, it is equally evident that a small but growing number of younger women, especially at the denomination's colleges, objected to the denomination's failure to address (or even acknowledge) both ambivalence in its own stance on women and issues raised by evangelical feminists.[33]

Feminism was integrally related to a larger discussion about the family that emerged in evangelical ranks in the seventies. Assemblies of God leaders looked askance at rising divorce rates and at a widening array of marital problems affecting relationships in local churches. The women's movement's apparent link to the breakdown of core values that seemed inherent in moral pluralism prompted the Assemblies of God to reiterate in numerous ways its commitment to the traditional family and its opposition to feminism.

Another dilemma of the postsixties era was divorce and remarriage. In spite of frequent lively discussions about alternatives, the Assemblies of God had consistently opposed the remarriage of a divorced person with a living spouse, and Assemblies of God ministers were forbidden to perform such marriages. In 1973 the denomination acted to permit Assemblies of God ministers to perform marriages in which one or both partners had been divorced. As divorce became more common in the culture, divorced people formed an increasing segment of Assemblies of God adherents. Their appropriate roles in local churches among a constituency that has a long tradition of unqualified disapproval of divorce has prompted uneasy accommodations. The Assemblies of God continues to refuse to ordain to the ministry any married person with a living former spouse.

In 1973 the denomination not only redefined the Assemblies of God stance on divorce and remarriage, it also implemented a rehabilitation program that had been developed over the past decade. In 1963 R. J. Carlson, district superintendent from Washington, suggested that the denomination consider "preventative" and "redemptive" phases of rehabilitation. Noting that "the greatest endowment we have in our Movement are men whom God has filled with the Holy Spirit" and that "everyone we lose is an irreparable loss," Carlson moved the appointment of a committee of "mature men" to address the subject.[34] The resulting report of the "Rehabilitation and Morals Study Committee" urged "great care" in the examination of ministerial candidates not only in testing biblical knowledge but also in probing character and self-discipline.[35] The report recommended a distinction between "moral weakness"—"repeated acts which have gone unconfessed"—and "those who may have been subjected to unusual temptation, resulting in a fall."[36] It was the latter group the men recommended for rehabilitation.

The report recommended as well that homosexuality be grounds for permanent dismissal: "Psychotherapy," the committee noted, "indicates that for a homosexual to be cured, he must get a new image of himself and undergo a personality reconstruction."[37] Insisting that, from a biblical perspective, such a personality reconstruction should occur at regeneration, the report maintained that ministers whose conduct required discipline for homosexual offenses should not be reinstated because they had presumably "not allowed [Christ] to effect the necessary transformation of personality."[38] In 1973, after several refinements to the original proposal, the denomination instituted a full rehabilitation program. Administered by the denomination's fifty-seven districts, the multifaceted program and its relationship to discipline determined Assemblies of God response to the well-publicized scandals involving media personalities Jim Bakker and Jimmy Swaggart.

Theological Trends

In recent years Assemblies of God leaders have frequently expressed concerns about numerous teachings with apparent appeal in the popular Pentecostal milieu. In partial response the General Presbytery has authorized the release of "position papers" reaffirming the denomination's commitment to healing, the rapture of the church, eternal punishment, and tongues speech as uniform initial evidence of Spirit baptism. Other such papers have attempted to provide guidance on issues raised largely by the charismatic movement: positive confession, discipleship and submission, and demon possession.

By the late seventies denominational leaders sensed growing diversity in their ranks and opted to impose a greater degree of uniformity by acting on the widely shared conviction that faculty members at some Assemblies of God colleges did not personally subscribe fully to the denomination's rigid premillenarian eschatology.[39] J. Philip Hogan, head of the foreign missions program, complained that his interviews with missionary candidates revealed that some failed to commit themselves on the rapture of the church and other elements within the basic dispensational premillenarian framework long approved by the Assemblies of God.[40] In response, the 1979 General Presbytery authorized the appointment of the Committee on Loopholes to explore how theological deviations surfaced.[41] The committee recommended that doctrinal purity be assured in all denominational schools, but it promptly found that diversity was far broader than had originally seemed indicated.[42] Not only did the denomination's stance on the pretribulation rapture seem impaired, so also did its views on the initial evidence of Spirit baptism and the inerrancy of Scripture. The latter issue had been raised in the larger evangelical community, and Harold Lindsell's *The Battle for the Bible* (1976) and *The Bible in the Bal-*

ance (1979), with their indictment of shifting attitudes in many evangelical institutions on the subject, seemed to support the worst fears of the
conservative denomination's leaders. The General Presbytery appointed
a larger committee and solicited a new report.[43]

In 1981 the committee report urged district officials to examine candidates for ordination more thoroughly. Before long, ministers were required to indicate annually any differences with the denomination on
specific doctrines that seemed most critical to the denomination's identity: initial evidence, baptism by immersion, premillennialism, divine
healing, eternal security, and sanctification.[44]

Efforts to assure that Assemblies of God colleges promoted right views
took the form in 1984 of urging faculty to use books published by Gospel
Publishing House.[45] The denomination's Board of Education instituted "a
careful, ongoing review of curricular offerings of our Bible colleges and
institutions, with particular attention to . . . detecting textbooks that
would include unscriptural philosophies leading to humanism, or other
faith-destroying teaching that would undermine the acceptance of the
supernatural."[46] The Board of Education recommended that each Assemblies of God school establish a textbook review process "to assure com-
patibility with our Movement's commitment to the supernatural moving
of God's Spirit."[47] For endorsed colleges, reports on textbooks became
part of the required annual questionnaire and statistical report. In addition, tenured faculty at Assemblies of God colleges were required to be
members of Assemblies of God churches and to conform to the moral
standards for Assemblies of God ministers.

Such attempts to assure doctrinal purity represent as well a further
narrowing of identity. One-time participants in a fluid and surprising restoration could by the eighties isolate six issues on which right belief was
critical. Only one of these was distinctively Pentecostal: tongues speech
as initial evidence of Spirit baptism. Clearly the movement's context and
expectations had changed. The social complexion of the denomination
had changed rapidly, too; the percentage of college graduates in the constituency, for example, nearly tripled between 1960 and 1970. Balancing
a heritage that valued individual autonomy and a measure of diversity
with the growing felt need to demand consensus provided ongoing
challenge.

The Assemblies of God at the Grass Roots

Like many other forms of evangelicalism, Pentecostalism is a popular
religious movement. As an audience-conscious popular expression of
Christianity, Pentecostalism has adapted itself to the themes and styles

running through American popular culture.[48] While denominational records document concerns and triumphs, the picture they present often bears little resemblance to the Pentecostalism with which the rank and file identifies. The Assemblies of God is by legal definition a ministers' fellowship; most of the vital history of the Assemblies of God, however, is the story of hundreds of thousands of unnamed men and women who never spoke at General Councils or voted on denominational questions. Their commitments keep local churches thriving; their giving keeps mission efforts flourishing; their behavior determines denominational norms. Although organizational development has modified some traits of popular Pentecostalism, the tradition continues to attract those who hope that faith will enable them to transcend life's difficulties and that the Spirit's indwelling will enlighten and empower them.

Unprecedented national visibility came late in the eighties when the activities of Jim and Tammy Faye Bakker and Jimmy Swaggart (both men held Assemblies of God credentials) became the subject of countless news stories, many of which explored the history and character of the Assemblies of God.[49] Bakker and Swaggart were part of a much larger group of televangelists and broadcasters whose efforts gave cohesion to the hopes and dreams of hundreds of thousands of Pentecostals, both denominational and independent, and charismatics. The content of their programs captured the essence of important dimensions of popular Pentecostalism in ways that denominational procedures could not.

Significant elements in the denomination had for years identified with the political rhetoric of televangelists who called the nation to repent and work for a Christian America. The relationship between televangelism and the new Christian political right is a fascinating one that has become the subject of scholarly inquiry.[50] In recent years, the Assemblies of God clearly included some who were moving from cultural alienation to endorsing Christian alternatives, a trend that was accelerated by prominent televangelists. They tended to "sanitize" the secular popular culture by adding "Jesus language," and they marketed everything from Christian rock and soap operas to Christian exercise videos, sex manuals, and diet programs. Instead of perceiving the church as an alternative to the popular culture, they regarded it as a forum for Christian forms of the secular. They took their cues from the popular culture and minimized (if they did not obliterate) differences between the church and the world.

A long-simmering feud between Bakker and Swaggart erupted early in 1987 when Bakker was accused of adultery, financial scams, and homosexuality and Swaggart called him "a cancer that should be excised from the body of Christ." The two understood better than most how to appeal to the popular culture that had been an integral part of the Pentecostal ethos since the movement's inception. On the surface, each represented an approach to ministry that had a long history within the movement. Deep down, the two were strikingly similar—egotistical, insecure, domineering, and calculating. Several fundamental assumptions help explain the appeal of such media ministries for Pentecostals. Some are ideological, others social.

First, Pentecostals respond readily to rhetoric that urges support for evangelistic outreach, and both Bakker and Swaggart exploited that inclination. Given their premillennialism and their emphasis on evangelism as their sine qua non, it has been easy to convince some that televangelism is the most effective way to carry out the worldwide proclamation of their message that they believe will prepare the world for Christ's return. It is obviously more attractive to give financial support to one who claims to be doing the job than to subscribe to the older Pentecostal emphasis on "each one win one."[51] And Swaggart claimed precisely that. Televangelism, he declared, was the only efficient way to proclaim the gospel around the world.

Second, many Pentecostals enjoyed seeing their own become stars. Having gone unnoticed for many years, they took pride in and lavished funds on those who gave them visibility and reshaped their public image. Like Bakker and Swaggart, many of them recalled years of deprivation. They seemed inclined to revel in possessions and to find appealing emphases that emanated from independent Pentecostal centers urging the reasonableness of health and wealth for believers. Swaggart's opulence did not disturb most of them, and when Jim and Tammy Bakker decided to open a lavish Christian amusement park and offer their devoted supporters the opportunity of participating in a setting that featured the stars of Christian pop culture, the faithful responded with enthusiasm. The setting, after all, brought them about as close to the country club milieu as they were likely to get. David Edwin Harrell, Jr., astutely observed that Pentecostals in the eighties "dressed in $500 suits to sing the old songs of longing for escape from the hardships of life." While some were "torn between love for simple God-fearing parents and a dazzling beckoning world," others had long abandoned the disdain for the world that had fueled early Pentecostal separatism.[52] They related, rather, to a movement that had moderated through the years, a movement with a message that remained similar at the core but that had been substantially redefined, clarified, and amplified at the grass roots.

Third, the Pentecostal fascination with modern technology should not be overlooked. Although the movement has historically used antimodern rhetoric, its members have been among the first to embrace modern technology and to adapt it for their ends. Television, once a suspect (and in some Assemblies of God districts formally condemned) medium, became a means to an end, and thus found its place in Pentecostal homes. Whereas the first generation of Pentecostals resisted the attractions of secular society to preach a culture-challenging gospel, recent generations have tended to accommodate readily to the technology and values of middle America.

Certainly the Pentecostalism modeled by these popular televangelists was demonstrably different in significant ways from that of earlier years, but there were continuities as well. Bakker's amiable religion, with its stress on Christian parallels to popular amusements, fashions, and communications, appealed to many who had at one level made their peace with this world. Bakker modeled what many classical Pentecostals had come to suspect: one could speak in tongues and exult in the thrill of a sense of power while embracing much more of this world than had previously been supposed. His was a mellowed brand of Pentecostalism that replaced the old idiom of the gospel hymns of the past with the new idiom of charismatic worship choruses devoid of much of the rhetoric that nurtured understandings of the personal and public meaning of Pentecostal experience for generations. PTL became a forum in which the Bakkers and others could present their case for the "liberation" of the movement from the vestiges of "separation" thinking. By featuring the stars of Christian pop culture, they set out to assist the ongoing "Christianization" of the arts and other pastimes. In so doing, they accelerated the permeation of the Assemblies of God with the view that the Christian life allowed more self-expression than had previously been acknowledged. PTL's agenda had affinity for the New Christian Right, dominated in the 1980 election by Jerry Falwell's Moral Majority. Although support for individual candidates was sometimes absent, conservative political causes—like reviving and preserving moral values, prayer, and creationism in the public schools and support for Israel and military spending—was strong.[53]

In accordance with established denominational procedures, the denomination's North Carolina District dismissed Jim Bakker in 1987 for conduct unbecoming to a minister, including fraud and allegations of homosexuality. They could not as readily expunge the influence of his style, however, for he symbolized a popular redefinition of how Pentecostal experience should influence one's relationship to culture and of how that experience should be understood. With its earlier eschatological context significantly eroded, an emphasis on celebration of the Spirit often seemed more inviting than a stress on the imminence of the end. The vocabulary of self-help best-sellers and the entertainers of the pop culture circuit gained widening acceptance in the Anglo Assemblies of God constituency in the eighties. To such Pentecostals, the religious experience that had often brought their grandparents social ostracism seemed a ticket to health, prosperity, and general well-being. God commanded them to live out the American dream, they insisted. Pentecostalism became a means to an essentially selfish, individualistic end. This version of the faith, as Frances FitzGerald has noted, fit easily into a decade that also gave the American people Reaganomics and the Iran-Contra Affair.[54]

In contrast to Bakker, Jimmy Swaggart, a talented music star whose style was rooted in his southern experience, used the rhetoric of early Pentecostalism and talked about holiness, separation, and evangelism in Pentecostal self-understanding. His language struck a responsive chord in thousands of Pentecostals who felt bewildered by the growing acculturation of their movement. His warm style and honky-tonk sound attracted hand-clapping crowds who regarded him as the ablest exponent of the true Pentecostal message. David Edwin Harrell, Jr., has called him the "foremost international salesman of traditional pentecostalism" and proposes that he was probably the most widely known Protestant preacher of the twentieth century.[55]

Yet however much he thundered against contemporary Christian rock music, pastoral counseling, the charismatic movement, Catholics, and those Pentecostals he thought compromised with modernity, his opulent lifestyle did not reflect his heritage, his harsh criticism of others revealed his insecurity, and his fascination with pornography and prostitutes toppled him at the peak of his fame.

Despite pressure to treat Swaggart's sexual indiscretions differently from those of other offending ministers, the denomination demanded Swaggart's compliance with a typical rehabilitation program. The pressures for special consideration came from within and outside the constituency. Prominent charismatic personalities such as James Robison and E. V. Hill urged that restoration to ministry should quickly follow confession of wrongdoing. Some thought Swaggart's multimillion-dollar annual financial contributions to the denomination's foreign missions assured him rapid reinstatement. Others thought his various ministries too vital to world evangelization to jeopardize by silencing him. But the Assemblies of God rejected its Louisiana District's plea for lenience.

At the same time that the titillating Bakker and Swaggart scenarios unfolded, several other once-powerful Assemblies of God leaders were involved in scandals. Marvin Gorman of New Orleans and David Crabtree of Des Moines, pastors of large, affluent congregations and, as part of the denomination's Executive Presbytery, members of the Board of Directors of the Assemblies of God Theological Seminary, were caught in adultery and refused rehabilitation. They and Richard Dortch, who was convicted and imprisoned for his part in the financial scandals that rocked

PTL in the 1980s, had seemed poised for the denomination's highest office. Disgrace was sudden and complete, and many within the Assemblies of God were bewildered by the apparent leadership crisis. The public disgrace of these popular Pentecostals challenged Assemblies of God adherents to evaluate their personal motives and priorities.

The sexual and financial scandals and power struggles of the 1980s served as a reminder that Pentecostals do not guarantee immunity from human failure. Rather, Pentecostalism offers health and prosperity in this life, the opportunity to be "of the world" through the parallel Christian culture, and hope for the future. Certainly this constituency is as subject as any other to moral and spiritual flaws. In this fluid, Spirit-oriented culture, Pentecostal prophets, writers, artists, and publishers cater to the whims and wishes of a huge constituency that includes many who worship in Assemblies of God churches. They have accelerated a transformation in music, dress, and life-style to conform to the trends of the times. Assemblies of God adherents have glimpsed a broader and attractive world and have evolved a hopeful affirmation that has muted older themes of judgment and found wide appeal. Assurance that people are never beyond hope from Christians who offer the Pentecostal message as the way to peace, forgiveness, healing, prosperity, and wholeness attracts drug addicts to the denomination's inner-city Teen Challenge Centers as well as middle-class professionals to crowded megachurches.

Responsiveness to the popular culture is both a strength and a weakness. It helps account for surges of growth. Casual, warm, relaxed friendliness attracts crowds that clap to the rhythm of contemporary Christian music while dressed in blue jeans and sneakers. Assemblies of God personalities are featured in independent charismatic contexts where a new Pentecostal idiom has come to terms with modernity. The new idiom illustrates how far Assemblies of God congregations have moved from their millenarian restorationist past. Institutional leadership is increasingly irrelevant to the courses Assemblies of God congregations chart for themselves; on the other hand, centrifugal forces are also at work, demanding more conformity and accountability from leadership. The Assemblies of God—as the sociologist Margaret Poloma recently noted—stands at a crossroads.[56]

As the Assemblies of God moved into the last decade of the twentieth century—a decade that, at its end, will mark the centennial of the American Pentecostal movement—the denomination mobilized for a "Decade of Harvest." Adherents were being challenged to involvement in a mammoth traditional evangelistic thrust. The Assemblies of God hopes to swell the ranks of its 30,552 ministers by training 20,000 more, to add 5,000 churches to the 11,000 that were scattered across the United

States in 1989, to disciple 5 million new converts, and to enlist nearly half of its adherents to function as 1 million prayer partners.

While the eschatological implications of the proclamation of the Decade of Harvest are unclear, much of the denomination has rallied to the summons. Over 1,600 missionaries cooperate with Assemblies of God national associations around the world to expand a worldwide membership that is rapidly approaching 23 million. This huge constituency retains a diverse character that assures the persistence of alternative models of the personal and public implications of its message.

The Assemblies of God has grown, broadened, and adapted and in the process become a prosperous denomination. Its members contribute more per capita to world ministries than do the members of any mainline denomination. The denomination's annual world ministries budget far exceeds $200 million. Its megachurches can be found in many states. Its members have the resources to support the large-scale evangelism for which they are currently poised. But acculturation has taken its toll on the denomination's dynamic and its stance toward culture. Early Assemblies of God adherents urged a sharp distinction between the holy and the unholy, and for them the unholy was not limited to the proscriptions of conservative, white, middle America. In the old frame of reference of "us against them," the "them" has changed. Perhaps the denomination's growing non-Anglo units more clearly retain the earlier ethos. In sharp contrast to the contemporary hopes of a constituency that has largely yielded to civilizing trends and come to terms with parts of the culture they once opposed, the past suggests that the Assemblies of God, like American Pentecostalism more generally, grew at first not in spite of its culture-challenging message but because of it.[57] At least partly because it was out of step with modernity, it attracted people who were convinced that its message would bring them into step with God's end-times purpose. In the process, it contributed extensively to the rich diversity that energizes American religion and became the world's largest Pentecostal denomination.

NOTES

1. "Why the Plan of Advance," in *Our Mission in Today's World*, eds. Richard Champion, Edward Caldwell, and Gary Leggett (Springfield, Mo.: Gospel Publishing, 1968), 11, 13, 14.

2. Ibid., 14.

3. Victor de Leon, *The Silent Pentecostals* (Taylor, S.C.: Faith Printing, 1979), 43–44.

4. Alice Luce File, Assemblies of God Secretariat, Springfield, Mo. (hereafter AGS), contains letters that document the growth of these Spanish-language ministries.

5. De Leon, *Silent Pentecostals,* 45–48.

6. The story of Hispanic Pentecostalism is told in de Leon's *Silent Pentecostals.*

7. An interesting footnote to this is that in the midtwenties Mason apparently launched efforts to create a white branch of the Church of God in Christ. Assemblies of God minister August Feick resigned his credentials to direct Mason's white branch. Nothing is known about the immediate fate of these efforts. It is evident, however, that a viable white branch did not take shape.

8. Report of the General Secretary for Presentation to the General Presbytery, General Presbytery Minutes, 1949, 5, AGS.

9. Ralph Riggs to Frank Lindquist, 12 Sept. 1956, 1, Race Relations File, Assemblies of God Archives, Springfield, Mo. (hereafter AGA).

10. Ralph Riggs to Nicholas Bhengu, 12 Oct. 1955, Race Relations File.

11. Riggs to Lindquist, 12 Sept. 1956.

12. Kenneth Roper (pastor, Assembly of God Church, Covelo, Calif.) to Ralph Riggs, 16 Jan. 1956, Race Relations File.

13. Ralph Riggs to Kenneth Roper, 24 Jan. 1956, Race Relations File.

14. Ibid.

15. Ibid.

16. "The 'Colored' Question," 2, Race Relations File.

17. General Presbytery Minutes, 1958, 36, AGS.

18. "Report of the Committee to Consider a Colored Fellowship," General Presbytery Minutes, 1959, 17, AGS.

19. Ibid.

20. See "An Appeal to the Conscience, Concern, and Commitment of the Organized Religious Community," Oct. 1957, Race Relations File; James Varner (Congress of African Peoples) to Assemblies of God Executives, 12 Aug. 1970, Race Relations File.

21. Ernest G. Jones to the editor, *Christianity Today,* 10 Apr. 1964, 17–18.

22. John Garlock to Thomas Zimmerman, 18 May 1964, Race Relations File.

23. General Presbytery Minutes, 1965, 32–33, AGS; General Council Minutes, 1965, 60–61, AGS.

24. General Presbytery Minutes, 1965, 32.

25. An early effort in the recent attempt to focus attention on African Americans was the conference Ministry to the Blacks in America held in October 1980. See list of participants and schedule in Race Relations File.

26. Resolution 20, General Council Minutes, 1989, 117, AGS.

27. General Presbytery Minutes, 1968, 24–25, AGS.

28. Ibid., 25.

29. Ibid.

30. Virginia Hogan to Thomas F. Zimmerman, 31 July 1978, Women's Movement File, AGA.

31. Ibid.

32. These quotations are taken from a draft of Sand's address, 4, 5, Women's Movement File.

33. Zimmerman made his opposition to the ERA clear in a letter to Mr. and Mrs. R. T. Highfill, 10 Feb. 1977, Women's Movement File. Declining numbers of active ordained women (i.e., those who have responsibilities apart from their husband's charge) have characterized the recent past. Robert Cunningham, "Let George Do It," *Advance*, Feb. 1987, 4–6, noted the decline with concern; Richard Dresselhaus, "The Place of Women in the Church," *Pentecostal Evangel*, 18 Feb. 1990, 4–5.

34. General Presbytery Minutes, 1963, 14–15, AGS.

35. "Report of the Rehabilitation and Morals Study Committee," General Presbytery Minutes, 1964, 66, AGS.

36. Ibid., 67.

37. Ibid., 68.

38. Ibid., 69.

39. See James Hunter, *Evangelicalism: The Coming Generation* (Chicago: University of Chicago Press, 1987).

40. General Presbytery Minutes, 14 Aug. 1979, 36, AGS.

41. Ibid., 37.

42. Ibid.

43. General Presbytery Minutes, 19 Aug. 1980, 13, AGS.

44. General Presbytery Minutes, 17 Aug. 1981, 10, AGS.

45. General Presbytery Minutes, 24 Aug. 1984, 27, AGS. Appended to the minutes was a list of titles, courses, and schools showing in which courses specific books were used. This followed an Executive Presbytery action in November 1983 suggesting that presidents and academic deans encourage the use of such books as texts and required supplementary reading.

46. General Presbytery Minutes, 6 Aug. 1985, 27, AGS.

47. Ibid.

48. For a consideration of the character of popular religion in America, see Peter Williams, *Popular Religion in America: Symbolic Change and the Modernization Process in Historical Perspective* (Englewood Cliffs, N.J.: Prentice-Hall, 1980).

49. For Bakker, see Charles Shepard, *Forgiven: The Rise and Fall of Jim Bakker and the PTL Ministry* (New York: Atlantic Monthly, 1989).

50. For example, Robert C. Liebman and Robert Wuthnow, eds., *The New Christian Right* (Hawthorne, N.Y.: Aldine, 1983).

51. Some of this material was previously published in two articles for *Christian Century*, "Divided Pentecostals: Bakker vs. Swaggart," 6 May 1987, 430–31, and "Swaggart and the Pentecostal Ethos," 6 Apr. 1988, 333–35.

52. David Edwin Harrell, Jr., "American Revivalism from Graham to Robertson," in *Modern Christian Revivals*, ed. Edith L. Blumhofer and Randall Balmer (Urbana: University of Illinois Press, 1993).

53. See the brief essay "Radical Right: Electronic Fundamentalism" based on David Edwin Harrell, Jr.'s, work in *A Documentary History of Religion in America since 1865*, ed. Edwin S. Gaustad (Grand Rapids: William B. Eerdmans, 1983),

539–44; Grace Halsell, *Prophecy and Politics: Militant Evangelists on the Road to Nuclear War* (Westport, Conn.: Lawrence Hill, 1986).

54. Frances FitzGerald, "Reflections: Jim and Tammy," *New Yorker*, 23 Apr. 1990, 45–87. For the Bakkers, see also Charles Shepard, *Forgiven: An Inside Account of the Battle for PTL* (New York: Atlantic Monthly, 1989).

55. Harrell, "American Revivalism."

56. Margaret Poloma, *The Assemblies of God at the Crossroads: Charisma and Institutional Dilemmas* (Knoxville: University of Tennessee Press, 1989).

57. See Grant Wacker, "America's Pentecostals: Who They Are," *Christianity Today*, 16 Oct. 1987, 21.

The Challenge of Conserving and Expanding

I N RECENT MONTHS, as I have participated in discussions among professionals in widely diverse settings about religion in the United States, I have often heard members of America's historic denominations refer with evident wistfulness to the apparent health of American Pentecostal denominations. In other places, I have listened as Pentecostals stereotyped "dead" historic denominations and adopted a thinly masked "we told you so" attitude toward apparent mainstream Protestant decline. The following paragraphs summarize my reflections on the inadequacy of both perceptions. Stimulated by misleading statistics released by the Assemblies of God and by years of reflection on the Assemblies of God in the context of the broad landscape of American religion, they indicate the dilemmas that denominational leaders face in the nineties. Much of what follows first appeared as "Decade of Decline or Harvest?: Dilemmas of the Assemblies of God" in *Christian Century*, 10–17 July 1991, and was co-authored with Dr. Paul B. Tinlin.

In recent years, much has been written about declension in American Protestantism. Historians, social scientists, and theologians have explored the changing landscape of the historic mainstream and offered diagnoses and remedies. Pentecostal denominations, on the other hand, are widely perceived to be thriving, and statistics offered by David Barrett and others seem to support the view that Pentecostalism has resilience and vitality. It is instructive to take a closer look, however. In general, American Pentecostals have not found the courage to subject their faith communities to critical scrutiny. The Assemblies of God, the world's largest Pentecostal denomination, has long been recognized as the leading predominantly white classical Pentecostal denomination in the United

States. That perception merits inquiry; even a cursory review suggests that the Assemblies of God is not immune to the numerical and spiritual stagnation more typically associated with mainstream Protestantism.

In August 1991 the Assemblies of God convened its forty-fourth General Council in Portland, Oregon. Delegates assessed the first reports of outreach under a decadal program for evangelism in the nineties, the Decade of Harvest. Preliminary figures give reason for concern rather than celebration. For at least the past decade the Assemblies of God has been stagnant, and major efforts to recover momentum have not succeeded. Still widely perceived as a rapidly growing, vibrant denomination, the Assemblies of God is in fact facing problems far deeper than those suggested by the Bakker and Swaggart scandals that caught media notice several years ago. Like many other denominations, it is beset by bureaucratization and bewildered by cultural change. In well under a century it has moved from a millenarian restorationist identity to make its peace in significant ways with this world. It retains a "them against us" mentality, but the meaning of "them" has changed. Much of its rhetoric has been functionally stripped of its early meaning. Selected denominational statistics can be introduced to indicate apparent success and expansion in recent years. Examination of the full numbers, however, suggests that the Assemblies of God needs to take a hard, critical look at itself and at current social and demographic shifts if it hopes to regain momentum.

Early in the eighties religious analysts noted the Assemblies of God as one of the fastest-growing denominations in the United States. A decade of denominational focus on evangelism in the seventies combined with gains from the burgeoning charismatic renewal to propel the once-ignored denomination into the public eye. Most Americans had long been suspicious and wary of Pentecostals and had simply preferred to ignore a movement that had nonetheless stubbornly refused to go away. By 1980, however, favorable journalistic coverage—sometimes by evangelical reporters who had themselves only recently been surprised to discover that many Pentecostals behaved much like evangelicals—had begun to dispel myths of bizarre conduct, severe economic deprivation, and inane theology.

In 1982 the *Saturday Evening Post* featured a story that maintained that Assemblies of God constituents were, in fact, middle-class evangelicals. Participants welcomed the recognition as vindication of the claim they had always made that theirs was a biblical, relevant message that met basic human needs. The story presented the denomination as growing and thriving and reassured readers about its intentions. The Assemblies of God had it reprinted and distributed it proudly and widely: the denomination had finally been recognized for its success and growth. Hindsight suggests, however, that elation was premature. Growth was at best uneven, confined largely to the denomination's Hispanic and Korean outreaches. Even in those sectors it did not keep pace with population growth. Entire geographical regions of the denomination had experienced no net growth at all; some had actually declined.

By the mideighties stagnation was apparent to thoughtful participants, but the Assemblies of God was still widely acknowledged by the religious press to be thriving. Official statistics, too, seemed to attest growth. In part, better reporting mechanisms had been devised, and numbers for the first time reflected more accurately the denomination's composition. In 1987 the televangelists' holy war and related disgrace of two of the denomination's best-known media stars brought unprecedented news coverage that further revealed the denomination's extent and increased public awareness of its working. It also clearly evidenced the tensions and uncertainties that concerned thoughtful adherents.

A change in national leadership that immediately preceded slowed growth and media scandals set the stage for reevaluation of Assemblies of God goals and programs. Serious financial strains resulted in a self-study yielding unavoidable evidence of declension, and denominational machinery was set in motion to devise a program to revitalize all aspects of Assemblies of God life. It is likely as well that the thought of deflecting attention from media scandals with a major denominational program of evangelism was appealing. The timing seemed right, too: most major denominations, along with many small religious bodies, were mobilizing their resources to launch growth-oriented programs for the nineties. The nineties represented not only a new decade but also the closing decade of the century and the millennium.

The Decade of Harvest suggests how far the Assemblies of God has come from its humble restorationist roots. Once it had seemed pure because it had been at odds with the culture; now its message had the ring of truth because so many believed it. Once adherents had been called to live in prophetic tension with their society; now they were typically conservative white working- and middle-class Americans whose life-styles resembled those of other Americans of similar social standing. Success, a word the constituency had once used to include connotations of uneasiness in this world, was, for the Decade of Harvest goals, described numerically.

The Decade of Harvest was launched at the Assemblies of God seventy-fifth anniversary extravaganza in Indianapolis in 1989. Assemblies of God youth ran with a lighted torch from Hot Springs, Arkansas, to Indianapolis, arriving at the Hoosier Dome to climax the anniversary celebration. The program called for 1 million prayer partners from within Assemblies of God ranks, 20,000 new ministers, 5,000 new churches, and

5 million new converts. The denomination's representative governing body, the General Council, did not vote on the Decade of Harvest. Rather, the program was adopted by the smaller General Presbytery on the recommendation of the denomination's executive leadership. It required substantial expenditures and presumed—in the best "fire 'em up" church-growth style—that the constituency could be excited by an imposed program that mandated a preplanned focus and defined goals. It came from the top down rather than from the grass roots.

Assumptions about the constituency's cooperation were perhaps misfounded. Early reports indicated a slow start at best. Barely 16 percent of the anticipated prayer partners signed on. The Assemblies of God reported that 340 new churches (considerably short of the goal of 500) had been opened. But 179 were closed, so the net gain stood at a fairly typical 161. The announcement that the Decade of Harvest goal of 2,000 new ministers had been exceeded, with 2,089 newly credentialed workers in 1990, failed to take into account that 2,036 had been lost through death, discipline, withdrawal, and transfer. The net gain stood at a far less impressive 53. The denomination reported 319,000 new converts in 1990, 181,000 fewer than its goal of 500,000. First reports indicated, then, that all of the energy that leadership had poured into the Decade of Harvest had merely enabled maintaining—or slightly improving—the status quo.

Other statistics raise related concerns about the selection of numbers to represent situations and trends in the denomination. The 1990 National Council of Churches decadal report, for example, cited the Assemblies of God as the denomination that had made the most progress over the past decade in affirming the ministry of women. The figures adduced to substantiate the claim seemed irrefutable, but the experiences of women in the Assemblies of God simply did not confirm them. The denomination has four basic forms of ministerial credentials: Christian Workers licenses, specialized licenses, preaching licenses, and ordination. On closer examination, it became apparent that the Assemblies' progress was largely due to the method of reporting, not to any sociocultural forward leap. For 1980 the Assemblies of God submitted the number of ordained women to the National Council of Churches' survey. In 1990 it volunteered the total number of licensed and ordained women. The comparison seemed to show dramatic change: it derived, however, from the contrasting of two very different figures. By far the majority of credentialed women hold licenses rather than ordination certificates; more than half of these are retired. Longer life expectancy confuses the issue, inflating the numbers of ministering women but assigning most of them retirement status. Progress on questions relating to ministering women has been slow and painful in the Assemblies of God as elsewhere.

Sunday schools and related activities are also faltering, as they are in many denominations. Sunday evening services, once the largest of the week, have experienced substantial declines in attendance; some Assemblies of God churches have canceled them completely. Wednesday evening adult services, once set apart for prayer and teaching, attract far smaller crowds than they did a generation ago. The tradition of altar services and prayer meetings, nurtured on Sunday and Wednesday nights and providing blocks of time for prayer, has virtually disappeared. Pentecostals once yearned for spiritual formation that they believed took time, discipline, and effort. Contemporary insistence on instant gratification makes some of the customs that once molded Pentecostalism's reason for being seem outmoded and irrelevant. Ever in tune with popular culture, of course, Pentecostals have responded by exploiting the part of their tradition that can be twisted to yield a theology of instant gratification. Deliverances and manipulative prayers often replace the priority earlier generations placed on spiritual discipline.

When they cover the Assemblies of God, both the secular and the religious press tend to focus on megachurches dominated by charismatic, independently minded pastors. In fact, more than half of Assemblies of God congregations have fewer than one hundred worshipers on any given Sunday. In one such instance the *Wall Street Journal* in December 1990 singled out First Assembly of God in Phoenix, Arizona, and its pastor, Tommy Barnett. While it is true that Barnett, whose church is the largest Assemblies of God congregation in the country, is promoted by the denomination as a successful pastor, it is not true that either he or his method is typical in the Assemblies of God. Megachurches easily achieve visibility, but their affluence and ethos do not fairly represent the Assemblies of God.

In other parts of the world, over 1,600 Assemblies of God missionaries work with national leaders to nurture some 23 million adherents of nationally led Assemblies of God organizations that the American denomination regards as "sister churches." United States world ministries giving in 1990 totaled some $283.5 million, more per capita than contributions in any mainstream denomination. Vitality abroad contrasts sharply with apathy at home. But the denomination's strength abroad is uneven, too; the largest Assemblies of God overseas constituencies are in Brazil (over 14 million) and in Korea, where Full Gospel Church, Seoul, alone accounts for close to 1 million. In some of its numerically successful mission fields, the Assemblies of God, at the invitation of national leaders or of other missionaries, took over efforts that already existed or systematized the energies of ongoing renewal. The dramatic growth of Pentecostalism in Latin America, for example, must be understood in the context of the growth of other social movements that both empower and affirm their adherents. Pentecostalism is a viable option for the poor and the powerless: it offers a sense of self-worth and the self-discipline necessary for success in other facets of life. In this context, the Assemblies of God is reaping some of the benefits of a wider social revolution.

Assemblies of God leaders have insisted for decades that foreign missions stand at the core of what the denomination is about. Nonetheless, a surprising number of Assemblies of God churches make no regular contributions to the denomination's missionary outreach. Missionary candidates struggle to raise their budgets, often finding it necessary to stretch the traditional one year of itineration to two. And, in earlier years, enthusiasm for foreign outreach was not matched by awareness of stateside social trends that brought millions of new immigrants and saw millions of Americans move to a few huge metropolitan areas. In the United States, the denomination has not always been located where the population clusters. The cost-related decision many years ago to move its headquarters from St. Louis to southwest Missouri distanced leadership, headquarters staff (now numbering over one thousand), and denominational educational institutions geographically, socially, and in mind-set from the urban America that is the experience of a majority of the population. Relating to the real world of the megalopolis thus stands as a growing challenge.

Such problems are not unusual today, of course, but they are usually assumed to be mainstream Protestant dilemmas. In recent decades, Pentecostal and charismatic movements have been perceived as somehow transcending the crises that have beset virtually all of America's historic denominations. Pentecostals have been quick to assert themes of spiritual power and dominion that they think make them immune to declension; they have exploited modern technology and embraced the marketplace mentality of the church growth movement. Their idiom denigrates "cold, dead denominational churches" and points proudly to their buildings, programs, Christian day schools, media ministries, and publications to prove their own vitality. The Assemblies of God, however, faces predicaments similar in some ways to those of mainstream denominations. While specific issues, especially theological ones, may stand in stark contrast, the social dimensions of the Assemblies of God crisis can no longer be denied. Leaders propose a simple answer: they long for revival and for a recurrence of the mystery and power that marked the humble Azusa Street Mission in Los Angeles when the restoration was proclaimed in 1906. Perhaps, however, they have yet to define the problem.

In part, the predicament of the denomination in the nineties is rooted in uncertainty about identity. Early Assemblies of God adherents had no intentions of forming a denomination. They sought, rather, to construct a framework in which an end-times restoration of the full experience of New Testament Christianity could be cultivated. They perceived themselves as participants in a brief, intense, divinely inspired movement whose life would culminate in Christ's imminent return. In restorationist fashion, they claimed no creed but the Bible. Their motivation for association was essentially conservative: they believed that they needed to conserve Pentecostalism's essence by curbing common excesses. Expansion depended on conservation. Conserving the dynamic of a movement focused on religious experience necessitated structuring it beyond the local church. Despite their intentions not to stem the tide of their religious movement, the formation of the General Council of the Assemblies of God marked a step in the process of the institutionalization of Pentecostalism. By 1916 the Assemblies of God (which referred to itself as a fellowship or a movement) adopted the Statement of Faith. Eleven years later, the ratification of a constitution and by-laws evidenced the rapid progress of denomination building. Throughout its life, then, the Assemblies of God has lived with the tension between movement and denomination, with the challenge to conserve but expand. Adherents perceive denominations as "dead" and movements as dynamic, creative, and vibrant. Trying to be both has issued in tensions that have not always yielded their creative potential.

Unwillingness to come to terms with being a denomination has been exacerbated by uneasy relations with the multifaceted charismatic movement. In many ways the charismatic movement appropriated distinctives that had once seemed to belong uniquely to Pentecostals. Charismatics discovered spontaneity in worship and celebrated gifts of the Spirit without relinquishing worldly life-styles. Through contact with dynamic charismatics, Assemblies of God adherents discovered with considerable relief that people who spoke in tongues could also embrace forms of modernity Pentecostals had long deemed sinful.

Charismatics also modified some of the rigid theological premises with which thoughtful and perhaps better-educated Assemblies of God ministers are increasingly uneasy. Like other Pentecostal denominations, the Assemblies of God insists that the baptism with the Holy Spirit will always be evidenced by tongues speech. It also subscribes to futurist premillennialism and has long affirmed dispensationalism. Although the denomination provides Bible colleges and a theological seminary, increasing numbers of men and women training for ministry choose to do so in non–Assemblies of God seminaries such as Fuller, Gordon-Conwell, and Trinity. Those who attend such schools are much less likely to accept unconditionally two of the denomination's historic cardinal doctrines:

initial evidential tongues and futurist premillennialism. The denomination responded early in the eighties to an evident surge in the percentage of candidates for ministry who did not unequivocally support these positions by tightening requirements for ministerial credentials and increasing pressure on denominational schools. The denomination became more rigid, but this could not counter the trend toward honest intellectual questioning of some long-cherished assumptions by people who wanted to remain deeply loyal to the tradition. A series of position papers emerged from the headquarters, defining what leadership deemed appropriate responses to theological and social issues they perceived to be of contemporary concern. The status of these papers is ambiguous; some districts use them as addenda to the Statement of Faith and demand adherence, others view them as nonbinding opinions of a committee. Since for the most part they are not a response to grass-roots demands for clarification, they carry little weight.

By the eighties, then, the struggle to expand while conserving had become limiting rather than creative. The risks of inquiry and scrutiny seemed too dangerous; openness, it was assumed, inevitably led to an amorphous threat—liberalism. The denomination chose to mask its vulnerability by sponsoring conventions and promoting popular personalities. Increasing numbers of educated young people with deep roots in the denomination felt alienated by the reluctance to grapple with real issues and an apparent growing inclination to define, codify, and prescribe.

The expulsion for adultery of several highly visible Assemblies of God ministers in the eighties—some of whom were elected to denominational office while in ongoing adulterous relationships—revealed deep character flaws. The Assemblies of God disclaimed the fallen, stressing the individual's responsibility for indiscretion without acknowledging the culpability of the broader constituency. Certainly leadership had contributed as well to the wide acceptance of Bakker and Swaggart by giving them visibility and authenticity through denominational periodicals and programs. Nor was it widely acknowledged that character flaws permeated Pentecostalism more generally. Amid the noise and bustle that have tended to mark Pentecostal movements, introspection and humility are sorely lacking. Like many other evangelicals, Pentecostals feel confident that they have the answers to every problem; in addition, they also claim to wield spiritual power. Instead of accepting responsibility and setting aside time for repentance, critical reflection, and prayer, the Assemblies of God turned directly to a major promotional evangelistic program that distracted attention from the serious issues that had been raised.

Despite these problems, although the steady growth of earlier decades slowed, the Assemblies of God had reached impressive proportions by

1990. It had 2.2 million adherents in 11,353 churches, served by over 30,000 ministers. But there is increasing evidence of the detachment of the grass roots from the national and district headquarters. The denomination's governing body, the General Council, is composed of all ordained ministers (18,060) and one delegate from each duly constituted, self-supporting congregation (6,524). Far fewer than 25 percent of the total possible voting delegates have participated in the voting process at recent General Councils. A similar turnout in a Chicago election would elicit strong media commentary; in the Assemblies of God it passes without comment.

Recent figures indicate that the only denominational sectors experiencing consistent growth are Hispanic. Yet that growth does not approach the percentage of Hispanic population increase. The 1990 census cites Florida, Texas, and California, three states with substantial Hispanic populations, as the fastest-growing in the nation. Each has historically had a relatively strong Assemblies of God presence. In order to assess current trends, the Assemblies of God needs to examine its outreaches and growth in relation to the percentage of population increase in these and other growing areas.

There has been much recent discussion about the influence of the baby boomer generation on American society. That discussion has not often been taken into account in Assemblies of God planning of programs and strategies. The baby boomers' lack of loyalty to a tradition; disinterest in attendance at Sunday school, Sunday evening, and midweek church activities; relaxed styles of dress; affinity for a contemporary musical idiom; demands for the latest technology; desires for instant gratification; and the yearning for affirmative rather than prophetic preaching have subtly but relentlessly affected average Assemblies of God congregations. The common identification between baby boomers and blue jeans runs counter to Assemblies of God habits of dress for church and has far-reaching implications for the themes of holiness and separation that long dominated Assemblies of God preaching. Outmoded programs and outdated methods on which the denomination—like other such organizations—continues to rely often fail to produce the desired results.

Until recently, the Assemblies of God was gratified by the free-lance success of some of its preachers in televangelism. The denomination as a whole, however, chose not to focus on video technology but to pour its media efforts into a radio program called "Revivaltime." Waning effectiveness suggests that a format suitable for the fifties may no longer be effective in the nineties. Alternative uses of technology for video education and outreach remain to be explored. The Assemblies of God lags far behind other evangelical organizations in efforts to make creative use of modern instructional technology.

Family-oriented programs, too, seem to require modernization. Models offered by Women's Ministries may ignore contemporary working women and the issues raised by the social revolution they represent. Today's typical family, in which both parents are employed and the children are latch-key kids, the proliferation of single-parent families, and the realities of divorce and remarriage present situations far different from those in the fifties when denominational family programs originated. As the denomination attempts to target inner-city constituencies, its family programs must be reevaluated.

Compounding the situation is the reality of aging leadership. While all institutions benefit from the rich experience derived from years of service, they also require the infusion of new ideas and approaches.

Theological issues, too, demand clarification in the nineties. Dissatisfaction with the traditional answers that have validated the denomination's position on tongues speech as uniform initial physical evidence of Spirit baptism comes at a time when Pentecostal scholarship offers theological alternatives. Premillennialism has been questioned by many evangelicals, and pressures mount within the Assemblies of God, too. The denomination's Statement of Fundamental Truths, crafted to meet a specific theological challenge in 1916, is silent on such key issues as the understanding of spiritual gifts. Proof-texting and codifying cannot suffice indefinitely. The Assemblies of God will be stronger when it finds the courage to raise theological questions for which it may not have ready answers. Without that, the Assemblies of God may well be facing a decade of decline rather than a Decade of Harvest. Of course, facing tough questions does not guarantee numerical growth, either. But the point is not numbers, but being faithful to the tradition's calling. And even more, it is confronting and engaging that calling regardless of whether or not such confrontation issues in numerical growth.

In spite of the perception in the religious community and the news media in general that the Assemblies of God is healthy, growing, and contemporary, then, analysis of denominational figures demonstrates that stagnation has been in progress for some time. The Decade of Harvest provided the Assemblies of God with a slogan for the nineties but not necessarily with a program that dealt with the real issues that called the Assemblies of God into being. It expressed the natural desire of every denomination for numerical and spiritual growth.

Early attempts in the Assemblies of God to balance the instinct to conserve with the mandate to expand have given way to decisions that make conservation and expansion mutually exclusive. Conserving what leadership perceives to be the denomination's essence often runs counter to the spirit of evangelism that summons the church to expansion. Evangelism and expansionism jeopardize the status quo. Some large congregations are willing to take the risk, but the denomination as a whole is not. As long as the protection and conservation of the denomination is the priority, the Decade of Harvest, which demands expansion with all the accompanying risks, may not produce the desired results.

Declining membership and finances have forced mainstream denominations to engage in self-scrutiny. Perhaps turning from noisy diversions to quiet introspection would yield among Assemblies of God adherents as well as other Pentecostals the sobering, painful awareness that the crisis in America's communities of faith runs far deeper than they supposed. It is not a mainstream problem; it is, rather, a dilemma faced by all who strive to be faithful in a modern, secular world.

BIBLIOGRAPHIC NOTE

In recent years numerous significant resources for the study of American Pentecostalism have become available. The most comprehensive guide to sources is Charles Edwin Jones, *A Guide to the Study of the Pentecostal Movement* (Metuchen, N.J.: Scarecrow Press, 1983). See also Grant Wacker, "Bibliography and Historiography of Pentecostalism (U.S.)," *Dictionary of Pentecostal and Charismatic Movements*, ed. Stanley M. Burgess, Gary B. McGee, and Patrick H. Alexander (Grand Rapids, Mich.: Zondervan, 1988). For a guide to literature on the broader context of which Pentecostalism is part, see Edith L. Blumhofer and Joel A. Carpenter, *Evangelicalism in Twentieth-Century America: A Guide to the Sources* (New York: Garland Publishing, 1990). Several reprint series, especially *The Higher Christian Life*, ed. Donald W. Dayton (New York: Garland Publishing, 1984–85), have greatly expanded the accessibility of relevant primary sources.

On the Assemblies of God, the most perceptive scholarly work is by the sociologist Margaret Poloma, *The Assemblies of God at the Crossroads: Charisma and Institutional Dilemmas* (Knoxville: University of Tennessee Press, 1989). Several sympathetic accounts of the Assemblies of God have been written by members of the denomination. These include Carl Brumback, *Suddenly . . . from Heaven* (Springfield, Mo.: Gospel Publishing House, 1961); William Menzies, *Anointed to Serve* (Springfield, Mo.: Gospel Publishing House, 1970); and an institutional history of Assemblies of God foreign missions, Gary B. McGee, *This Gospel Shall Be Preached*, 2 vols. (Springfield, Mo.: Gospel Publishing House, 1986, 1989).

INDEX

Cashwell, Gaston Barnabas, 74–75, 76
Catholicism, 229, 234, 235, 241n54;
    charistmatic renewal, 223
Central Bible Institute, 150
Charismatic renewal, 4, 218, 222, 223–
    26, 232, 270
Chisolm, Rueben Benjamin, 120
Christian and Missionary Alliance, 17, 95,
    134; baptism of Holy Spirit, 77–78;
    premillenialist views, 18; tongues,
    views on, 102–5, 111n86
Christian Catholic Apostolic Church, 72
Christian Evangel, 119, 120, 124, 131, 132,
    143, 144, 145, 147, 153, 154, 210,
    216, 228
Christian Science, 37n32
Christian Workers Union, 97
Church of God in Christ, 73–74, 83, 117,
    134, 247, 248
Coe, Jack, 214–15, 224
Collins, Arch, 123, 132, 148
Cook, Glenn, 129
Crabtree, David, 258

Darby, John Nelson, 16
Davis, Ralph T., 182, 184
Decade of Harvest, 259, 260, 265, 266,
    274
Divorce, 120–21
Dortch, Richard, 258
Dowie, John A., 15, 20, 22–23, 46,
    48, 72
Duncan, James, 78
Du Plessis, David, 6, 224, 230, 233, 234,
    235, 237, 238n3, 243; Assemblies of
    God, departure from, 231–32,
    240n39; ecumenical views, 226–29
Durham, William, 80–81, 99, 114, 116,
    128, 134, 205, 206; sanctification,
    views on, 125

Easton, Susan, 154
Elim (Rochester Bible and Missionary
    Training School), 78–79, 173, 205,
    210
Elim Pentecostal Herald, 210
Erickson, Clifton, 214
Evans, William I., 148
Ewart, Frank: baptism, views on, 128–30,
    131

Farrow, Lucy, 55, 86n44
Federal Council of Churches, 182, 183,
    186, 190, 191, 192, 193, 194, 195,
    201n45, 225, 229, 230, 233
Finney, Charles G., 32
Fisher, Warren, 129
Flower, J. Russell, 118, 119, 123, 141n85,
    155, 157, 208, 247; baptism, views on,
    131, 132, 133; National Association of
    Evangelicals, association with, 184,
    189, 194, 200n30; Pentecostal Fellow-
    ship of North America, 196; Pentecos-
    tal World Conference, 197; tongues,
    views on, 91, 92
Fosdick, Harry Emerson, 190
Freeman, William, 214
Frodsham, Stanley, 145, 147, 160
Full Gospel Business Men's Fellowship,
    218, 225–26

Gardner, Velmer, 211, 214
Gee, Donald, 197, 225, 226, 227
Gordon, A. J., 18, 19, 20, 36n19; heal-
    ing, views on, 20–21, 37n36
Gortner, J. Narver, 153
Gospel Publishing House, 124, 153, 154,
    246, 254
Gospel School, 120, 123
Gospel Tabernacle, 102
Goss, Howard, 67n78, 82, 83, 92, 117,
    130, 132

Hagin, Kenneth, 217
Hall, L. C., 130
Hardin, Ben, 189
Harris, Thoro, 92
Hawtin, Ernest, 204, 206
Hawtin, George, 204, 206, 207, 224
Haywood, Garfield T., 92, 129, 130,
    132
Healing, 5, 19–20
Herald of Faith, 206
Hicks, Tommy, 216
Holiness, 26–29, 124–27
Holt, Herrick, 204
Holy Spirit, 24–25, 91. See also Baptism,
    Holy Spirit
Hopkins, Evan, 58
Horne, J. W., 26, 27
Hunt, Percy, 204, 206

Note on the Author

EDITH L. BLUMHOFER received her Ph.D. from Harvard University. Her previous publications include *The Assemblies of God: A Chapter in the Story of American Pentecostalism*, *Twentieth-Century Evangelism: A Guide to the Sources* (with Joel Carpenter), and *Modern Christian Revivals* (coedited with Randall A. Balmer).